R.C.M.P. SECURITY BULLETINS

THE WAR SERIES, 1939-1941

R.C.M.P. SECURITY BULLETINS

THE WAR SERIES, 1939-1941

Edited by Gregory S. Kealey and Reg Whitaker

St. John's: Committee on Canadian Labour History

Committee on Canadian Labour History
Department of History
Memorial University of Newfoundland
St. John's, Newfoundland
A1C 5S7

Typography and book design by
VHA Publishing Services (7814)

Printed and Bound in Canada

Canadian Cataloguing in Publication Data
Main entry under title:
Royal Canadian Mounted Police security bulletins

Contents: no. 1. The war series, 1939-1941
ISBN 0-9692060-5-4 (v. 1)

   Subversive activities—Canada. 2. Communism—
Canada. 3. World War, 1939-1945. 4. Internal
Security—Canada. 5. Royal Canadian Mounted Police.
I. Whitaker, Reginald, 1943-   . II. Committee on
Canadian Labour History

HV7641.A6 1988   332.4'2   C88-090461-5

TABLE OF CONTENTS

PREFACE

Our goal in publishing the *Bulletins* has been the creation of a volume which would be accessible to the general reader and useful to the specialized researcher at the same time. The documents we received presented two sets of problems. Those who gathered the information originally were quite casual about consistent and accurate nomenclature. While a complete annotation of the text to clarify and correct these matters was not possible, we have provided a comprehensive and corrective index. It was felt that the documents would be clearer without what would have been an awkward and confusing reliance on *sic*.

There were other elements of the documents that needed to be drawn to the reader's attention. As the introduction explains in detail, a great deal of material was judged exempt under the Access to Information Act and was deleted from the copies we received. To provide the reader with an accurate picture of what is missing, it was necessary first to indicate the location of page breaks. Each *Bulletin* begins with an unnumbered title page. Page breaks have been inserted at their proper location in the text in brackets (e.g., ...[6]...).

Exempt material has been deleted in three ways. Some pages containing such material were simply not included in the copies we received. We have indicated such omissions in the text in brackets (e.g., ...[6][Page 7 is missing.]...).

A second method of deletion was to cover the material with a white mask and an "exempt" stamp before copying (see Figure 1). We have in-

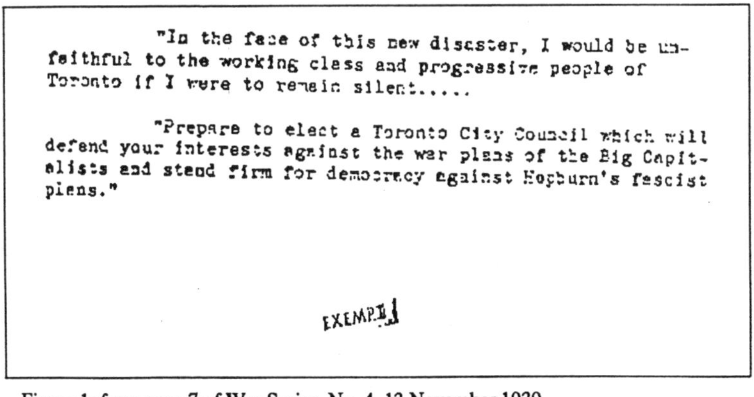
"In the face of this new disaster, I would be unfaithful to the working class and progressive people of Toronto if I were to remain silent.....

"Prepare to elect a Toronto City Council which will defend your interests against the war plans of the Big Capitalists and stand firm for democracy against Hepburn's fascist plans."

EXEMPT

Figure 1: from page 7 of War Series, No. 4, 13 November 1939 dicated such deletions with an outline scissor symbol at the appropriate place in the text (e.g., ...[✂blank][6]...).

A third technique was used to excise shorter passages. Words, lines, and whole paragraphs were simply covered over with black marker on the copies (see Figure 2). Here it was possible to give a better sense of the

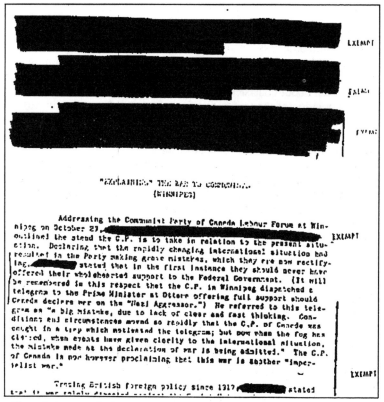

Figure 2: from page 8 of War Series, No. 4, 13 November 1939

amount of material withheld. We have used a black scissor symbol combined with a brief report of the number of lines missing to indicate such deletions (e.g.,...[✂deletion: 1 paragraph: 6 lines]...). We have defined a line as any part of a line in the original text. We have also made an effort to format such deletion symbols and reports as if they were text. For instance, lines which are obviously titles have been formatted as titles.

These devices should alert the reader to both the nature and quantity of what is missing without adding more distraction than is necessary.

INTRODUCTION

On 21 August 1939, the Nazi-Soviet Pact was disclosed. On 23 August Prime Minister Mackenzie King announced that Parliament would be called into session at once if efforts to prevent the immediate outbreak of war were to fail.[1]

Two days later, King's Minister of Justice, Ernest Lapointe, received a letter from the Commissioner of the RCMP, S.T. Wood, outlining the state of war readiness of Canada's national police force and internal security agency. The Mounties reported that they had prepared lists of "all known potential enemy aliens" and of all espionage suspects: these could be arrested "at a moment's notice" once the word was given. "Suspects of lesser importance" were to kept under surveillance. A registry of enemy aliens would be supplied with information from the RCMP files. Although concerned with fascists and Nazis (and Ukrainian nationalists sympathethic toward the Hitler regime), the RCMP also anticipated a "more rigid and extended surveillance of Communist Agitators, particularly those active among industrial workers" and recommended the outlawing of the Communist party by Order in Council under the War Measures Act. The Commissioner also spoke of close co-ordination between the RCMP, military intelligence, External Affairs, and the departments of transport, justice, and immigration, and added that "liaison is being maintained in all matters of mutual interest with M.I.5, London, England."[2]

Canada was just days away from entering a global conflict for which it was ill-prepared in almost every way except one. The economy, battered by a decade of depression, was hardly in a promising state to wage war. Military preparations were, according to the official historian of the Canadian Army, "utterly inadequate by comparison with the scale of the coming emergency."[3] Nor did Canada have any external intelligence capacity of its own, apart from scraps gathered by its small number of

[1] J.W. Pickersgill, *The Mackenzie King Record*, vol. 1: 1939-1944 (Toronto 1960), 15.

[2] National Archives of Canada [NAC], Ernest Lapointe Papers [MG 27 III B10] vol. 50 file 50, S.T. Wood to Ernest Lapointe, 25 August 1939.

[3] Col C.P. Stacey, *Six Years of War: the Army in Canada, Britain and the Pacific* (Ottawa 1955); James Eayrs, *In Defence of Canada: Appeasement and Rearmament* (Toronto 1965), 134-53.

diplomatic representatives abroad. For foreign intelligence Canada was dependent upon Britain's Foreign Office and its Secret Intelligence Service, or M.I.6. During the war, Canada would carve out a small, if subordinate, role in signals intelligence gathering,[4] and would host the celebrated (and rather over-romanticized) Camp X for training secret agents.[5] But this was small potatoes in what Sir Winston Churchill called the "wizard war" of espionage and codebreaking. In only one area was the Canadian state ready for war—internal surveillance and control. Foreign enemies would await national mobilization and conversion of the economy to war production. The Canadian state was, on the other hand, well prepared for the enemy within.

There was some question, however, regarding the identity of this enemy within. Pro-Nazis and pro-Fascists would seem to be the obvious candidates in a war against the Axis powers. There were such groups in Canada, a few homegrown and others rooted in the German and Italian communities. There was general suspicion among Canadians regarding the German and Italian ethnic communities (justified or unjustified) and later in the war, outright racism would engulf the Japanese-Canadian population of British Columbia. Yet in the late 1930s, with fascist armies on the rise in Europe, it took the specific urging of Norman Robertson, a senior civil servant, to draw the close attention of the RCMP to pro-fascist activities.[6] Charles Rivett-Carnac, head of the RCMP's Intelligence Branch, tried to assure Robertson in early 1939 that fascism was much less of a threat than Communism since the former guaranteed at least a "modified form of capitalism."[7] The official historian of the RCMP has recently written that the Communists were the "principal target of RCMP intelligence" in the interwar years, while at the end of the 1930s pro-fascist groups became a "secondary objective."[8]

The weight of state repression did fall most heavily on those judged to be sympathetic to Canada's enemies.[9] Yet to the RCMP and to many prominent civilian officials in both Ottawa and the provincial capitals, it

[4] Wesley K. Wark, "Cryptographic innocence: the origins of signals intelligence in Canada in the Second World War," *Journal of Contemporary History*, 22 (1987), 639-65.

[5] David Stafford, *Camp X: Canada's School for Secret Agents, 1941-45* (Toronto 1986).

[6] Reg Whitaker, "Official repression of Communism during World War II," *Labour/le Travail*, 17 (1986), 137; J.L. Granatstein, *A Man of Influence* (Ottawa 1981), 81-6.

[7] NAC, Norman Robertson Papers, vol. 12 file 137, Rivett-Carnac to Robertson, 24 January 1939.

[8] S.W. Horrall, "Canada's security service: a brief history," *RCMP Quarterly*, 50:3 (Summer 1985), 45.

[9] Just under 24,500 residents of Canada were interned or forcibly relocated, not counting another 5,400 so-called 'enemy aliens' from Britain interned in Canada

was obvious that Communism was the permanent and enduring enemy within. The Nazi-Soviet pact and the opposition of the Communist party to the "imperialist" war (which lasted until precisely 22 June 1941, the day the Nazi armies poured over the Soviet borders), offered valid grounds for targeting the Communists under the Defence of Canada Regulations. They also offered a pretext for intensified intrusive surveillance which the RCMP was eager to grasp.

The Intelligence Section of the RCMP was, on the eve of the war, run by a tiny six-man headquarters attached to the Criminal Investigation Branch. Yet despite its small numbers, its agents and sources had deeply penetrated the Canadian Communist party. One of its stalwarts was John Leopold who, as undercover agent "Jack Esselwein," had successfully played a prominent Communist agitator in the 1920s before making a dramatic appearance as a Crown witness in the case of *Rex v. Buck et al*, the 1931 prosecution of party leaders under Section 98 of the Criminal Code. Clearly one of the reasons for its relative success in Red-hunting was that it had marshalled its resources and limited its targets. War against Nazi Germany and Fascist Italy provided it with opportunities hitherto undreamed of. By 1943 the headquarters staff of the Intelligence Section had risen to 98 and in the field there was a sharp increase in personnel: 20 in Toronto, 19 in Montreal, 9 in Vancouver, for example.[10] It seems to have acted competently in counter-espionage operations against the enemy, but Canada was far away from the centre of hostilities and unlikely to be a major target for Axis espionage. The main thrust of RCMP activities was mounted against the enemy within, and here the RCMP itself took a strong role in defining the tasks of security and intelligence.

The RCMP was represented on a high-level, top-secret committee of civil servants which mapped out plans for wartime emergency powers before hostilities actually began. Thus the police were able to contribute directly to the shaping of the laws and regulations they were later to enforce.[11] The Commissioner was appointed Registrar General of Enemy Aliens, responsible for registration of tens of thousands of Germans, Italians, and Japanese. Rounding up and interrogation of internees was a major task, as was the investigation of complaints from citizens regarding possible espionage or subversion cases. Guarding sites judged impor-

---

at the UK's request. 22,000 of the interned residents were the Japanese Canadians forcibly relocated from the West Coast to the interior. Of the remainder over 90% were of German, Japanese or Italian origin or were native fascists. 133 Communists were interned (more were ordered interned but went into hiding), although Communists escaped such attention in Britain and the United States.

[10] Commission of Inquiry Concerning Certain Activities of the RCMP, Second Report, *Freedom and Security Under the Law*, vol. 1 (Ottawa 1981), 58-9.

[11] Whitaker, "Official repression," 136; Ramsay Cook, "Canadian Freedom in Wartime," MA thesis, Queen's University, 1955.

tant to the war effort and countering potential sabotage to war production made great demands on time and resources. When regular police work within the national jurisdiction (much expanded in wartime under the War Measures Act), and the Mounties' role as provincial police in most provinces, excluding only Quebec and Ontario, are taken into account, it is apparent that the RCMP had a major role to play in wartime Canada.

The Intelligence Bulletin, produced within the Intelligence Section and circulated to the Prime Minister's office and to the senior levels of federal departments, offers an invaluable insight into RCMP thinking on its rapidly expanding security and intelligence role. Intelligence gathering is an activity which requires a certain degree of analytical skill in interpretation and preparation of a finished intelligence product for its consumers— the latter being the senior RCMP brass and the government of Canada. Criminal investigation may not necessarily induce analytical reflection upon its practicioners, and certainly not literary expression. But intelligence work does lead in this direction. It is perhaps no accident that Inspector Charles Rivett-Carnac, head of the Intelligence Section, was also the editor of the *RCMP Quarterly*, and subsequently a published author following his retirement. The Intelligence Bulletins offer an insight into the RCMP mind as well as into the kind of intelligence they were pursuing in wartime Canada: who and what was considered dangerous and why.

Not everyone in official Ottawa in the select circle which received the Bulletins was impressed by their contents, or by the RCMP's concept of intelligence. Harry Ferns was serving as a young official in Mackenzie King's office in the spring of 1940 when he came up against the face of Canadian intelligence. As Ferns later recollected:[12]

Political intelligence in the Canadian government was characterized by boneheaded stupidity. I was not alone in this opinion. A few weeks after I entered the Prime Minister's Office, an RCMP constable came to my room bearing a large brown envelope marked SECRET. He saluted and asked me to sign a receipt. This I did. With some awe I carried the envelope to Pickersgill[13] and asked him what to do with this. Jack gave one of his loud guffaws, waved his hand with a flourish and said, "That's the *Perils of Pauline*. Throw it in the file, but read it if you want a laugh."

I went back to my room and opened the envelope. Inside was another envelope together with a receipt returnable to the RCMP attesting to the fact that I was about to open the second envelope. Inside this envelope I found a mimeographed pamphlet bound in a green cover bearing the arms of the RCMP. About 80 per

---

[12] H.S. Ferns, *Reading From Right to Left: One Man's Political History* (Toronto 1983), 182.

[13] J.W. Pickersgill, the second ranking official of the PMO under W.A. Turnbull, the Prime Minister's Principal Secretary. Pickersgill was later to become Clerk of the Privy Council and a cabinet minister under Louis St. Laurent and Lester Pearson, as well as Mackenzie King's literary executor.

cent of the items were extracts from Canadian newspapers concerning the movements and utterances of Communists, supposed Communists, and various trade union officials. Some of the items I had already seen among the daily circulation of the Prime Minister's clipping service. There were a few items on various priests and pacifists, and nothing at all about various splinter groups in Quebec opposed to Canada's entry into the war. It was something of a mystery to me how the RCMP ever found the home-grown Fuhrer, Adrien Arcand, let alone arrested him. After reading this intelligence bulletin a few times I began to follow Pickersgill's advice. I simply "threw it in the file."

Ferns goes on to note that the discovery of Soviet espionage in wartime Ottawa came not through the counter-espionage activities of the RCMP but through the defection of the Soviet cypher clerk, Igor Gouzenko in 1945. The RCMP, he suggests, were instead "taught to see Communists at work wherever men and women assembled to talk about civil rights, trade union problems, poverty and peace." Ferns was not an entirely neutral observer. He had himself become a Communist while studying at Cambridge in the 1930s amidst that famous generation of Cambridge Communists. He maintains that his party ties had dropped away before he took up his duties in the PMO, but he retained a certain distance from some of the conservative shibboleths of official Ottawa. Indeed, he was later driven out of the civil service and later yet out of Canada for his alleged left-wing sympathies.[14] But his doubts about RCMP "intelligence" were shared by others in the PMO.

Jack Pickersgill had prepared an analysis of the Intelligence Bulletin for the Prime Minister in late November 1939. This was passed on to King a year later by James A. Gibson, another PMO official, with approval.[15] Pickersgill noted that in wartime, "the detection of espionage, of plans for sabotage, and of subversive activities is the most important aspect of intelligence work in connection with the maintenance of internal security." Such work was "presumably divided" between the RCMP and military intelligence. The latter reported no information to the Prime Minister. The RCMP on the other hand reported regularly through the Intelligence Bulletin. Pickersgill's analysis of a single issue of the Bulletin (30 October

---

[14] These difficulties are recounted at length in *Reading From Left to Right*. Some of the problem seems to have stemmed from an alleged mention in one of the documents that Gouzenko stole from the Soviet Embassy: this turns out to be an absurd case of mistaken identity based on a mistaken transliteration of Russian into English. See Reg Whitaker, "Spy story: lifting Gouzenko's cloak," *The Globe and Mail*, 6 November 1984.

[15] NAC, Mackenzie King Papers, J4 Series, vol. 372 file 3913, 'J.A.G.', memorandum to King, 16 November 1940; Pickersgill, "Note on a War-time intelligence service," 27 November 1939 and "Analysis of the Intelligence Bulletin issued at R.C.M.P. Headquarters, October 30, 1939" (C257902-C257910).

1939—'War Series No.2') revealed a number of serious deficiencies:

(1) an inability to distinguish between 'facts' and 'hearsay';
(2) an 'anti-Red complex' which has a striking resemblance to that of the notorious Dies Committee[16] in the United States, with the same tendency to label labour organizers, mild radicals, etc., as Communists. It may be noted, for example, that a French Canadian Liberal candidate in a recent provincial by-election was described in one of the Bulletins (not the one analysed) as a member of a Communist-controlled organization;
(3) no discrimination between legitimate social and political criticism and subversive doctrine;
(4) an almost exclusive pre-occupation with so-called subversive organizations, and, even in this field, very little information about Nazis or Fascists;
(5) no evidence of any suspected sabotage or espionage;
(6) no suggestion that there is any co-ordination with the Military Intelligence, or with the Immigration authorities, or with the Department of External Affairs, or even with the Censorship.
It is evident that the police are attending and reporting on often completely harmless meetings, and spying on the daily activities of peaceful and law-abiding citizens. In itself this may not be very serious, although it would seem to be undesirable in a free country. It is, however, somewhat disturbing to discover that the police are setting themselves up as self-appointed censors of political opinion in the Community, especially when they regard the mildest expressions of liberal views as evidence of Communism.
What is more disturbing is the evidence of a total lack of capacity, education and training required for real intelligence work, and a failure to appreciate the direction from which serious danger may threaten us.
It may well be that there are Communists in Canada who are engaged in espionage or in planning sabotage, but they will presumably be working secretly and will obviously not be among the so-called "agitators" who are sufficiently well-known. It is more likely that there are secret German agents in the country....From a casual reading of these "Intelligence Bulletins" one would scarcely realize that Canada was at war with Germany; there is not the slightest hint that anything is being done in the way of intelligent and well-directed "anti-espionage" work.

Pickersgill went on to suggest greater co-ordination and liaison between various government agencies with an interest in aspects of intelligence and security under the overall direction of an Intelligence Branch located in the Department of Justice, to which the RCMP would report. The civilian Director of Intelligence, "with an adequate conception of the real function of intelligence work in war-time, could probably direct the energies of the police into channels which would enable them to contribute effectively to our internal security without creating public uneasi-

[16] The House Committee on Un-American Activities which under the chairmanship of Congressman Martin Dies of Texas investigated Communism in America in the late 1930s with scant attention to fact but a sharp eye for headlines.

ness about the development of a police-state."[17]

In his analysis of the October 30 1939 Bulletin, Pickersgill pointed out specific examples of the kind of problem to which he was alluding. For instance, its item on the Russian-language Communist organ *Kanadsky Gudok* refers to "seditious attacks." "To illustrate these seditious articles," Pickersgill notes, "a paragraph is quoted criticizing the Chamberlain government in terms which, to say the least, would not be considered outside the limits of legitimate criticism in England." Indeed, Britain was often cited by liberal Canadian officials as an example of relative tolerance of dissent, despite the close proximity of Britain to the Nazi threat.[18] Canada, far from the direct threat of invasion, was apparently more jittery. The RCMP expressed a mood which had far wider roots than the police alone. Indeed, despite the existence of some critics with liberal reservations within the government, and despite the private expressions in his diary of Mackenzie King's liberal conscience, the King government in general and the Justice Department in particular, strongly supported the Mounties.[19]

The obsession with Communism, evident from the pages of the Bulletin in these years, was only tenuously related to the CP's anti-war propaganda during the life of the Nazi-Soviet pact. That propaganda was, in any event, pretty marginal and unimportant—as is evident from what the best efforts of the RCMP were able to uncover as revealed in the Bulletin. Although the Mounties had warned in the very first issue of the Bulletin's War Series [23 October 1939] that "we are of the opinion that there is more to fear from acts of espionage and sabotage on the part of the Communist Party than from Nazi or fascist organizations and adherents," no evidence of sabotage was ever adduced, and the espionage on behalf of the USSR revealed in 1945 by Igor Gouzenko did not seem to have been initiated until the arrival of a Soviet mission in Ottawa in 1942.

In February 1941, the Commissioner of the RCMP, S.T. Wood, went

[17] This would not be the last time that civilian direction or control over RCMP activities in security and intelligence would be suggested. Only after two Royal Commissions, one reporting in 1968 and the second in 1981, would the RCMP security service be 'civilianized' under the Canadian Security Intelligence Service Act of 1984. Pickersgill was thus ahead of his time by about forty-five years.
[18] In the spring of 1941 His Majesty's Commander of Prisons for England and Wales had testified before the secret hearings of the House of Commons Committee on the Defence of Canada Regulations that 'there was not much trouble in Britain with Communists as the British sense of humour was somewhat inclined to view them as a joke rather than a menace...': 20 May 1941, Papers of the Committee, Office of the Clerk of the Committees of the House of Commons.
[19] Whitaker, "Official repression of Communism," 163-4.

public with the anti-Communist message. In *The Canadian Spokesman*, under the title 'TOOLS FOR TREACHERY', Wood confided to his readers that

many may be surprised to hear that it is not the Nazi nor the Fascist but the radical who constitutes our most troublesome problem. Whereas the enemy alien is usually recognizable and easily rendered innocuous by clear-cut laws applicable to his case, your 'Red' has the protection of citizenship, his foreign master is not officially an enemy and, unless he blunders into the open and provides proof of his guilt, he is much more difficult to suppress....Most of his work is carried on under cover of other organizations and associations pretending to be, or in reality, loyal to the Constitution.

Wood cited, as examples of such witting or unwitting fronts: labour unions, groups of the unemployed, the "criminal and weakminded classes," youth clubs, civil liberties associations, dupes in the press who criticized government policies, and even "a few parliamentarians, who are apparently sincere but obviously un-informed or indifferent to facts" who were "greatly encouraging the subversive elements by attacking the Defence [of Canada] Regulations."[20]

This diatribe roused the ire of the leader of the CCF, M.J. Coldwell. Coldwell's question in the House of Commons came to the attention of Pickersgill in Mackenzie King's office. The latter passed on a copy of the article to the Prime Minister with a handwritten note attached: "It seems to reveal the same kind of attitude which the Nazis fostered so successfully with the *Anti-Comintern Pact*, and which did so much to weaken the morale of France."[21] King's reaction is not recorded, but there is no evidence that Wood was chastised.

After 22 June 1941 the Communists did a sharp U-turn and became instant enthusiasts for a total war effort of the democracies against fascism. The RCMP could not care less. The Bulletin for 16 August 1941 [War Series No. 46] had this to say:

Until Germany invaded Russia Canadian Communists were the relentless enemies of democracy and of anything that made for its defence. Now, because the Fatherland of Communism is in deadly peril, they deign to join forces with us against the common enemy—*until the enemy is destroyed*. Thay have turned their coats but not their hearts and their hatred of democracy burns as fiercely as ever. Should their interned leaders be freed again to stab us in the back?

The question was obviously rhetorical. And indeed the interned

---

[20] *The Canadian Spokesman: the Magazine on National Affairs*, 1:2 (February 1941), 1-6.

[21] King Papers, J4 Series, vol. 355 file 3815, Pickersgill, memorandum to King, 18 February 1941 [C245668]; *Hansard*, 17 February 1941, 878.

"leaders" [*sic*—the leaders had gone into hiding, it was mostly lower level party operatives who ended up in jail], remained interned in many cases for almost a year after the USSR had become an ally.[22] Moreover, the Communist party remained illegal throughout the duration of the war on the advice of the RCMP (as well as the Catholic church and the Quebec Liberal caucus). Canada was thus the only Western ally to maintain a ban on the local CP during the era of the Soviet alliance. A convenient fiction was worked out whereby the party was recreated as the Labour Progressive Party which could legally run candidates and its banned newspaper resurfaced as the *Tribune*. This peculiar protocol was necessary to appease the diehard opponents of Communism who savoured their symbolic, if not substantive, relegation of the party to illegality.

Yet once the USSR had become an ally, and once Mackenzie King began appearing before Canadian Aid to Russia rallies where rousing renditions of the Internationale and God Save the King opened proceedings, the diehard anti-Communism of the RCMP was bound to wear thin in the eyes of many officials. It even became embarrassing when the Communists in the unions began volunteering no strike pledges on behalf of war production, and such old Red-baiters as Ontario premier Mitch Hepburn started turning up on platforms beside prominent Communists to preach the virtues of a total war effort. By 1942, the Prime Minister's Principal Secretary, W.J. Turnbull, was complaining to his boss about the Mounties still engaging in "'red' hunting." "Apparently there are in the...Mounted Police, some men like the notorious Sergeant Leopold, whose jobs would seem to depend on continuing to uncover bolshevik plots. They may have some grounds for their suspicions, but I would think that a change of policy might well be indicated to them, with Russia a valiant ally."[23]

It may have been the attitudes of prime ministerial advisers like Turnbull and Pickersgill, given a strong boost by the international situation, which led to a sudden change of policy with regard to the circulation of the Intelligence Bulletins. At the end of 1941, all distribution beyond the RCMP security service itself came to a halt. Moreover, Mounties came around to offices where the Bulletin had previously been transmitted and removed all earlier editions dating back to the beginning of the war. Since documentary evidence is lacking on this decision, it remains unclear just what was behind it. Probably the government no longer found the regular anti-Communist litany of much interest. The Mounties went back to talking to themselves—if indeed, given the earlier testimony of Harry Ferns,

---

[22] See William and Kathleen Repka, *Dangerous Patriots: Canada's Unknown prisoners of War* (Vancouver 1982).

[23] King Papers, J4 Series, vol. 328 file 3490, Turnbull, memorandum to the Prime Minister, 6 July 1942 [C227104].

the Bulletin had ever actually had much of an external readership. Intelligence is a product to be consumed, normally by the governments that employ intelligence agencies. The RCMP Intelligence Bulletin was a product consumed in-house.

Are these Bulletins then worth our attention almost a half century later, if the government of the day could scarcely be bothered to consult them? There are strong arguments for republishing them today—perhaps, ironically, for the very reasons that critics rejected them in the early war years.

The Bulletins provide us with a considerable amount of information on the very subject that the government of the day was growing tired of hearing about: Communism and Communist activities in various sectors of Canadian life. Not only is party activity, as such, chronicled, but trade unions and other organizations are surveyed as they relate, or allegedly relate, to Communist penetration. Particularly valuable as source material are RCMP studies of various ethnic organizations in Canada, including material which has never been in print (at least in English) before. The Mounties maintained sources in some of these organizations; their reports thus constitute first-hand accounts of the politics of ethnic communities. Pro-fascist activites were being reported upon, even though Communism held pride of place.

There are also interesting insights to be gained into the outlook of the RCMP: that, for instance, the force did not approve of free-lance vigilante groups attacking alleged "fifth-column" traitors [10 June 1940—War Series No.33], and that it preferred to see anti-alien hysteria in the population die down, rather than fan the flames. In Canada, questions of subversion and treason were to be dealt with by the accredited authorities of the state, not by unofficial entrepreneurs. In the United States, J. Edgar Hoover's FBI was happy to feed Congressional and private witch-hunters with material from the Bureau's files. This tendency, later to grow into McCarthyism by the early 1950s, was not at all to the taste or inclination of the RCMP. As is evident from a number of items in these Bulletins, the Mounties were not averse to quoting approvingly from the findings of the demagogic House Committee on Un-American Activities. But they would not have welcomed a Canadian equivalent. Such a body would itself have been rather un-Canadian.

***

The Bulletins which are reproduced here represent a very early use of the Access to Information Act. In 1983, shortly after the Act came into force, I directed a request to the RCMP for specific numbers of the Bulletins from October 1939 through December 1941. In the course of research I had come across a notation in the records of the External Affairs Department that in December of 1941 a representative of the Mounties had removed the War Series Bulletins which had been transmitted to the Department. The Bulletins taken away were itemized by date. I could thus make my request very specific. After paying $164.00 for photocopying charges, I received copies of the Bulletins early in 1984.

Numerous deletions had been made on the texts, but complaints to the Information Commissioner (as provided for by the Act) were of no assistance. Among the complaints I raised were that material was exempted on the grounds of s.19(1) of the Act regarding personal information, even though the documents were some 40 years old and dealt with persons already of mature years. Presumably most would now be dead, and a good many dead for the 20 years or more required under the Act for the release of personal information. The response of the Commissioner to this point was that neither her office nor the RCMP (*sic!*) "have the capacity to ascertain the status of each individual mentioned in the documents." She went on: "If you believe that a given person might be mentioned in an exempted portion, and that that person died over 20 years ago, please let us have the details and we will check the record."[24] The catch-22 in this, of course, is that when names are removed, how can one possibly prove that these phantom presences died 20 years ago or more? Similarly, my attempts to draw attention to the RCMP's apparent failure to apply the "injury test" clauses of the exemption sections they had invoked—s.15(1) speaks of material which could "reasonably be expected to be injurious to...." and s.16(1)(c) uses the same language—failed to impress or interest the Commissioner, who declined to press any of my complaints, except for one technical one.

In regard to the deletions in the text, the Pickersgill analysis of the 30 October 1939 Bulletin [War Series No. 2], includes a summary of the contents of each item. In the text released to me by the RCMP, three items have been removed. The headings in the table of contents have also been removed so that the reader has no idea even of the subject matter (which of course makes it difficult to make a case against the exemption). In the Pickersgill summary, the three missing items are described as follows:[25]

There follows a report that a member of the Communist party has got a job as organizer with the Hosiery Workers Union in Hamilton. The next item reports the dismissal of the business manager of the Daily Clarion of Toronto for opposing the policy of the Communist party.
The next item records the resignation of the Mayor of Blairmore, Alberta, from the Communist party. In comment on the resignation, the report reads, "Whether this individual has an ulterior motive underlying his announcement, is not known as yet."

Readers may draw their own conclusions regarding the injury to the national interest or to the privacy of these individuals that would have been involved by the disclosure of these items 45 years after the event. It

[24] Letter from Inger Hansen to the author, 14 May 1984.
[25] See n.15, above.

may also be confidently assumed that much of the remaining exempted material falls into the same category.

At the end of 1987, the Canadian Security Intelligence Service, which since the passage of the CSIS Act in 1984 now houses the historical records of the RCMP security service, gave unrestricted permission to the Committee on Labour History to publish the Bulletins which Professor Gregory Kealey and myself had had released under various Access to Information requests. Under different names and formats, these declassified Bulletins run from December 1919 through December 1955. We plan to publish all of them in successive volumes, of which this present series is one.

R.W.

SECRET

INTELLIGENCE
BULLETIN

ROYAL CANADIAN MOUNTED POLICE
HEADQUARTERS, OTTAWA

WEEKLY SUMMARY
OCTOBER 23, 1939

CONTENTS

Fascism:
Communism:
General:
War Series
No. 1

FASCISM

ITALIAN SECRET SOCIETIES PREPARED TO SABOTAGE

Italian Consuls continue to be the centre for all Fascist activities among the Italian people throughout the Dominion, and it should be noted that it is no mere coincidence that practically all these Consuls have visited Italy and returned to Canada within a few weeks of war being declared. The Italian Consul General, Marquis A. Rosso-Longhi, has returned to his position in Ottawa since the declaration of war, and there is much expectation among the Italian population as to the nature of the instructions which he will send out to his staff and, in turn, the Italian organizations throughout the Dominion. The Italian secret societies, which are not Communist, continue to be very anti-British in their attitude, in spite of the fact that Italy is neutral. These Italian secret organizations are definitely prepared to carry out sabotage, more particularly on the railways and harbours. At this stage, it appears to be more likely that the Italian Anarchists and Black Hand Organizations in Canada of both Communist and Fascist leanings are definitely committed to acts of sabotage. Such professions of loyalty from Italian groups as have been forwarded to the Government are from Communist controlled organizations and are to be treated with

21

suspicion, since the Communist Party is supporting the policy and action of Russia in the present conflict, and to this end is prepared to engage in a campaign of sabotage.

SABOTAGE

No definite acts of organized sabotage have been committed so far. It can hardly be expected that such will take place until the movement of troops and war material overseas are well under way. We have knowledge of instructions, [?<deletion: 1 line] giving details of methods to be employed in the sabotage of rolling stock on railroads and the transportation system as a whole; likewise sabotage in industry. It may not be out of place here to mention that instructions have gone out to members of the Communist Party to join the Defence Forces in preparation for the Revolution which they anticipate will follow at the conclusion of hostilities. We are of the opinion that there is more to fear from acts of espionage and sabotage on the part of the Communist Party than from Nazi or Fascist organizations and adherents, for the reason that the Communist Party is much better organized and has cells in practically every industry.[2]

INTERNMENT OF ENEMY ALIENS

Of 335 enemy aliens (German) listed by this Force for internment prior to the outbreak of war, 300 have been interned, which includes some that have been interned since the declaration of war. A number left the country shortly before war was declared. There is a noted tendency on the part of mining companies and others who have been employing Germans for years to endeavour to have the Police intern these men, in order to relieve them of the responsibility of discharging them. Evidently they fear acts of retaliation.

REGISTRATION OF ALIENS

Registration is well under way, and actual figures will be given in the next bulletin. Registration is being conducted by members of all Police Forces, with the exception of the Ontario Provincial Police, and with the co-operation of Postmasters in remote districts. There has been no indication of any exodus of enemy aliens.[3]

COMMUNISM

POLISH CANADIAN SITUATION

The destruction of Poland as a national entity and its dismemberment by Hitler and Stalin have had the effect of widening the breach in Canada between the Polish patriotic groups and the Polish Communists. Previous to Russia's invasion all classes of Poles were united in rescuing their fatherland from the Nazis by loyal co-operation with Canada's war efforts. Today the Marxists are acclaiming the "salvation" of half of Poland by the Red Army and are eagerly anticipating the day when the whole country will become a "New Socialist Poland" under the protection of Soviet Russia.

While, fortunately, the great majority of our Polish-Canadian citizens are unswervingly loyal to their adopted country, the revolutionary minority is bitterly antagonistic and must be segregated and rendered harmless. This can be accomplished by, first, encouraging and supporting the loyal majority in their own "house-cleaning"; second, by keeping close surveillance of Communist leaders and, when necessary, putting them under restraint.

The Polish radical offensive is lead and inspired by the POLSKE TO-WARZYSTWO LUDOWE (Polish Section of the Communist Party of Canada) and their political organ the "Glos Pracy." The invasion of the German Army had first inspired the radical Poles here to vehement anti-Fascist slogans, and it seemed that they would discard political dogmas for patriotic sentiments. Thus, when a Polish Legion was proposed by the P.T.L., the Dabrowsky Legion members who had returned from the Spanish War hurried to join in another anti-Fascist war. (The idea was killed by patriotic Poles who were mistrustful of the good intentions of their compatriots.) They also flooded the Canadian Government with their resolutions of loyalty and offers of support against Hitler Germany. But when it became clear that behind the mask lurked the ulterior ends of the Communist Party of Canada the semblance of patriotism was dropped for more subtle methods of campaigning.

Stalin's betrayal and the "stab in the back," fully justified by the speeches of Molotov and other Red leaders the world over, were then approved by the Soviet official press and Polish radical opinion. Marxists in Canada fell in line with the Red Army in Poland in an endeavour to exterminate the remaining vestiges of Polish class nationalism or sympathy for the "wretched class government of Poland" expressed by patriotic Poles in Canada. In this [4] onslaught the speech of Lloyd George is profusely used as a maxim for the accepted British opinion.

Thus we see today an unusual spectacle of calumny, contempt, and malevolent indictments heaped upon the heads and regime of the defeated Poland by the Polish radicals in Canada—an attack more vicious and damaging in nature than the propaganda ever aimed at Poland by her Nazi enemy. The Polish ruling class is branded by this propaganda as "rotten, spineless, and traitorous," who betrayed and handed the country over to Hitler (no mention of the Soviet invasion). The whole social system of Poland is indicted. The landed gentry, clergy and reactionary elements are blamed for contributing to the fall of Poland by setting up a semi-Fascist state and perpetuating the rule of aristocracy which oppressed and exploited the workers and 8,000,000 of the landless peasants. This government is again charged with sabotaging Polish defences and fearing the common people's co-operation in defense because "they might upset the

government and then prosecute a 'democratic war' against Hitler along
the lines and slogans of republican Spain...defeat the Nazi and establish
a Socialist Poland."

This offensive of the Polish Marxist camp in Canada has two definite
aims: justification of the Soviet action, as a prerequisite for the existence
and growth of the Polish Communist Party in Canada, and support of the
movement to establish a Socialist Poland.

The evident purpose of the attacks on the Polish ruling class and its
protaganists in Canada is to distract the opinion of the Poles from the actual crime committed against their nation by the Soviet Union and shift
the onus of the crime on the victim—the ruling class of Poland—or on
Hitler. Like other Canadian Communists, Polish radicals cannot conceive
of rebelling against their spiritual fatherland, the Soviet Union, or the
mighty Stalin. As a result of this blind faith the criminal is represented as
a "saviour," and the invasion of Eastern Poland a blessed act.

Indeed, the Red Army occupation and the subsequent Sovietization of
the territory serve as grist for the mills of propaganda in Canada. Within
a short period of the first confusion the Polish Communists had succeeded
in justifying the Soviet treachery and are now consolidating their position
and penetrating the ranks of patriotic organizations with added zeal. The
full force of class arguments has again been turned against the "reactionary element" among the Poles in Canada, with the obvious purpose of confusing, demoralizing, and converting them to the Communist Party. They
argue that the Polish Communist group is the only anti-Fascist organization which has been warning and struggling against the Nazi plans of aggression. Now that Nazi Germany has justified their early warnings, their
appeals sound more plausible.[5]

In recent issues of the "Glos Pracy," notice has been served upon the
patriotic camp that the radicals are withdrawing their co-operation from
the Polish Defense Committees, set up throughout Canada at the start of
the war, and will henceforth conduct an independent action of raising Red
Cross funds, etc. They charge the patriotic leaders with a general boycott
of their "patriotic" endeavours and for efforts made to dissolve the P.T.L.
by secret denunciations to the authorities in Ottawa. But it would seem
that the prime purpose of their withdrawal is to build up a new "democratic
front" heralding a "new Poland" under a Socialist or Communist regime.
As soon as such a regime is established in Poland, it has been stated in the
"Glos Pracy," the Soviet Union will withdraw its army from the occupied
territory, apparently as a comradely gesture. As for Britain and France, it
is suggested that it is not too late for them to make up with the Soviets, in
order to break Hitler, so that "Poland may soon arise without the necessity of smashing the Siegfried Line or our people against it."

It appears that the political gulf dividing the patriotic and Marxist
camps is gradually widening. The first are displaying at the present a pug-

nacious hatred of their Communist compatriots because of propaganda justifying, on one hand, Stalin's stab in the back, and, on the other, the besmirching of leaders of the old Polish regime. If the Polish Communists get too aggressive in their promotion of Communism and a Marxist Poland among their resentful compatriots, serious friction may result.

C.I.O. EXPELLED FROM TRADES AND LABOUR CONGRESS

The 55th Annual Convention of the Trades and Labour Congress of Canada was held in the Masonic Temple, London, Ontario, from September 25th to 30th, 1939, with 432 delegates attending. Of these, [⸲<deletion: 2 lines]

The main issue before this year's convention was the "outlawing" of the Committee for Industrial Organization Unions, and delegates representing any of its affiliated bodies were barred from participation in the Congress. All delegates attending were warned that voting in favour of the C.I.O. might disbar them from further activity and cause the suspension of their Union Charter. Voting on all questions was done "publicly" as against previous "secret" balloting, in order that every delegate's stand should be known. On the C.I.O. resolution a great many delegates refrained from voting so that their stand, if opposed to the Union which they represented, should not be publicised. Though the vote on the expulsion of the C.I.O. Unions showed a great majority, it apparently did not portray the true feeling of the Congress, as many were "forced" to vote against the C.I.O. who would have voted otherwise had the balloting been secret.[6]

Commenting on the action taken by the Congress, the Communist Party remarks:-

"The Congress failed in its duty, although a strong block of delegates stood firm by their principles, including many who for many reasons could not vote as they believed."

[⸲<deletion: 2 lines] is quoted from the "Clarion," Communist weekly published in Toronto, Ont.:-

"A sober analysis of the London gathering leads us to the regretful conclusion that the 55th Annual Convention failed to live up to the historic obligations which the present critical situation placed upon it as the expression of the largest trade union center in Canada. In fact the London Convention adopted certain measures which only the rank and file of the International trade union membership can prevent from having a seriously damaging effect upon their vital needs and conditions.

"The previous three Congress Conventions showed a definite trend towards greater inner union democracy...but this course was changed at the London meeting..... It was a harmful return to the days of machine controlled conventions.....

"Despite the pressure of the international offices to bring along 'safe' delegates, they were by no means sure of the delegates when they arrived.... A shameful orgy of ganging up was immediately launched. The 'heads' herded together their respective delegates and appealed, cajoled, and threatened them with expulsion and removal if they did not 'vote right'....."

Defeated in the question of the expulsion of the C.I.O. unions, the Communists tried to have elected a "progressive" executive, but were again outmanoeuvered. Referring to this Communist "catastrophe" Salsberg writes:-

[ℰ<deletion: 1 paragraph: 6 lines][7]

Because of the extensive lobbying carried out to enlist the support of all delegates in order to elect those sponsored by the American Federation of Labor, the Communists claim that the Congress was controlled by choking discussion. In all the resolutions the Communist Party was overridden. Regarding the war resolution, [ℰ<deletion: 1 line] states:-

"The war resolution betrayed the leadership's eagerness to please the high and mighty and outdo the worst jingoists in the country who pretend to speak in the name of the trade unionists. As for the masses of workers they will look in vain if they will seek in the adopted resolution any trace of labour independence or sound labour policy to guide them on the war question and during the war period."

Referring to the outcome of the Convention, [ℰ<deletion: 1 line] regrets that "progressive" people in Canada have temporarily been checked, but adds "We will down them yet." His article concludes with a denouncement of "imperialist war aims."

"Those who succeeded temporarily to check the flow of progressivism through the Convention channels will either change or they will be washed away. For the Canadian workers in the international unions as well as in all other trade union centers want unity. They want large scale organization drives to win hundreds of thousands of new recruits to their side. They want to defeat fascism but they have no interest in wars of an imperialist character. They desire a just and a lasting peace. They want to achieve a higher standard and want to exercise a decisive influence in the government councils for the welfare of the whole people instead of being used as the hewer of wood and drawers of water. Around these vitally urgent needs of all workers and of all people unity will be forged, joint drives will be undertaken, mutual support will be granted, and learning from the sad experiences of the last war and from the last post-war period Canadian labor will emerge with greater strength and clearer in aim than ever visualized before."

[ℰ<deletion: 1 paragraph: 3 lines][8]

CONFUSION AMONG COMMUNISTS

The hatred of Communists for Hitlerism seems, in recent days, to have been counter-balanced by blind trust in Stalinism.

Out of the confusion and welter of almost daily fluctuations in Communist policies there emerges a not undivided front committed to combat the Allies now by every possible means and to be prepared to destroy them utterly after they emerge weakened from the world conflict.

Following Canada's declaration of war, the Party staged a "black-out," issuing orders to destroy all incriminating documents and literature and their leaders going into hiding. This has seriously disrupted their lines of inter-communication, weakening central control over individual members and hampering united action. In fact, so great is the apprehension of many of the leaders, that only the inner circles of the Party know of their whereabouts. Public meetings have been cancelled SINE DIE and all districts have been split up into sections comprising not more than five or six members.

Although Communism in Canada has been temporarily weakened, it is far from being dead. We know that Party members have been urged to gain admission into "key" industries and Defence Forces, in order to sabotage and cause disruption at an opportune time. The Party is also urging its membership to extend their operations in the various trade unions to influence their policies.

Directives issued from Toronto Headquarters refer Party members to the "line" adopted by the leadership of the Communist Party in England and the United States, as well as Canada. However, there is a great deal of confusion and the Canadian membership are showing more curiosity than belief in the various statements issued by the Party. If, as they seem to think, the Communist Party is declared illegal, the Headquarters of the Canadian Section will be moved to New York, from where they will direct all activity. If this should happen, it is anticipated that many of the Party will sever their connections with the organization. Meanwhile, a great number of erstwhile members, mostly of the Jewish faith, have left the ranks, disclaiming the "good intentions" of Russia in its fight against the Jew-baiting Nazis.

All members of the Communist Party have been warned against making any statements about the Party's stand. "It is in order to discuss these matters within the unit, but they must avoid discussion with outsiders," is the subject of a directive issued from Party headquarters.[9]

Communist Party circles are rather bewildered over [&<deletion: 1 line] recent statement before the Dies Committee on Un-American Activities in Washington, to the effect that the American Communist Party did not support the war. This was, according to the majority of opinions, very different from statements that had been given out by the Canadian Communist Party Headquarters.

Though there has been no further official announcement of a change in policy here one gathers from the Communist press that again they will be forced to step into line, this time to denounce the war altogether "before it has brought death and destruction to millions of people, before the flower of our youth are slaughtered." In a further declamation of Imperialist aims, the Communist press declares:-

"This is not a war for democracy and against Fascism. This is not a war for the liberties of the small nations. This is not a war in defence of peace against aggression. The war is a fight of imperialist powers over profits, colonies and world domination. It will bring only suffering and misery to millions of working class homes. The immediate issue is cessation of hostilities and the calling of a peace conference."

The reception of this latest effort of the Communist Party to portray the international scene has not, so far, brought any comments from its membership, but they will, on all probability, denounce their previous policy with as much determination as lack of foresight; by placing implicit faith in "Joseph Stalin, inasmuch as he can be relied upon to have taken the best means to further the cause of the workers of the world."[10]

GENERAL
STRIKE IN ESTEVAN COAL FIELDS

The breakdown of efforts of the Saskatchewan Provincial Government to mediate for a settlement in this coal mining area at a conference between company officials, United Mine Workers of America and government officials, prompted the local union to formulate plans for a strike affecting the Western Dominion Coal Mines Limited, Manitoba and Saskatchewan Mine, Eastern Collieries, Baniulis Brothers and the Lignite Coal Company. The strike was called for October 16th.

The main factor involved is the refusal of the above mines to recognize the United Mine Workers of America in preference to the Canadian Federation of Labour with whom they have a "closed shop" agreement. The coal companies allege that the men concerned are perfectly willing to continue working, but are prevented from doing so by the action of the U.M.W. of A. in placing pickets around the various mines.

The mine management concerned are anxious to have a strong police force in the vicinity, and this was stressed at a conference with Provincial officials on October 18th at which the mine operators suggested the use of the troops stationed at Weyburn. Display of force, representatives of the Western Coal Mines Limited contended, would defeat the operation of the strike. It was pointed out to them that such action would in all probability lead to an outbreak of violence. So far there has been no destruction of property and the several assaults that have been reported have been dealt with successfully by members of this Force presently stationed in that area. Despite the many conflicting reports appearing in the press and from other sources, the strikers appear to be conducting themselves with reasonable regard for the law, and unless the pickets become more aggressive no action will, apparently, be taken by the Provincial Government, who are trying to maintain a neutral stand on this question.[11]

EDUCATIONAL CAMPAIGN FOR "BETTER CANADIANS"

It is our opinion that a National Educational Campaign might be undertaken to point out the benefits of democracy and responsible government in order to offset the insidious and poisonous teachings spreading throughout our social structure. This campaign should be extended not only to the English-speaking Canadians but to those of foreign extraction, such as Ukrainians, Austrians and those from other central European countries, where recent events have been the means of dividing their opinions and leaving them in a state of mind which makes them easy prey to subversive propaganda.

In these weekly bulletins we hope to be allowed to advance further suggestions and perhaps elaborate definite schemes that may prove helpful in the strengthening of our civil security menaced by the "enemy within."

SECRET

INTELLIGENCE
BULLETIN

ROYAL CANADIAN MOUNTED POLICE
HEADQUARTERS, OTTAWA

WEEKLY SUMMARY
OCTOBER 30, 1939

CONTENTS

General:
Communism:
Fascism:
Note:

War Series
No. 2

GENERAL

INCREASING COST OF GUARD DUTY

A survey has been carried out by members of the R.C.M.Police commencing in March, 1939 and covering 1,685 vulnerable points in Canada. These points include power companies, communication points, transportation, food supply, industrial concerns and miscellaneous, such as water works, filtration plants, magazines, etc.

As a result of the survey, private companies and municipalities have expended many thousands of dollars in providing protective equipment such as fencing, floodlighting, screening and other items, in addition to which they have also provided guards at points where recommended.

The responsibility of the R.C.M.P. covers national harbours, radio stations, government grain elevators, international bridges and Dominion public buildings and in addition, points of vital importance are now being transferred from the Department of National Defence to this Force for guarding, which includes railway bridges, canals, dry docks, cable stations, etc.

The R.C.M.P. are at present employing in the neighbourhood of 900 members of the veteran organizations and it is expected that a further 800 will be employed in the course of the next two weeks, in order to relieve the Department of National Defence of the responsibility.

Arrangements are at present under way for the protection of hydraulic works in international waters, which will include certain hydro projects and international dams. This will require approximately a further 225 war veterans, bringing the total to the neighbourhood of 2,000 Special Constables.

The equipment furnished to the war veterans employed as Special Constables costs in the neighbourhood of $20 per man, and the pay and allowances for single men amount to $2.60 per diem, for married men $3.20 per diem and Supervisors $4.60 per diem. Therefore on an average basis of $3.20 per diem, the cost of 2,000 Special Constables will be $2,336,000 per annum, and with the cost of equipment added it will be in the neighbourhood of $2,400,000.

Requests have already been received to have guards furnished for certain radio coast stations, radio range stations, also a number of [1] international bridges, but these items have not been included in the above mentioned summary.

Considering the above facts it would seem that the Dominion Government were assuming an ever-increasing and perhaps disproportionate share of the responsibility and cost of guarding public works and strategic spots throughout Canada.

SERIOUS ASPECTS OF ESTEVAN COAL STRIKE

The strike called by the local union of the United Mine Workers of America on October 16 in the Estevan-Bienfait area, involving approximately 400 miners, has assumed a more serious aspect, inasmuch as the Western Dominion Coal Mine have obtained an injunction restraining the U.M.W. of A. from interfering in any way with the free work of the mine for three weeks. The mines affected by the strike are:

Taylorton, Sask. - Western Dominion Coal Mine, 75-100;
Manitoba & Saskatchewan Mine, 180; Lignite Mines Ltd., 30; Baniulius Brothers, 30; Eastern Collieries Ltd., 6;
Bienfait, Sask. - Western Dominion Coal Mine, 50.

Picketing has continued around the Strip Mine owned by the Western

Dominion which is located about two miles south of Bienfait, with approximately 250 miners taking part, and working in eight hour shifts. The other mines in the district, though idle, have not received the attention of the pickets.

A recent report on the situation reveals that the men are "striving for an organization that would protect them in other matters besides salary," and the strike leaders contend that the signing of an agreement with the United Mine Workers in preference to the Canadian Federation of Labour would bring this about. [ɜ<deletion: 3 lines] other than minor disturbances during the early stages of the tie-up. [ɜ<deletion: 1 line] claims that the U.M.W. of A. has the almost unanimous support of the miners, and that "there was no need for pickets so far as the local miners were concerned, but that the U.M.W. of A. was afraid that the operators were going to import 'scab' labour from Brandon or Winnipeg." In this[2] connection it is interesting to note that two miners from Brandon, in response to a "Help Wanted" advertisement, reported for work, but "upon being advised of the real situation" they jointed the picket line.

[ɜ<deletion: 1 paragraph: 5 lines]

So far the Attorney General has not ordered police reinforcements into the strike area, but the situation is being closely watched.

BRITISH COLUMBIA TEACHERS ON WAR

Popularization of Communist doctrines within the British Columbia Teachers' Federation has been observed for some time now and, although the group of "Progressives" within the said Federation is not in a controlling position, it is interesting to note the attitude of this body of organized teachers on war as reflected in its official organ "The B.C. Teacher."

In a leading article appearing in its September issue entitled "Armageddon-And The Teacher," "The B.C. Teacher" declares:

"We did not learn much in 1914-1918, but those of us who at that time had already reached adult years learned never again to accept at face value the accusations and rebuttals with which the directors of wartime propaganda darken the counsels of the multitude. We remember too well the devilish fairy tales that came to us, ostensibly from Belgium, to whet our generous indignation into the unreasoning hate which war lords, of whatever breed, seem to think a necessary condition of military efficiency. It is the business of the teacher, now as formerly, to refuse to be stampeded and to train pupils in the dispassionate weighing of evidence and pursuit of truth.

"We are profoundly convinced and have been teaching that people everywhere are very much like people anywhere; that the differences between men as individuals are much greater than the differences between men as races and nations; that the human nature of men as spiritual beings entails possibilities of control of their human nature as quarrelsome animals. We believe and have been teaching that war is an insane device [3] for the extermination of peace-loving people of one land by peace-loving people of another land; that neither the British nor the French nor the Poles nor the Germans nor the Italians nor the people of any other country desire war but that, on the contrary, the overwhelming majority in every land ardently wish to live peaceably with all their neighbours. These things we must continue to teach, no matter how unpopular such doctrines for a time may be.

"It is for the teacher to hew to the line, let the chips fall where they will. If the rising generation is left blind to our own sins and follies, then, even if our armies prevail, war will again be followed by another Versailles and by other policies that, like those adopted by the democratic powers subsequently to 1918, will make the only possible peace a mere armistice. If we had done our duty when Streseman was valiantly endeavouring to establish a German democracy, we might now have 90,000,000 German friends instead of 90,000,000 German enemies.

"This is everybody's war and therefore everybody's business. The British Commonwealth of Nations, the France, the Poland, the Germany that are going into the war will not be the Commonwealth, the France, the Poland, the Germany that will emerge from the war. Nor will the conflict and resultant revolutionary changes be confined to this group of nations. Even if it were possible to evade revolutionary change, such evasion would be disastrous. At present we are not the kind of nations nor is ours the kind of organization that can ever ensure a just peace. Teachers everywhere will have their part to play if we are to be transformed into something better and if foundations are to be laid for such economic and political machinery and organization as may justify the sacrifice of indefinite multitudes of helpless noncombatants and of the world's sturdiest and bravest sons."

[⸺deletion: 1 paragraph: 5 lines][4]

COMMUNISM
EARL BROWDER INDICTED

Earl Browder, General Secretary of the Communist Party of the U.S.A., was indicted on October 23 by a Special Federal Grand Jury in the United States Court on two counts: charging him with using a passport obtained on false representations, and making false statements to obtain a passport.

Browder's indictment marked the climax of American sentiment against the Communist Party engendered by the Nazi-Soviet Pact and by statements given before the Congressional Committee investigating un-

American activities to the effect that, in addition to travelling on false passports, Communists had obtained money directly and indirectly from the U.S.S.R. The indictment of Browder is said to be only the first step in what promises to be widespread action against influential Communists in the United States suspected of having travelled abroad in recent years on fraudulent and forged passports obtained through what is described as a "Passport Mill" in New York.

Representative Martin Dies, Chairman of the Special Congressional Committee investigating un-American activities, issued a statement that unless the State and Justice Departments took immediate action he would take independent action to bring about the prosecution of the Communist Party and the German-American Bund for not registering as agents for foreign governments, as required by Federal law. Representative Dies has maintained throughout the investigations carried on by the Committee that the Communists and the German-American Bund were directly connected with the Governments of Soviet Russia and Germany.

RIFTS IN THE COMMUNIST INTERNATIONAL

Displaying great consternation over the removal of Harry Pollitt from the leadership of the British Communist Party and fearing that it is an indication that the English membership are not in agreement with the policy of the Communist International, Canadian Party members are anxiously awaiting further developments regarding the situation. This, coming on top of a series of very disquieting news concerning French relationships with the Soviet Union is particularly depressing. Inasmuch as the French Party [5] is the biggest delegation to the Comintern and supplies the majority of officials to the Central Committee, their national policy is regarded with as much interest as that from British sources, and the loss of approximately 40% of the French membership over the signing of the Russo-German Pact, is considered by many of the Party a failure of the Soviet Union and the Communist International. Their belief that the Party was firmly entrenched on French soil has been seriously shaken over the action of the French Government in declaring the Party illegal, and the arrest of so many prominent individuals. The principal topic of conversation within the Secretariat and amongst the rank and file, is the utter breakdown of the Comintern's consistent attack on Nazism by the expansionist action of the U.S.S.R. Failure to understand the changed political standpoint and retain their faith in the Soviet Union is very difficult for all but the most ardent supporters, and one member is reported to have remarked concerning the above situation: "That's what I've been doing, just travelling on my faith."

Complaints that the leadership are not providing sufficient political enlightenment to the membership, appears to be one of the main troubles in Party circles, and seems to be justified from a Communist viewpoint, inasmuch as Headquarters are reticent over any definite policy because of "rapidly changing conditions."

CAUTION PERVADES FINNISH COMMUNISTS

Since the days of the Soviet-Nazi "betrothal" and consequent flurry of consternation in the Red camp, it seems that Canadian Finnish followers of dictator Stalin have either not sufficiently recovered from the shock or else are playing possum.

Unlike the English-speaking Reds who are clamouring for Hitler's head, as well as for the heads of some of the Canadian and British statesmen and "reactionaries," the Finnish Communists appear mysteriously hesitant. They trail far behind their dogmatic brethren, the Ukrainian and Polish Reds, who are closely allied to Tim Buck and his "Clarion." A careful perusal of the reports, based on the summaries of the editorials and news accounts appearing in the "Vapaus," fails to reveal anything but a policy of cautious reservation and endeavours to camouflage Finnish links with the Communist Party by a heavy veil of pseudo-Canadian patriotism. The official organ refrains from any out-spoken attitude on any national and international question. Its editor has apparently lost his initiative in the matter of treating editorial problems in the direct manner of other Communist editors in the country, confining himself [6] to subjects discussed by such papers as the "Toronto Star" and "Winnipeg Free Press," and denying that the C.F.O., as such, propagates Communist ideals. At the same time the "Vapaus" cannot resist giving prominence in its editorial discussions to all the important events and problems affecting the Communists and more blatantly handled in the "Clarion" and other Communist papers.

The news dispatches from Moscow are published in most of the issues of "Vapaus." The "Izwiestia" and "Pravda" are quoted as saying that continuation of war is a foolish butchery and that Hitler's peace proposals should be considered. The "Izwiestia" news item and editorial published in the "Vapaus", September 5, regarding the event of the decoration of 930 Red Army soldiers are reported in part as follows:

"The land of socialism is victoriously marching toward communism and there is no force in the world which could block that march of millions of Stalinists along the road of progress."

All events marking the progress or "glory" of the Soviet Union are faithfully lauded in "Vapaus."

It is true that the Canadian Finnish Organization has officially declared itself by the resolution of the Central Executive to the effect that "Nazis are the foes of mankind and must be speedily destroyed, and having this aim in sight to support the Government's war measures is offered." But this support however, as in the case of the parent organization, the Communist Party, and its language sections, is strictly conditional the "joker" being that before any move towards the support is made they must be convinced that people's social rights and liberties are preserved, even in war times, and of course profiteers and reactionaries abolished.

C.C.F. STEALS COMMUNISTS' THUNDER

Claiming that the "Canadian Commonwealth Federation has encroached on Communist territory," the Party membership are reluctantly admitting their failure to be included on C.C.F. platforms advocating "Civil Liberties" for the Canadian people, and the slogans "Not a man for Overseas," "No Profiteering," etc., are considered to be a stronger political lead than previous Party planks. Recent issues of the respective Western publications of the two organizations appeared with headlines sponsoring such efforts for the preservation of Canadian democracy. However according to reports from Communist sources, the C.C.F. has "stolen our thunder."[7]

"KANADSKY GUDOK" (CANADIAN WHISTLE) ATTACKS CHAMBERLAIN

The Communist Party organ in the Russian language, published in Winnipeg, is becoming particularly seditious in its vehement attacks upon British institutions. Adhering to the policy of the Communist Party as enunciated from Moscow, this publication has been most daring in pronouncing this an imperialist war. It is clearly implied that the prosecution of this war means the liberation of Polish and German peoples, as well as British, French and Canadian peoples from their governments and bourgeois institutions.

An article appearing in a recent issue supports the "working class movement" and states that workers have been driven to an impasse, forcing them to support such governments as headed by Chamberlain, whereas under other leadership they could have had "peace" by accepting the overtures of the Soviet Union:

"The direct responsibility for the present situation lies on the English politicians and reactionaries represented by Chamberlain, who have persistently sabotaged the peace front and helped fascism and the fascist aggression, because they hoped to turn the fascist countries upon the Soviet Union and thus solve the problems of British imperialism by deviating the attacks of the fascist countries and converging them upon the Soviet Union. This disastrous policy which was openly expressed in Munich was not abandoned during the five months of insincere negotiations with the Soviet Union. These negotiations have only been a diplomatic means of pressure on the fascist countries to accept the British conditions."

The article further denounces the workers' movements for "peacefully tolerating the Chamberlain policies." It is suggested that the workers should have taken the initiative and acted boldly against the policies of their national governments. Approving the agreement between the Soviet Union and Germany, it states that it is a "proper reply to the betrayal,

sabotage and swindle of the peace front." In conclusion the article calls
upon the workers and the true democratic elements to follow the example
of the Soviet Union and to lead an attack against Chamberlain and his
reactionary policy:

"The blow of the Soviet Union along the whole front of the
Munich policy has created for us the most favourable conditions to
achieve a victory.[8]

"The present situation does not demand a so-called national unity
which in fact would be betraying the people, but an intensified
struggle against Chamberlain.

"It is necessary for an immediate democratic welding of forces
of the whole workers' movement against the demoralization. It is
necessary to muster all the democratic forces of the workers for the
rout of Chamberlain and for the defense of democracy against reaction within the country and abroad."

[჻<deletion: 1 line]

[჻<deletion: 1 paragraph: 7 lines]

[჻<deletion: 1 line]

[჻<deletion: 1 paragraph: 6 lines][9][჻<blank]

CANADIAN TRANSIENT WORKERS' UNION

The Canadian Transient Workers' Union of Vancouver held its first
organizational meeting on October 11. Leaflets were posted throughout
the east end of the city, enlarging upon the problem of the single unemployed and assuring them that their attendance at this meeting would
have the effect of combatting the authorities and bringing "our condition
before the public."[10]

The attendance at the above meeting was approximately 140 persons
but it is believed that the majority of these came solely out of curiosity,
as a great number were not eligible for membership. Steve Brodie, a leader
of the sit-down strike in Vancouver about a year ago, addressed the meeting. No definite plan of action was formulated, and the meeting resolved
itself into a discussion of the grievances of the gathering. This group considers that the Relief Project Workers' Union has done nothing to help the
single men and that another union is necessary to get some action. The
R.P.W.U. will have nothing to do with this "outlaw" group, and are planning to register their membership in order to ascertain their relative
strength.

The present membership of the new organization, numbering between
50 and 60, are being cared for by local relief authorities. (It is understood
that they were expelled from the Cultus Lake Relief Camp, following a
strike there this year.) [჻<deletion: 2 lines][11]

FASCISM
THE ITALIAN FASCIO

The leaders of the Italian Fascio in Canada continue to pursue a policy of "watchful prepared waiting." While activities are being carried on in a quiet unobtrusive fashion, it has been noted that the leaders in the chief cities are in constant touch and consultation with the Italian Consuls. Developments in Europe are being followed very closely, with the Italian Consuls and the Fascio remaining in readiness pending instructions from Italy.

INTERNMENTS DISRUPT NAZI ORGANIZATIONS

With the internment upon outbreak of war of the known leaders of the National Sozialistische Deutsche Arbeiter Partei, the Deutsche Arbeitsfront and the Deutscher Bund fur Kanada, and the more prominent disseminators of pro-German propaganda, together with the departure of German Consular officials, many of whom were actively engaged in the promulgation of Nazi ideology, the activities of these organizations were rendered ineffective or entirely stopped. Only isolated cases of support of the present Nazi regime have come to the notice of the authorities and these have been appropriately taken care of. At the present time, the Germans in Canada are silent or else are disclaiming any anti-British feeling and only ask to be left alone to their peaceful pursuits.

It is a matter of interest that among the ranks of the Deutscher Bund fur Kanada dissatisfaction has resulted from the recent Pact between Germany and Russia. Membership in the Bund consists of both Germans and those of German origin (such as Russo-Germans and Mennonites), many of whom were attracted to the Deutscher Bund only on account of their anti-Communistic feelings, and not as a result of their pro-Nazi leanings. The same may be said of many German Canadians, especially those who are guided by their religious tenets. Therefore the Russo-German Pact naturally weakens the Bund structure. A recent survey conducted among the Germans in Saskatchewan bears out this supposition and discloses that a feeling of actual enmity is formulating against the present regime in Germany.[12]

NOTE
EDUCATIONAL CAMPAIGN FOR "BETTER CANADIANS"

Last week we advocated, in brief, the organization of a Nation-wide Educational Campaign.

Through the system and facilities of our Force we would be in a position to supply information as to the direction in which to concentrate action. It is shown in the earlier pages of this week's bulletin that some of our school teachers are radically and revolutionarily inclined. This condition exists in several of the Provinces. The responsibility for remedy lies, of course, with the Provincial Departments of Education, and it would be the duty of the Dominion Government Department to carefully approach the Provincial Department with facts and suggestions.

The CBC News Summary 11 p.m. of the 23rd instant announced that Canadian authors had offered their services to the Government. We ask, To what better purpose could the abilities of these volunteers be applied than the preparation and publication of articles, in many languages, on the subject of becoming better citizens in this our Dominion of Canada? Such articles could be disseminated via the press, radio stations, lecture platforms, pulpits and classrooms.

Under the heading of this proposal we are not suggesting that action be directed against any particular organization or "ism." The effort would be to teach the advantages of good citizenship as against all other teachings foreign to sound Canadian ideas and ideals.[13]

INTELLIGENCE
BULLETIN

ROYAL CANADIAN MOUNTED POLICE
HEADQUARTERS, OTTAWA

WEEKLY SUMMARY
NOVEMBER 6, 1939

CONTENTS

War Series
No. 3

LABOUR UNREST

POLICE SENT TO BIENFAIT AREA
(ESTEVAN)

Throughout the past week picketing has continued over the Western Dominion Coal Co.'s Strip Mine at Bienfait, and efforts of the mine management to send sufficient workers through the picket lines have not met with any success. The injunction restraining the local union of the United Mine Workers of America from interfering until November 14 with the continued operations in the mine has failed to disperse the strikers, who maintain that they are justified in "peacefully" picketing the property. No trouble occurred during last week's activities. The local union of U.M.W. of A. intend to carry the injunction into Court.

On October 27, Mr. Lind, K.C., counsel for the mine management, had warrants sworn out for the arrest of a number of pickets who obstructed strike-breakers, but the execution of these were withheld pending the outcome of a conference between Premier of Saskatchewan, Major Mac-Pherson, K.C., counsel for the United Mine Workers of America, and Mr. Stokaluk, U.M.W. of A. organizer for District 18. The conference proving fruitless, the acting attorney general for Saskatchewan requested the officer commanding the Royal Canadian Mounted Police at Regina to send in sufficient police to ensure peace and order as the company intended to continue operations. Later a "full force" was requested.

On October 30, 150 members of the R.C.M.P. and 16 horses were dispatched to Bienfait, and it is hoped that this show of strength will have the effect of averting a clash between the various factions. Arrival of police brought no signs of hostility and mine traffic remains unimpeded. The mines started work on October 31, without interference or trouble.

Present indications suggest that the strike may be a long-drawn out affair because of the inability of the mine operators to compromise and recognize an all-embracing union in the field.

The management of Western Dominion Coal Company have stated that they do not intend to import labour.[1]

LEADER, TRANSIENT WORKERS UNION, ARRESTED
(VANCOUVER)

The first act of the new Canadian Transient Workers Union of Vancouver (see Bulletin 1) was to forward a letter to the Minister of Labour requesting that "Civic assistance be given to between 3,000 and 4,000 men in desperate straits." Failing to elicit Government aid (inasmuch as the majority of the signatories to the letter represented the Cultus Lake strikers who were repatriated to their home provinces last year, but have returned to Vancouver), these men under the leadership of Steve Brodie marched on October 17 to the Provincial Relief Office and demanded aid. In view of their past activities and their grossly exaggerated claims, relief was refused. They attempted a "sit-down" strike, but were dispersed after Mayor Telford of Vancouver interceded and spoke to the men. Their exit resulted in several arrests, amongst whom was Brodie, who was later sentenced in police court to "three months I.H.L."

The Relief Project Workers Union are taking this opportunity of Brodie's absence to gain their former prestige amongst the unemployed in Vancouver.

AGGRESSIVE ACTIONS OF NEW UNION
(KIRKLAND LAKE)

[≫deletion: 1 paragraph: 7 lines]

The first issue in this union's campaign will be a demand for an increase of 15 cents per hour in wages, to meet the rise in the cost of living. It was decided to draw up a petition to be presented to the Federal Labour Minister asking that a Conciliation Board be set up to act in this grievance between the company and the employees. The petition will read somewhat along the following lines:

"We, the undersigned workers, do appoint the International Mine, Mill and Smelter Workers Union, Local No. 240, to represent us in this petition."[2]

[℈<deletion: 1 paragraph: 3 lines]

B.C. LABOUR DESIRES WAR AIMS
(VANCOUVER)

The Vancouver and New Westminster District Trades and Labour Council recently gave approval to a resolution adopted at the last annual convention of the Trades and Labour Congress held at London, Ontario, stating "that labour gives whole-hearted support to the Allied war effort," but contended that it must demand a definite statement of British and Canadian war aims.

[℈<deletion: 1 paragraph: 7 lines][3]

COMMUNISM
COMMUNISTS' PART IN QUEBEC ELECTIONS

Running as an independent Communist but with the full support of the Communist Part in Montreal, Evariste Dube, candidate in the St. James Riding in the recent Quebec Provincial elections, polled only 193 votes out of a total 7073 cast in the riding. This defeat reflects the failure of the French-Canadians in that district to support the Communist "ticket," and to some extent is attributed to the operations of the so-called Padlock Law.

The campaign leading up to the election was devoted, in the main, to the issuing of leaflets indicating Communist Party policy, taking full advantage of this opportunity to criticize the Government and its "imperialist war policy" clearly manifesting the views of the Communist Party on conscription and participation of Canada in this war.

In this campaign the defeat of Duplessis was the primary object of the Communists. Though disagreeing with past policies of the Action Liberale Nationale of Mr. Gouin, they were ready to give him full support in his denunciation of the actions of the two major parties and anti-participation sentiments of a large number of his adherents are fundamentally progressive."

The C.P.'s attitude towards the major political bodies in the field and the situation in general was outlined by Dube in an address on October 23 as follows:

"Measures were adopted by the Government with a view to centralizing the powers at Ottawa and in such a way as to endanger the rights of provincial autonomy and to threaten the freedom of speech of French-Canada on conscription and participation.......

"The Communist Party is firmly convinced that the Quebec people cannot have faith in L'Union Nationale of Duplessis and in the imperialists supported by St. James Street, King, Lapointe and

Godbout. Neither a Duplessis nor a Liberal victory would serve the cause of the popular struggle against conscription and the trusts......

"The position of the party (Communist) on the imperialist war is well known. We have always fought for the maintenance of peace and against those who have sabotaged collective security in the period just gone by.......[4]

"These war aims have the full support of Canadian 'big business' because it hopes to reap another mass of profits in the blood of tens of thousands of young Canadians fallen in the prosecution of a futile and criminal war........

"Under the false pretext of War against Hitlerism, Canadian 'big business' has worked hand and hand with English imperialists and capitalists in bringing our country into an European conflict, the result of which can only bring suffering and misery to our Canadian people....

"Resolutely opposed to conscription and devoted to the cause of liberty and peace, the people of Quebec know today that the present war is a war for imperialist profits, a war which will not serve the cause for liberty but will bring instead only destruction and suffering to the working class.....

"Be prepared for liberty and the speedy conclusion of a just and democratic peace.......

"Let us end the imperialist war, and call for a conference of the belligerent and neutral nations, including the Soviet Union."

"WE ARE STRONGER THAN YOU THINK" (TORONTO)

[℈<deletion: 1 line] discussing the international situation declared:

"Stalin will help Hitler to defeat Britain and France by sending the Red Army to the Western Front, then when France is defeated, the Russian Army returning home will stop in Germany long enough to establish Communism there, also part of the Red Army will remain in France for the same purpose. By making friends with the small Baltic countries, Russia hopes to be able to hit at Britain. In Canada and the U.S.A., Communists are advocating democracy, and are telling the Canadian people that they are more than willing to help and support the Canadian Government in crushing Hitlerism, but this is only to cover up Communist activities among the workers, as it is very hard to convince Canadian workers that Communism is the best thing for them......"

When asked if he thought the Communist Party in Canada and the United States was strong enough to put up a fight against the Governments of those countries, [℈<deletion: 1 line] stated:[5]

"We are stronger than you think. Our Party can take this country over in 24 hours, but this is not the time yet. The time will come when all these Canadians and other patriots have gone overseas and are getting killed as fast as they get there, and the country is weak. That is the time to act, because that is the time when women will be all against capitalism and its wars. We have good leaders. Our leaders are not sleeping. They are watching every move made by the Government, and will know when the time is ripe." [✂blank][6]

NAZISM

REGISTRATION OF ENEMY ALIENS
(As Reported Up To October 16)

Province	No. of registrars appointed	No. of registrars who have reported	No. of alien enemies registered	Estimated no. of aliens to be registered
British Columbia	31	15	554	1405
Alberta	96	57	837	1809
Saskatchewan	101	77	647	1719
Manitoba	56	46	584	677
Ontario	164	103	1794	2835
Quebec	30	18	51	1098
New Brunswick	32	12	30	44
Nova Scotia	16	12	66	116
Prince Edward Island	7	1	—	10
North West Territories	12	—	—	—
Yukon Territories	7	—	—	—
	552	341	4563	9713

Internments to date, under Defence of Canada Regulations: B.C., 54; Alta., 35; Sask., 65; Man., 19; Ont., 72; Que., 99; N.B., 7; N.S., 16; P.E.I., 1. Total, 368.

NATIONAL UNITY PARTY REMAINS INACTIVE
(MONTREAL)

[✂deletion: 1 paragraph: 7 lines][10]

SECRET

INTELLIGENCE
BULLETIN

ROYAL CANADIAN MOUNTED POLICE
HEADQUARTERS, OTTAWA

WEEKLY SUMMARY
NOVEMBER 13, 1939

CONTENTS

War Series
No. 4.

SABOTAGE

Preparations for the sabotaging of war material and personnel have been disclosed in the following cases:

1. A dynamite electric time bomb of expert workmanship, consisting of 30 sticks of 60% Polar dynamite, was found in the coal chute of a Toronto Oil Service Station. It is believed that the bomb was hidden there to await removal to some strategic point, such as a munitions factory or bridge. Police investigation was frustrated by publication of this incident in the press. This is the first indication of use of explosives in sabotage.

2. Broken glass and metallic substances have been found in cargoes of grain leaving Montreal for the British Isles. These acts of sabotage

were discovered on board the "SS Lysaker V" and "SS Letitia." The former with 24880 bushels reached its destination before an "admixture of glass" was discovered and the cargo rejected by the consignees. The latter was ordered back to Montreal by the British Government to arrange for the transfer of her grain cargo to a tramp. When unloading, the grain was found to contain broken and whole bottles and empty tin cans.

3. A well-organized Fascist plot for wholesale sabotaging of Montreal Harbour works, in the event of Italy becoming an enemy.

STRIKES TO SABOTAGE INDUSTRY
(VANCOUVER)

The Communist Party are making every endeavour to further their activity in the various unions throughout the country. [<deletion: 2 lines] recently stated that "the masses of the people did not understand why the miners should come out on strike at the present time, but we as communists under[1]stand that to tie up industry at the present time is the best way for the workers to get their demands. The war machine needs what we produce, and now we can show our strength by demanding higher wages and better living conditions for the toilers." In this connection the Party intend to use their influence in the various branches of the Housewives League and have them "get behind the men in their struggle and better the conditions of workers in all walks of life."

Ted Gunrod, of the International Woodworkers Union, stated that he has been very busy making trips to the lumber camps in an effort to convince some of the workers that now is the time to go on strike for better wages and living conditions. "Great Britain has ordered a huge lumber shipment, and this must be ready in three months, and if the camps would stick together they would soon get their demands."

CANADIAN SEAMENS UNION ORGANIZE STRIKE
(NOVA SCOTIA)

[<deletion: 1 paragraph: 9 lines]

The companies involved—Swimm Brothers, and The Lockport Company— have refused to recognize the union. Upon notices being served stating that temporarily the companies would not buy any more fish, the fishermen necessarily being thrown out of work, the Canadian Fishermens Union called a strike and, with the aid of some 500 pickets, prevented shipments of fish by non-union employees.

A committee, consisting of several civic officials and provincial government authorities, was appointed by the union, who placed before the companies a proposal for settlement signed by [<deletion: 1 line] and two local union officials. The proposal was unacceptable to the companies concerned, who would have nothing to do with outside organizers but were willing to meet members in their employ.

[⸓<deletion: 1 paragraph: 3 lines][2]
[⸓<deletion: 1 paragraph: 6 lines]

STRIKE CONTINUES IN ESTEVAN-BIENFAIT MINES

150 men and 20 horses of R.C.M. Police have remained tied up at Estevan on strike duty since October 30, on orders of Attorney-General of Saskatchewan. Things have been quiet during the past week. The pickets on duty over the Western Dominion's Strip Mine have remained in position, but have not attempted to stop miners from proceeding to work. The court injunction restraining the strikers from picketing was amended, making it clear that peaceful picketing would be permitted. In this connection the strike leaders have assured the Police of their full co-operation in respecting the situation.

It is reported that it is the intention of the strikers to "boycott" the mine—possibly endeavouring to secure the co-operation of the railway unions and have them refuse to move any coal while the strike continues.

Two small strip mines reopened on November 6, with about 20 men reporting for work. At the present time the Western Dominion Strip Mine is operating at approximately 50% capacity.

Referring to the strike, the "Mid-West Clarion," communist publication for the Prairie Provinces, is endeavouring to attach ominous significance to the presence of the R.C.M. Police in the area—relating this strike to that of 1931, when three miners were killed. The front page of a recent issue of this publication is devoted to the Estevan strike, the editor twisting the situation to suit Party ends, which include the fomenting of trouble and removal of the Police. To quote some of the more prominent headlines:

"Estevan Citizens angry as 100 Mounties arrive to break Miners' Strike."

"Withdraw the R.C.M.P. from Estevan.... The last time Mounties were sent to Estevan, in 1931, bloodshed followed and three innocent miners were shot to death."[3]

"A contingent of 100 R.C.M.P., equipped with steel helmets and all regalia of war, stood guard as a handful of imported strikebreakers wound their snaky way through the miners' picket lines."

STRIKE AT GENERAL STEEL WARES PLANT
(TORONTO)

The strike at General Steel Wares plant, Toronto, formulated by the Steel Workers Organizing Committee under the leadership of [⸓<deletion: 2 lines] was concluded on November 2. In the settlement agreement collective bargaining and grievance procedure arrangements were set out and seniority arrangements were confirmed. The agreement is to extend until December 31, 1940.

According to a report from Toronto, this quick settlement is entirely agreeable to the Communist Party because of their lack of strength in the plant concerned. In this connection Steele was severely reprimanded by the C.P. for agreeing to strike action before a strong strike sentiment and organization were developed.

[ɜ҃deletion: 1 paragraph: 3 lines]

No disturbances occurred during the duration of the strike.

STRIKE AT PIONEER GOLD MINES ILLEGAL
(BRITISH COLUMBIA)

The strike at the Pioneer Gold Mines, Bralorne, (perhaps the most important gold mine in B.C.), called by Local No. 308 of the International Mine, Mill and Smelter Workers Union on October 8, was declared illegal by the Government under the terms of the Provincial Industrial Conciliation and Arbitration Act. The demands presented by the Union included:

(1) "Recognition of the Union executive as the sole bargaining agent for Pioneer employees;

(2) "A check-off system under which dues would be deducted from the payroll;

(3) "A $1 per day increase in all departments."[4]

The company were given one-half hour to accept the Union demands after their presentation; otherwise the men would strike. Company officials refused, contending that it was entirely a matter for the Government to settle.

The situation at the Pioneer Gold Mines and the events leading up to the strike had been thoroughly investigated by the British Columbia Department of Labour, who stated that the Union had no grounds to warrant taking action.

A perusal of reports submitted on this strike would indicate that it was wholly unwarranted and unjustified. The men employed are in receipt of the highest wages paid in the metalliferous mining industry in Canada, and their demands are ridiculous. Moreover by calling a strike without waiting for conciliation, the Union leaders committed, knowingly, an infraction of the Conciliation and Arbitration Act and rendered themselves and their members liable to heavy fines. As the men did not appear in Court to answer charges of violating the B.C. Industrial Arbitration and Conciliation Act, warrants have now been served for the arrest of 6 executives of the Pioneer Local of the M.M. & S.W.U.[5]

COMMUNISM

HOW STEWART SMITH APPEALS TO ELECTORS
(TORONTO)

"Defeat Hepburn's Attack on Municipal Democracy," boldly headlines a recent pamphlet by Alderman Stewart Smith of Toronto, provincial secretary of the Communist Party, issued apparently as a "feeler" for the Government's attitude towards the C.P. and as one of a series of articles to precede the "Party Manifesto." The pamphlet reads in part as follows:

"Hepburn's Fascist Record. This disastrous attack upon civic democracy is the high point of the whole fascist line of policy of the Hepburn Government.

"This is the Government which refused relief to our transient unemployed youth calling them 'Bums'. This is the Government that enforced starvation on the 350,000 men, women and children on relief in Ontario. This is the Government that led the crusade of the big corporations to destroy the trade unions under the threat of force and to keep wages at starvation levels in the interests of big business. This is the Government that blocked public works in Ontario to give jobs instead of starvation relief. This is the Government which linked up with Duplessis in Quebec to sell out to the Quebec power trust and undermine Canadian democracy.

"The Hepburn policy means fascism, for fascism (or Hitlerism) is unemployment, forced labour, suppression of trade unions and economic hardship enforced upon the people in the interest of Big Capital by state coercion......

"By annuling the municipal franchise, they desire to deprive the people of all means of expressing opposition to the unlimited profiteering and corruption, increasing unjust taxation of the masses, lowered living standards, poverty, misery and ruin which will be the fruit of capitalist war.

"Save Municipal Democracy.

"When they speak of 'war to save democracy' they are obviously lying. They are using the war to destroy democracy and to attack the living standards of the people so that the capitalists may make fortunes out of the war.[6]

"In the face of this new disaster, I would be unfaithful to the working class and progressive people of Toronto if I were to remain silent.....

"Prepare to elect a Toronto City Council which will defend your interests against the war plans of the Big Capitalists and stand firm for democracy against Hepburn's fascist plans." [✂blank][7]

[✂deletion: 1 paragraph: 3 lines]

[✂deletion: 1 paragraph: 4 lines]

[✂deletion: 1 paragraph: 4 lines]

"EXPLAINING" THE WAR TO COMMUNISTS
(WINNIPEG)

Addressing the Communist Party of Canada Labour Forum at Winnipeg on October 29, [✂deletion: 1 line] outlined the stand the C.P. is to take in relation to the present situation. Declaring that the rapidly changing international situation had resulted in the Party making grave mistakes, which they are now rectifying, [ℬ<deletion: 1 line] stated that in the first instance they should never have offered their wholehearted support to the Federal Government. (It will be remembered in this respect that the C.P. in Winnipeg dispatched a telegram to the Prime Minister at Ottawa offering full support should Canada declare war on the "Nazi Aggressor.") He referred to this telegram as "a big mistake, due to lack of clear and fast thinking. Conditions and circumstances moved so rapidly that the C.P. of Canada was caught in a trap which motivated the telegram; but now when the fog has cleared; when events have given clarity to the international situation, the mistake made at the declaration of war is being admitted." The C.P. of Canada is now however proclaiming that this war is another "imperialist war."

Tracing British foreign policy since 1917, [ℬ<deletion: 1 line] stated that it was solely directed against the Soviet Union; that the Allies would never destroy Hitlerism and Nazism, even if they won the war, but that Nazism could be destroyed only by the German working class. He predicted that the war would be of short duration and that the dangers of peace are far greater than those of war. Furthermore, it would mean the abolition of capitalism in many European countries as an aftermath of the war and the increased power of the working class.[8]

At the conclusion of the address the meeting was open for questions, but few took advantage of this opportunity. There were 54 persons in attendance.

R. L. CALDER SNUBS COMMUNISTS

Notwithstanding his defeat in the recent Quebec Provincial elections, R. L. Calder, K.C., president of the Civil Liberties Union, had "let down the Communist Party" by accepting nomination as Canadian Commonwealth Federation candidate at Verdun, P.Q. Only recently Calder made a tour of Canada championing the Civil Liberties drive and denouncing the so-called "Padlock Law" under the sponsorship of the Communist Party of Canada, and it was hoped that he would therefore be their standard-bearer in Quebec Province. The Party are disgusted over the fact that in this instance, as in a great many others, the C.C.F. has scored very heavily over the Communist Party.

It has been earnestly hoped that the endeavours of certain factions within the C.C.F. to form a "united front" with the Communist Party would be beneficial, but with the arrival in Vancouver of the article "British Labour's War Aims in the Nation," by Professor Harold J. Laski, until recently a leading member of the C.P. of Great Britain, there has been a distinct coolness between these factions and the Party leadership in Canada. The article in question derides Russia's entry into the international situation, which is the antithesis of communist belief in soviet policy. The book particularly stresses the probable longevity of the present conflict, and places the blame on Russia.

[ᢞ<deletion: 1 line]
[ᢞ<deletion: 1 paragraph: 5 lines]
[ᢞ<deletion: 1 paragraph: 3 lines][9][Page 10 is missing.]

CIVIL GUARDS

10,000 GUARDING VULNERABLE POINTS

The Civil Security Survey of vulnerable points, commenced in March, 1939, now covers over 1700 points, of which only about 10% are the responsibility of the Federal government for guarding, and the remaining 90% are of provincial municipal or private responsibility.

As a result many thousands of dollars have been expended by provincial, municipal and private concerns to provide wire fencing, screening, floodlighting, etc., for protection, based on the recommendations of the R.C.M.Police, and in addition guards are now employed to an estimated strength of 10,000 throughout the Dominion. The City of Toronto alone claims to be spending at the rate of $325,000 per annum for guards.

The Dominion Government provide guards obtained from the Veterans' Organizations as Special Constables at the following Dominion Government and other properties:

8	Ship Canals
43	Railway Bridges and Tunnels
8	Dominion Govt. Grain Elevators
11	National Harbours and Dry Docks
10	Can. Govt. Broadcasting Stations
7	Wireless and Direction Finding Stations
9	International Dams
	International Hydraulic Works at Niagara, Ontario
3	Cable Stations
1	International Bridge
1	Dominion Govt. Building (outside Ottawa)

The protection of the above mentioned points requires the employment of approximately 1800 veterans, costing with equipment about $2,500,000 per annum. A considerable reduction has already been made in the original number of guards recommended at several points, and it is expected that further reductions can be made after a re-survey.

A few of the points of vital importance have not been taken over from the Dept. of National Defence as yet, but it is expected that the handing over will be complete by November 15, 1939.[11]

ENEMY ALIENS
REGISTRATION OF ENEMY ALIENS

Province	No. of Regis-trars	Reports Re-ceived, Oct. 1-16	No. Reg-istered Oct. 1-16 from Returns to Date	Reports Re-ceived Oct 17-31	No. Reg-istered Oct. 17-31 from Returns to Date	Total Regis-tered During Oct. from Returns to Date	Esti-mated No. to be Reg-istered
B.C.	31	26	655	22	244	899	1405
Alta.	96	88	918	72	739	1657	1809
Sask.	101	95	847	65	401	1248	1719
Man.	56	51	592	46	671	1263	677
Ont.	168	131	1905	100	2327	4232	2835
Que.	29	24	345	20	626	971	1098
N.B.	33	13	30	8	11	41	44
N.S.	16	16	90	15	45	135	116
P.E.I.	7	2	—	1	1	1	10
N.W.T.	12	—	—	—	—	—	—
Y.T.	7	—	—	—	—	—	—
	556	446	5382	349	5065	10447	9713

In explanation of fact that actual registrations exceed the estimate in several instances, only unnaturalized Germans were included in the estimate whereas the registration now taking place includes Czechs, Austrians, etc. [12]

SECRET

INTELLIGENCE
BULLETIN

ROYAL CANADIAN MOUNTED POLICE
HEADQUARTERS, OTTAWA

EXTRA

WEEKLY SUMMARY
NOVEMBER 14, 1939

CONTENTS

Communism:

"Moscow Speaks"
Communist International declares war on
democracies; calls on working people to
fight war.
Dimitrov explains new "line" of Comintern.
Communist Party of Canada manifesto calls
on Canadian people to end the war and
open road towards "socialist life."
Numbers arrested throughout Canada for
distributing manifesto and charged under
Defence of Canada Regulations.

War Series
No. 4-A

MOSCOW SPEAKS

Down with the imperialist war!

Down with Capitalist reaction!

Down with the instigators of war, the profiteers and freebooters!

No support for the policy of the ruling classes directed towards continuation and spread of the imperialist slaughter!

Long live the fraternal alliance of the workers of the entire world!

Long live the U.S.S.R., the bulwark of peace, freedom and Socialism, the fatherland of the working people of all lands!

These are some of the slogans issued by the Executive Committee of the Communist International in its manifesto on the occasion of the 22nd anniversary of the October Revolution on November 7th. To those who adhered to and insisted in the belief that Communist Russia had abandoned its idea of world revolution, the manifesto brings little comfort. The document dispels all contentions that Soviet Russia has abandoned the principle of the "Class struggle" and world revolution. It is a virtual dec-

laration of war upon the democracies and is an appeal to workers throughout the world to rise against their governments.

The Comintern manifesto is in complete harmony with the speech delivered by the Premier and Foreign Commissar Viacheslav M. Molotov
at a meeting of Communist Party members in the Bolshoy Opera House
on the very evening of the day the manifesto was issued; it is, on the whole,
a repetition of Molotov's address.

Molotov accused the British and French ruling classes of doing "their
utmost to protract and extend" the war, "with the purpose of utilizing it
to consolidate their world supremacy." He said Soviet Russia stood
against this with her "policy of peace and her ardent efforts to secure rapid
termination of the war." "The names of Lenin and Stalin," he declared,
"arouse bright hopes in every corner of the world and resound as a call to
fight for the peace and happiness of nations, to fight for complete emancipation from capitalism." The accusations made in the manifesto are of
a similar nature. In this respect the document declares:[1]

"Do not believe those who are dragging you to the war under the false
pretext of the defence of democracy. What right have those who oppress
India, Indo-China, the Arab countries, who hold half of the world in the
chains of colonial slavery, to speak of democracy? The bankers of London and Paris have in the past by their loans saved, and they continue to
save, the most reactionary regimes in Europe.

The Lords of Britain maintain reaction on all the five continents of the
earth. The boasted democrats of France throw Communist deputies into
jail, suppress the Communist press and abolish political liberties. It is not
for the freedom of the nations that they are fighting, but for their enslavement. Not for the preservation of democracy from fascism, but for the triumph of reaction. Not for a stable peace, but for new imperialist conquests
fraught with new wars."

In the manifesto, the Communist International calls on the "proletarians and working people" to struggle against the imperialist war; to be
true to the end to the cause of proletarian internationalism, to the cause of
fraternal alliance of proletarians of all countries; to strengthen the fraternal alliance with the toilers of the city and the countryside, with the
enslaved peoples of the colonies; to rally closer around the Soviet Union.

It is important to note that both Molotov and the Comintern refer only
vaguely to Germany; their main attack being directed at Great Britain,
France and the United States of America.

Gregorie Dimitrov, General Secretary of the Communist International, writing in the official organ of the International called on Communists
throughout the world to join other Left-Wing elements in a new united
front to resist the "Imperialist War." He said the united front would include only those who opposed war.

The article appeared soon after War Commissar Klementi Y. Voroshilov, addressing army units massed in the Red Square on November 7th, declared that Russia "must be ready for war, although we shall not take part in war."

Outlining the new Comintern 'line,' Dimitrov said that the old united front had become obsolete. He declared that the new united front could be organized "by a most decisive struggle against Socialists and Radicals for the purpose of liquidating the influence of those agents of the bourgeoisie in the labour movement.

"Communists must not be frightened by persecutions or repressions, and must adjust themselves to war conditions, purge doubtful elements from their ranks and establish iron discipline," he said.[2]

Acting upon instructions from Moscow similar manifestos were issued by the Communist Parties of the United States and Canada. Earl Browder, General Secretary of the American Party, in his speech in Boston celebrating the anniversary of the Bolshevik revolution urged the people of the United States to duplicate the feat of the Russians. He further declared that his followers must achieve Socialism in the U.S.A. by a quick transition.

The Communist Party of Canada, the Canadian Section of the "foreign legion" of the Soviet Union, on the eve of Remembrance Day, issued, in pamphlet form its own manifesto entitled "The People Want Peace." The pamphlet, issued officially by the Dominion Executive Committee over the signature of Tim Buck, General Secretary, and which was distributed simultaneously throughout Canada by members of the Party especially selected for the task, reads in part:

"THE PRESENT WAR is a catastrophe for Canada. Twenty-one years after the 'war to end all wars' which claimed 10 million lives, and before we recovered from the consequences of that war, Canada is engulfed in a foreign war and Canadians are being exhorted to throw away their lives on foreign fields.

"For the capitalists this war means fabulous profits; but for the Canadian workers, farmers and middle classes the war means death, misery, exploitation, crisis and ruin.

"The Canadian people wanted national recovery, jobs and security and peace.

"The Mackenzie King government and the bankers and capitalists who were strangling national recovery in peace, are now the promoters of imperialist war. There was no money in peace, so they said, to pay decent wages to the workers and fair prices to the farmers; no money or public works; no money for jobs for our youth; no money for adequate relief.

"But today, Premier King and the capitalists say there is unlimited money for destructive war. Your scanty income, your dinner table, your sugar, tobacco, your bread, are heavily taxed to provide the first $100,000,000 of the billions that they say they will spend on war.

CANADA SOLD INTO ECONOMIC BONDAGE

"Canada is being sold into economic bondage to the war-profiteers by the government. Canada will be impoverished as our children for generations will pay tribute to the 50 Big Shots.[3] Profiteers are given free rein. Purchasing power and the living standards of the masses fall while the Wartime Prices and Trade Board blames the housewives and consumers for the rising prices, thus shielding the profiteering monopolists. The masses will bear the entire brunt of the war.

"To enforce this war policy the government has annulled all democratic rights. The British North America Act is suspended. The Quebec people, opposing conscription and the war, are being threatened with martial law. Provincial and municipal rights, freedom of trade unions, the rights of free speech, assembly and press are being wiped out.

"In the name of 'war to save democracy' every democratic movement of the workers, farmers and consumers to defend themselves against the profiteers and big business sharks will be ruthlessly attacked.

"The most reactionary capitalist cliques, who have been long undermining Canadian democracy, have seized upon the war to consummate their aims. The nation is being sold into political bondage to the most imperialistic, most chauvinistic and most fascist circles of big business. This is the real essence of fascism...

"The people know the truth. This was is not a war to save democracy but is the inevitable result of imperialist intrigues against democracy....

"Had the international working class succeeded, despite the reformist splitters, in forcing the establishment of such a Peace Front, there would have been no war today.

"The Chamberlain circles deliberately prevented such a Peace Front of the peoples and governments.

"Chamberlain, and the pro-Chamberlainites in Canada, prevented a Peace Front in Canada because they approved the merciless suppression of the German and Italian working-class and democratic movements by Hitler and Mussolini; they supported the fascist war against the liberation movement of the Spanish people; they welcomed the robber war against China. For, to them, fascism was the saviour of crisis-stricken, dying capitalism!.....

HOW POLAND WAS SACRIFICED

"We are told that this is war to save Poland. The truth is that Poland was chosen to be the final link in the conspiracy to instigate the long-planned German-Soviet war. Poland was the [4] pathway for the Nazi war machine to attack the Soviet Union.....

THE REAL AIMS OF THE WAR

"Chamberlain's aims in this war are identical with his aims during the past two years—to maintain the supremacy of British imperialism, to continue the exploitation and suppression of the workers and colonial peoples, and above all to find the way to transform this war into a joint imperialist attack against the Soviet Union.....

"The guilt for this criminal war rests equally upon the shoulders of the imperialists of Berlin, London and Paris. And 'our own' Canadian imperialists, with their eyes upon markets and huge profits, have played and are playing, their ignoble independent role in the tragic crime as willing partners of Chamberlain and Daladier, thus threatening to embroil the Americas in the war.

WHY CANADA IS AT WAR

"Canada is plunged into war because it is hitched, through the ruling groups, to the war policy of Chamberlain; because the government of Mackenzie King, and before that, of Bennett, refused to pursue an independent foreign policy based on the needs of the Canadian people—on Canadian security!

"Mackenzie King's slavish support of Chamberlain inevitably meant that when the war came Canada was plunged into it without any regard for the real interests of the Canadian people.

"That it took our people by surprise and shocked them, is to be seen by the absence of that wild jingoism which accompanied August 4, 1914, by the questions asked by the people everywhere (and for which they are jailed under the War Measures Act), by the events in Quebec.

"The Canadian nation did not want war; its security as an American nation demanded that Canada keep out of it.

"The Canadian government, supported by the Tories and by the opposition parties in Parliament, plunged the country into war because it was tied to the tail of the Chamberlain government, and because the small handful of already rich profiteers saw in war the chance for those great contracts which would heap their vaults with gold, as in the last war—in short, because [5] they are ready to sacrifice Canadian lives and jeopardize Canadian security if only they can reap a golden harvest as partners in British imperialist war.

"All of this shows that the Communist Party was mistaken in the first weeks of the war in creating the illusion that this could be made 'a different kind of war.' These opportunist illusions could only help the capitalists to create the confusion necessary for them to carry through their imperialist aims against the people.....

U.S.S.R. — BEACON OF PEACE

"The U.S.S.R. in this crisis has acted firmly and swiftly to save its people from invasion and to strengthen the people of the whole world who long for peace. It has kept its millions out of war. It has refused to be a catspaw for imperialist schemes, knowing that its duty to the people of the world is to stand firm for peace.

"Once Hitler, stopped in the east by the Red Army, sued for peace, the Soviet Union in proposing that peace be considered by all the belligerent powers acted in the best interests of all peoples.

"The Soviet Union stands for peace. So do the working people of the world—a peace which will stop the advance of imperialism and the destruction of millions of lives!

"We call on the Canadian people to fight for the restoration of their liberties; the right to a free press; the right to freely criticise government policy and war aims; the right to speak and assemble; the right to unite for the restoration of peace!

"We call on the Canadian people to fight profiteering by the big monopolies who want this war for their own greedy ends.

"Declare an end to the imperialist war!

"Fight for a lasting and democratic peace!

"Immediate measures against the profiteers to bring down prices!

"For immediate increases in wages, farm prices and unemployment relief to meet the rise in the cost of living![6]

"Hands off democratic rights and social services!

"For the establishment of a new government which will carry out these demands, begin peace negotiations and represent the interests of the people against the armament kings and plundering 50 Big Shots!

"Banish the spectre of war and open the road towards a new, free, Socialist life!"

The distribution of the Communist Party pamphlet constitutes part of a gigantic International Campaign initiated by Moscow in an attempt to block the war efforts of Great Britain and France. It marks the beginning of a movement, in Canada, calculated to undermine the morale of the people and their faith in the British Empire.

The Communist Party of Canada stands convicted as an agency of Stalin and his methods.

Mass distribution of the Communist Party pamphlet containing the manifesto was halted by this Force acting in conjunction with Provincial and Municipal Police. A number of the distributors were arrested throughout the country and charged under the Defence of Canada Regulations.[7]

SECRET

INTELLIGENCE
BULLETIN

ROYAL CANADIAN MOUNTED POLICE
HEADQUARTERS, OTTAWA

WEEKLY SUMMARY
NOVEMBER 20, 1939

CONTENTS

Communism:
General:

War Series
No. 5

COMMUNISM

PROMINENT COMMUNIST ARRESTED

Arrested on November 15 by the Toronto City Police on a charge of contravening Section 39A of the Defence of Canada Regulations, Douglas Stewart, business manager of the "Clarion," communist weekly published at Toronto, was released on bail of $2000. Subsequently the Attorney General of Ontario instructed the Crown Attorney to raise the bond to $5000, as it is intended to proceed against Stewart under indictment. According to the Attorney General, the Provincial Government is taking a very serious view of this case.

LABOUR DEFENCE LEAGUE TO THE RESCUE

Lying dormant for the past few years, the Canadian Labour Defence League, Communist controlled organization in defence of workers' "civil liberties," has again been resurrected. [᠈<deletion: 3 lines]

In the November 11 issue of the "Mid-West Clarion," published at Winnipeg, the full particulars relative to this organization are stated. According to this article "the labour movements stand in need of a Dominion-wide Labour Defence League at the present time." "For all signs today point to the fact that labour must stand on guard and fight hard to protect its cherished democratic rights of free speech, press and assembly." "There is no time to lose for the danger signals are flying."

Anticipating the arrest of individuals caught distributing the recent manifesto issued by the Communist Party, this league has taken on the task of advising them should they be apprehended. All arrested are ordered to immediately ask for the help of the C.L.D.L.

Carefully disguising their affiliation with the Communist Party under the role of a Labour Democratic organization, they demand the right of all democratic privileges. Part of a statement issued by [᠈<deletion: 1 line] reads as follows:[1]

"The suppression of the French-Canadian labour-progressive journal, Clarte, the suspension of the right of Habeas Corpus, the reactionary attacks against elected representatives of the people in Toronto, Windsor and other municipalities, the threat to the 75 pacifist ministers of the United Church who took an anti-war stand and the many prosecutions and convictions under the War Measures Act all go to prove that labour must zealously guard its long-established rights.

"The C.L.D.L. will provide that broad, non-party, non-sectarian defence movement which the labour movement of Canada needs today. I appeal to all those interested in the defence of the democratic rights of the Canadian workers, farmers and middle classes to co-operate in the building up of the C.L.D.L."

SOWING DISAFFECTION IN ARMY UNITS

Disturbing reports have recently been received relative to the activities of Communists in Canadian National Defence forces. It is a generally known fact that the intentions of the Communist Party are to develop and exploit disturbances with a view to undermining discipline and causing widespread dissension amongst the men. To this end members of the Party are filtering into the various units so that when opportunity occurs they will be ready to act.

A recent report from Toronto shows their manner of working. [᠈<deletion: 2 lines] circulated a rumour to the effect that this unit would be transformed into infantry as soon as it arrived overseas. Fortunately, this

rumour was immediately checked; otherwise it might have led to serious dissatisfaction, as a number of men are engaged on technical work who, no doubt, would not relish the thought of being assigned to infantry duty. Later this same member received a number of leaflets issued by the Communist Party for distribution to the members of this unit. Several of these however were seized by the authorities and the propaganda was dropped.

In Montreal similar methods are being used. [∂<deletion: 2 lines] He told of widespread feelings of discontent prevalent in his unit and of a disturbance which recently occurred during meal hour, presumably caused by an insufficient quantity of food given the soldiers at a charge of 35 cents per meal. He also said that verbal accounts of the riots which occurred in [2] France and in Great Britain after the Armistice in the last war are quite common topics of conversation amongst the men.

He stated "that the spirit of the troops is far different from that of the troops at the beginning of the World War, that insofar as morale and spirit are concerned the troops of today are staring where the troops of 1914-1918 left off. He contends that 99% of those who enlisted did not do so out of a feeling of duty or of patriotism but rather because they had nothing worth-while to look forward to, and further, that they had brought with them into the army a spirit of revolt with which they were animated because of the bad economic conditions under which they have lived for years."

According to [∂<deletion: 1 line] the seeds of revolt are clearly widespread and when the "big day" comes, which he thinks is not very far off, "the Communist Party will have the opportunity of fertilizing these seeds."

"YES, WE ARE COMMUNISTS," BOASTS DUSHNICKI
(TORONTO)

[∂<deletion: 1 paragraph: 4 lines]

"This war between Britain and France on one hand, and Germany on the other, is nothing else but a fight between Imperialist powers over profits, colonies and world domination. But it won't last long, because workers and the members of the Communist Party in Canada and the whole British Empire will not allow themselves to be used as the tools of Chamberlain's reactionary aims. We cannot be satisfied to fight for democracy under the leadership of those who betrayed Spain and Czechoslovakia and who are betraying democracy in England and France. Britain is the chief oppressor of small nations in the world today. Britain has betrayed Ethiopia, Austria, Spain and Czechoslovakia, and she will continue to betray until the workers get around to give the Bum's Rush to the Downing Street Dracula. The people of the Baltic States have now said goodbye forever to the German and British capitalists, they are now joining with the Soviet Union because warm friendship with the

Soviet Union has banished the nightmare of war. Some of our members have reported to Comrade O. Melnyczenko that they have been called Communists by the members of the Ukrainian Nationalist organization. What if they are called Communists? Yes, we are Communists,[3] and we are proud of it. We are proud of being members of the Communist International of Lenin and Stalin. We are proud and happy that in all the countries of the old capitalist world hundreds of thousands of members of our International struggle, like the French Communists, against their own war-mongering Imperialists. We are proud to be members of the same International as the Communist, Dimitroff. We are proud to be members of this world party of Communists which has overthrown capitalism forever on one-sixth of the earth and established in its place a Socialist regime of prosperity and peace."[4][⊱blank][Page 5 is missing] [⊱deletion: 1 paragraph: 4 lines]

[⊱deletion: 1 line]
[⊱deletion: 1 line]

[⊱deletion: 1 paragraph: 7 lines]

DISTRICT VIGILANCE COMMITTEES

Vigilance Committees are composed of trusted members of the Communist Party who investigate the activities and complaints of communists in their respective sections. These Section Vigilance Committees are subordinated to the District Vigilance Committee which in turn comes under the Control Commissioner of the Communist Party.

[⊱deletion: 1 line]

[⊱deletion: 1 paragraph: 6 lines]
[⊱deletion: 1 paragraph: 2 lines][6]
[⊱deletion: 1 paragraph: 7 lines]
[⊱deletion: 1 paragraph: 4 lines]
[⊱deletion: 1 paragraph: 5 lines]

"KANADSKY GUDOK" PREACHES REVOLUTION
(WINNIPEG)

Recent issues of foreign language publications in Canada sponsored by the Communist Party, have cast aside reserve and are vehemently attacking British institutions and Government action. In particular, this is true of "Kanadsky Gudok," Communist organ in the Russian language published at Winnipeg, Man. Late issues of this paper have been running a serial entitled "The Teaching of Lenin and Stalin about Scientific Foresight." According to this article it is possible to foresee the outcome of political events. To quote:

"The Party of Marxism, the Party of Communism, the Party of the working class, knew how to establish the rules of social development, the rules of a state which is to be at the service of revolutionary realities. This party has not only foreseen the march of events in the future, but has also organized the fight of the working class against capitalist subjection and has achieved a victory of socialism on one sixth of the terrestrial globe."[7]

The article is based on the teachings of Marx, Lenin and Stalin and stresses the necessity of "carrying on by means of an open political struggle the fight for a victorious Communist regime," and quotes paragraphs devoted to the "coming revolution of the workers." It contains teachings, not only on the science of foresight but how to organize and conduct reprisals and revolutions in the same way as the Bolshevist Party did in Russia.

Another article devotes considerable space to the position of Canada in the Soviet sphere of influence and states:

"In Canada the same as in other countries the toiling people decidedly no more believe the capitalist press..... This is particularly true since the war. The toiling masses clearly see that where nations really struggle for their independence the Soviet Union gives them the maximum assistance."

"Kanadsky Gudok" asserts that Great Britain and France have failed in their attempt to draw the U.S.S.R. into a "war bloc." Several articles are distinctly pro-German. One paragraph reads:

"The German submarines carry on a quiet energetic war against the enemy commercial ships, mainly against the British. In the short time from the beginning of the war the German submarines have not only given a vital blow to the British commercial fleet but also to the British Navy to a very significant degree. Germany has thus clearly proved that it represents all along an earnest threat not only to the British Merchant Marine but also to the British Navy."

WHAT EVERY COMMUNIST SHOULD READ

In order to impress upon the Communist Party membership the full significance of their work at this time, personnel have been instructed to digest the policy of the Party as contained in its many official text books. In particular, they are to study "The History of the Communist Party of the Soviet Union." As this publication is banned in Canada, attempts are being made to smuggle copies through the Customs, and thus augment the considerable number already on hand. To quote from a letter issued by the District Bureau at Toronto stressing the importance of education:[8]

"It is now more necessary than ever that our members carry on systematic self study and educational activity. Our groups must study and discuss, not only the rapidly changing international and domestic situation, but also the basic Marxist-Leninist works on Imperialism and Imperialist war. No clear understanding of the international situation and the war crisis can be obtained without mastery of the classics of Leninism.

"The most important textbook for reading and group study is the history of the C.P.S.U., copies are now available and can be ordered through your group. Every member should strive to buy a copy of this invaluable work and every group should begin a thorough study of its contents, particularly with the sections dealing with the imperialist war of 1914-1918....

"Two books which will make valuable supplementary reading are 'Fascism and Social Revolution' by Palme Dutte, and 'Military Strength of the Powers' by Max Werner. Cheap editions of these are available or you can get them from your public library."

COMMUNISTS SPLIT OVER POLITICS
(VANCOUVER)

The Russo-German Pact continues to sow dissension in the Vancouver Party. It is becoming increasingly evident that Party discipline suffers while members openly criticize functions and policy. One side dares to question the foreign policy of the U.S.S.R. while another believes blindly that Stalin can do no wrong! Unit meetings are being held but the progress made is negligible. The leaders are finding it difficult to convince members that the expansionist policy being pursued by Stalin in the Baltic and the support given the Nazis are directed toward the emancipation of the workers of the world. Members are also critical of the "Advocate," communist publication at Vancouver, and [⊱deletion: 1 line] recently stated that it is merely "aping the C.C.F. publication," (The Federationist), and the Party is not conducting a campaign "half as hot as the C.C.F."

Discussing the distribution of leaflets, [⊱deletion: 3 lines][9]

SUPPORTING THE HOUSEWIVES LEAGUE
(VANCOUVER)

Assisted and abetted by the Communist Party who are surreptiously defining their policy, the various housewives' leagues throughout the country are organizing to "defeat war-profiteering" as it affects the consumer.

A "delegate conference" was recently called at Vancouver, to which representatives of church and service clubs were invited, in order to set up a council, the object of which will be "to act in the interests of the consumer both provincially and municipally, in conjunction with the Wartime Prices and Trades Board of the Dominion Government." The league particularly condemns the rise in necessary commodities, but also undertakes to fight for the raising of wage scales, pensions and relief allowances.

While it is realized that the Communist Party will take a great interest in this work and many persons will enlist solely on "patriotic" grounds, on the other hand the Party sees in the "good name" of the league an excellent cover for the promulgation of subversive policies.[10]

GENERAL

ALL QUIET ON THE ESTEVAN FRONT

During the past week few developments have occurred in the Estevan-Bienfait lignite area. Pickets, though reduced in number, have continued at their positions. [&<deletion: 2 lines], and these meetings were attended by between 500 and 600 men. It was stressed that the strikers intend to continue co-operation with the authorities in every respect and that the strike must be won "acting within the law." While the neutrality of the police is above criticism, the mine operators are bitterly assailed for using unfair tactics and being out "to drive the men back to work by fair means or foul."

A conference was called on November 8 by the Attorney General of Saskatchewan at Regina, with the result that all of the operators, except the Western Dominion management, are willing to accept an all-embracing union in the field. The United Mine Workers of America are agreeable to this.

20 members of the R.C.M.P. were withdrawn to Regina on November 11, and three days later the Attorney General authorized the withdrawal of 30 more members of the force, including the personnel and horses of the mounted section, numbering 16 men. The remainder of the force, approximately 100, will continue on duty in the field until further orders are received.

"COUNTERACT INSIDIOUS PROPAGANDA"

"This war, in a very special sense, is a war of ideas. It is accepted by our people and Allies as a crusade for great principles" and it is essential "to strive to counteract insidious propaganda against us" as well as "to keep a watchful eye on every movement inimical to our interests."

"These words—spoken recently by Lord Macmillan, Minister of Information, on being freed from British censorship control so that he could devote himself to his "real task" of propaganda—apply as fittingly to Canada and other parts of the British Commonwealth as to Great Britain.[11]

The continuous dissemination of "right" information would seem to be as vital to our present security and our ultimate success as is the suppression of "wrong" statements. Up to the present however, only the latter duty has been officially recognized.

We know that in Canada internal enemies are insidiously boring into the foundations of our social and political structure, with the expectation of eventually accomplishing its overthrow. At present we are doing little more than following a policy of watchful waiting for individuals to actually run foul of the War Measures Act and the Defence Regulations based thereon. We are not carrying the war into the enemy's country with a counter-barrage of wholesome and convincing truths calculated to forestall and counteract the lies.

The pressing need of such a campaign is being demonstrated in the case of the Communist manifesto with its violent tirade against the war and the Allied Governments. Undoubtedly, the attack will have an injurious affect on such ignorant and wavering minds as have not been fortified with the knowledge of facts and are only too ready to believe the worst of any given situation.

The Czecho-Slovak situation is another case in point. The presence among the Czecho-Slovaks of one competent to explain the reasons for registration would have allayed suspicious and encouraged confidence in Canadian democracy.[12]

INTELLIGENCE
BULLETIN

ROYAL CANADIAN MOUNTED POLICE
HEADQUARTERS, OTTAWA

WEEKLY SUMMARY
NOVEMBER 27, 1939

CONTENTS

War Series
No. 6.

[Page 1 is missing.]

COMMUNISM
"CLARION'S" REACTIONS TO SUPPRESSIVE MEASURES

Notwithstanding their apparent failure to disturb Canadians over the wholesale distribution of their recent manifesto, the Communist Party are congratulating themselves over the fact that very few individuals have been apprehended by the authorities and, with the exception of Douglas Stewart, manager of "The Clarion," all the leaders are still at large. In this connection the November 18 issue of "The Clarion" states:

"So well was the distribution organized that only 24 arrests were made by the police—4 persons were arrested in Toronto, 9 in Montreal, 3 in Winnipeg, 5 in Vancouver, 2 in Regina and 1 in Calgary."

According to an article in this paper, 10,000 persons participated in the distribution across Canada of 175,000 anti-war manifestos, 25,000 of which were printed in French. It denounces the capitalist press for their assuming certain facts relative to the originality of the Party manifesto, "The People Want Peace":

"Replying to blasts in the capitalist press that the Canadian Communist manifesto was issued on the basis of the recently-issued manifesto of the Communist International, a leading official of the Communist Party of Canada told The Clarion that the statement distributed last week had been prepared and ratified for distribution in the second week of October, whereas the C.I. manifesto appeared in the second week of November, a month later."

It is rather interesting to note certain references made by "The Clarion" to the publication of the manifesto. On several occasions this document is referred to as coming from an outside source and the paper disclaims all knowledge of its publication. One statement reads:

"The leaflet was signed 'Dominion Executive Committee, Communist Party of Canada, Tim Buck, General Secretary,' and purported to be printed by the Contemporary Publishing Association, Montreal, Que. Police state they have been unable to locate any such company."[2]

Referring to the arrest of Douglas Stewart, "The Clarion," under the headlines "Freedom of Press Dealt First Blow by Hepburn Stooges;" "Stand by the Clarion! Protect Labor's Rights!" declared that its warnings regarding attacks on Labour "rights" had been vindicated by the seizure of papers and arrest of personnel. It accused the Ontario Government of being the most reactionary of provincial administration in its suppression of free speech and free press and, under cover of the war, of attempting to destroy the very democracy we are supposed to be fighting for.

Hepburn, says "The Clarion," is trying to take away the municipal franchise! He is trying to stifle Canada's oldest and most authoritative labor paper! He is, along with Ottawa, trying to stop men and women telling the truth about this war, and he with the federal government, under the fascist provisions of the War Measures Act, is marching towards the establishment here of a totalitarian state replete with political prisoners, concentration camps, a terrorized population and the unbridled rule of the big capitalists who shout for joy at the thought of making millions out of this war."

According to this weekly, every attack upon communism today is an attack upon every labour organization tomorrow. It exhorts workers to rally around the Canadian Labour Defence League.

(On November 21 the publication of "The Clarion" was prohibited, under Regulation 15 of the Defence of Canada Regulations.)[3][ℵblank]

LEAGUE FOR PEACE AND DEMOCRACY
(MONTREAL)

A recent report from Montreal states that the League for Peace and

Democracy, an affiliate of the Communist Party of Canada, will close its various offices throughout the country. This is due, apparently, to the control exercised under the War Measures Act which precludes the possibility of this organization disseminating agitation and propaganda. Party leaders realize that because of the composition of its membership,[4] part of which is not communist, the league cannot carry on its agitation for peace in the face of the present stand of the U.S.S.R. and that of the Communist Party without confessing its communist control and leadership. [5][✂blank][Page 6 is missing.][✂blank]

COMMUNIST PARTY CLOSES NATIONAL OFFICES

The Communist Party at Toronto have decided to close immediately both the district and national offices. The reasons given are lack of funds, and the offices are not longer essential since the Party has gone "underground."[7]

STRIKES IN CANADA INCREASING

Elated over the success of their efforts in the labour field, the Communist Party headlines a recent issue of "The Clarion" "Strikes on Rapid Increase in Canada," to advertise the effect of their endeavour to "help the working class." An article devoted to labour conditions stresses the importance of the great number of strikes (25) which occurred during October of this year. Undoubtedly, many of these were due to Party agitation for "better working conditions," and, comparing the number with other monthly totals, it would seem that the Party have some cause for jubilation. At the same time unfavourable working conditions, in many instances, played into the agitators' hands.

(Such activities as the above serve to emphasize the pressing need for legislation to outlaw as illegal such an organization as the Communist Party of Canada and its affiliates.)

"DER VEG" BITTERLY HOSTILE

"Der Veg," communist weekly published at Toronto in the Yiddish language, has recently, in conformity with other publications controlled by the Communist Party of Canada, scathingly denounced the leadership given by the British and Canadian Governments to the people, and has declared its opposition to this stand in no uncertain terms. It expresses satisfaction over the policy enunciated by the Soviet Union concerning the international situation, recent speeches of prominent Soviet leaders quotes and stresses the necessity of workers having implicit faith in the Soviet Union and the "mobilization of the masses for the struggle against the war which is now on."

> "The working class today has the mission of conducting a decisive struggle against the regime of relentless terror, oppression and plundering of the populations which have been introduced. The task of the working class today is not to allow the ruling class to lay

the burden of the war on the backs of the labouring people. Today the working class must set as its immediate task the abolishment of Capitalistic slavery, this task becoming more urgent as the crisis deepens in consequence of the war....."

"The Communist Parties in the Capitalistic countries will get enthused with the heroic example of the Russian Bolsheviks, the example of Lenin's party, of Stalin's party, which in the years 1914-1918 showed the way to the workers, and the way out, then assured the victory of Socialism. The Communists shall fulfil their historic mission."

As the trend of the various articles is extremely anti-British the continued publication of "Der Veg" might arouse serious disaffection.[8]

GENERAL

"DEMOCRATIC RIGHTS MOVEMENT" LAUNCHED

Purported to be sponsored by the Co-operative Commonwealth Federation, the Democratic Rights Movement, (Victoria) recently came into being at Victoria, B.C. This organization, upon its inception, endeavoured to obtain the co-operation of the two major political parties in Canada and other patriotic organizations. A perusal of the aims of this movement resulted in these bodies refusing to lend their support, on the ground that the aims of the movement "were likely to prejudice the war efforts of the British Empire." These aims are:

(1) That true democracy in Canada is threatened by the state of war which now exists and suggesting a tentative programme of action.

(2) A far-reaching campaign demanding the maintenance of peace time democratic rights during the war.

(3) Freedom of conscience. This involves opposition to conscription of man-power for war purposes.

(4) Freedom of assembly and maintenance of the right to organize.

(5) Freedom of expression.

(6) Recognition by the Canadian Government of the right of individuals to have actual information placed before them through the press and radio. The elimination of distorted news accounts.

(7) A public demand that the Canadian Government state its war aims clearly.

(8) Elimination of war profiteering. As an immediate step effective regulation of commodity prices to the consumer at pre-war levels must be affected. A further essential is that there be consumer representation on price control boards.

(9) A campaign to minimise hatred of the German peoples and do all that can be done to work towards a fairer peace treaty than the Treaty of Versailles. This to include education of the public to resist misleading propaganda and discounting obviously exaggerated

atrocity stories.

(10) The investigation of the possibilities of service of a strictly impartial nature for the relief of suffering.[9]

This organization's purpose appears to be the repeal of the majority of censorship regulations, which are alleged to be an infringement of the people's rights. With this end in view, a recent meeting of the association severely criticized certain censorship regulations with the intention of having certain sections deleted. The movement will carry out an intensive campaign throughout Vancouver Island to organize the people in the fight for "their rights," as Canadians.

[⊱<deletion: 1 paragraph: 4 lines]

FIRST SESSION OF TORONTO YOUTH PARLIAMENT

Convened at 8.30 p.m. of November 9, the Toronto Youth Parliament opened its session with the "Government" presenting the following National Emergency Act to be passed by the house:

1. The mobilization for effective aid to the Allies of Canada's entire industrial agricultural and other economic resources shall be the primary contribution of this Country in the struggle.
2. For the prosecution of these ends committees with the following functions shall be appointed:
    (a) To survey Canada's resources and industries for the purpose of mobilizing them for wartime needs.
    (b) To nationalize for the duration of the war all armament manufacture and allied heavy industries.
    (c) To prevent hoarding of necessities and undue rise in the price of consumer's goods or profiteering in government contracts and to publish its findings from time to time.
    (d) To ensure the maintenance of the present Dominion-Provincial Youth Training Programmes for the improvement of technical standards in industry. These shall be planned with a view to the future restoration of peace-time conditions.
3. Insofar as overseas military service may be necessary at the present time, enlistment is to be free from legal or economic coercion.[10]

There were about 18 delegates from the Young Communist League present, [⊱<deletion: 1 line] This body confined its discussion to the demand for aid to unemployed youth as the first responsibility of the Government. War aims and opposition to the war itself were not injected because of the overwhelming majority of patriotically minded youth. The first session ended in a defeat of the amendments sponsored by the C.C.F. and Y.C.L.

ENEMY ALIENS REGISTERED AND INTERNED

Registrations to November 15, 1939, (returns
incomplete) 12,734
Total internments 387
Less releases 16
Total interned (November 25)...............................371

(Of the above internments, the Commissioner as Registrar General has ordered the internment of 36.)[11]

INTELLIGENCE
BULLETIN

ROYAL CANADIAN MOUNTED POLICE
HEADQUARTERS, OTTAWA

WEEKLY SUMMARY
DECEMBER 4, 1939

Communism:
   C.I.O. Boasts Successful Strike
   Stewart Smith Leads Cheers for Stalin
   In Defence of the Manifesto
   Fur Workers Break from Communism
   Letter Discloses Underground Methods
   To Fight Defence of Canada Regulations
   Party Leaders Dread Arrests
   "Slobodna Misao" Plans Special Edition
   "Be Friends with the Soldiers"
   C.I.O. Fostering Mine Strikes
   Coal Strike Continues at Estevan
   "Party Will Continue to Provoke"
   New Party Weekly Contemplated
General:
   Atlas Coal Strike Settled

War Series
No. 7

COMMUNISM
C.I.O. BOASTS SUCCESSFUL STRIKE
(OTTAWA)

Joyce [⁊<deletion: 1 word], reporting as a delegate of Local 195 to the Ottawa convention of the Committee for Industrial Organization, said that the parent body was bent on increasing its membership in Canada to 100,000 (or to twice its present standing) within a year. He mentioned some of the gains made by the C.I.O. in Canada and referred to what he called the "little Wagner Act" in Nova Scotia, and also to the recent strike at the General Steel Wares plant at Toronto, which he stated was the first successful strike in Toronto in 10 years. He boasted proudly that the strike was conducted by the C.I.O.

Regional Director Burt of the C.I.O. spoke of the poor legislation in Canada for "protecting the working man," stating that "the C.I.O. is demanding that the Government set up a Labour Board in order to protect

discrimination cases," and that "under existing laws the working men have
no chance of protecting themselves or of prosecuting a company in any
discrimination case."

Morris Fields of Detroit, Mich., of the United Automobile Workers'
Association, an affiliate of the C.I.O., was the main speaker. He went into
considerable detail in attempting to justify the union's position in the
present automobile strike in Detroit which has resulted in unemployment
for a great number of automobile workers.

It is interesting to note that the C.I.O. are making every endeavour to
establish the Canadian organization with a view to ousting the Canadian
Federation of Labour which recently demanded the exclusion of C.I.O.
affiliates from the Trades and Labour Congress.

STEWART SMITH [⊰deletion: 1 line]

At a recent meeting held by the Dukowinian-Bessarabian Society of
Toronto, Alderman Stewart Smith of the Toronto City Council was one
of the principal backers. [⊰deletion: 3 lines] who is backing Hitler in the
fight against Great Britain and [1] the Chamberlain Government. He is
said to have stated that as long as Stalin is behind Hitler the workers under
their leadership will see that Great Britain and her possessions, including
Canada, will be sovietized by our Party. He received great applause from
the audience, which numbered about 700.

[⊰deletion: 2 lines] referred to the part women play in the communist
movement. She stated that as long as the Ukrainian women are members
of the C.P. they will do their best to obtain new members for its organizations, to educate the workers how best to fight for their freedom. Women,
she said, are the best means for getting communist propaganda spread
among foreigners, and their main objective at this time should be the organization of women workers engaged in the textile industry now being
used for war needs.

Reporting on C.P. activities in metal and textile industries, O. Melnyczenko, [⊰deletion: 1 line], stated that the time is coming when this organization will take a leading position in the ranks of the workers who
will be led to a better life in Canada. "The Hepburn Government is trying
to stop us from spreading our propaganda among the workers but it is too
late now. Our organization is strong enough to stop any government, and
all members of the communist organizations in Canada will see that this
is done. Our main duty just now is to organize workers in the metal and
textile factories. Workers in the lumber industry are well organized."

[⊰deletion: 2 lines]

"Our organization has worked for the past 22 years to bring
workers into our movement, and today we can be proud of our members—they take leading and responsible positions during all strikes
and are the sponsors of all strikes, and at almost every strike they
assume financial responsibilities. All employed members must or-

ganize workers in the shops where they can come in contact with them, showing these workers that our duty is to stop this war spreading and that we as loyal members of the International must do all in our power to stop the war, and this can easily be done when production of war material is curtailed or stopped altogether through our efforts."

He added that the time is rapidly approaching in Canada when the workers under the leadership of the C.P. will close all churches and Christian organizations and will sovietize them.[2]

Referring to the part played by the Canadian Labour Defence League, which is a section of the International Red Aid, with head office in Russia, [⊰deletion: ? words] stated his views as to what should be done towards stopping the war in Europe. "All members of the C.P. must stick together and not be afraid of being arrested, as the C.L.D.L. was reorganized a few days ago and will defend all members who have been arrested for anti-war activities in Canada." He said that all members must try to circulate the "People's Gazette" because "the paper is the best organizer of the Ukrainian workers in Canada." (The policies of this publication are directed by the Communist Party of Canada.)[3]

FUR WORKERS BREAK FROM COMMUNISM
(TORONTO)

Communist control of certain unions sometimes suffers humiliating defeats. The "Fur Workers' Union" of Toronto, an affiliate of the American Federation of Labour organization, that has been under the domination of the Communist Party for the past several years, recently awoke to the fact that it was being used solely for political manoeuvres and that the Party have little interest in the improvement of conditions amongst the workers. The November "Bulletin" of the union now calls upon all members of their organization to disassociate themselves from the yoke of Communism:

"Fur Workers: Now is the time to free yourselves from the Hitler-Stalin henchmen. Act now! Do not delay! Manifest your loyalty to Democracy against Communism and Fascism. Join the A.F. of L. Fur Workers' Union of Toronto."[⊰blank][4][⊰blank]

"SLOBODNA MISAO" PLANS SPECIAL EDITION
(TORONTO)

In order to celebrate its eighth anniversary, "Slobodna Misao" (The Free Thought), communist paper published in the Croatian language at Toronto, is planning a special issue. It is anticipated that about 40 contributors will write special material for appearance in this edition. The date of issue is being kept secret but 1000 extra copies are to be printed.

[℁<deletion: 1 line]

[℁<deletion: 1 line]

[℁<deletion: 1 paragraph: 4 lines][6][℁<blank]

C.I.O. FOSTERING MINE STRIKES
(KIRKLAND LAKE)

On November 19 the local Mine, Mill and Smelter Workers' International Union (C.I.O. affiliate) called a "strike vote" of the Teck-Hughes Mines employees at Kirkland Lake, with a view to having the miners individually register their desire to have the union represent them in a request for higher wages.

To date union officials claim that 500 miners have signed the petition, out of approximately 750 employees. From reliable information it has been ascertained that this statement is greatly exaggerated and that a large percentage of the Teck-Hughes miners did not wish to strike but "they are being high-pressured by the union organizers and already the slurring work "Scab" is being flung at them." [℁<deletion: 2 lines][7]

COAL STRIKE CONTINUES AT ESTEVAN

Conditions have remained unchanged during the past few weeks in the Estevan-Bienfait lignite area. Striking miners continue to picket the coal properties. No disturbances have occurred and the Royal Canadian Mounted Police reinforcements on hand, originally numbering 150 men, have dropped to about 30. Latest reports would indicate that pickets also have decreased and interest is waning.

Operations at the Western Dominion Strip Mine, Poage's Strip Mine and the Estevan Collieries are being continued without interference or molestation. Baniula's Brothers Mine commenced operations in a small way on November 18. To date no further attempt has been made to operate the other mines in the district.

Arrested on a charge of assault during the early part of the strike, Max Pasoka was found guilty in Magistrates Court on November 16, fined $15 and costs and ordered to keep the peace or serve six weeks hard labour in Regina jail. John Elchyson, charged under the Criminal Code with unlawfully watching and besetting, elected trial before jury and was remanded on $2,000 bail to appear at the next assizes. Other charges against William Knight and Robert McLean for causing damage to property were withdrawn because these individuals have already been sent up for trial on charges of robbery and violence occasioning bodily harm.

On November 23 pamphlets represented as being issued under the joint auspices of the Winnipeg and District Trades and Labour Council and the Winnipeg National Council of the All-Canadian Congress of Labour were distributed in an attempt to acquaint the general public with the strike situation existing in the Estevan coal fields. This literature contained no seditious material and represented the "necessity of collective bargaining by unions, which principle has been approved by the Federal and Provincial Government as a means of maintaining peace in industry." Good feeling between striking miners and R.C.M.P. has existed throughout the strike.

[⊱deletion: 1 line]
[⊱deletion: 1 line]
[⊱deletion: 1 paragraph: 2 lines][8]
[⊱deletion: 1 paragraph: 8 lines]

NEW PARTY WEEKLY CONTEMPLATED

With no Eastern publication available at the present time the Communist Party are preparing to distribute copies of the "Mid-West Clarion," published in Winnipeg, to Party members this week. Efforts are being made to arrange for the issue of a smaller weekly sheet under another name during forthcoming weeks. In this connection a special distributing corps is being organized in Toronto to circularize Party news and literature.[⊱blank][9]

GENERAL
ATLAS COAL STRIKE SETTLED
(EAST COULEE, ALTA.)

On November 21, miners employed at the Atlas Coal Company, East Coulee, Alberta, went out on strike over what appeared to be a very minor disagreement. The walk-out affected three shifts, totalling 150 men.

The mine management contacted [⊱deletion: 2 lines], who advised the members of Local 7331 of this union to return to work, pending subsequent negotiations with the operators. The management claimed that the miners had broken regulations in their "wage agreement" wherein it was provided that in all cases, while disputes are being investigated and settled, the miners, mine laborers, and all other parties involved must continue to work pending investigation and until final decision has been reached, and they refused to discuss this situation with the miners until such time as they returned to work. They agreed to negotiate. No disturbance occurred although picketing of the mine prevented the men from returning to work. The arrival of [⊱deletion: 1 line] resulted in a conference between the parties concerned and a satisfactory settlement was reached on November 23.[10]

INTELLIGENCE
BULLETIN

ROYAL CANADIAN MOUNTED POLICE
HEADQUARTERS, OTTAWA

WEEKLY SUMMARY
DECEMBER 11, 1939

CONTENTS

Editorial (General Survey)

War Series
No. 8.

GENERAL SURVEY

The situation along the European Front is reflected here in our hidden war "behind the lines." Our internal enemies are wary, alert, undismayed, but uncertain as to where and how best to strike. Evidence that their hatred of British laws and institutions is stronger than of opposing ideologies is seen in a growing sympathy, or at least toleration, between Nazis and Communists.

Just as Stalin and Hitler have formed an "unholy alliance" in Europe so in Canada all "antis" are merging their respective hates against Democracy with the declared aim of undermining morale, sabotaging war efforts and eventually destroying society in a bloody revolution.

That the general public, and indeed many of the enemy's milder followers, are blissfully ignorant of the real motives of the leaders does not refute the gravity of the situation, but rather heightens it. Officials who are responsible for our civil security know that from coast to coast throughout Canada paid agents of Red Russia are tirelessly at work subverting individuals, organizing Communist groups, penetrating into Labour organizations and into many social, educational and church clubs and societies, inciting strikes in mines and factories and attempting to fan every small grievance into a major issue. These officials know that if it were not for municipal, provincial and federal police protection and the authority granted under the Defence of Canada Regulations Canada's war activities would be seriously crippled.

It seems clear, however, that our inner defences must be greatly strengthened, not only for the duration of the war but for the peace time that will follow. With armistice will come our real test of strength! The Communists, realizing this, are demanding peace at any price. They remember the social unrest that followed the last armistice and are preparing to take fuller advantage of the one to come. We too must prepare![1]

COMMUNISM
FRENCH CANADIAN COMMUNISTS DENOUNCE THE WAR (MONTREAL)

On November 27 the Communist Party at Montreal undertook a further distribution of C.P. leaflets in conjunction with their policy of denouncing the war aims of the allied nations. This new leaflet, printed in French, is decidedly anti-British. Translated, it reads as follows:

IS THIS THE REASON FOR WHICH WE ARE AT WAR?

Seven men and two women have just been arrested under the War Measures Act for having distributed circulars demanding peace.

However, all the agents of the High Finance, all the leaders of Parliament connected with Trusts, agree in telling us that the present war is a war for the defence of our democratic liberties.

What an irony!

For those who dare favour peace, those who proclaim Chamberlain's fatal politics and that of the English Imperialists, those who proclaim the voracious profiteers who are enriching themselves in this war see themselves menaced by the most ferocious repression, by long years of imprisonment.

Is that the "Democracy" for which we have to let ourselves be slaughtered?

IS THAT THE REASON FOR WHICH WE ARE AT WAR?

Hardly the war had started when the 'liberal' imperialists of Ottawa ordered the suppression of the labour newspaper "Clarte" because it dared to place in doubt the sincerity of the war propaganda of the big interests of the King-Lapointe Government. The newspaper "Clarion" printed in the English language was also suppressed for the same reasons. And the distributors of the pamphlet of the Communist Party on the war are arrested because they are pleading for peace.....[2]

IS THIS THE REASON FOR WHICH WE ARE AT WAR?

In Ontario, the great "democrat" who is the inveterate imperialist Hepburn, threatens to abolish the municipal elections for the length of the conflict. However, the municipal vote is the cornerstone of the democrat regime. In the federal field one wishes to eliminate the full liberty of expression for the members of the legislative assemblies in order to gag every expression of desire for peace or of opposition to the imperialists. The War Measures Act allows the federal authorities to do away completely with the rights of the provinces in order to establish at Ottawa a war dictatorship!

This dictatorship also extends over the industrial domain for the greatest safeguard of profits. The granting of the Industrial Disputes Act to war industries is a first step towards the abolition of the right to strike. It is the point of departure of a general offensive against the freedom of the working class.

The King-Lapointe War Budget was the first blow against the consumers, a present for the imperialist war profiteers. And these politics are only at the beginning. Do you know that for the past three months ending September 30, the International Nickel has pocketed $15,000,000 of profits 5 million of dollars per month 60 million dollars per year and the slaughtering "for the democracy" is only starting!

It is for all this that we are at war

It is for this reason that the honest people who do not want this imperialist war and who dare express it loudly are sent to prison!

This attack led against our popular liberties strikes at all the working class people in Canada. But its menace is directed particularly against French Canada. Because it is here where the imperialist bloodsuckers fear to meet most resistance, it is here where the project for CONSCRIPTION, the BLOOD-TAX which is now prepared at Ottawa, meets with the strongest opposition!

We stand against the direct, immediate danger, the danger of a brutal attack on our French-Canadian liberties, against the rights of national survival of our people by imposing upon the Province of Quebec a regime of martial law, in order to allow them to smother every popular opposition and [3] to send to the criminal slaughter in Europe the best of our men, the best of our youth to pay with their blood and their lives for the criminal folly of the monopolist interests, the imperial profiteers.

Ask for the liberation of those who were arrested for defending peace.

Join in order to put in check the conscription which is prepared by King — Lapointe!

Denounce everywhere the criminal character of this imperialist war.

FOR THE DEFENCE OF OUR LIBERTIES MORTALLY MENACED.

FOR THE DEFENCE OF THE RIGHTS OF FRENCH CANADA.

FORWARD!

Provincial Committee of the Communist Party
of Canada.

NOTE

According to reliable information emanating from Quebec the Communist Party are recruiting new members into the French sections, while recruiting into the English sections has almost stopped. French Canadian members are becoming increasingly anti-British when addressing small Party meetings.

STRONG COMMUNIST SUPPORT IN C.I.O.
(WINNIPEG)

At a recent meeting of the C.I.O. in the Fort Garry Hotel at Winnipeg, [⊱deletion: 2 lines] It was pointed out that through the help of the steel workers and miners in the United States, and also of the Communist Party, "the C.I.O. are now going to give the Canadian Federation of Labour a ride in this Province."

Stating that the C.I.O. have been interested in the way that the C.F. of L. have been playing with the companies and the workers [⊱deletion: 1 line] said that it is the intention of the C.I.O. to organize the unorganized [4] in Manitoba. Referring to the part played by the Communist Party within the C.I.O. he said: "We are sure getting a good deal of help from the Communist Party as to workers working in different plants in Manitoba and we have the sympathy of the trade unions after they see what they are up against."

In regard to manner of organizing [⊱deletion: 1 line] explained:

"The plan will be for us to work in pairs and to pick up loose talk around the plants or halls, then get into the conversation and get him to come to our office and tell us the inside story; from this we can call a meeting by printing some of the facts that this man has told us; I am going to get the committee to prepare a leaflet for a campaign when this Estevan strike is over; we have now $4,000 to fight with, stated P. Conroy and we intend to follow Mr. Meikle and Russell (C.F. of L. organisers) around and upset their 'scabbery' plans with these companies. We are going to set up the Steel Workers Organizing Committee in this city and start where Russell left off or was bought off."

The question was brought up concerning the action recently taken by the American Federation of Labour against Communism within the C.I.O. [⅜<deletion: 1 line] stated in this respect that "we do not intend to use the Communists in the front, they will work their old game of under pressure."

ANOTHER STRIKE IN PREPARATION
(TORONTO)

The Communist Party are making renewed efforts to organize the workers in the General Steel Wares plant at Toronto. They are not satisfied with the results of the recent strike at the Toronto plant, and [⅜<deletion: 3 lines]
Thus the C.P. are anticipating another strike at the General Steel Wares plant within the near future.[5]

[⅜<deletion: 1 line]
[⅜<deletion: 1 line]

[⅜<deletion: 1 paragraph: 7 lines]
This decline in faith in C.P. ideals can be traced directly to A. C. Campbell, Party secretary at Saskatoon, for his apparent disinterestedness and (according to reliable information) for becoming an inveterate "drunkard." His exact whereabouts are unknown.

FISH SHIPMENTS STILL HELD UP
(LOCKPORT, N.S.)

The strike of fishermen and fish handlers at Lockport, N.S., has changed little since its inception last October. Probably because the strike is sponsored by the Canadian Fishermen's Union (an affiliate of the communist controlled Canadian Seamen's Union) and is led by [⅜<deletion: 2 lines] all attempts of the government to mediate the dispute have proved futile.

Picketing continues with few disturbances, but with effective blocking of shipments, only one truckload of fish having broken through the picket lines in recent weeks.

From Halifax Herald:

"Fishing out of Lockport in recent years, Nova Scotia fishermen have put an annual catch of nearly 30 million pounds through the plants of the Lockport Company and Swim Brothers. During the five weeks of Lockport's industrial dispute, the fish have been having an easier time, but nobody else has been enjoying it. The fishermen are earning nothing. The fish-handlers at the wharves are unemployed. Valuable plant is lying idle. Markets are being lost. Serious loss is threatened to the whole community.

"Normally a thriving town, Lockport's purchasing power has been woefully reduced. Sturdily avoiding relief during the long years of depression, the families of many workers in the [6] fishing industry face a bleak prospect, with Christmas approaching, unless an early settlement is reached."

WORKERS EDUCATIONAL ASSOCIATION
(TORONTO)

Recently reorganized for the purpose of instructing the workers along "progressive" lines, the Workers Educational Association at Toronto, an affiliate of the Communist Party of Canada, is appealing to the public to attend its weekly meetings for a better "understanding of the best means by which we can get security for all against want in the midst of plenty." This organization has been able, according to reports, to procure several prominent individuals in Toronto as speakers at these meetings. This movement is appealing openly through the medium of letters to the press for the support of the public.

"IS IT WAR ON THE PEOPLE?"
(EDMONTON)

A pamphlet with the above caption was recently distributed in Alberta by the Communist Party. [≻deletion: 2 lines] Sections of the pamphlet are considered to contravene the Defence of Canada Regulations, and MacPherson's apprehension is being sought. The pamphlet reads, in part:

The Camp of reaction howls and the cringing subsidized Press whines against the forthright and truthful exposure of the present War by the Communist Party of Canada. But hundreds of citizens and soldiers welcome the sentiments of the Communist leaflet, because it merely expresses what 90% of the Canadian people say in private today.

Never was there so much suspicion of the war aims of the British and Canadian Capitalist class, as today. The man in the street asks, "Can the men who destroyed collective security and turned deaf ears to the needs of their own people be trusted to conduct a 'war against Hitlerism'?"......

While the power and advantages of munition and industrial kings is strengthened, steps are being taken to strip the people of every semblance of political liberty. UNDER THE MASK OF FIGHTING FOR "DEMOCRACY" MONOPOLY CAPITAL INTENDS TO INTRODUCE HITLERISM INTO CANADA.[7]

.....Truly the actions of the Chamberlain and MacKenzie King Governments are dictated by the interests of greedy Capitalistic monopolies. This is the trend of Hitlerism. It is out of such a brood of munition kings and Profiteers that Hitlerism was nourished and grew to its present stature.

AGAINST THESE GROUPINGS, THE ENEMY OF DEMOCRACY AT HOME, MUST THE FIGHT BE DIRECTED. TO SAVE OUR PEOPLE, OUR HOMES, OUR DEAR CHILDREN

FROM DISASTER, WE MUST FIGHT THE TERRORS OF DE-
CAYING CAPITALISM!
FIGHT HITLERISM AND THE PROFITEERS IN CANADA!
PEOPLE OF EDMONTON! FIGHT THE PROFITEERING BY
THE BIG MONOPOLIES WHO WANT THIS WAR FOR THEIR
OWN GREEDY ENDS!
TRADE UNIONISTS! USE YOUR ORGANIZED POWER TO
DEMAND GOVERNMENT ACTION AT ONCE AGAINST THE
BIG CORPORATIONS! TAX THEM HEAVILY TO PROVIDE
SOCIAL SERVICES FOR OUR PEOPLE!
WORKERS! ORGANIZE AND FIGHT TO GET THE WAGE IN-
CREASES NECESSARY TO CARE FOR INCREASED LIVING
COSTS!
UNEMPLOYED WORKERS! ORGANIZE AND FIGHT FOR
INCREASED RELIEF — MAKE THE PROFITEERS BEAR THE
COST!
MOTHERS OF EDMONTON! BEFORE IT IS TOO LATE...
BEFORE YOU MUST SHED TEARS OF BITTERNESS.... DO
NOT LET YOUR SONS BE MADE CANNON FODDER FOR
PROFITEERS!
WE PLEDGE OURSELVES TO FIGHT HITLERISM AND
STAND ON GUARD FOR THE CANADA THAT IS TO BE —
FREE AND STRONG — A SOCIALIST CANADA THAT WILL
BANISH POVERTY AND WAR.

[ℛ<deletion: 1 line]
[ℛ<deletion: 1 line]

[ℛ<deletion: 1 paragraph: 6 lines][8][ℛ<blank]

COMMUNISTS IN MUNICIPAL ELECTIONS
(WINNIPEG)

Although taking an active part in the various municipal elections
throughout the country, the Communist Party were unable to return their
full quota of candidates.

An extensive campaign conducted by non-communist candidates to
unseat three members of the Winnipeg City Council resulted in only two
members of the Party being returned for the 1939-40 Council in the elections held on November 25. The Party was successful in re-electing both
their candidates in Ward 3 — Alderman J. Penner and Andrew Bilecki,
school trustee. In Ward 2 the communists were not so fortunate, Jock Mc-
Neil, aldermanic candidate, receiving only 1,454 votes—less than half of
his last year's vote of 3,030. His defeat, however, is more significant than
the victory of those elected inasmuch as Ward 2 is an English-speaking
district. McNeil ran as an Independent Labour candidate, although his
connection with the C.P. was well-known in the district.[9]

Reviewing the election campaign, indifference in voting proved evident in every party group and faction. The total vote including communist had dropped form 61,125 in 1938 to 46,121. One could not ascribe the decrease in the communist vote to indifference in the communist ranks, as they all zealously strove in the campaign. Therefore it must be considered as due to serious losses in membership. Despite that they are elated over their success, and reports indicate that they are giving a great deal of credit for it to the speech delivered by Mayor Queen in which he severely condemned the C.P. machinery, as they believe that this verbal assault only rallied votes to the Party's aid.

(REGINA)

Public fear that the late Labour Party of Regina was controlled by the Communist Party defeated the communist-supported Labour candidates on every count in the municipal elections on November 27. With the exception of J.M. Toothill, who has still one year to run as alderman, all members of the Regina City Council are detached from C.P. influence.

(MELVILLE)

The election by acclamation of I.S. Hillworth, [⅛<deletion: 2 lines], to the school board at Melville, Sask., is being referred to in the Communist Party press as a great achievement for progressive forces in Saskatchewan.

(CALGARY)

In Calgary, Tom Roberts, [⅛<deletion: 1 line] in the civil elections held on November 22, received only a little more than 1,000 votes for the position of alderman. The failure of the Party to elect their candidate is apparently due to Roberts himself, who is very little known to the general public and who has not the personality or ability to put himself over; and also to the rivalry at present existing between [⅛<deletion: 1 line] This rivalry, noticeable in the past, has of late been increasing to the point of open friction.[10]

SECRET

INTELLIGENCE
BULLETIN

ROYAL CANADIAN MOUNTED POLICE
HEADQUARTERS, OTTAWA

WEEKLY SUMMARY
DECEMBER 18, 1939

CONTENTS

War Series
No. 9.

EDITORIAL

A WAR OF WORDS

Physical combat hangs fire, but the mental onslaughts continue with increasing fury. Barrage after barrage of "poison gas" is being loosed by the enemy in their attempts to stultify our war efforts, subvert our loyalty and beguile us into a convenient peace that would be more perilous for the democracies than open war.

This propaganda campaign cannot be ignored or belittled. Its insidious effect is spreading not only among the unemployed and the more ignorant elements but often finds fertile soil in "high places." No less a personage than [⊰<deletion: 2 lines] He says, in a great American newspaper, "Russia's desire for peace is profound. It is so integral a part of its policy that it would, I feel personally convinced, throw its whole weight into the scales for peace and the construction of a new world order......Russia's

86

every action shows that it loves peace."

We have abundant evidence completely refuting such a belief and proving that Stalin's sole ambition is destruction of nationalism and individual rights in a world revolution of regimented workers. In this current issue leading Canadian Communists are quoted verbatim shouting for "a Socialist Canada"; "Work with Italy, Germany, and Russia" for "independence" (that is, the overthrow of democracy); "The peace slogans are clever designs for the purpose of spreading Communism."

This is indeed a "war of words" and we must fight it as efficiently and courageously behind the lines as along the Maginot Line and in the North Sea.[1]

COMMUNISM
"VAPAUS" LAUDS INVASION OF FINLAND
(SUDBURY)

Notwithstanding the various Press announcements by Finnish organizations throughout the country denouncing the Russian invasion of Finland, a certain element within this organization is extremely pro-Soviet and are celebrating what they term the "Russian victory over Finland." This section have openly stated that as soon as Russia gains control of this Scandinavian country they intend to return and this general situation prevails amongst the Finnish Reds in Canada, especially at the more important Finnish centres, Sudbury, Port Arthur and Toronto.

The Canadian-Finnish Red newspaper "Vapaus", published under the auspices of the Communist Party, Sudbury, applauds the U.S.S.R. in its various articles and is extremely anti-British. Loyal Finns have requested the Canadian Government to declare the activities of these Reds illegal and to ban their newspaper; also to seize all the property owned by them and restore it to the legitimate Canadian-Finnish organization.

The attitude adopted by the newspaper "Vapaus" has resulted in a raid being conducted recently by the Ontario Provincial Police, on orders of the Attorney General of Ontario, and all copies of the issue were seized.

[ꝺ<deletion: 1 line]
[ꝺ<deletion: 1 line]

[ꝺ<deletion: 1 paragraph: 8 lines][2]
[ꝺ<deletion: 1 paragraph: 5 lines]
[ꝺ<deletion: 1 paragraph: 5 lines]

BETRAYING UKRAINE TO RUSSIA
(WINNIPEG)

A leaflet issued at Winnipeg by the Association for the Defence of the Western Ukraine states that this organization sent $25,000 and over 10,000 letters to political prisoners and their families in the Western Ukraine. In winding up its activities in Canada the association urged its members to transfer their activities to the Ukrainian Labour Farmer Temple Association and the Association for the Defence of Bukowina and Bessarabia, and to continue to work for the people's happiness and the protection of democratic rights and freedom in this country. The leaflet also reminded its readers that some of the Ukrainian lands are still outside the Soviet Union and that it is essential that they be given aid to enter into one great Soviet-Ukrainian family.

[ℨ<deletion: 1 paragraph: 1 line]

"THE HOUR HAS STRUCK"

"The long awaited hour of a struggle to revolutionize Europe has struck. The Comintern urges British and French workers to inaugurate their own war against the imperialist war, which must end, it states, in the Socialist peace. The aim of Stalin since 1924 has been centred in his government's efforts to rebuild the Soviet Union into a mighty power and then wait for the proper moment to use it for a world revolution. The peace slogans urging the working masses to [3] struggle against war and reaction, have been in fact clever designs for the purpose of spreading Communism and ideas of the world revolution."

[ℨ<deletion: 1 paragraph: 1 line]

[ℨ<deletion: 1 line]

[ℨ<deletion: 1 paragraph: 7 lines]
[ℨ<deletion: 1 paragraph: 2 lines]

"YOUTH MUST FIGHT THE IMPERIALIST WAR"
(TORONTO)

A recent edition of "The Beacon," a Young Communist League publication mimeographed in Toronto, contains the usual denunciations of Allied war aims. Its feature article, "Canada's Youth Must Fight the Imperialist War," demands:

"What kind of a war is this?"..... This is an imperialist war! This is a war in which Canadian youth is to be sacrificed by the Mackenzie King government in the interests of the millionaire bankers and profiteering capitalists, in the interests of the British and Canadian imperialists.

In the Name of Freedom

A barrage of propaganda and lies drenches Canada. Taking advantage of the people's hate of fascism, Premier King exhorts the youth to fight Hitlerism. George McCullagh,[4] the publisher of the reactionary paper, the Globe and Mail, demands the extermination of the German people. Colonel Drew demands the setting up of militarised labor camps to regiment the Canadian youth.

The War Measures Act which gives full dictatorial powers as in any fascist country has destroyed Canadian democracy. It abolishes freedom of speech, press, assembly and freedom of conscience. It grants arbitrary powers to any official to arrest and imprison without warrant or trial by jury. People have been jailed for opposing the imperialist war. The Clarion and the Clarte, independent labor-progressive newspapers, have been banned. One hundred and fifty Royal Canadian Mounted Police terrorise striking coal-miners in Estevan, Sask. As in the last war Quebec youth opposing conscription and the war have ben threatened by repressive measures.....

The ruling class of Canada, those in control of the great industries, the banks, the railroads, forests, and fields of our young and bounteous country made a sorry mess of internal affairs. And now they hurl the nation into imperialist war abroad.....

After comparing this "imperialist" war with the last, "The Beacon" cries upon youth of all lands to

"Rally with the rest of the Canadian people in a united militant struggle against the imperialist warmakers," and to

"Join with us to organize the working youth, young students, farmers, middle class youth against the warmakers, for a free Socialist Canada."

It concludes with the ringing exhortation:

"Defend your civil liberties and democratic rights, freedom of speech, freedom of the press and association, freedom of conscience! Organize against the fascist-militarism of the Drews. Fight for higher wages, for jobs, education and security! Organize into Trade Unions to defend your interests. Fight for a Socialist Canada. Join the Young Communist League."[5]

ESTEVAN COAL MINES' STRIKE ENDS

On December 7, after a seven weeks' shut-down of coal mines in the Estevan-Bienfait area, union officials and mine owners agreed to recognize the presence of one all-embracing union in the field and the strike terminated.

Six members of the R.C.M. Police will remain on the scene in case of further dissension, as requested by the Attorney General for Saskatchewan.

B.C. LABOUR REBUFFS THE REDS
(VANCOUVER)

The Vancouver and New Westminster District Trades and Labour Council recently tendered the Communist Party a considerable shock by opposing Communist inroads into the organization. Party leaders at Vancouver had planned to give T.L.C. endorsement to the Consumers Research Council, a [⊱deletion: 1 line] and were greatly upset when the opposition in the Council managed to obtain a majority vote.

The Boycott Committee set up by the T.L.C. under the chairmanship of Sam Shearer, [᠍᠍᠍<deletion: 1 line] was practically liquidated over the attempt to circulate their "Save our Union" leaflet which was written by members of the Communist Party and contained the same material as the Trade Union leaflet which was confiscated in Edmonton recently. The leaflet purported to show that the executive of the T.L.C. subscribed to the view that the present European conflict was an "imperialist" war and that the trade unions of Vancouver and New Westminster demanded the cessation of hostilities. Members of the Council took the floor and exposed the Communist inspiration of the leaflets and left the question of "If Hitler should have been stopped a few months ago, why shouldn't he be stopped now?" with the delegates to think over.

Members of the Party rose and commenced a long tirade about the murder of civilians in China, with materials supplied by Canada, and furthermore protested the sale of Japanese and German goods in Vancouver. They, however, made no reference to Russia as an aggressor nation. The delegates were unmoved and the executive confiscated the leaflet as misrepresenting the views of the Trades and Labour Council. The activities of the Boycott Committee have been suspended indefinitely.[6]

DISCOURAGE YOUTH FROM ENLISTING
(VANCOUVER)

[᠍᠍᠍<deletion: 1 paragraph: 4 lines]

The Communist Party expects Germany and the Allies to agree to a truce and combine their forces to fight the Soviet Union. We must, therefore, stop or discourage our young men from joining the army as we do not want to see the Soviet defeated.

Referring to the Canadian Labour Defence League and the Civil Liberties Union, [᠍᠍᠍<deletion: 2 lines]

The work of the Communist Party at the present time must be to organize, so that when the capitalist countries attack the U.S.S.R. we can organize revolts in our own country and refuse to fight against the Soviet Union. This is the reason we want our comrades in industry, so that they can organize their work-mates and when the class war between capitalist and socialist arises, they will come out on strike and refuse to manufacture arms and other materials to use against the Soviet.

This is yet another reason why some of our party members should be in the army and air force. They should enlist in order to organize within the armed forces and explain to these poor fools who have joined to fight Naziism, the true nature of the war and have them refuse to fight the Red Army.

[᠍᠍᠍<deletion: 1 line] states that most of the Party members were unfortunately too well known for this work and therefore must endeavour to work more closely with trade unions and mass organizations, pick out sympathizers and train them without actually making them members of the

Party. She said that "the Party did not want to sacrifice any of its members when we can get outsiders to do our work in the trade unions and in cultural organizations." Referring to the possibility of arrests for carrying out Party work, she thought that those receiving jail sentences "will become more bitter against capitalism and long for the day when it will be overthrown by the U.S.S.R. who will free them and all other workers from the bonds of slavery." [7]

[≫deletion: 1 line] concluded her educational talk with "The Party will not lose any prestige by adopting the above methods; instead they will rally the friends and families of these prisoners and thus gain many new members."

MALICIOUS WHISPERING CAMPAIGN
(VANCOUVER)

A "whispering campaign" is in progress at Vancouver. A report indicates that this singular system of agitation is being employed to undermine Canadian war efforts. It is noted further that this campaign is not only prevalent amongst those active in subversive movements and the unemployed but is also being used by individuals employed in stores, mills and factories. It is definitely not being spread by the communists of the British Columbia district, neither does the whisper emanate from the so-called Trotskyists. As a typical example:

"Why should the unemployed join the army to fight for something they have never had, food, etc?

"The unemployed of the dictatorships are fed and put to work and the unemployed of Canada would be no worse off under a Nazi government than they are under the present government."

The campaign seems to emanate from one source up to the present untraceable.

POLICE PROTECTION AT FISHERMEN'S STRIKE
(LOCKPORT, N.S.)

With the exception of union meetings and continued picketing by members of the Canadian Fishermen's Union, the strike situation continued during the past week with little change and no further shipments of fish have been made. However, on December 9 a request was received from the Attorney General of Nova Scotia by the Officer Commanding Royal Canadian Mounted Police at Halifax to afford protection to the fish companies when they attempted to move their products, and 40 men were despatched to Lockport on December 10.[8]

In an endeavour to shift a crowd of more than 600 blocking efforts of the companies to move loaded railway cars of fish a clash occurred during which no one was seriously injured. After a half hour struggle police were forced to interfere in order to protect women and children in the crowd. No weapons were used by the police in this instance.

For nearly two months Swimm Brothers and Lockport Co. Ltd. have been closed as a result of their refusal to recognize union demands. [ଡ଼deletion: 3 lines] stated that if more police arrived "the union's answer will be the call in more men," and that 800 union men were available for picket duty. However, as there was an insufficient number of police on hand, 50 additional men have been despatched from various centres in Eastern Canada to Lockport for temporary duty and will remain there as long as the necessity exists. (Police protection, now totalling 150 men, was given at the request of the Attorney General of Nova Scotia.)

(Note: Wire received December 15 advising dispute has been settled and police withdrawn.)

[ଡ଼deletion: 1 line]

[ଡ଼deletion: 1 paragraph: 7 lines]
[ଡ଼deletion: 1 paragraph: 6 lines][9]

WORKING WITH ITALY, GERMANY, RUSSIA
(WINDSOR)

At a meeting of the Macedonian Political Organization held at Windsor recently, [ଡ଼deletion: 2 lines]

"I am very glad to see so many members of our organization together tonight. I know that we have different beliefs and different political opinions in our organization, like Anarchists, Communists and Nationalists. Everyone is able to be a member of our party irrespective of his political opinion or to what political party he may belong. We are the Macedonian Revolutionary Organization. Everyone is welcome. We have to work all together for our independence, for our beliefs, and the only way to get our independence is to work with Italy, Germany and Russia. These three countries will help us to get our independence."

Other speakers adopted similar lines, "stressing the fact that Italy and Germany are our friends." [10]

NAZIISM

REGISTRATION OF ENEMY ALIENS

From reports received to date, the following registrations by provinces have been recorded up to and including November 30, Several registrars have yet to be heard from.

British Columbia	1259
Alberta	2495
Saskatchewan	1705
Manitoba	1605
Ontario	5409
Quebec	1580
New Brunswick	43
Nova Scotia	178
Prince Edward Island	3
Northwest Territories	10
Yukon Territories	14
Total	14301

Number interned (the majority under Section 21) is 394. Since outbreak of war 46 of the interned have been released. Of these 32 were successful in their appeals and the rest were released as not coming under the Act.

All interned aliens are now concentrated in the camps at Kananaskis and Petawawa.[11]

INTELLIGENCE
BULLETIN

ROYAL CANADIAN MOUNTED POLICE
HEADQUARTERS, OTTAWA

WEEKLY SUMMARY
DECEMBER 26, 1939

CONTENTS

EDITORIAL

"ENEMIES IN FACT"

Revolutionary minorities among our foreign nationality groups are meeting with increasing opposition from their own people. Evidence of this is strikingly shown in two articles in this issue in which Red Finns attack and loyal Finns defend their adopted country.

It appears obvious that the large majority of Germans, Ukrainians, Poles, Finns and other "groups" are being embarrassed by the traitors in their midst and would gladly welcome sterner Government measures for their elimination.

In the meantime public opinion throughout Canada continues to urge the outlawing of all subversive movements. The "Globe and Mail" says editorially:

"Inasmuch as they are well organized and are known to be inspired from Nazi and Communist sources, the simplest way to deal with them is by outlawing them during the period of the war by Federal legislation. It is not sufficient to have them banned in Ontario and neglected elsewhere. It is little use to have an organ of the Communist Party put out of business in this Province merely to appear in Manitoba and be circulated from there. There should be more rigid nation-wide legislation to show that Canada is not fooling about her single-mindedness in this war".....

"It will not be possible to ignore the Reds in this country as actual enemies. To pretend to separate them from this fountainhead is ridiculous at any time. Canada should not only list them with Nazis as potential enemies, but be prepared to deal with them as enemies in fact" .....

"At this critical time we cannot take chances even on an incipient revolution or a campaign to this end".[1]

COMMUNISM

LOYAL FINNS DENOUNCE RED TRAITORS
(SUDBURY)

Despite the revolutionary actions of the Finn minority and their organ "Vapaus," the majority are loyal to their new "Fatherland." At a mass meeting of "the loyal Finnish people," held in Sudbury on December 7, a resolution exposing and denouncing "Communistic cutthroats" was unanimously adopted and afterwards mailed to the Minister of Justice by the Chairman and Secretary.

The resolution reads:

"We, the Finnish people of Sudbury District who do swear our allegiance to His Majesty the King and to the government of this, our Dominion of Canada, assembled in the Sampo Hall at Sudbury on December 7, 1939, do hereby resolve that the attention of the Hon. Gordon Conant, attorney-general of Ontario be called to the situation obtaining our midst, which could develop into very serious danger to Britain and her allies in their struggle against their atrocious and merciless enemies. By this we mean Communism which had crept into our midst and which hides under the name of the Finnish Organization of Canada. This same Communistic movement is also serious peril to our endeavour to raise funds to aid the land of our fathers, which endeavour has recently been started because our Fatherland has been invaded by Communistic cut-throats. For those, who have betrayed their old as well their new Fatherland, are trying to poison the minds our fellow nationals against Great Britain as well as Finland.

Therefore, be it further resolved that we ask the attorney-general of Ontario to take immediate action to put an end to the Finnish Organization of Canada, which has halls and branches all over Canada, and also their newspaper 'Vapaus' published at Sudbury, Ontario."

The resolution was amended to cover confiscation of "all property owned by Vapaus Publishing Co. Ltd., the Finnish Organization of Canada, the Trustees of the Finnish Hall on Spruce Street or any individual who may hold property either real estate or chattels in trust for the Communistic movement or any organization with Communistic aims or leanings;" and further amended to include "pamphlets and publications in Yugoslav, Ukrainian, Russian and other foreign languages as well," several speakers charging that considerable subversive literature is being circulated in those languages. The meeting was attended by about 250 people.[2]

RUSSIA, THE SAVIOUR OF FINLAND!

A Communist bulletin entitled "The Significance of the Finnish-Soviet Developments" is being secretly circulated among dependable Communists throughout Manitoba. It is the usual flimsy fabric woven of falsehood and hate, but calculated to provide "copy" for the ignorant faithful. Starting with a tirade against this Second Imperialist War, instigated by world Capitalists under the leadership of British Imperialism ("The sinister figure behind the attack upon the Soviet Union"), it swings into a glorification of the Soviet Union, whose task since its inception was twofold: "1. To preserve its security as a state, as the base of world socialism, and 2. to aid the workers and colonial people throughout the world to break the chains of Imperialist oppression and exploitation."

To this end:

"The Soviet Union, knowing the aims of the Imperialists, carried through its policy of guaranteeing peace for the people of the Soviet Union as the best guarantee to bringing this Imperialist War to an end, implements its call for peace with the guaranteeing of peace to its immediate neighbours. She signed mutual assistance pacts with the people of the Baltic States and offered a similar agreement with Finland. She was prepared to grant Finland concessions that would have been of great economic benefit to her in exchange for certain concessions that would have contributed greatly to the peace of the Soviet Union and the general peace of Europe."

The bulletin asserts that Finland was never an independent state, but soon will be, with Russia's help.

"The forces of Proletarian and National revolution are on the march. The question of the workers, peasants and soldiers in a number of European countries taking power and establishing their own government without Capitalists is on the agenda and is fast becoming a fact. This is the working class answer to Imperialist war and counter-revolution. It is with such perspectives that we must view the events in Finland. The success of the peace policy of the Soviet Union gives encouragement to the peoples of other countries. The day of final socialist victory is being brought nearer."

Ignoring the bitter hatred of the overwhelming majority of Finns for their "rescuer," the bulletin insists that the latter still wants to have peaceful relations with the people of Finland and [3] "both it and the people of Finland will fight for these peaceful and friendly relations."

However, "the reactionaries are opening up the floodgates of hate. The Canadian Capitalists who have millions invested in Finland will fight to safeguard these investments. It is our task as Communists to increase the struggle against these war plans a thousand fold, by explaining to the masses the real meaning of the present situation and furthering the revolutionary struggle for peace, a peace that will bring socialism." [✂blank] [4][✂blank]

DOUKHOBORS BEING TAINTED WITH COMMUNISM

Doukhobors are rallying to the support of "Kanadsky Gudok", Russian language newspaper published at Winnipeg, which covered the recent Progressive Doukhobor Convention. A speaker at this convention urged his comrades, "as class conscious members of our Progressive Organizations," to make every effort to provide financial assistance to the 'Kanadsky Gudok'. He outlined the object of the Doukhobor page ("The Doukhobor Life"), declaring that there is a very close co-operation between their section and the rest of the paper.

"It is the newspaper of the working masses and it fulfils its task fully and honestly with regard to all the toilers," as compared with what he called the bourgeois press, which misinterprets and falsifies the news in favor of the capitalist class. He said the "Kanadsky Gudok," being a newspaper of the labouring masses, throws light on all the events according to reality.[5]

"Look how the bourgeois press gives the news and comments on the Soviet Union, and then look how the workers' press does it," he continued. He charged the bourgeois press with falsifying the international situation and the capitalist governments for the failure of negotiations between the Allies and the Soviet Union. "What would happen to the world if the Soviet Union had not acted the way it did?" he demanded, and asserted that every agreement between the Soviet and small countries guarantees and safeguards the independence of the latter from the enslaving capitalist nations.

Resolutions were passed by the Progressive Doukhobor Association with the purpose of uniting all members and groups into one Doukhobor family.

Note: ("Kanadsky Gudok" is published by the New World Publishing Co., Winnipeg, Man. [ℰ<deletion: 3 lines][6][Page 7 is missing] [ℰ<blank]

[ℰ<deletion: 1 line] WINDSOR ELECTIONS

The [ℰ<deletion: 1 line] candidates were defeated in the Windsor elections held on December 12, 1939. Alderman Reg. Morris, [ℰ<deletion: 1 line] was ousted from office in Ward I. His defeat, which was a great loss to [ℰ<deletion: 1 line], and that of other Leftist Labour council members, wiped out the labour front majority and a sizable share of support for Mayor Croll and the city council. From all reports the election results will probably mean a general realignment in the council faction and considerably more opposition to the Croll command.

Insofar as [ℰ<deletion: 2 lines] is concerned, he ran for alderman in Ward 4, but spent election day in the local jail, having been arrested for alleged violations of the Defence of Canada Regulations. Whether his sojourn in a public institution had anything to do with his election defeat is not known. Nevertheless, he was hopelessly defeated, having polled only 200 votes.[8]

PENETRATING PUBLIC SCHOOL SYSTEM
(TORONTO)

A new high school student organization is being formed in Toronto under the name of the High School Student's Council. There are two more of these organizations in Canada one in Montreal and one in Winnipeg. Their purpose is student administration of the high school and they work on the same system as the city council. Each collegiate elects an alderman and they all vote for a mayor.

On the surface this organization appears harmless and even Mayor Day of Toronto has endorsed the move. It is, however, being [ℰ<deletion: 5 lines]

[ℰ<deletion: 1 paragraph: 5 lines]

[ℰ<deletion: 1 line]

[ℰ<deletion: 1 paragraph: 8 lines]
[ℰ<deletion: 1 paragraph: 4 lines][9]

[ℰ<deletion: 1 line]
[ℰ<deletion: 1 line]

[ℰ<deletion: 1 paragraph: 8 lines]

"SLOBODNA MISAO" JOINS THE RED CHORUS

A recent publication of the Croatian language newspaper "Slobodna Misao" (The Free Thought) in conformity with other communist controlled publications in Canada, declares itself against Canada's war aims in no uncertain terms. One article denounces the bourgeois and Canadian authorities as follows:

"We have been slandered by the bourgeois and discriminated against by Canadian authorities. We have been put in prisons and deported. Spies have been placed against us and we were constantly attacked by the reactionary press. But it was to no avail... We have continued and still continue the struggle. We know that we have to suffer in the struggle for an ideal....

This is the time when the colonial and semi-colonial countries expect to regain their freedom and when the workers and farmers boldly put forth the demands for their rights, and hundreds of millions of people yearn for peace and are against bloodshed."

ALBERTA BEET WORKERS TO JOIN C.I.O.

The Picture Butte local of the Alberta Beet Workers Union is seeking affiliation with the C.I.O. With this end in view, John Beluch, addressing a meeting, spoke on the negotiations now under way between the union and the C.I.O. He explained that the C.I.O. has a branch in the [10] U.S.A., known as the "United Cannery, Agricultural and Packing House Workers Association," with a membership of 60,000. He read a number of C.I.O. pamphlets in respect to the constitution of this Association. The members discussed the matter and agreed to apply for a charter of affiliation.

Similar meetings are to be held by other union locals in this area for the same purpose.

[ℨ<deletion: 1 line]

[ℨ<deletion: 1 paragraph: 5 lines][11]

GENERAL

COST OF GUARD DUTY

As mentioned in our issue of October 30, 1939, the R.C.M. Police are employing over 1500 returned veterans as Special Constable Guards on 88 vulnerable points throughout the Dominion, at a cost to this Department of over $2,000,000 per annum. These veterans are paid and clothed on a scale considerably exceeding that of regular Special Constables employed elsewhere throughout the Force, and this scale of pay and clothing has the approval of the President and officials of the Canadian Legion.

It was known from the commencement of hostilities that certain of the duties of these veteran guards were seasonable, in that on the close of navigation the number of guards of harbours and canals would be reduced, as an economic measure, and this policy is now being put in effect with the co-operation of other Government Departments. These guards are now being reduced after four months' employment, having been given the usual advance notice. This action is meeting with some opposition in the Press and elsewhere.

No acts of sabotage have been committed since the outbreak of hostilities.[12]

SECRET

INTELLIGENCE
BULLETIN

ROYAL CANADIAN MOUNTED POLICE
HEADQUARTERS, OTTAWA

WEEKLY SUMMARY
JANUARY 2, 1940

CONTENTS
Editorial: "Freedom" of the Press.
Communism:
What is the Mid-West Clarion?
Disruption of Nova Scotia Industries Planned.
"Subscribe to the New Advance"
[⧼deletion: 1 line]
Labour Council Torn by Politics.
[⧼deletion: 1 line]
Communists Rebuked at Memorial Meeting.
Party Excuses for Civic Defeats.
General:
Registration of Enemy Aliens.

War Series
No. 11.

EDITORIAL
"FREEDOM" OF THE PRESS

There is a wide gulf between freedom and license, particularly in time of war. The Clarion was suppressed because it was an enemy of the State, weakening our war efforts and encouraging our enemies. The "right" of Free Press was not meant to include the right to defame, destroy and incite to violence. But this right is still being claimed by the Mid-West Clarion and a dozen more Communist organs which are disseminating propaganda from Red Russia in the name of "truth".

Recently a Communist pamphlet was issued for the purpose of increasing the circulation of the Mid-West Clarion not only in Manitoba but throughout Canada, on the ground that it is a "splendid medium" for combatting the "enemy's propaganda". Condemning the "reactionaries" in Canada for following the footsteps of Hitler, the pamphlet urges Canadian people to fight for the freedom of the press. Here is a typical paragraph:

"You are aware of the attack made on our labor press. The Toronto Clarion, the French paper, Clarte, as well as a number of progressive and radical papers and magazines from England and the United

States have been suppressed....Conant, the Minister of Justice of Ontario, is clamouring to also have the Mid-West Clarion suppressed. The Capitalist newspapers are playing a most despicable role in the present situation. Deliberate lies are being manufactured against the Soviet Union. What a farce. The people are told to give their all for democracy, while right here, at home, democracy is being trampled. Every effort is made to rob the people of free speech and a free press. The only thing that will convince the Government that they cannot silence the people is for us to see that more and more people read the Mid-West Clarion."

The real status of the Mid-West Clarion is revealed in this Bulletin.[1]

COMMUNISM

WHAT IS THE MID-WEST CLARION?

Originally intended to serve the three Prairie Provinces, the Mid-West Clarion, published at Winnipeg, has, since the banning of the Clarion by the Secretary of State, enlarged its circulation to include Eastern Canada as well and attempts have been made to introduce it to former Clarion readers in Southern Ontario and Quebec. The circulation is not known but it is considerably greater than hitherto.

[><deletion: 1 paragraph: 5 lines]

The circulation of the Mid-West Clarion is general; reaching all sections of the population, though the paper particularly stresses that it is the medium of the working class. The financial resources of this paper are Communist, and in this respect the publishing association holds periodical press drives to obtain funds.

With regard to the policy of the Mid-West Clarion, it will be seen that it advocates Soviet foreign policy. The majority of its international news is pro-Soviet and emanates from Moscow. It carries on a tirade against all things British and its main editorials are particularly vehement in this respect. Leading members of the Party throughout Canada, the United States, the Soviet Union, England and France are regular contributors. The majority of these articles are supposed to alleviate the ills of the working class movement, but with emphasis attached to Communist ideals as enunciated by the Soviet Union, and the paper actively agitates for a change in Government.

At the present time the paper is strongly urging a repeal of the Defence of Canada Regulations and especially a removal of the bann imposed on other Communist publications, asserting that the Government has destroyed all the rights of the Canadian people, and urging "The public of Canada to rise in thunderous protest against [2] this blackout of democratic liberties in our country. Unless action is taken immediately, unless the labour movement and all democratic-minded people compel the government to retreat, reaction equal to the blackout fascism will overwhelm our people..... The powers taken by the government of Canada under the War Measures Act are a negation of all democratic rights. The actions of the censor department, the actions of the Minister of Justice, are a denial of civil liberties and of the freedom of the press."

The Mid-West Clarion is being used and will continue to be used by the Communist Party in their attempt to undermine the Canadian Government and institutions; to lessen the public's faith in the reasons for this war and to stop it at all costs and, at the same time, endeavour to institute Soviet policy into Canadian affairs.

This paper is being used as a medium for the election of Communists and "Progressives" in all municipal, provincial and federal elections.

That this paper is having a detrimental effect upon its readers, there can be little doubt. The continued libelous statements made through the medium of its various articles in an attempt to cloud the real aims and policy of the Government have a tendency to confuse the real issue and subvert the loyalty of many otherwise well meaning people.

DISRUPTION OF NOVA SCOTIA INDUSTRIES PLANNED

J. A. Pat Sullivan and Charlie Murray, [≫deletion: 2 lines], and leaders of the Canadian Seamens Union, are in Nova Scotia organizing locals of the Canadian Fishermens Union, an affiliate of the C.S.U. Their first endeavour in this respect was the organizing of the fishermen and fish handlers at Lockport, N.S.

These two Communists have also made a tour of the important industrial centres in N.S. with a view to obtaining information regarding the prospect of strikes in the spring. According to information, Sullivan recently stated that "he will organize every fisherman on the coast of N.S. for a big push this coming spring." He said further that one of their big time organizers will take part in the final drive. To this end he is going to Cape Breton at an early date, following which he will proceed to other parts of the province.[3]

It should be recalled that previous to the recent strike at Lockport, conditions there were most satisfactory, Lockport being one of the many prosperous small towns where tie-ups, unemployment and relief were unheard of. While the Red agitators succeeded in organizing a satisfactory union they have sown seeds of discontent and unrest with the ultimate object in view of reaping a revolutionary harvest. The C.S.U. organizers have no intention of letting the matter rest at this stage either at Lockport or at any other vulnerable point they subsequently attack, and their activities should be curtailed before there is further trouble, not only among fishermen but also in the coal mining and steel industries of Cape Breton.

"SUBSCRIBE TO THE NEW ADVANCE"
(MONTREAL)

The Communist Party members at Montreal have been urged to subscribe to the "New Advance", a magazine published by the Young Communist League, in view of the fact that it is one of the few remaining Canadian Communist periodicals available. Its circulation should be one of the main tasks of the members of the C.P.

[❧deletion: 1 line]

[❧deletion: 1 paragraph: 3 lines]
[❧deletion: 1 paragraph: 3 lines]
[❧deletion: 1 paragraph: 1 line]
[❧deletion: 1 paragraph: 2 lines]
[❧deletion: 1 paragraph: 1 line][4]
[❧deletion: 1 paragraph: 2 lines]
[❧deletion: 1 paragraph: 1 line]
[❧deletion: 1 paragraph: 2 lines]
[❧deletion: 1 paragraph: 2 lines]
[❧deletion: 1 paragraph: 1 line]
[❧deletion: 1 paragraph: 3 lines]

LABOR COUNCIL TORN BY POLITICS
(VANCOUVER)

At a monthly meeting of the Trades and Labour Council at Vancouver there was considerable discussion over the merits of Russia's invasion of Finland. A resolution passed by the Milk Drivers and Dairy Employees Union condemning Russia's attack on Finland gave rise to dispute. A number of delegates objected to the resolution and requested that it be filed instead of endorsed. The vote on this matter was upheld by a considerable majority. [❧deletion: 3 lines] Upon a delegate asserting that this was not a political meeting, the vice president suggested that the council attend to its own business and leave politics alone. The delegate of the Hotel and Restaurant Employees Union, however, continued the discussion, saying "This is not the first time Russia has invaded Finland. Last time she was supported by American, British and German capital. Let us understand the histories of these countries before we start adopting resolutions of this kind." There were angry protests from several parts of the hall to [5] which the president, [❧deletion: 4 lines]

A lengthy resolution was submitted by the Street Railwaymens Union Local, but on a vote only one section of it was endorsed. This section urged that a protest be sent to the B.C. Minister of Labour and the Premier against the arrest and conviction of the union leaders at the Pioneer Mine. The remainder of the resolution, not endorsed, dealt with the "reactionary forces" in Canada taking advantage of the war situation to profiteer at the expense of the "toiling population." The resolution also referred to the same reactionary forces taking advantage of war sentiment to curtail civil liberties as an aid to still more intensive exploitation of the Canadian workers.

This union further protested the banning of the two working class papers, "Clarion" and "Clarte", and the arrest of citizens whose only crime was to distribute a leaflet explaining the cost of the present war.

Charles Stewart and Peter Munro, [⊱deletion: 2 lines] and delegates of the Street Railwaymens Union, strongly protested the shelving of the latter part of this resolution. "If we allow these papers to be suppressed," said Munro, "the Government will go further and suppress our own Trade Union papers."

[⊱deletion: 1 paragraph: 4 lines]

Again the question of politics was brought before the meeting, being introduced by D. McPherson. He stated, "I hear nothing at these meetings that is constructive to the labour movement which I represent." He added that the working man's problems were infinitely more pertinent to the business of the council. "If this is going to become a political meeting, let us know in advance so that we can go somewhere else and form a labour movement."[6]

[⊱deletion: 1 line]

[⊱deletion: 1 paragraph: 3 lines]
[⊱deletion: 1 paragraph: 4 lines]
[⊱deletion: 1 paragraph: 3 lines]

COMMUNISTS REBUKED AT MEMORIAL MEETING (WINNIPEG)

In conformity with Communist Party policy to utilize every means at its disposal to elicit public attention, the Party at Winnipeg held a memorial meeting for Dr. Bethune on December 17 under the joint auspices of four organizations—Chinese Patriotic League, Friends of China, Winnipeg Committee to Aid Spanish Democracy and Friends of the Mackenzie-Papineau Battalion. Between four and five hundred people were present at the meeting, which was conducted under the joint chairmanship of L. St. George Stubbs, former Judge of the Winnipeg Congress and a prominent member of the Communist Party, and Dr. T. Quong. Brief addresses of tribute were made by the following speakers: R. C. McCutchan, Dr. A. Magid, E. J. McMurray, Charlie Foo, Wm. Kardash, Prof. W. F. Osborne and Marshall J. Gauvin.

St. George Stubbs eulogized Dr. Bethune's work as physician and surgeon in Canada, Spain and China, and other speakers continued the praise. The meeting was in full accord until William Kardash spoke. He began by paying tribute to Dr. Bethune and all that he had done to help humanity, then stated that the doctor was a Communist and that "it takes a Communist to do what Bethune did." His concluding remarks were received with resentment by a great many of the Communists as well as others, and the applause after his speech was somewhat sporadic.[7]

Professor Osborne of the University of Manitoba followed and stated that this gathering is not to glorify any Communist and that many present were taking part in this memorial meeting solely because of Bethune's splendid deeds. His further remarks were a denunciation of the Russian invasion of Finland, at which murmurs arose from the Communist section of the audience. The last speaker, Marshall J. Gauvin, condemned Stalin and warned the worshipping enthusiasts of diabolic diplomacy not to be quite so sure of themselves. As the Communist Party had been chiefly responsible for the meeting and most of the audience were Party sympathizers, the remarks of Prof. Osborne and Marshall Gauvin were received with bad grace.

A collection amounting to $96 was taken at the door.

PARTY EXCUSES FOR CIVIC DEFEATS
(WINNIPEG)

Regarding the recent civic elections held at Winnipeg, the Communist Party have published a bulletin to explain the reasons for their defeat at that time. According to this bulletin "the weaknesses revealed in the work of the Party during the elections indicate that they have not yet learned to react quickly and boldly to the attacks of the counter-revolutionary forces. The leading committees of the Party in Winnipeg accept their responsibility for the mistakes made in the elections and are taking the necessary measures to improve the work of the city committee and of the Party as a whole."

It is urged in this pamphlet that the Party membership must take stock of the present situation in order to have a clear understanding of the tremendous events that are now shaking the world and "be in a position to influence the workers and to clear their minds of confusion and from a bourgeoisie ideology. The Imperialist war is now rapidly changing into a counter-revolutionary war, a war against the Soviet Union, a war of bourgeoisie against the revolutionary forces of the working class in every capitalist country." It is stressed that the Party must realize the full reality of the war and "these facts must become the property of wide masses of working people in order that they may fully understand the blows that the Soviet Union is now directing against the counter-revolutionary forces that we may deal blows at these same forces in our own country, which we failed to do during the elections campaign."[8]

The bulletin further states that the Party membership was inefficiently organized for the election campaign, with an almost complete absence of initiative on the part of members. "The main weakness of the groups and membership is still the lack of initiative and the fact that a section of the Party is still taking a position of retreat, showing timidity, lack of confidence and confusion, which creates pacivity at a time when the most urgent need in the present period is a bold advance to the offensive."

The general opinion has existed that the Jewish element within the Communist Party ranks has withdrawn a great deal of its support. Insofar as members of the Party are concerned, there was at first a great deal of dissension and several of the minor Jewish lights left in disgust. However, the majority of the more important Jewish leaders have remained, as is seen in this statement:

"A very encouraging exception to the general weakness of the campaign is the good election work carried on by an active group of our Jewish comrades and by a considerable number of our Jewish comrades and by a considerable number of our Jewish sympathizers and by the 'Veg.' The result of this good work was reflected in the vote our candidates received in the Jewish polls. It was on the Jewish field that the heaviest guns were directed against us, but when the ballots were counted it was revealed that our loss in the four Jewish polls compared with last year's vote, was much smaller than the loss of I.L.P. candidates sustained.

"This was a smashing defeat for Queen, Blumberg and their reactionary allies. The Communist Party candidates in Ward 3 came out at the top of the poll once more. The reactionary onslaught was successfully repulsed. A quick liquidation of the shortcomings and weaknesses of our work, as revealed during the election campaign, will lay the basis for a broad advance of the Party on all fields."[9]

GENERAL

REGISTRATION OF ENEMY ALIENS

Number of Enemy Aliens registered up to and including December 15:

British Columbia	1315
Alberta	2680
Saskatchewan	1837
Manitoba	1636
Ontario	5478
Quebec	1858
New Brunswick	43
Nova Scotia	181
Prince Edward Island	3
Northwest Territories	10
Yukon Territory	14
Total	15055

INTELLIGENCE
BULLETIN

ROYAL CANADIAN MOUNTED POLICE
HEADQUARTERS, OTTAWA

WEEKLY SUMMARY
JANUARY 8, 1940

CONTENTS

War Series
No. 12.

EDITORIAL
IS COMMUNISM DEFEATED?

Judging by the contents of this issue the Communist Party of Canada has been suffering reverses comparable to those of their Russian "comrades" in Finland. The recent municipal elections throughout Ontario succeeded in eliminating a large proportion of the Reds from boards and councils, including the much-advertised Alderman Stewart Smith of Toronto. The great shrinkage in the number of votes cast for Communists in almost every ward denotes wholesale deflections in the ranks of former sympathizers. Even the United Mine Workers and the C.I.O. are turning cold shoulders on these extremists.

The cause for this access of unpopularity is, of course, the war and Stalin's partnership with Hitler. For instance, since the signing of the Russo-German pact the Party membership among Toronto Jews, originally about 3500, has dropped off 70%. The invasion of Finland has widened the splits in the Red ranks.

It would be a serious mistake, however, to think that the Communist Party is out as well as down. Their leaders are as active as ever and even more virulent. Russian successes in Europe, backed by fresh propaganda barrages from Moscow, might succeed in rallying the Party's ranks to former strength and even greater opportunity for mischief.

Partial eradication of this "tapeworm" in the body politic will only leave segments to develop again and perhaps make our last state worse than the first.

And in the meantime our enemies continue to hate and to threaten, promising to "leave no stone unturned to save the working class from being butchered for profits."[1]

COMMUNISM
COMMUNIST LOSSES
IN ONTARIO MUNICIPAL ELECTIONS

Recent municipal elections throughout Ontario have resulted in grave loss of communist prestige. Communists, especially in Toronto, met such opposition from various civic bodies as to ensure their defeat from the start.

(a) [⊱<deletion: 1 line] Defeated at Toronto

Efforts of [⊱<deletion: 1 line] in Toronto centered largely around the task of electing Alderman Stewart Smith to the Board of Control. This year Tim Buck, General Secretary of the C.P. of Canada, was not a candidate.

[⊱<deletion: 1 line] in the field were ex-Alderman J. B. Salsberg, Fred Collins, Jean Laing, George Harris, Harry Bell. No communist was elected to public office. The Party has lost more than 50% of its following since the 1939 election.

It is presumed that Smith [⊱<deletion: 2 lines] and from this it would appear that their support has declined since last year by over 25000 votes. William Dennison was defeated as a C.C.F. candidate, [⊱<deletion: 2 lines] On the other hand, William T. Lawson, a [⊱<deletion: 1 line] was elected School Trustee in Ward 4. The Party also supported a number of progressive candidates in the various wards. The vigorous opposition encountered by the communists was largely due to the Soviet-German pact, the Russian invasion of Finland and the present war. With virtually no supporters in the Toronto City Council, a serious blow has been dealt the Communist Party of Canada. The vote in Toronto was lighter than previous years.[2]

Board of Control

	1940	1939	1938
Stewart Smith	19,641	45,112	44,148
(Replacing Tim Buck)			

Aldermen

	1940	1939	1938
Ward1 - Harry Bell	1,717	4,374	1,509
" 2 - George Harris	933	6,563	1,735
" 3 - Jean Laing	1,217	1,604	1,429
" 4 - J. B. Salsberg	2,154	5,859	4,725
" 5 - Fred Collins	2,729	8,121	8,025

(b) Scarboro Voters Reject Communist Council

James Wilson, [>deletion: 1 line] was defeated at the polls in Scarboro township. He came third and last in the voting in Ward 2, with a total of 878.

(c) [>deletion: 1 line] Elected at Hamilton

Sam Lawrence was returned in the recent Civic elections as head of the Board of Control, receiving a total vote of 18,096, approximately 500 more votes than last year. To head the polls, Lawrence drew heavy support from the labour wards. Harry Hunter, seeking election as Alderman in Ward 7, was again successful and received a vote of 1613. Both these individuals are held in very high esteem by the Communist Party. Several other individuals were successful in receiving a small percentage of the Communist votes in the various wards.

(d) Reverses in the Mining Districts

In the mining districts in Northern Ontario the Communist Party conducted an extensive campaign to elect Party members and supporters in the various municipal elections. In the majority of cases they suffered reverses as against last year's figures.[3]

At Kirkland Lake Tommy Church, organizer for the Mine, Mill and Smelter Workers Union and [>deletion: 1 line], did not run openly as their candidate. However, he was elected to the Council, receiving 1,701 votes (second highest number of votes cast) as against 2,629 cast for him last year. He has the only known candidate in the running.

At Timmins A. B. McCabe and H. R. Anderson, running on a labour representation platform, [>deletion: 2 lines] and the mass organizations. Anderson [>deletion: 2 lines] and union organizer for Northern Ontario for the I.M.M.S.W.U., whilst McCabe, [>deletion: 2 lines] controlled Workers Co-operative Society of New Ontario. The latter was a Councillor in 1939 when he polled 1,802 votes. In this election he received only 1,538 votes and was defeated. Anderson, not previously a member of the Council, was also defeated, receiving only 1,380 votes.

At Sudbury, Joe Billings, J. M. Thompson and Dr. G. Davidson, polling respectively 149, 228 and 406 votes, were defeated in the election for the City Council. [%<deletion: 2 lines] J. M. Thompson was the only member who ran for a seat in the Council last year, receiving 265 votes.

In the above three elections, it will be noted that, though a few Communists were elected, there was a considerable drop in their support.

C.P. IN CIVIC ELECTIONS, NOVA SCOTIA
(SYDNEY)

In conformity with Communist Party policy throughout the Dominion at the present time, prominent Party functionaries at Sydney, Nova Scotia have approached a leading labour member with the purpose of having him run in the coming municipal elections.

Norman MacKenzie, president of Lodge 1064, Steel Workers' Organizing Committee [%<deletion: 1 line] has been asked to run under the auspices of [%<deletion: 1 line] in Ward 5 in the next Civic elections. Whether MacKenzie will be boosted as a [%<deletion: 2 lines] is not known. It is anticipated that he will run as a Steel Workers' candidate, in order to insure his election.[4]

The seriousness of communists gaining control in civic bodies, especially in important industrial centres such as Sydney, because of the international situation, need hardly be emphasized. In view of recent reports to the effect that prominent members of the Party will endeavour early this year to organize steel workers and miners in Cape Breton, the position of one communist member on a civic board (especially if he ostensibly represents the interests of the steel workers) may be viewed with apprehension. Nearly all their recent efforts have caused strikes of serious proportions. At the present time, with the steel works in Sydney running at full capacity on "war orders," a strike would be costly.

C.I.O. ORGANIZING IN THE BORDER CITIES

The C.I.O., under the instigation of regional director Burt and organizer Napier are contemplating advancing grievances in all industrial plants where there is union representation in the Border Cities. This will be a preliminary step in developing agitation against employers and subsequent appeals to the labour department. This method is being used by the C.I.O. in an endeavour to apply the Industrial Disputes Act in such a manner that it will be of assistance to them in organizing. So far it has had no success.

Burt claims to have been authorized to spend more money on organizational efforts at the international executive board meeting of the U.A.W. held at Pittsburg recently. He has not divulged any definite plans in this respect.

"THE CLARION, BY ANY OTHER NAME—"

A new newspaper, the "Canada Tribune," will be published in Toronto in the course of the next week or so. This publication will take the place of the newspaper "Clarion," chief organ of the Communist Party, which was recently banned by the Secretary of State. A. A. MacLeod, [≫deletion: 1 line] and former national chairman of the Canadian League for Peace and Democracy, will be managing editor; J. G. King, [≫deletion: 2 lines], is business manager. The editorial board of this paper is composed of two well-known Montreal individuals, R. L. Calder, K.C., member of the C.C.F.[≫deletion: 1 line][5][≫deletion: 1 line], and vice-president of the Montreal branch of the Canadian Civil Liberties Union; and R. A. C. Ballantyne, [≫deletion: 2 lines] and secretary of the Montreal branch of the Canadian Civil Liberties Union.

It is not known as yet what the policy of this paper will be. It will, however, be subsidized by the C.P. of Canada and will carry on to a great extent the work of the late "Clarion."

MORE ENGLISH-SPEAKING MEMBERS WANTED
(MONTREAL)

It has been decided that the English-speaking section of the Communist Party at Montreal must start recruiting immediately. Consequently a sympathizers' meeting will be organized on a large scale. This information shows a change in policy of the Communist Party at Montreal, who a few weeks ago issued instructions that recruiting into English-speaking sections of the Party would be discontinued until further notice.

[≫deletion: 1 line]

[≫deletion: 1 paragraph: 7 lines]
[≫deletion: 1 paragraph: 7 lines][6][≫blank]

A BLAST FROM OUR RED FURNACE

Leaflets dealing with the peace-front adopted by the Communist Party of Canada have been published and distributed in Nova Scotia by the Maritime Committee during the latter part of December. These leaflets represent the latest attempt of the Party to oppose the war aims of the Canadian Government, and it will be seen from the following excerpt that the views expressed are as corruptive and disruptive as anything previously issued:[7]

"The present situation in Northern Europe is the result of the intrigues and schemes of the reactionary Finnish government, who agreed to serve as a tool for British imperialism, and who were in agreement with the British ruling class for allowing Finland to be used as a base in Northern Europe for an attack on the land of Socialism.... They hide the fact that it was the Russian Workers' revolution and its Party of Lenin & Stalin who gave independence to Finland, and it was Baron Mannerheim, friend of the Tsar's court, decorated with the iron cross by Kaiser Wilhelm of Germany supported by German and British imperialist bayonets, who drowned in blood the newly born Workers' and Farmers' government of Finland.....

"This Imperialist war is being fought to decide who will dominate Europe for colonies, natural resources, work markets to enrich the exploiters and to prevent the workers from gaining their freedom.... The main consideration above all others is capitalism's efforts to crush Socialism and to prolong their own greedy exploiting system.....

"The Hitlers, the Chamberlains, the Daladiers are all to blame for this Imperialist War. They shamelessly conduct the war under the disguise of fighting Fascism, agression and defending democracy. They who strangled democratic Spain, who betrayed Ethiopia, Austria, Czechoslovakia, Albania and Memel; they who filled the concentration camps of Europe with hundreds of thousands of the best working class fighters. They who hold the responsibility for the murder of tens of thousands of the flower of the working class.....

"The War Measures Act at one blow wipes out Magna Charta and every vestige of Canadian democratic rights and liberties that took centuries of working class struggle to gain. It is designed to crush all opposition, all protest, against the scandalous profits that are being piled up by the rich exploiters the dealers in blood. The Clarte and the Clarion working class papers are suppressed and the management arrested, dragged into court for daring to criticize the government and the munition kings. Trade Union leaders are arrested, ministers of the church are persecuted for voicing the sentiments of the "prince of peace." The blood thirsty war mongers bare their fangs and snarl and snap at any who mention peace.[8]

"Sixty thousand of the best sons of the Canadian working class were killed in the 'war to end wars' 1914-1918. Sixty new millionaires were created. The war mongers are out to improve on this. They are trying to place the whole burden of the war onto the backs of the working class, by increasing their profits. Your dollar today is worth no more than 70 cents at the corner store. To put this over they must weaken working class resistance by attempting to smash trade unions as evidenced by Premier MacDonald and his police terror against the Lockport Fishermen's Union, and by Dosco's offensive assisted by the government against the steel workers and coal miners.

"With honourable exceptions practically the whole leadership of the C.C.F. have climbed onto the Imperialist war chariot. They outdo the capitalist's venal press in slanderous attacks against the Soviet Union. They execute all forms of gymnastics in trying to fool the people that this Imperialist war is a war for democracy. They speak of reconstruction after the war is over, ignoring the fact that millions of workers are condemned to be slaughtered in the meantime. They are playing a more treacherous role than their colleagues of the 2nd International did in the 1914-18 blood bath....

"The Communist Party is opposed to Imperialistic war and will leave no stone unturned to save the working class from being butchered for profits.....

"Workers—Build your trade union and a struggle for higher wages to meet the increased cost of living. FIGHT the War Measures Act and every infringement on your democratic rights and liberties."

"FOR FREEDOM OF SPEECH AND PRESS
DOWN WITH THE IMPERIALIST WAR"[9]

GENERAL

ILLEGAL STRIKES BANNED BY UNITED MINE WORKERS

As a result of the numerous unofficial strikes and petty disturbances of recent occurrence in the Nova Scotia mining district the United Mine Workers (District 26) have issued a circular declaring they would no longer countenance petty strikes or any other breaches of contract entered into between United Mine Workers and operating companies.

"For the past two years," reads the circular, "irrespective of the fact that there exists a joint signed agreement by and between the United Mine Workers of America, District 26, and the International Union, and the Dominion Coal Corporation, Limited, there have been many stoppages of work by tie-ups and strikes. These stoppages are open and defiant violations of the 3rd clause of our joint agreement....

"Illegal tie-ups, strikes, or stoppages of work will no longer be tolerated on the part of our membership. If one more member of the United Mine Workers of America feels that he is unjustly dealt with by the company, he must take up his grievance as provided by the joint agreement, remaining at work until same is adjusted as provided by the terms of our joint agreement.

"The executive board of District 26 and your International Union will no longer countenance or condone violation of its joint contract. Any failure to subscribe to its provisions by our membership whose economic welfare is protected and preserved under its provisions and the provisions of our district and International Constitution will be dealt with forthwith in harmony with the laws of our union."

The above official action of the U.M.W. should have a healthy effect throughout the Nova Scotia mining industry and do much to offset the disruptive work of such [⊰deletion: 1 line] as Pat Sullivan and Charlie Murphy, who, (as explained in our last Bulletin) are planning "a big push this spring" on Cape Breton steel and coal industries.[10]

INTELLIGENCE
BULLETIN

ROYAL CANADIAN MOUNTED POLICE
HEADQUARTERS, OTTAWA

WEEKLY SUMMARY
JANUARY 15, 1940

CONTENTS

War Series
No. 13.

EDITORIAL

A LESSON FROM DIES

The reports of the Dies Committee on un-American activities, together with Representative Martin Dies' series of articles now appearing in "Liberty" are of vital significance to Canada, whose social and political problems are for the most part accurate reflections of its neighbour's.

Dies has exposed "more snakes than I can kill," in the guise of Communists, Nazis and Fascists. He has shown that these traitors to democracy, over 1,000,000 strong, are striving by fair means and foul to destroy every right and privilege free peoples have fought for and won down through the ages. He has shown how these traitors penetrate wholesome progressive movements and corrupt their personnel into enemies of the State—how the leadership of many C.I.O. and Federation of Labour Unions, of youth, church and educational associations is Communist, drawing its pay and control from Russia. He has shown how all these subversive elements "borrowed the fundamentals of their cults from Karl Marx, the greatest expounder of the philosophy of materialism the world has yet produced."

What about Canada? Our investigators have found evidence of similar methods and conditions. The audacity and virulence of our traitors are in no wise behind their's. Because, however, we are actually at war, Americans can afford to confine themselves to "investigations" and political controversies regarding their internal enemies, while we must act with decision and force, upon the evidence at hand, to defeat these enemies before they have defeated us.

Weakening the power of the Defence of Canada Regulations (at the indirect instigation of the enemy) is like boring holes in our boat while crossing a stream!

Clinging to our peacetime rights (as demanded by the enemy), while they are being used as weapons to destroy all freedom, is national suicide!

Leniency towards traitors is abject betrayal of our own people![1]

COMMUNISM
THE OLD "CLARTE" BECOMES "THE NEW"
(MONTREAL)

"La Clarte Nouvelle", successor to the French Communist newspaper "La Clarte" which was banned by the Acting Secretary of State on October 5, 1939, appeared the latter part of December in Montreal. This publication is mimeographed and carries no indication by whom or where it is published. It flouts the Canadian Government's authority to initiate and enforce the Defence of Canada Regulations. The main article is a repetition of the one issued by the Central Executive of the Communist International on the occasion of the 22nd Anniversary of the October Revolution. Another stresses the position of French Canada among the other provinces and warns:

"Do not believe those who call you for war under the flag of national unity. What may there be in common between yourselves and those who make a commerce of cannons and of human blood? What unity can there be between exploiters and exploited?"

Other articles severely criticise the dictatorship powers bestowed upon the Canadian Government, "in the interests of the millionaire profiteers and the imperialists.......the regime of profits made on the blood of the people."

It is reported that the paper is to be published weekly. Seventeen hundred copies of the first issue were mimeographed—probably in Montreal.

POLISH PEOPLE'S ASSOCIATION STILL ACTIVE
(TORONTO)

Since its organization in Canada, the Polish People's Association has received financial aid from the Ukrainian Labour Farmers Temple Association. The former organization, like the latter, is [2] exclusively under Communist leadership and both organizations have similar ends and objects, namely to attract to and educate as many members as possible in the doctrines of communism. This fact directly contradicts the assertions frequently made in public that the P.P.A. is not a Communist organization.

During the Spanish Civil War this organization recruited about forty of its members for service in Spain with the Mackenzie-Papineau Battalion. Upon arrival overseas, however, they were transferred to the Dombrowski Polish Battalion.

The P.P.A. is continually collecting money from its members and sympathizers for the purpose of furthering communist propaganda in Canada, Poland and other parts of the world. Financial aid was sent to political prisoners in Poland and also to Spain for the purpose of equipping Polish members of the Mackenzie-Papineau Battalion. This aid was in some instances sent abroad openly by the organization, but more often it was sent through a selected individual so that the organization should not be involved. Leaders of this association have stated publicly that thousands of dollars have been collected from the Poles in Canada and used as stated above.

Since the outbreak of war, the organizational personnel of the Polish People's Association have been divided into two sections. The less important organizers have remained in Toronto, but the leaders are reported to be now in Winnipeg. With the signing of the Russo-German pact a number of members severed their connections. Most of these have since returned and the incident has had no serious effect upon the organization.

Leaders are Arthur Morski, editor of "Glos Pracy", Wasyl Dutkewich, J. Maitchak and Tadeusz Lewandowski. The activities of the P.P.A are of similar nature to those of the U.L.F.T.A.—meetings, dances, socials, children's schools, etc.[3]

YOUNG COMMUNISTS' CHALLENGE TO GOVERNMENT

Twenty-five hundred copies of a mimeographed pamphlet, issued for Toronto and Eastern Ontario by the National Executive Committee of the Young Communist League of Canada, were distributed recently. Further copies of this leaflet are to be printed or mimeographed by the Young Communist League districts in Quebec, Western Canada and Northern and Western Ontario. Funds are not available for a central printing of this circular. The leaflet was written by Sam Walsh and Dave Kashtan. [³<deletion: 2 lines]

The leaflet is entitled "Youth Must Fight For Life, Not Die For Profits" and is contained in two sheets, written on both sides and appropriately decorated with rough drawings. There is a similarity in this and all other leaflets issued recently by the Party and their affiliate organizations which denounce the Canadian Government for their support of the "Imperialist War" and the "Blackout of Civil Liberties."

Under the sub-title "Lest We Forget", the article states, "In 1914-18 our fathers were led and conscripted into the terrible slaughter of imperialist war under the false slogans of 'save democracy', 'a war to end all wars', 'a land fit for heroes to live in.' Now again we are expected to uphold an empire that holds 500,000,000 human beings in virtual slavery, to defend capitalism, which breeds imperialist war and poverty for the people......It is a brutal, unjust robber war of rival imperialisms."

Urging the "young people of Canada" to "rally with the Canadian working class in a united militant struggle against the imperialist war-makers", the article calls for "a free social Canada", and concludes:

"END THE IMPERIALIST WAR!
JOIN THE YOUNG COMMUNIST LEAGUE!"[4]

WAR'S THREAT TO LABOUR
(VANCOUVER)

The British Columbia Coast District of the International Woodworkers of America (C.I.O.) held their annual convention at Vancouver, commencing on Janaury 3. Some fifty delegates attended from Vancouver Island and the interior, whilst about half a dozen were present from locals in Washington and Oregon, U.S.A. The meeting was opened by Mayor Lyle Telford who wished them "all the success in the world in their fight for humanity."

Stressing the fact that although sawmills and camps were expanding operations under the stimulus of war orders and that employment was at a ten-year high, Hjalmer Bergren, president of District Council, said that in very few cases have wages risen correspondingly whereas the cost of living was going up. He pointed out that industrial safety in the woods and manufacturing centers was at a low ebb owing to speed-up systems, power saws and outworn machinery. Bergren submitted the following resolutions which were adopted by the meeting:

1. Definite steps for a wage increase.
2. Obviate speed-up systems and the power saw.
3. Work to establish the C.I.O. lumber locals as an organizing force throughout all B.C. Industries.
4. Eliminate war profiteering.
5. Increase safety precautions.

The District Council secretary and provincial representative on the international executive board of the C.I.O., Nigel Morgan, supported Bergren. He declared that a "war, as it always has done, threatens labour. We have failed in China, Spain, Austria and Czecho-Slovakia and now in England and France. Our greatest war is to prevent Canada's fifty bigshots from destroying democracy at home. Since hostilities commenced we have embarked upon regulations we used to think characteristic of dictatorship. Public orders have been passed which can, and in some cases in eastern Canada have, destroyed trade unions, one of the corner stones of democracy." He also criticized the Department of Labour in British Columbia, and emphasized the importance of amendments to the Defence of Canada Regulations.[5]

The second session developed into a discussion of the "Blackout of the fundamental rights of the Canadian People." A resolution in favour of civil liberties was adopted.

The resolution receiving the most enthusiastic endorsement was that calling for $1.00 a day wage increase for woodworkers.

"KANADSKY GUDOK" ATTACKS AGAIN
(WINNIPEG)

The December 28 issue of "Kanadsky Gudok", published at Winnipeg in the Russian language and under the auspices of the Communist Party, scathingly attacks the so-called capitalist press, charging it with spreading abominable lies about the U.S.S.R.

The main article, entitled "Dimitroff About Stalin", is a eulogy of the latter by the General Secretary of the Communist International and apparently emanates from Moscow. The writer urges the workers in capitalist countries to follow the teachings of Stalin. He further says "the Communist Party learns and will learn from Stalin the art of successfully overthrowing the capitalist orders and introducing a workers' system." The article continues:

"There is no greater honour for the Revolutionary Workers than to closely follow Lenin and Stalin. The Bolshevists know that victory will never come by itself, that it must be achieved, conquered and, therefore, the revolutionary Workers must prepare. They must, therefore, learn from Stalin how to fight, how to fight in a revolutionary realistic way and must learn to be fearless and ruthless in the class struggle with the enemy."

In conformity with other Communist publications in Canada, the various articles call for the defence of the rights of Canadian people. The efforts of the Canadian Labour Defence League are extolled.[6]

"TRUTH ABOUT THE IMPERIALIST WAR"
(HAMILTON)

Apparently each district of the Communist Party throughout Canada has been authorized to print and circulate its own pamphlet containing "facts" relative to the present war. In the main, these various documents differ very little in content, which, in recent weeks, has been almost exclusively the Soviet-Finnish war and the attitude Canadians should take toward it.

In this connection the Hamilton executive of the Communist Party of Canada has issued a small four-page circular headed "Truth About The Imperialist War" which has been distributed in the Hamilton area. The pamphlet discusses the "miraculously resurrected League of Nations" and "the campaign of hate, lies and incitement against the Soviet Union." Questioning the reasons for the sudden interest being taken in the League of Nations by "Imperialist powers", the pamphlet declares that "collec-

tive security and the League of Nations were scuttled by the ruling class
of England and France." This policy of the Allied nations means "a war
in which the mass of people are the sufferers in terms of death, privation
and loss of liberty; a war for the glory of munition kings, bankers and bosses." Declaring that England is directly responsible for the war in Finland,
the pamphlet states that "the British government which sold Czecho-
Slovakia down the river at Munich and starved a genuine democratic
Republic into submission (Republic of Spain) overreaches itself in its zeal
to use the capitalist class of Finland to lead the Finnish people to destruction in war upon the Soviet Union."

The pamphlet ends with the following appeal to the working men and
women of Hamilton:

"Smash the plans of the Canadian reactionaries to involve the
Canadian people in an anti-Soviet war! Fight against the imperialist
war-makers! Demand the repeal of the War Measures Act, which
has taken away the democratic rights of the people, suppresses the
press and is intended as a weapon to keep the truth from the light
of day! Fight against profiteering and the high cost of living!
Demand wage increases![7]

"Greetings to the Finnish people, who together with the Red
Army of Liberation and Freedom will rid Finland once and for all
of its exploiters and ensure a friendly co-existence between the
people of Finland and the U.S.S.R."

"CANADIAN TRIBUNE"

Subscribers to the new publication, the "Canadian Tribune", which is
being issued under the auspices of the Communist Party at Toronto, have
been notified that this paper would not appear until January 20, two weeks
later than expected. The "Tribune" is the proposed resurrection of the
defunct "Clarion."

COMING CONVENTION

The 1940 Communist convention is to be held in New York city this
coming Spring. In the meantime arrangements are being made to discuss
the election of delegates and other business in this connection.[8]

AFTER-EFFECTS OF TORONTO ELECTIONS

[deletion: 2 lines] In all instances they had anticipated a higher vote
and even believed that J.B. Salsberg might be elected in Ward 4. [dele-
tion: 1 line] had estimated that Stewart Smith would poll at least 25,000
votes. The 19,000 odd votes which he did poll has been a depressing shock
to the Party. Deflection of the Jewish support also was a blow.

The election of William Thomas Lawson, [deletion: 1 line] Board
of Education, came as a great surprise to members of the Party. Prior to
the election little was known of Lawson's connections with the Communist Party and his election in Ward 4 is considered a real victory. In all

probability the Party will endeavour to use his influence to offset the Communist defeat in the aldermanic field and the Board of Control.

The result of the polling at Toronto this year may more than ever represent the true support of the Communists at that point. In view of the intensive campaign conducted to oust Communists from the municipal board, it is hardly probable that many others than Party members and sympathizers voted for their own candidates. [ℳdeletion: 2 lines] Stewart Smith's vote may be looked upon as a fair indication of [ℳdeletion: 1 line] support among the electorate at Toronto.

The Communist Party plans to issue a post election leaflet, outlining the reasons for its reduced vote, but at the same time terming it a victory. The leaflet will deal with the need for "progressive labour action" to release the program outlined and advocated by Stewart Smith [ℳdeletion: 1 line] It will also attack the recently elected civil administration as a return to "Family Compact" administration and the issues and methods used by anti-Communist Party candidates in the elections.[9]

LABOUR REBUKES COMMUNIST TACTICS
(VANCOUVER)

The Trades and Labour Council at Vancouver held their first meeting of 1940 on January 2. Members were addressed by a former president of the Council, Arthur Crawford, who is now stationed in the east. In his address, Crawford roundly condemned the Communist Party, with special reference to those members representing the various local trade unions. He charged that the C.P. is the only political party in Canada that has not offered to co-operate with the Government in the prosecution of the war. He stated that Communists sitting as delegates on trades councils throughout the Dominion have been able to advance themselves through their association with trade union movements. He declared that these individuals have taken this opportunity to expound through the press that the trade union movement in Canada is "Red" and that it is not adherent to the policies it has laid down.

"The time has come", Mr. Crawford continued, "for the trade union movement to take a stand on its policy. Trades and labour councils throughout the Dominion should decide to carry out the policy of labour as laid down by the constitution of the movement and deal only with business relative to labour instead of discussing matters that may prove detrimental."

The president of the Council, E.A. Jamieson, rebuked a reporter from the "Advocate", Communist Party organ in British Columbia which had prophesied that the policy presently enunciated by the council would be "out of line" in a few months.

Recent meetings of the Vancouver and New Westminster Council have strongly opposed the Communist Party faction and influence therein and this opposition to the C.P. is steadily gathering strength.[10]

INTELLIGENCE
BULLETIN

ROYAL CANADIAN MOUNTED POLICE
HEADQUARTERS, OTTAWA

WEEKLY SUMMARY
JANUARY 22, 1940

CONTENTS

War Series
No. 14.

EDITORIAL
"THE STRUGGLE WILL BE LONG"

When Major-General A. G. McNaughton, commanding our First Division, said that "the struggle will be long and bitter, and its successful outcome largely depends on a steady stream of leaders in all walks of life" he was probably speaking with more truth than even he knew. Obviously he was estimating the struggle in terms of vast hords of Germans and Russians let loose upon Western Europe in an attempt to destroy this thing called Democracy and make this world a better place to live in—for Dictators.

But we venture to say (with indisputable evidence to prove it) that what we see with the eye is but the surface manifestation of an inward and "spiritual" struggle transcending in violence anything the world has experienced. This is not an imperialist war, a race war, a religious war nor even an economic war. In the last analysis it is the ageless struggle between good and evil, between spirituality and materiality, between individual self-expression and mind enslavement. That is why there is no paradox in Soviet Russia and Nazi Germany joining forces and making mutual pacts with Japan and Italy or any other dictatorship. Eventually, if victorious, these thieves would fall out among themselves and destroy each other, but for the present they are glad to sink their minor differences in an unholy alliance against the only authority that can check their growth.

The real war is a mental war—its bullets are words, its most deadly offensives are comprised of lie barrages, its shock troops are behind the Allied lines sabotaging morale and the will to resist. The enemy reasons that attacks from the rear will be more effective and far less costly than breaking the Maginot lines of guns and cement. That is why its uniformed armies hold, why its spies and agents disseminate peace manifestoes and other subversive matter among our civilian population and promise the World Revolution for universal salvation.[1]

Nazis and Communists are convinced that this revolution is imminent. They will frankly tell you so. Unless you have inside knowledge you may scoff at their boasts, but the fact is they have a certain amount of reason for the faith that is in them. All the totalitarian states (not only those at open war with us) are organized throughout the democracies for the violent overthrow of government at the opportune time. Only a few days ago in New York Edgar Hoover of the F.B.I. exposed such a plot. It is too much to expect that we will always be forewarned and forearmed and that this hidden struggle will not be "long and bitter" before we have indeed made the world safe for democracy.[2]

COMMUNISM
[ᣔ<deletion: 1 line] ELECTED TO SYDNEY CITY COUNCIL

[ᣔ<deletion: 2 lines] Norman Mackenzie, President of Lodge 1064 of the Amalgamated Iron, Tin and Steel Workers Union at Sydney, Nova Scotia, was elected to the City Council in the recent civic elections. In Soliciting support, MacKenzie [ᣔ<deletion: 2 lines] and is considered a fair agitator. Running in Ward 5, (Steel Workers' Ward) MacKenzie polled 677 votes against that of his opponent who polled 540.

As a leader of the Steel Workers' Union, he wields considerable influence. [ᣔ<deletion: 2 lines] Should he undertake this task, as ostensible representative of the Steel Workers of Sydney, he might create a great deal of trouble and dissension. In view of the importance of the district, due to the war contracts at the steel plants, any dissension which might cause a strike at this time would be most regrettable.

MacKenzie's [ᣔ<deletion: 2 lines]

The following telegram was received by Norman MacKenzie on January 12 from Pat Sullivan, [ᣔ<deletion: 1 line] and President of the Canadian Seamen's Union.

"Montreal, Que., Jan. 12, 1940.

Norman MacKenzie,
President Steel Workers Union, Sydney, N.S.

Congratulations upon your election to the City Council stop this is one more victory for the workers in your district and is the only assurance that the Trade Union Government will carry on its existence in the face of the opposition by Dosco stop keep up the good work.

Pat Sullivan
President Canadian Seamens Union."[3]

LUNENBURG BOYCOTTS RED AGITATORS

During the latter part of December, J. A. (Pat) Sullivan, Charles Murray and Douglas Betts, [⊰<deletion: 2 lines] and officials of the Canadian Seamen's Union, an affiliate of the Communist Party, arrived at Lunenburg from Halifax. They endeavoured to arrange with Captain Angus Walters, President, and Mr. Lawrence Allen, Secretary-Treasurer of the Fishermen's Federation at Lunenburg, to address a meeting of this Federation on December 28. The request was refused.

The following news item in this connection appeared in the local press on January 3, which outlines the feeling which has arisen against the tactics employed by these members of the Communist Party who instigated the strike at Lockport (settled several weeks ago).

"LUNENBURG, December 29 — Officials of the Fishermen's Federation, Station No. 101, of Lunenburg, issued a statement here today that they would have nothing to do with the Canadian Seamen's Union and therefore would not grant representatives of that Union permission to speak at any of their meetings.

Can Look After Itself.

Capt. Angus Walters and Capt. Lawrence Allen, President and Secretary-Treasurer of the Lunenburg Station, stated that as a result of investigations and the settlements made at Lockport, they do not believe in the methods used by the C.S.U. They said: 'We will do things in our own way with no outside help and the things we do will be of benefit to the fishermen only. Lunenburg can look after itself, without any outside help, as it has done in the past.'"

Their failure to influence the Fishermen's Federation necessitated these individuals making other arrangements to address a local gathering. They hired the Anglican Church Hall at Blue Rocks,[4] but only one person, the caretaker attended. The meeting was postponed for two days, but on this occasion the organizers did not put in an appearance and it is reported that they had entrained for Halifax.

While in Lockport, the above named members of the Canadian Fishermen's Union endeavoured to obtain the use of the Town Council Chambers and the Badminton Club quarters, but both these halls were refused to them.

It is not known whether these organizers intend to return to Lockport, but it would appear from the above that it would be hardly expedient in view of the cold reception which they have received.

[ℑ<deletion: 1 line]
[ℑ<deletion: 1 line]
[ℑ<deletion: 1 paragraph: 9 lines][5]

ALL QUIET ON THE PACIFIC WATERFRONT (VANCOUVER)

It is interesting to note that the labour troubles at San Francisco, which have occupied the headlines in the United States and certain Canadian newspapers, have had little effect at Vancouver. The men continue to work with no thoughts of striking or causing dissension; content apparently in the belief that if the San Francisco longshoremen force another wage increase it will necessarily be applied to Canadian (Maritime) labour.

The agitation during the early part of the war against the German element (naturalized) amongst the longshoremen has almost entirely died out. There was some effort put forth at that time to have these men thrown out of waterfront employment, but the matter was finally left in the hands of the executives of the unions and the Shipping Federation. No further mention has been made of the subject and the rank and file seem to have forgotten about it. Altogether there were only about 30 out of 150 foreign born longshoremen on the Vancouver waterfront who were found to be aliens. Any individuals who could not satisfactorily prove their naturalization, to the Shipping Federation, have been suspended.

AMONG FRENCH-CANADIAN COMMUNISTS

A few months ago when it became known to the world that Germany had signed a treaty with Russia, Party members in Canada were completely demoralized, and it required several weeks to reoriente their line of attack. Now that the U.S.S.R. has invaded Finland, Communist Party members feel more confident, realizing "that Russia can do something and will show the world that she is not afraid of England."

The spirit is so high in certain branches of the Communist Party, and in particular in the French-Canadian membership, that they believe a Canadian revolution is inevitable and in a not too distant future, and that it can only result in victory for the progressive forces. The Reds are therefore more cheerful than usual.

The French-Canadian leaders are making every endeavour to stress upon their followers the necessity of defeating any move by the Government to enforce conscription.[6][Page 7 is missing].

EXPLAINING THE WAR SITUATION
(TORONTO)

A public meeting under the auspices of the Communist Party was held at the Labour Temple, Church Street, Toronto, on January 12 with Harry Bell acting as chairman. The speakers included William Lawson, [ɜ<deletion: 1 line] who was recently elected to the Board of Education in the city of Toronto, Tom Hill and Fred Collins.

The meeting opened with Bell stating that the speakers would explain the war situation regarding the U.S.S.R. and Finland. He urged all Communists to explain Party doctrines and denounce the lies that the press are spreading regarding the Russo-Finnish war.

The other speeches were rather lengthy and contained the usual Communist propaganda.

ELECTING REDS TO LABOUR COUNCIL
(TORONTO)

In order to ensure the election of at least one [ɜ<deletion: 2 lines] to the executive of the Toronto and District Trades and Labour Council, special efforts are being made to foist Fred Collins into this position as the elections are to take place in the near future and as [ɜ<deletion: 2 lines] of Collins, all Communist Party delegates to that body have received instructions to be in attendance. No excuses for non-attendance will be accepted, it is stated.

[ɜ<deletion: 1 line] Dewar Ferguson, secretary-organizer of the Canadian Seamen's Union at Toronto, and Sam Lapedes, an executive member of the International Union of Needle Workers, [ɜ<deletion: 2 lines]

It is felt by the Party that should Collins be re-elected, besides giving the C.P. voice in this labour organization it will at the same time be a setback for anti-Communist Party elements in the Trades and Labour Council.[8]

[ɜ<deletion: 1 line]

[ɜ<deletion: 1 paragraph: 7 lines]

ATTACKING DEFENCE OF CANADA REGULATIONS
(MONTREAL)

A pamphlet was recently circulated in Montreal by the Canadian Civil Liberties Union which comments upon the Defence of Canada Regulations and states the position of the union towards them. R.A.C. Ballantyne, Executive Secretary of the C.C.L.U., has instructed as wide a distribution as possible of this first published commentary on the regulations.

The pamphlet is entitled "The War and Civil Liberty" and the cover depicts a great many restrictions which the regulations are empowered to deal with. The contents declare that certain regulations having regard to the safety of the state in guarding against espionage, sabotage, etc., are necessary, but "many others authorize flagrant invasion of the basic constitutional rights and liberties of the citizen." Although the regulations state that freedom of an individual will be interfered with as little as is necessary "no provision is made for the carrying out of this principle by submission to the courts or by the control of the officers and Ministers charged with the administration of the Regulations".

Dealing particularly with Sections 15, 39, 39A of the Defence of Canada Regulations, which "prevent freedom of expression and criticism either orally or in writing", the pamphlet states "we have ample security against disaffection in the law of treason and sedition. If anything further is desired, let it be proposed to Parliament in the form of a bill and duly scrutinized".[9]

Regarding Section 21, which deals with "the liberty of the subject", the article declares "that this regulation is undeniably a gross 'interference with the liberty of the subject'. Under it the Minister of Justice is given the most absolute power, by detention orders or otherwise, to deprive the Canadian people of every one of their fundamental liberties acquired since Magna Carta. Nor may the exercise of this power be submitted to the control of the courts. Under Section 22, an appeal is provided to an Advisory Committee set up by the Minister, but the Minister is perfectly free to reject any opinion given by the committee."

While these four sections are the "most dangerous of the Regulations", the pamphlet denounces the others as they also "abolish habeas corpus and they threaten the right of labour to strike by authorizing the use of the army to eject persons from places where they have been forbidden to go."

The article remarks upon the fact that Canada is far more stringent with her regulations than England has been. "Can Canada", it has been asked, "afford to be less democratic than Great Britain?"

Under the sub-heading "Unwarranted Violation" the article comments:

"After long scrutiny and discussion of the Regulations, the Canadian Civil Liberties Union, Montreal Branch, has gone on record as condemning them as an unwarranted violation of fundamental civil liberties. The Union does not concern itself with the form which criticism of the Government's Policy takes, but it emphatically takes the position that Canadians must not be deprived of their right to criticize.

Basing itself on this policy, the C.C.L.U., Montreal Branch, has voted to take every means at its disposal to remove certain of the Regulations in order to test the constitutionality of the Regulations in the courts, the Union has undertaken the defence of a number of persons charged under them. It has approached the Governor-General in Council seeking repeal or satisfactory amendment of the objectionable Regulations, and it has undertaken a campaign to ac-

quaint the people of Canada with the danger to their liberties represented by the Regulations.[10]

The Union has resolved to oppose every attempt to take advantage of times of war to restrict unnecessarily the civil rights of
Canadians. It invites the assistance of all patriotic and public spirited citizens in this fight. But if the fight is to be successful, it must
be organized. You can join it by filling out the form on the next
page."

[ℐ⊲deletion: 1 paragraph: 6 lines]

<u>GENERAL</u>

ENEMY ALIENS

Registrations:

   Total to Dec. 31, 1939...15,055
   Given Exemption Certificates..................................1,371
   Exacts granted to date...154

Internments:

   Total interned or detained since Sept. 4..................... 403
   Released immediately 3
   Released after appeal 56
   At present interned or detained 344

[11]

SECRET

INTELLIGENCE
BULLETIN

ROYAL CANADIAN MOUNTED POLICE
HEADQUARTERS, OTTAWA

WEEKLY SUMMARY
JANUARY 29, 1940

CONTENTS
Editorial: The Canadian Situation
Communism:
  [⊱deletion: 1 line]
  C.I.O. Seeking Official Recognition
  "Finland the Facts" (As They See It)
  Poles Rally to Support of "Glos Pracy"
  [⊱deletion: 1 line]
  First Issue of "The Canadian Tribune"
  Communist Activity Amongst the Unemployed
  Brown Addresses Labour Defence League
  Dissension Splits Western Party
  [⊱deletion: 1 line]
                                    War Series
                                    No. 15.

EDITORIAL

THE CANADIAN SITUATION

The contents of this issue disclose considerable dissension and disor-ganization throughout the Communist Party of Canada. Rather frantic ef-forts are being made to rehabilitate a structure that has been badly shaken by "capitalist press propaganda" and by the turn of events overseas. Against such revolutionaries the continuous barrage of written and oral facts constitute the most effective defence both here and abroad. For this is largely a battle of ideas rather than of physical forces. [⊱deletion: 3 lines]

[⊱deletion: 1 paragraph: 9 lines]

After the Armistice, what? There may follow a period of military peace, but this civil war will surely continue until we have set our house in such scrupulous order that agitators can find no serious social or economic grievance to use as a convenient weapon against the State. In the meantime the true meaning of democracy and the vital necessity of unified defence of it must be impressed upon all Canadians until there is a lasting victory behind the lines, founded upon peace, order and good

government.[1][Pages 2 and 3 are missing.]
  [℈deletion: 1 paragraph: 3 lines]
  [℈deletion: 1 paragraph: 5 lines]
  [℈deletion: 1 paragraph: 4 lines]

C.I.O. SEEKING OFFICIAL RECOGNITION
(WINDSOR)

It is reported that the C.I.O. is making every effort to reorganize the employees at Windsor and also to increase its membership. Bob Stacey, new organizer at Windsor, stated that the situation at that point is better than in some other parts of Canada prior to the beginning of reorganizational campaigns.

Speaking to a recent meeting of Local 195 at Windsor, Stacey discussed briefly the question of the C.I.O. affiliating with the All-Canadian Congress of Labour in Canada. He told those present that it was his opinion that it would be a very good thing for the C.I.O. to affiliate, because at the present time the C.I.O. is not an officially recognized labour organization. He meant that the C.I.O. is not officially recognized by the Government, being expelled from the Trades and Labour Congress of Canada at that body's recent convention. According to Stacey, affiliation with the A.C.C.L. would give the C.I.O. closer contact with the Government.

It was reported that the Canadian Automobile Workers Association will publish an official bulletin for its membership. A motion was carried at the meeting requesting that money received from the International (C.I.O.) in the United States be spent for publicity in the furthering of the C.I.O. interests in Canada. It is understood that this will amount to approximately $300.00 each month.[4]

"FINLAND THE FACTS" (AS THEY SEE IT)
(TORONTO)

Under the caption "Labor Truth" and subtitle "Finland The Facts," a leaflet was distributed on January 20 by the Communist Party of Canada throughout the Toronto District, which denounces the Capitalist Press in reporting the Russian-Finnish hostilities. According to this leaflet "a deluge of bare-faced lies and manufactured atrocity propaganda about Finland is being flooded upon the Canadian people as part of the imperialist plan of intervention and war against the Soviet Union."

In conclusion it says:

"The interest of the Canadian people are united with the interest of the Finnish working class, led by the COMMUNIST PARTY of Finland, to stop their country from being used by the imperialist fire-bugs in their mad plans of war against the Soviet Union. Our country too must be saved from the fate of a pawn of the capitalists war-incendiaries against the Land of SOCIALISM.

FIGHT THE IMPERIALIST WAR PLANS WITH ALL YOUR MIGHT. BACK THE FINNISH WORKING-CLASS AND THE SOVIET UNION AGAINST THE IMPERIALIST WAR-MAKERS AND THEIR LACKEYS. THE FRENZIED ANTICS OF THE IMPERIALISTS WILL PROVE TO BE THEIR DEATH DANCE."

POLES RALLY TO SUPPORT OF "GLOS PRACY" (TORONTO)

A concert was held recently by the Polish People's Association in connection with the press campaign for "Glos Pracy" at Toronto. The direction of this concert was personally supervised by the editorial staff of this Polish newspaper published by the P.P.A., [≈<deletion: 2 lines] Taking part in the program were the U.L.F.T.A. Brass Band and a choir from the C.U.Y.F.

The main speaker on the program was W. Dutkewich, Assistant Editor of "Glos Pracy" and Toronto organizer for the P.P.A. He stated that about nine years ago a publication known as "Budzik" (The Awakener) [5] brought about the beginning of the P.P.A.; the name of this paper being later changed to "Glos Pracy." According to Dutkewich, this publication has greatly aided the progressive and liberation movement of the working class in Canada and Poland. Speaking about the "Imperialist War," he stated that there was every likelihood that it would be extended next spring and that "repressive measures against the workers could be expected." Referring to Great Britain, he said that "the greatest power in the world which claimed to be all powerful was trembling in fear for its integrity and supremacy. This great power is at present confident that there is no power on the continent who could challenge its strength. Nevertheless, this great power was trembling and the workers' movement steadily growing."

Dutkewich stated that it was up to the forces of the workers to consolidate themselves and be ready for the coming storm which was imminent. To this end they should give all their support to "Glos Pracy." The workers should organize and unite to withstand the reactionary forces which were going to attach the workers' democracy.

Approximately 500 persons attended this concert, and it is of interest to note that the U.L.F.T.A. gave considerable assistance in order to ensure its success. A silver collection taken at the conclusion of the concert was not particularly successful.

[≈<deletion: 1 line]
[≈<deletion: 1 line]

[≈<deletion: 1 paragraph: 4 lines]
[≈<deletion: 1 paragraph: 8 lines][6][Page 7 is missing.][≈<blank]

FIRST ISSUE OF "THE CANADIAN TRIBUNE"
(TORONTO)

The "legal" Communist Party newspaper which is taking the place of the banned "Daily Clarion" made its appearance in Toronto on Saturday, January 20. Terming itself to be a "journal of democratic opinion," this first issue can hardly be considered a contravention of the Defence of Canada Regulations. Several articles in its contents are quoted from other newspapers and are critical of the powers enacted under the D.O.C.R. One page (of the eight pages) contains a one-sided discussion of the situation in India. The last page contains the editorials from which a judgment of the standard set by the paper may be ascertained.[8]

The newspaper is published weekly by the Canadian Tribune Publishing Company and is printed by the Ever Ready Printers at Toronto. Its editor is A. Albert MacLeod, a member of the Communist Party. Contributing editors are C. H. Huestis, R. A. C. Ballantyne, H. K. Gordon and Margaret Fairley. Its business manager is J. G. King, also a member of the Communist Party.

COMMUNIST ACTIVITY AMONGST THE UNEMPLOYED
(REGINA)

Notwithstanding the fact that the election of officers does not ordinarily take place until May of the current year, a provincial conference of the Saskatchewan Union of Unemployed is being held this month in Regina at which representatives from every branch of this organization will be present. In order to speed such election, the entire executive resigned on Friday, January 12, with the hope of the Communist Party leadership that members of the new executive would be more aggressive than those who have taken a leading part in the S.U.U. during the past.

[≈<deletion: 1 paragraph: 6 lines]

BROWN ADDRESSES LABOUR DEFENCE LEAGUE
(SASKATOON)

Speaking to a meeting of the Canadian Labour Defence League at Saskatoon on January 12, Reverend W. G. Brown, recently elected Federal Member of Parliament for Saskatoon, representing the United Reform Movement, adopted as his theme the right of every citizen to "free speech and free actions." He dwelt "for some time on the consequences of suppression of civil liberties" and said that "recognized authority who denied the citizens the right of freedom of speech and actions must be afraid to hear the truth." He urged everyone to fight for his civil liberties, and quoted the Bill of Rights.[9]

Other speakers were Robert Bell (alias "Buster") Nuttal, [≈<deletion: 2 lines], who dwelt at length on the Defence of Canada Regulations and urged the audience to fight for the release of those individuals who have been arrested under the War Measures Act. W. S. Borland, representing

the Brotherhood of Locomotive Engineers, also spoke.

From all appearances the majority of the audience attended with the purpose of hearing Mr. Brown speak, as many left immediately thereafter.

DISSENSION SPLITS WESTERN PARTY
(SASKATOON)

Dissension is rife within Communist Party circles at Saskatoon. As a result of the election of the United Reform Movement candidate, Rev. W. G. Brown, [⅜<deletion: 1 line] T. G. McManus, Provincial Secretary of the Party has had to appear before a C.P. meeting at Saskatoon. [⅜<deletion: 4 lines]

[⅜<deletion: 1 paragraph: 2 lines]

A motion was moved at the meeting by Robert Dochterman, prominent member of the C.P. at Saskatoon, that the action of McManus be thoroughly investigated. This motion was defeated, but a decision was reached to investigate [⅜<deletion: 1 linc] for demanding the investigation. The bureaucratic manner in which this meeting was held has incensed many members of the Party and a few have severed their connections, with others signifying their intentions of doing likewise. Those members that have tendered their resignations are Harold Miller, Robert Dochterman, Fred Birch, Victor Beech, Art Abrahams and Merle Fredrichs.

Robert Dochterman and Fred Birch have written letters to the Dominion Committee at Toronto asking that they investigate the whole matter. Further, Birch wrote Stewart Smith protesting the actions of McManus and asking for his removal as Provincial Secretary.[10]

INTELLIGENCE
BULLETIN

ROYAL CANADIAN MOUNTED POLICE
HEADQUARTERS, OTTAWA

WEEKLY SUMMARY
FEBRUARY 5, 1940

CONTENTS

War Series
No. 16.

EDITORIAL
"PREPARING FOR A LAST CRUSADE"

Lies and rumors of lies increase in intensity and ingenuity. Bulletins printed and mimeographed, issue from hide-outs in every town from Halifax to Vancouver in a desperate attempt to "politicize" unwary Canadians into becoming adherents of Communism and vassals of Stalin.

But Canada is only one small section of the world-wide battlefront in this relentless (perhaps "final") war that is challenging all the best in humanity. And humanity is gradually awakening to this ominous truth.

A semi-official report on world conditions, emanating from London, contains the following warning and admonition:

"The truth is that we are face to face with evil forces which are bending all their considerable energies and exercising all their wits in order to destroy that which is best in our highest conception of life and its meaning. Such a struggle cannot be abandoned, even if we wished it so, nor indeed can it easily be resolved.

"History seems to teach that sometimes a man or a family is evidently destined to perform one single task in preparation for which there seem to be almost endless, even meaningless, years of vicissitude and trial which must be faithfully endured until the appointed time if the task is to be accomplished. The clearest minds see in this present strife the consummation of a great conflict which has been raging for countless centuries. It is a struggle between evil and chivalry. The course of the struggle can be traced through history in the deeds of men and nations. Almost it would seem as if certain peoples, driven by some terrible force to which they had given hostages, had been [1] preparing themselves to become the supreme instruments of that evil, while other nations, as if following a fiery cross at times bright and clear and at others dim and almost lost to sight, had been preparing for a last crusade.

"If indeed the conflict is of such a nature, and few doubt it, it may yet be that we shall be stripped of our confidence in political theories and much of our hope in material forces and because of this, after passing through a cleansing, we shall fulfil our appointed task, for which all that has gone before, the best and the finest deeds in our history like the hardest and the most difficult, has been a preparation."[2][Page 3 is missing.]

LENIN MEMORIAL MEETING AT TORONTO

A public meeting was held on January 21, in the Labour Temple, Toronto, under the auspices of the Communist Party, to commemorate the 16th anniversary of the death of Lenin. Fred Collins, recently defeated [ఇ<deletion: 1 line] for alderman in Toronto, acted as chairman; the other speakers being Walter Dent and William Lawson, [ఇ<deletion: 2 lines] the latter school trustee in Toronto.

Collins gave a brief biographical outline of the life of Lenin and stated that "if the Canadian people applied the teachings of Lenin they would be able to do in Canada what the Russian people had done in Russia."

Walter Dent, who ostensibly spoke on behalf of the progressive youth of Toronto, dealt mostly with the "growing opposition to the war", claiming that "the French-Canadian people had provided an object lesson by their struggle which had prevented conscription as far as Quebec was concerned." He said that "millions of people had been killed during the last Great War, all for the lust of war profiteers and financiers." Answering his own question, "What was the heritage of youth following the last war?" he told his audience that unemployment and miserable economic conditions had been the outcome, and extolled the great heritage that Lenin had left to the youth of the Soviet Union in educational facilities, etc.

The main speaker, William Lawson, eulogized Lenin as a profound thinker whose ideas had found expression and realization in the creation of the Soviet Union. He said it was important at this time, when the capitalist nations were passing from secret diplomacy to open armed intervention against the Soviet Union, to study the truth and to realize that under capitalism we are living in the Dark Ages as compared with the Soviet system.

Engels and Marx had shown the way out from capitalism by means of the dictatorship of the proletariat. Lawson asserted that Lenin had followed a policy of revolutionary opposition to the last Great War, and that "the workers and soldiers had stopped the war themselves."[4]

He lauded the Soviet constitution as being the most democratic in the world and explained that the dictatorship of the proletariat was only a temporary measure. Mentioning the Padlock Law and the War Measures Act, Lawson said that in view of these laws, some people still had the nerve to call Stalin a dictator.

The working class, he continued, needs a party which will follow Lenin's teachings. "The Communist Party still lives and will never give up the struggle until Socialism has been achieved....The Canadian capitalist will not give up without a struggle and when the time comes that they use force, the Canadian people will know how to deal with it." In this connection, he read a quotation urging Communists to be leaders of the Lenin type, "merciless to the enemy."

From recent reports relating to the Communist Party and their activities, it appears that the Party are making very strenuous efforts to develop an "agit prop" department, and the word "revolutionary" has been making its appearance in a great many other recent statements attributed to Communist Party leaders.

[ℑ<deletion: 1 line]

It is understood that Leslie Morris [ℑ<deletion: 2 lines] in the absence of Tim Buck, [ℑ<deletion: 1 line]

[ℑ<deletion: 1 line]

[ℑ<deletion: 1 paragraph: 7 lines][5]

PREPARATIONS FOR THE GENERAL ELECTION
(VANCOUVER)

The Communist Party of Canada is already preparing to take part in the forthcoming Federal election campaign. The Vancouver branch has been given preliminary instructions as follows:

With a Federal election in the offing the main tasks of C. P. members will be to expose the Imperialist war aims and Canada's part in it, and link this up with the economic difficulties of the workers. Discussions should include how the role of the Mackenzie King Government has changed, and that by carrying out Canada's war aims, they are slowly but surely taking away our democratic rights. All members must arouse public opinion against profiteering by agitating against high prices. This should be continually brought up with acquaintances and fellow-workers. Our new slogan will be

"Make the Rich pay for their own war." Stickers and leaflets bearing this slogan will soon be printed. These are to be stuck on store windows, placed in street-cars, in magazines and books, and any other place that can be thought of where they can come to the attention of the workers.

NEW PRESS CORRESPONDENT

The death of Pat Forkin, Canadian Communist press correspondent, was reported several weeks ago from the Soviet Union. In his place, Shachno Epstein, formerly one of the editors of the "Freiheit", Jewish Communist daily at New York, has been appointed correspondent at Moscow. Articles reported emanating from Epstein have been appearing in recent issues of "Der Veg" (The Road), Canadian Yiddish language paper, published at Toronto.[6]

NAZI ATTITUDE TOWARDS COMMUNISM

A close watch has been maintained on the relationship existing between Nazi followers in Canada and the Communist Party. Whereas before the commencement of hostilities there was hardly a Nazi who would have associated with a Communist, now reliable information discloses that these "isms" are more or less fraternizing, that their views about causes and aims in the present war are on a common ground and directed against Great Britain. They agree that the present war is a war between working classes and international capitalism and between Socialism and Capitalistic Democracy. The capitalist countries, especially Great Britain, must be defeated.

It is interesting to note that prior to the last municipal election in Toronto, several adherents to the Nazi policy were reported to have stated that "if they were entitled to a vote they would vote only for communist candidates."

DIES' OBJECTIVES ENDORSED

Canadians note with interest that the work of the Dies Committee has been endorsed in the House of Representatives by a vote of 345 to 21. The Committee's part in exposing and jailing Earl Browder (Communist leader) and Fritz Kuhn (American Bund leader) was widely acclaimed.[7]

ANNIVERSARY DRIVE FOR CONVERTS
(WINNIPEG)

A bulletin emanating from Winnipeg, but similar to one published in other parts of Canada, has been mimeographed and circulated amongst members of the Communist Party and sympathizers.

It urges all Party members to commemorate the anniversary of the three great working-class leaders, Lenin, Liebknecht and Luxemburg, and to impart to youth the great Leninist teachings on "Imperialist War" as "powerful weapons in the hands of the revolutionary movement of today".

Declaring that the history of the Young Communist League is closely bound up with the struggle of the revolutionary socialist youth against the Imperialist war, the bulletin urges the League "to fight against the treacherous social democratic leaders of the 'Socialist' youth leaders".

It also stresses the necessity of an intensive anniversary drive to distribute the "history of the communist party and the communist union" (Bolshevik), as their fundamental textbook.

[⅜<deletion: 1 line]

[⅜<deletion: 1 paragraph: 5 lines][8]

ORGANIZING FOR MORE LABOUR TROUBLE
(SYDNEY)

At a meeting held recently at the Steel Union Hall, Sydney, Nova Scotia, delegates from the coal mining locals unanimously decided that a branch of the Trades and Labour Council should set up at Sydney. George McEachern, [⅜<deletion: 2 lines] was elected Provisional President. Other provisional officers included Clarence MacInnis, Secretary, and Rankin McDonald, Treasurer.

It was suggested by a delegate from Glace Bay that a Provincial Federation of Labour should be organized in preference to a county Trades and Labour Council, in accordance with the Ottawa Conference of the C.I.O. In this connection, McEachern explained that similar councils will be organized in the Province and from this will emerge a Provincial Federation. Application for a charter will be forwarded to the C.I.O.

A resolution emanating from the Glace Bay Branch of the Army and Navy War Veterans Association, demanding an investigation into the high cost of living and low wages, was approved by the meeting. A similar resolution will be dealt with by the council at its next meeting and submitting to the proper authorities.

The formation of the above Trades and Labour Council is in conjunction with expressed Communist Party policy at this time. It is of especial interest to note that prominent Communist organizers intend to agitate in the mining districts and in the steel industry this spring, and are building their plans accordingly.[9][⅜<blank]

UKRAINIAN COMMUNISTS HAVE SUCCESSFUL YEAR
(WINNIPEG)

The annual meeting of the Winnipeg Branch of the Ukrainian Labour Farmer Temple Association was held on January 21 with approximately [10] 200 persons in attendance. From the report, it is indicated that a very successful year has ended for the Ukrainian Labour Farmer Temple Association and that very close to $20,000 was received by the Winnipeg Branch, giving a credit balance of over $850.00. According to the report, most of the receipts had been spent on educational work.

If the figures quoted are correct, it would appear that the Association has lost little prestige over the Russo-German pact and its later ramifications, despite the fact that it is dominated and controlled by the Communist Party. As suggested, the majority of money collected by the U.L.F.T.A. is spent on "educational work" amongst the Ukrainians practically all propaganda in some form or another.

MORE PROPAGANDA CAMPAIGNS
(MONTREAL)

In an effort to disseminate as much propaganda as possible, the Communist Party throughout Canada are publishing a wide variety of pamphlets and newspapers. The majority of these publications are in mimeograph form and are circularized by local districts of the Party. In Quebec Province and particularly Montreal, the French-Canadian membership of the Communist Party are undertaking one of the most intensive drives in the country in order to propagate dissension and disclaim the "Imperialist War".

One of the more recent publications in the French language, "L'Eclaireur" (The Scout), published by the Young Communist League of Quebec, carries the manifesto of the executive committee of the Communist international which appeared last November and contains a vicious onslaught upon the Allied nations and their war efforts. One paragraph of this manifesto discloses the trend:

"If the youth fights in revolutionary unity it will be in a position to rally the whole working class in the struggle against the war. Therefore, working youth, raise high the banner of combat for unity. Follow the example of the heroic youth of Spain which cemented its unity in the revolutionary war of liberation."[11]

INTELLIGENCE BULLETIN

ROYAL CANADIAN MOUNTED POLICE HEADQUARTERS, OTTAWA

WEEKLY SUMMARY
FEBRUARY 12, 1940

CONTENTS

War Series
No. 17

EDITORIAL
"CONTAGION"

When a disease spreads until it affects a vital organ it is time for strong remedial action. The virus of Communism, long coursing, almost unopposed, in our social blood-stream has now reached the heart of our educational system as represented by undergraduates and even college professors in several of our leading universities.

This condition is not peculiar to Canada. The student mind has been the spear-head of countless revolutions, and the Red plague is not confined to the ranks of poverty and unemployed.

Representative Dies, head of the Dies Committee on Un-American Activities, writes in "Liberty":

"According to the testimony of Earl Browder, the majority of the members of the Communist Party are employed and hold fairly good jobs. Some of them are professors in colleges and universities, and many of them hold government positions, where their salaries range from $4,000 to $10,000 a year. Neither can it be said that education will prevent the spread of Marxism, because many professors are Marxists and they are sowing the seeds of Marxism disguised as liberalism in the minds of our youth."

140

We are discovering these truths for ourselves, as this Bulletin reveals. Evidence of a Communist "drive" upon our College youth is steadily accumulating. As yet the majority in every student body is loyal to Democracy but it appears to be waging an unequal fight against well organized foreign-controlled disruption and disaffection. Some educational leaders are alive to the peril and are endeavouring to combat it, as [1] illustrated by recent incidents:

1. The University of Toronto section of the Young Communist League staged a debate on the Russo-Finnish war and Professor Saunders was prepared to take the Finnish side of the question. Dr. Cody is reported to have refused Saunders permission to debate, claiming that Professor Underhill and Grube had already cost the University $100,000 in grants and he was taking no more chances on antagonizing the "powers that be". Saunders is known to have radical views and it is probable that the "debate" would have been merely Soviet propaganda.

2. The Student Council of the University of Manitoba dissolved the Third National Conference of Canadian University Students for its anti-British anti-war policy. The "Argosy Weekly" of Mt. Allison University carried the headline: "Mt. A. Delegates Condemn C.S.A."

3. In Montreal on February 6th, a body of McGill University students broke up a meeting of the McGill section of the Canadian Student Assembly for its anti-British sentiments.

Federal and provincial authorities might consider these futile efforts to combat the Red contagion, with a view to assisting in its complete eradication from our universities.[2]

COMMUNISM

COMMUNISM RIFE IN CANADIAN UNIVERSITIES

Communist activities in the Canadian Student Assembly constitute the most recent problem before the Intelligence Branch of the R. C. M. Police. In several of our leading colleges the C. S. A. is rapidly becoming a Communist organization — aggressively opposing the Allied war efforts and implanting the seeds of disloyalty and disaffection among the undergraduates. In several colleges, it is believed, the disaffection is being encouraged by professors and other members of the faculties.

There are two distinct university student groups in Canada, of which one, the National Federation of Canadian University Students, is reported as being "reputable and dependable". The other, the Canadian Student Assembly, is a partly organized body which grew out of a meeting called in Winnipeg for members of the S. C. M. (Student Christian Movement) a few years ago. It is under no authority nor are its groups in various universities under the official students' councils. It leans so strongly to the left that there appears little doubt but that it is thoroughly permeated by the Young Communist League of the Communist Party of Canada.

While the presence of these subversive elements in the C. S. A. has long been understood, attention has become focussed upon it as a result of the Assembly's Third Conference, held at Ste. Anne de Bellevue, Quebec, December 27-31, 1939.

Delegates from all the Canadian universities were present. Suspicion was early aroused among those from remoter points when they found that those attending from the universities more adjacent to Ste. Anne de Bellevue were permitted to increase their attendance by allowing additional delegates. Thus, while the Western universities were set with delegates of three, the University of Toronto was allowed 40 delegates, Queens 20, Western Ontario 10, McGill 30 and Montreal and Laval each 20. In view of the subversive nature of the matters discussed, it is not unreasonable to suppose that those attended from the Eastern universities were more or less those radical in thought, with the result that the Conference had all the ear-marks of having been packed.

The Dean of one university reports that he and others of the more conservative persons in the educational field were assigned to the subjects of extension of improvements, while those who were known to have [3] radical leanings were assigned as leaders to discuss "Canada and External Affairs" and "Canadian Unity". The Dean states that, in his opinion, some of the professors present voiced opinions that constitute a flat violation of the Defence of Canada Regulations, Section 39, and he was so disgusted with the obvious anti-British motives underlying the Conference that he decided to sever all connections with the Assembly. In all, student delegations of 5 universities have broken their connections with the C. S. A. for similar reasons; namely,

> University of Saskatchewan,
> University of Alberta,
> University of Manitoba,
> University of New Brunswick,
> Mount Allison University, Sackville, N.B.

It is reported that one of the most dangerous results of the C. S. A. is the projected referendum in universities and high-schools to take place on February 14. (In this connection it should be noted that Ken Woodsworth, member of the Y.C.L. and secretary of the Canadian Youth Congress, is calling for a referendum among this Congress on the same date). The effect of this referendum will, undoubtedly, be far-reaching. The question as to whether or not the youth of Canada votes for or against conscription is less important than that the referendum will have a definite effect on voluntary enlistments in the C.A.S.F. A leading college authority estimates that such a referendum will result in a large decrease, probably 40%, in the number of voluntary enlistments. In view of the fact that the government hopes to enlist thousands of young men in technical work in connection with the air training scheme and the C.A.S.F. generally, this is a serious situation. On the other hand, preventing the holding of the referendum will probably do more harm than good. Students are very jealous of their standing in the community, and it is submitted that legal action, either through the courts or by way of open police investigation, would result at the present time in swaying many of the thousands of students into an attitude of open sympathy for those against whom action is taken.

To glance at the brighter side of this whole picture, we are advised that the numerical strength of the subversive leaders is not very strong and that the Canadian Officers Training Corps in the universities is particularly well placed for the boosting of morale and as a starting point for anti-subversive propaganda. The immediate need of an educational drive among the students of all universities along patriotic lines, and perhaps the formation of a student organization to further these aims, and [4] particularly to nullify the effects of the proposed ballots and the subversive thought being engendered, is strikingly obvious.

While Toronto is probably the centre of these radical activities in the universities (although the offices of the C. S. A. are located at 772 Sherbrooke Street, West, Montreal), the scope of this association is national and requires national attention.

QUESTIONNAIRE

"Youth's Answer to Conscription"

At a recent meeting of the Montreal Youth Council, with guests and 75 representations of different organizations in the city present, the President of the Council submitted his resignation and Kenneth Woodsworth, [⊰deletion: 1 line] was elected to the vacancy. After his election, Woodsworth spoke on the questionnaire which youth groups are being urged to distribute throughout the country and which concerns "youth's answer to conscription, civil liberties, profiteering and conditions of youth." Woodsworth stated that it was the intention of the Youth Council to place results obtained from this questionnaire before the representatives in Parliament.

No Signatures Required!

According to a latter appearing in the February 7 edition of the Toronto "Daily Star" and signed by Kenneth Woodsworth, Secretary of the Canadian Youth Congress, this body have prepared and already distributed 50,000 copies of this questionnaire. It is interesting to note that no signatures are required, but only the occupation and ages of the signatories. The omission of personal identification permits, of course, the sponsors to "stuff" the ballot boxes as they will and to insure that Canadian Youth will appear to be in overwhelming support of the policies of the

Young Communist League (instigators of the questionnaire) and of the Communist Party of Canada.[5][✕blank]

WINNIPEG PUBLIC MEETING

The first Communist public meeting of any consequence for some time was held on January 28 in the Fisher Hall, Winnipeg, Manitoba. James Litterick was the main speaker and Jock McNeil acted as Chairman. Held to commemorate the 16th Anniversary of Lenin's death, the meeting was very similar to other gatherings held by the Party throughout Canada in this connection. Approximately 200 people were present, 90% of them being foreigners.[6]

LITHUANIAN COMMUNISTS HOLD MASS MEETINGS
(Toronto)

Little activity of major importance is being undertaken by the Lithuanian section of the Communist Party of Canada at Toronto. For the past two months, this young organization has centred its activities around these five main points:

"(1)   Belittling the press reports on the Soviet invasion of Finland and the Allies' War Aims;

(2)   defending the treaty between the Soviet Union and Lithuania;

(3)   the possibility of Sovietizing Germany and the world's revolution;

(4)   linking the Canadian Lithuanian Sons and Daughters of Mutual Aid Society with the Lithuanian Literary Association; and

(5)   recruiting the youth to the Canadian Lithuanian Sons and Daughters of Mutual Aid Society."

All these points have been discussed at regular meetings of the Lithuanian Literary Association and at a series of special mass meetings held for this purpose. Speakers at these meetings have been the more prominent Lithuanian Communist Leaders in the district. At least one mass meeting (forum) a week was held, with an average attendance of 70 to 80 people.

Press reports on war were branded as Capitalist press lies, provocations and Imperialist war propaganda spread by Imperialist war mongers who control sources of the world's information. This attack on the press is in conformity with the Communist Party drive for funds in support of their own press, which explains that the Allies' war aims are to set up another dictatorship in Germany which would co-operate with English-French Imperialists, in the destruction of the Soviet Union, and that Finland is being used as a tool in British interests.

Speakers defended the mutual aid treaty between the Soviet Union and Lithuania, the Russo-German Alliance pointing out that the trade and non-aggression pacts with Germany are merely Soviet strategy towards eventual Sovietization of Germany — and laid great stress on the ultimate collapse of Capitalism and the victory of Communism.[7]

The Canadian Lithuanian Sons and Daughters of Mutual Aid Society have begun to co-operate with the Lithuanian Literary Association more closely than heretofore, especially in municipal election campaigns and in the discussion of current events.

BAKERY WORKERS

A report emanating from Fort William, Ontario, states that the Bakery Workers at that point are negotiating for a closed shop and higher wages. Further, a representative from the American Federation of Labour Union at Minneapolis has been at Fort William endeavouring to arrange an agreement. He apparently failed to do so, but before returning to the United States is alleged to have instructed the Bakery Workers to strike within the month. The employers (bakers) are refusing either to consider a closed shop or an increase in wages.

A. E. SMITH TOURS CANADA

The recently reported provincial conference of the Saskatchewan Union of Unemployed is not taking place until February 20, 21 and 22 one month later than stated in a previous bulletin. It is noted that not ex-Alderman Stewart Smith but his father A. E. Smith, National Secretary of the Canadian Labour Defence League, will be in Regina for the conference.

A. E. Smith is now on a tour of Canada in an endeavour to enlarge the organization of the League. On January 28, he was the principal speaker at a meeting in the Goldfields Theatre, Timmins, under the auspices of the Porcupine District Trades and Labour Council. Other speakers included Robert Dickey, a member of the Executive of the Miners' Union, and William Brenan who acted as Chairman.[8]

CANADIAN FINNS FORM NEW CLUB
(South Porcupine, Ont.)

During the past three months the Canadian Finnish Organization of South Porcupine [?<deletion: 1 line] has lost a considerable number of its membership owing to its attitude towards Finland in the present International crisis. To offset this loss the organization has inaugurated a new club known as the "Finnadio Club of South Porcupine", ostensibly for the purpose of bringing together loyal people of Finnish extraction; and to be non-sectarian and non-political.

However, the executive positions of this new club have been filled by members of the C. F. O.

ORGANIZING FOR ELECTIONS

The United Reform Movement is organizing zone meetings for educational discussions throughout the city of Saskatoon, with the idea of building up a corps of people willing to work for the movement during the forthcoming federal election. Notifications of these meetings are carried in the local press from time to time.

ROBBING THE UNEMPLOYED

Charges are being laid against Sid Brown, one of the leaders of the unemployed at Toronto and a member of the Communist Party, for misappropriating the funds of the Single Unemployed, reported between $150 and $300. Whether these charges will be made in Court is not known, but in view of Communist Party activity amongst the unemployed, the latter are likely to take action themselves. Brown and several of his henchmen have left the Single Unemployed Association.[10]

EXCLUDING REDS FROM LABOUR COUNCILS

The Communist Party is to place greater emphasis on the tactics of the "United Front from Below" on issues they wish to popularize, such as higher wages and anti-war policy, especially in relation to the Trade Unions. With this end in view, Communist Party activities in the Unions will be concentrated toward winning the members of the locals over the heads of their leaders if necessary to support Communist Party inspired campaigns within the Trades Union movement.

In spite of an almost complete mobilization of Communist Party delegates (members delegating from Unions) to the Toronto and District Labour Council, not one important Committee seated a Party member. This was due to the anti-Communist strategy of Arthur Dowel of the Musicians Union in mobilizing sufficient delegates from the Fire Fighters, Teamsters and Truckers Unions. A member of this latter Union also aided in the Communist exclusion. Sufficient voting power was arranged to prevent any Communist election to the executive of any of the important committees. Delegates Collins and Lapedes [ಒ<deletion: 3 lines] They feel, however, that they may be able to influence Buckley, Watson and Kelly, members of the Council executive, to support the issues and campaigns that they bring before the Council.

It is understood that a further move is afoot to exclude members of the Communist Party from the Trades and Labour Council, even as delegates.

"MID-WEST CLARION"

The Communist Party at Winnipeg are encountering difficulties in the distribution of the "Mid-West Clarion" due to the general indifference of the public. A campaign to popularize the paper will be started. Addressing a meeting of the Winnipeg Clarion Committee on January 28, Annie Buller, the Clarion Manager, announced that by getting the people to read "The Mid-West Clarion", they would be given the proper guidance as to how to end this Imperialist War in the revolutionary way. "Until the masses read the truth in our press," she stated, "we cannot do much."[11]

THE HITLER-STALIN PARTNERSHIP

The relationship now existing between members of the Communist

Party and Nazi organizations is exemplified in the following statement made by Dillon O'Leary of Ottawa, [⊱<deletion: 1 line]

"Many people believe that Hitler is crazy. Hitler is a genius and his immediate aims are excellent. As the war goes on the integration of the French and British peoples will to some extent be more evident. Hitler knows it. He will strike hard with a 'blitzkrieg' which will aid to demoralize France and Great Britain. With a tremendous will power he will keep on until the French masses will break out in a revolution, which of course will spread. Hitler is also right when he claims that he crushed the inside enemies of Germany. Germany has had seven years experience dealing with various underground organizations and his secret service is extremely efficient. France and Great Britain show a different picture. Look at England! Powerful labour organizations have passed resolutions already against war on the Soviet Union, and this is only the beginning. England intends to bring in the Scandinavian Countries and spread the war. The Soviet Union will not tolerate Italian influence in the Balkans. The reports on the Finn-Soviet war are so ridiculous and exaggerated that people begin to laugh at them and make jokes about it. In Canada discontentment is evident already. Neither Germany nor England will win the war, but the working class."

The above is more or less in confirmation of other reports received at Headquarters which show a corresponding trend of thought between the two organizations which not so long ago were at each other's throats.[12]

SECRET
INTELLIGENCE
BULLETIN

ROYAL CANADIAN MOUNTED POLICE
HEADQUARTERS, OTTAWA

WEEKLY SUMMARY
FEBRUARY 19, 1940

CONTENTS

War Series
No. 18.

EDITORIAL
WHY THE BULLETIN?

Its office is two-fold:
1. Liaison between R.C.M.Police Headquarters and Heads of Government Departments.
2. Liaison between R.C.M.Police Headquarters and Commanding Officers throughout the field.

Its purpose (in the first category) is to keep the Government advised of all conditions, movements and acts that in any way tend to menace our Civil Security either by direct action or by indirect influence, and thus permit the framing of corrective laws and regulations founded upon evidence gathered largely from secret sources.

Its purpose within the Force is to knit all Officer in a common knowledge of present working conditions and activities throughout the whole Dominion and so aid them in the carrying out of their respective duties relating to Civil Security.

It is not the intention of the Bulletin to provide profuse details on any particular "case" such as are embodied in reports from Divisions, but rather to reveal at a glance the significance and motives underlying the case.

The Editorial usually calls attention to some major problem at present receiving or demanding action, or reviews unsocial and anti-Canadian trends of thought and frankly suggests ways and means of correcting them.

The "Style" of the Bulletin is dictated by one motive: to have the summary read. Therefore the articles are short and the contents to the point.

The need of protecting Bulletins from falling into "wrong" hands is obvious to all who read them.[1]

COMMUNISM

"SAVE CANADA FROM CATASTROPHE"

Under the above title the Communist Party of Canada have compiled a pre-election nine-page booklet that for violent invective and incitement to revolt against responsible government exceeds all previous outbursts. The Defence of Canada Regulations have never been openly and more defiantly challenged! This booklet is largely a compilation of the baldest accusations and denunciations contained in other pamphlets distributed recently from the Centre at Toronto and is being mimeographed in cities east and west for the widest possible distribution. We quote in part:

What lies behind the farce enacted in Ottawa on January 25th? What is the purpose of the snap election called for March 26th?

Under the virtual military dictatorship established by the War Measures Act, the King Government and the main capitalist groups, in agreement with Chamberlain, desire to carry through a mock election before the Canadian people gather their forces sufficiently to fight back against their criminal war. They have wiped out your democratic rights and set up a ruthless, despotic regime....They make it illegal for any candidate in the election to speak or publish the truth. They intend to arrest any honest working class candidate. Their election is no better than one of Hitler's "plebiscites". Through it they aim to secure a fake "mandate" to rule over you for the next five years and carry through their criminal war policy.

They want the election over before the massacre starts on the Western Front. They plan conscription, to herd hundreds of thousands of Canada's finest sons to slaughter in Europe. A quick election and then conscription—that is their plan....[2]

They want to get the election over as quickly as possible, before the Canadian people begin to realize that the war is really directed against them. Before the war, the government held secret conferences with the leading employers on ways and means of keeping wages down in time of war.....

The war offensive of the government and the capitalists is directed in the first place against you, the Canadian workers and farmers. These men of the capitalist class, who despoiled and laid waste our country before the war, jubilantly greet and support the vast human slaughter as an opportunity for greater robbery and plunder of the Canadian people. Their chief class aim is to devise ways and means of coining millions from your war suffering and exploitation.

They are holding down to starvation levels the prices they pay for the farmers' products, while bleeding the consumers through war prices. They intend to take the farmers' sons away from the cultivation of their homeland to drench the soil of Europe with their blood....

There will be no prosperity for you. They will rob and plunder you during the war, and leave you destitute and starving in the after-war ruin.

To save Canada and to save themselves, the Canadian people must unite to beat back this war offensive of the government and the capitalists. That is the only way to use the election for your own interests and the interests of your country. Only disaster awaits you, unless a truly powerful fight is waged to stop the war plundering of the nation......

In the elections, they will tell you they are fighting for the well-being of peoples in Europe. Do not believe such bare-faced lies! This class of capitalists who exploit you, who have condemned Canada to years of crisis for their profits, who condemn hundreds of thousands of Canadian children to misery and undernourishment, are not in war for the well-being of any peoples in Europe....

They will tell you they are waging war for "democracy". This is the most despicable lie of all. They are the [3] enemies of democracy.

For years they have conspired against Canadian democracy, stripping the Canadian people of the heritage of the revolutionary struggles of MacKenzie and Papineau...Now they have crushed all your democratic rights and have established their unbridled class dictatorship. In the face of all truth, they think the Canadian people are so gullible as to believe their brazen lies about "war for democracy".......

What are their REAL aims in the war with German Imperialism? They are clear.

First, to preserve their imperialist markets, dependent on the hegemony of British Imperialism in Europe, and endangered by German imperialism.

Second, to profit from the war tortures of Europe's peoples and to make fortunes by the barter of Canadian lives for European arms orders.

Third, to strengthen their own imperialist position in the world, seize new super-profit markets from Germany and Britain in South America, Africa and in British dominions and colonies, and acquire a creditor position in world finance by vast war exports of capital.

In this war the Canadian capitalists plan to revel in luxury at home, raking in the mounting piles of profits, while sending our best sons to rot and die in the trenches of someone else's war on a far-off continent. Greedily they count the millions that they will make from the life of every Canadian boy sacrificed on their barbarous altar of profits. A degenerate, begotten, parasitical class, they are carrying on a traffic in death. In exchange for war orders, they are bartering Canadian lives. What despicable pay-triots! Relying upon this vicious trade, the imperialists of Europe are refusing to make peace and are planning a long and ghastly slaughter, which will pile the battlefields with mountains of dead.

People of Canada! Do not permit this parasitical ruling class to make a mockery of your love of democracy, justice and truth by cloaking their bloody criminal war with these sacred words! In the name of all that we hold [4] dear, in the name of the rights bequeathed to us as a North American people by the struggles of our pioneer forefathers, determine to fight against this war, this ghastly crime against humanity.

Fight for Canada Against the War!

As a people, we, the Canadians, now face the greatest test of our national history. In the interests of our country, in the interests of world peace, in the interests of all humanity, we must wage a fight to the end against the criminal war aims of our parasitical ruling class. We must break their war alliance with British imperialism, which prolongs and extends the slaughter with the resources of Canada and the lives of her sons. We must extricate Canada from the war, and thus speed the termination of the slaughter, and save our country and ourselves from catastrophe and ruin.

This, and only this, position in the federal election represents the true interests of Canada and the Canadian people.....

Manion, Hepburn and Drew would "improve" upon the ruthless suppression of democracy, the heartless exploitation and robbery of the Canadian people, and push the nation more deeply into the morass of war......

The ruling class relies upon these lackeys in the C.C.F., in the Social Credit Party and in the trade union movement to help lead the masses to the slaughter under the fraudulent slogan that this is a "just" war. Their role is the most despicable one.....

Your problem is to build unity of the Canadian people in uncompromising struggle against the criminal war-makers and their hangers-on.[5]

COMMUNIST PARTY ELECTION PLATFORM

(As Quoted From Booklet "SAVE CANADA
FROM CATASTROPHE")

The Communist Party Holds High the People's Banner

The Communist Party, alone among the political parties, refuses to submit to the war dictatorship of big capital, disdains to conceal its principled adherence to the true interests of the working class and raises high the banner of struggle for the people's interests, for democratic rights, and against the criminal imperialist war.....

Now, in the face of the unbridled dictatorship of the capitalist warmakers, the Communist party calls upon you to unite and fight in the federal election for the platform that truly represents your interests:

1. No Conscription! Bring the Canadian boys back to Canada! Not a man must leave Canada's shores to die in imperialist war!
2. Repeal the War Measures Act! The real fight for democracy is here in Canada against the war dictatorship of reaction! Freedom for the honest working class press! Release Douglas Stewart of the Clarion!
3. Higher wages, union conditions, the 8-hour day. Fight back the bosses' war on living standards! Make the war profiteers pay living wages!
4. Parity prices for the farmers! Jail the war profiteers!
5. Repeal the Sales Tax. Tax the incomes and fortunes of the rich. They grow fat on war. Let them pay for it!
6. Non-contributory unemployment and health insurance; increased relief pending such insurance. Our children come first—not war profits!
7. A national works program of slum clearance and rehousing for the people, to provide jobs so that our youth can work to build Canada, not die for profits![6]

The Communist candidates, fearlessly taking their stand upon this platform of your interests, appeal for your support. Capitalism and the capitalist class, breeding crises, poverty and the horrible slaughter of war, are your enemies, are the enemies of humanity. Their fury is directed in the first place against the Communist Party because it is the vanguard of the working class and of the people in the fight for a new world, a world of Socialism, prosperity and human happiness, without profit-seeking, war-making imperialists. The Communists declare that the workers must not slaughter each other for the profits of their imperialist masters, but must unite to defeat the imperialists on both sides of the imperialist war....In the federal election, the Communist Party raises high the banner of Proletarian Internationalism, true to the end to the cause of the brotherly alliance of the working people of all countries....

The Canadian people have common cause with the Finnish and Soviet people against the Mannerheim war-instigators, whose careers will be terminated to stop the spread of the flames of war.

In the sharpening conflict between the old world of dying capitalism and the new world of growing Socialism in the Soviet Union, the Canadian people's interests lie with the Socialist world. Through all the sudden lies of the capitalist press, the beacon of Socialism in the Soviet Union lights the way of all humanity to peace and happiness!

People of Canada! Workers and Farmers, men, women and youth!

Unite your ranks, build up your popular united front to defeat the war offensive upon your living standards and democratic rights! Never submit to the virtual military dictatorship that has been established by capital! Not all their lies, nor all their persecution and suppression can defeat you!.....

Determine to fight and live in Canada for peace and social progress; not suffer and die for profits! Extricate Canada from the imperialist war!.....

Organize and fight, strike and demonstrate for higher wages, democratic rights, progress and peace!......[7]

Go to the polls and cast your votes for the Communist candidates, for those who fight for your interests against the imperialist war camp!

In constituencies where all candidates support the war, go the polls and use your ballot for the fight by writing on it the word "Peace"!

Prepare to fight with all means against conscription! Wives, mothers, sisters, wipe the tears from your eyes and demand—for all to hear—that your husbands, sons and brothers be returned to you form the carnage in Europe!

Join in one common front against this most criminal war of human history. Strike a blow in this federal election to save Canada, to end the war, for Peace!

Political Committee
Communist Party of Canada.

SMITH'S TOUR ITINERARY

The "Mid-West Clarion" publishes the itinerary of the National Secretary of the Canadian Labour Defence League (A.E. Smith) Western tour as follows:-

Brandon—Feb. 15; Regina—Feb. 15-24; Calgary—Feb. 24-26; Lethbridge—Feb. 26-27; Blairmore—Feb. 27-29; Vancouver—March 1-12.

Although the schedule of his return trip is not as yet published, it is stated that he will be back in Calgary on March 13.[8]

VOTE FOR PEACE OR SPOIL BALLOTS

The Communist Party is contemplating the organization of an intense campaign of agitation against war, war dictatorship, war economy and conscription. It is their intention to run candidates wherever possible in the coming election, and in constituencies in which they are not represented they will support those opposed to war, or, where such are not in evidence, will ask voters to go to the polls and void their ballots by writing on them "No Conscription", or "Peace".

The Party is planning to co-operate with the Nationalists on the basis of their opposition to war and will, if necessary, carry on an illegal campaign regardless of the risks involved.

Considering the C.C.F. conditional support of the war as highly unsatisfactory, the Party has resolved to oppose them.

According to reports received from Montreal, the Communist Party are undertaking another "somersault", with instructions being issued by the Quebec Provincial Secretary, E. Dube, that wherever the Communist Party are unable to place their own candidate in the coming Federal Election, members are to support candidates of the Nationalist Party. It is apparent that this is the outcome of Party belief that other political bodies in the field are pro-conscription.

[⊱deletion: 1 line]
[⊱deletion: 1 line]
[⊱deletion: 1 paragraph: 6 lines][9]

DISBANDING CANADIAN C.I.O. LOCALS

The Communist Party of Canada has set out in a guarded manner to disband Canadian C.I.O. Locals in favour of affiliation with the All-Canadian Congress of Labour. This move was undoubtedly promoted by the realization that the C.I.O. Locals, being international and particularly American, are decidedly unpopular during this present war period and do not afford an outlet for the energies of their membership; and also, as previously reported in this Bulletin, the C.I.O. is not officially recognized by the Government, having been expelled from the Trades and Labour Congress of Canada. Furthermore, organizers feel that they will be afforded a greater degree of safety under the colours of the A.C.C.L.

Tommy Church [⊱deletion: 1 line] and C.I.O. Trade Union organizer, is said to have been in the United States, working up the details with the American C.I.O. heads.

[⊱deletion: 1 line]
[⊱deletion: 1 line]
[⊱deletion: 1 paragraph: 8 lines][10]

COMMUNIST TICKET IN SASKATCHEWAN

Tentative arrangements have been made in Saskatchewan for several members of the Communist Party to run on a straight Communist ticket. This matter is being taken up with the Centre at Toronto for confirmation.

T.G. McManus, Provincial Secretary of the Communist Party [⊱deletion: 2 lines]

Walter Wiggins, Provincial President of the Party [ఌ<deletion: 2 lines]
[ఌ<deletion: 1 paragraph: 6 lines]

Niles Buchanan is to run in Wood Mountain on a C.C.F. ticket. C.H.
Williams Provincial Leader of the C.C.F. [ఌ<deletion: 2 lines]

STUDENT REDS IN MANITOBA

The Canadian Student Assembly at the University of Manitoba have
recently shown that they are wholly in favour of voluntary enlistment but
are against conscription. The Assembly at this point is largely composed
of Young Communist League members who are very militant. This faction is endeavouring to arouse in the C.S.A. a sentiment in favour of the
Soviet Union and, in particular, opposed to the attitude of the Allies
towards Finland, and are trying to create an impression that eventually
those who enlist with the Allied Forces will find themselves fighting
against Socialism, which means Soviet Russia.[11]

INTELLIGENCE
BULLETIN

ROYAL CANADIAN MOUNTED POLICE
HEADQUARTERS, OTTAWA

WEEKLY SUMMARY
FEBRUARY 26, 1940

CONTENTS

War Series
No. 19

EDITORIAL
"CONSCRIPTION"

So far as the major political parties are concerned Conscription is not an election issue. The enemies of democracy however have forged it into a most effective weapon for attacking Canada in the back. The war cannot be openly opposed with impunity. Weakening our will to war however by causing dissension in our ranks is a simple method of avoiding the law. Behind all this anti-conscription agitation stands the Communist Party of Canada, directed by Moscow. Many of its tools are loyal citizens who have no suspicion of the manner in which they are being used as enemies against the State. An apparently innocent questionnaire is distributed by college undergraduates and Youth Councils, inviting opinions on conscription, profiteering, free speech and implying that the liberty we are fighting for abroad is at stake at home. Fear and suspicion are engendered. Is this an imperialist war? Are French-Canadians going to be forced against their will to snatch Britain's chestnuts out of the fire? Is Fascism masquerading in the guise of Democracy? The whispering campaigns are fanned into open clamour, as professors, lawyers, college assemblies, clergy and others rise to the attack of fancied perils.

Quebec is proving a particularly easy mark for these hidden enemies. For instance the Youth Congress has issued a circular entitled "Conscription Conspiracy" signed by Prof. A.M. Angers of University of Montreal, in which he demands "an immediate campaign to mobilize public opinion of all the country against conscription", adding "This campaign is an urgent matter if English-Canadians want French-Canadians to feel that they are better considered in Canada than the Czechs and Poles in Germany".

The implication throughout the article that partiality exists as between these two great and equal races is as unjust as it is injurious to national unity. And yet this insidious disruptive agitation is spreading unchecked throughout every class of society in the name of Defence of Liberty, Free Speech, Free Press![1]

There are many ways of preventing it. Last week the students of McGill rose in sudden wrath to forbid the Canadian Student Assembly [≻deletion: 1 line] in their midst from speaking in the name of the University. A few loyal students had been shown the "hidden hand"!

In short, the mildest form of counter-propaganda would quickly destroy the Red Dragon so omnipotent is Truth! [2]

COMMUNISM

COMMUNIST ELECTION SLATE CONTINUES TO GROW

The Communist Party election campaign will be waged to the slogan "Bring the Canadian Troops Home." Stickers and leaflets will be used to popularize the various planks of the Communist Party and will be printed for national distribution under the editorship of Stewart Smith.

Stanley Ryerson, Secretary[≻deletion: 2 lines], has announced that Evariste Dube, [≻deletion: 1 line], has been nominated as the candidate in the St. Mary's riding [≻deletion: 1 line] It will be remembered that Dube was also a candidate for the Montreal St. James constituency in the Quebec Provincial election of October 25, 1939. In this election he received 193 out of 7073 votes registered.

[≻deletion: 2 lines] Stewart Smith, it is reported, will run in Trinity (Toronto), Joseph Salsberg in Spadina (Toronto) and a campaign is being considered for Tim Buck in Hamilton East. While Buck will not appear and his candidacy will not be valid, a campaign for the Communist Party program will be carried out and voters will be asked to mark Tim Buck on their ballots in that constituency. Efforts are being made to have progressive candidates nominated in Hamilton industrial constituency, Toronto, Windsor, Kitchener, Sudbury, Timmins, Port Arthur and Niagara Falls.

Straight Communist tickets will be presented in Saskatchewan and Winnipeg if sufficient support is available and no C.C.F. or Social Credit opposition appears.

The campaign for W. Halina, [ℌdeletion: 1 line] who is going to run in the forthcoming election in Vegreville, Alberta, is now being carefully arranged by the Party.

Stickers demanding Canadians to organize, stop the imperialist war, defend free speech, fight Hitlerism in Canada, capitalism means war, a socialist world will assure peace, make India free and stop the war for profits and colonies are being posted on billboards, buildings and motor cars throughout Vancouver as part of Communist Party propaganda.[3]

The Party at Vancouver intend to run three candidates, probably on a Labour ticket in Vancouver Centre, Vancouver East and the Comox-Alberni constituency. A candidate will run on a C.P. ticket in Hastings East.

The leadership have stated that Fergus McKean, [ℌdeletion: 2 lines] in British Columbia, is to run in the East Kootenay Constituency. The question arises over the fact that there will be no real indication of the strength of the Party unless he runs in this constituency. If, however, they undertake this task and lose their deposit, they will be equally responsible to the Centre.

There is a possibility that Malcolm Bruce [ℌdeletion: 2 lines] He is reported to be strenuously opposing taking the field, as the position of the present member of parliament (Mr. A.W. Neill) is well nigh impregnable. He urged, however, that all efforts be concentrated on electing a representative in Hastings, East, where the numerical strength of the Party is greatest and where there would be less expense in conducting a campaign.

FALSE OATHS ARE EASY

An interesting statement was recently made by Reginald Morris, former Labour Alderman for Ward 1, Windsor, Ontario, to the effect that he was not a member of the Communist Party. This statement was made in conjunction with an oath he was obliged to take before becoming a member of the United Brotherhood of Carpenters and Joiners of America, and received prominent publication in the local press. [ℌdeletion: 4 lines][4]

PAT SULLIVAN, [ℌdeletion: 1 line] FERMENTING STRIKES

The failure of negotiations instituted by the Steel Workers Organizing Committee in January at Sydney, Nova Scotia, was the main reason behind the strike involving 308 men in the Coke Ovens Department of the Dominion Steel and Coal Corporation which commenced on February 9. Union officials are apparently in the position that they must do something to justify their existence and their efforts are concentrated on calling a general strike. On February 12 a vote was taken over general conditions as outlined in a bulletin circulated which advocated seven points, including a wage increase and shorter hours, with the result that 2,263 members of the Union voted for and 297 against a strike. The Union Executive immediately announced that this did not mean an immediate general strike but, on the basis of this favourable vote, the company would again be approached with the demands of the workers. It was reported on February 16 that the strike had ended, pending negotiations. Should these discussion prove fruitless, a board of conciliation would be set up under the Industrial Disputes Act. The leadership of the Steel Workers Organizing Committee at Sydney are either [⊱deletion: 1 line] or sympathetically inclined toward this organization. Norman McKenzie, President was recently elected Labour Alderman to the Sydney Municipal Council [⊱deletion: 2 lines] Prior to the strike, McKenzie held a meeting of Union officials and, at that time, stated that the International would back the Lodge both financially and morally in the event of a general strike. Should this strike have commenced in the Steel Workers, it would undoubtedly have had serious repercussions in view of the relationship existing between the Steel Company and the Collieries in the district; tying up, as it would have done, the major industry of the whole industrial district of Cape Breton Island.

Undoubtedly the recent visit of John A. (Pat) Sullivan [⊱deletion: 2 lines] and President of the Canadian Seamen's Union, and his henchmen to Nova Scotia is the outcome of this present disturbance. They frankly stated, that they intend to organize and agitate in the Maritimes this coming spring. Several labour organizers, prominently connected with the Communist Party in Eastern Canada, are still in Nova Scotia conducting the affairs of the Party, which has, of late, considerably increased its activities.[5]

Sullivan is presently in Ontario endeavouring to organize the Seamen on the Great Lakes, (As was reported in a recent bulletin). Undoubtedly the Communist Party would attach great importance to such a strike on the eve of the opening of navigation. Already information has been received to the effect that the C. S. U. have managed to place several agitators on board Imperial Oil Boats. Conditions under this management are, however, particularly good and C. S. U. officials anticipate considerable trouble in overcoming this fact.

An ulterior purpose must be behind the increased activity of these prominent agitators who are organizing in basic industries from Fort William, Ont., to Sydney, N.S., and who are choosing this most opportune time to commence "hostilities".

Expected back in Nova Scotia early in March, Sullivan has definitely decided to run as a Labour-Liberal Candidate in the Federal elections at Lockport, N.S. (It will be remembered that last November he arrived at this point and conducted a fishermen's and fish handler's strike). It is quite possible that Sullivan's plans to run might, of necessity, be changed to a C.C.F. Ticket, in view of strong appeals which have been made by Lockport constituents to have a candidate run under this banner. According to Sullivan, he would not appreciate this fact in view of the "strings attached" while under the influence of C.C.F. leadership.

[&<deletion: 1 line]

[&<deletion: 1 paragraph: 5 lines][6]

"MILITANT ACTION AGAINST WAR AND CONSCRIPTION"
(Quebec)

The Provincial Committee of the Communist Party of Quebec have issued a circular to their branch secretaries regarding the duties of Communists in the Federal election, which is being distributed from house to house. This material has also appeared in the last issue of "L'Eclaireur" (The Scout), publication of the Young Communist League of Quebec. The last paragraph is of particular interest:

"Our party will participate in the election in order to be able to organize in a better way the masses against war. We must lead a flaming and agitated campaign, on a vast scale, with an intensity and a vigour increased tenfold IN ORDER TO INFORM THE PEOPLE OF THE IMMINENT DANGER OF CONSCRIPTION. TO GIVE RISE EVERYWHERE TO THE INDIGNATION AND HATRED AGAINST THOSE WHO HAVE BETRAYED US AND TOOK US INTO THE IMPERIALIST WAR, AND TO HELP ORGANIZING AS SOON AS POSSIBLE MILITANT ACTION OF THE WORKING CLASSES AGAINST WAR AND CONSCRIPTION, FOR THE CESSATION OF HOSTILITIES AND THE THROW-OVER OF THE REGIME OF THE IMPERIALISTS.

"Forward to Steady, courageous and bolshevik work!"

This Y.C.L. Publication has a circulation of 300 copies a week. However at the present time we have been unable to ascertain where the material is being printed.

[&<deletion: 1 line]

[&<deletion: 1 paragraph][7]

AFTER THE WAR — MORE COMMUNISM!
(Toronto)

An item appearing in "GLOS PRACY" (Voice of Labour) printed in the Polish language, dated Toronto, February 3, entitled "Before The Elections In Canada", reads in part as follows:

"The passing over of the Liberal and reformist elements to the banner of the war, left Communism, at least at the beginning of the war, as an exclusive and extreme opposition which thus far does not represent a competition in the Federal field. Not until the masses shall begin to feel the results of the war and ebb away from the Liberal, Conservative and Reformist parties may this camp (the Communist Party) become an influential force in the country, as it was in Russia and in Europe at the end of the last war.

"The last municipal elections in Ontario have shown that the masses will support those candidates who proclaim the slogans of opposition against the assaults on democracy and the interests of the people in war time. The number of such representatives in the new Parliament, and above all, the number of votes cast for them, shall constitute an expression of the people's tendencies at the beginning of the present war. In proportion to the pressure made upon the masses by the war burdens and sacrifices, and by the restriction of rights, the tendency will unquestionably grow in force and significance, veering gradually further to the Left."

AFFILIATING WITH THE C.I.O.

Negotiations are now proceeding between the C.I.O. and the All Canadian Congress of Labour concerning a possible affiliation of A.C.C. of L. Unions with the C.I.O. Should the A.C.C. of L. decide in favour of such affiliation it is almost certain that the Communist Party would endeavour to have all American Federation of Labour Unions in Canada under its control to sever their affiliation with the A.F. of L. so that they could link up with the C.I.O.[8]

"SAVE CANADA FROM CATASTROPHE"
(Regina)

The Communist Party leadership at Regina are reported very worried as to what the outcome will be when the pamphlet "Save Canada From Catastrophe" makes its appearance. They are quite certain that the Communist Party will be outlawed.

Insofar as Saskatchewan is concerned, 5,000 copies of this pamphlet have been mimeographed in Regina and are now ready for distribution 1,000 copies are for the McKenzie constituency; 1,000 for Maple Creek constituency; 1,000 for Regina and the remainder are to be split up through the various country branches in the Southern District.

[℈<deletion: 1 paragraph: 11 lines]

(Montreal)

Copies of a similar pamphlet, numbering approximately 5,000, were printed in Montreal and distributed by members of the Communist Party in various sections of the City on the evening of February 19. Whereas other Districts of the Communist Party in Canada are apparently distributing this leaflet signed by the Political Committee of the Communist Party, these French leaflets are signed by Evariste Dube, [℈<deletion: 1 line] in the Ste. Marie constituency and President of the Provincial Committee, and Stanley B. Ryerson, [℈<deletion: 2 lines][9]

BUILDING "AN ANTI-WAR FRONT FROM BELOW"
(Vancouver)

[℈<deletion: 1 paragraph: 4 lines]

[⸮deletion: 1 paragraph: 4 lines]
[⸮deletion: 1 paragraph: 12 lines]

Prominent in all Communist Party pamphlets is a vehement attack upon the War Measures Act in which efforts are made to compare these regulations with Fascism. Referring to the A.F. of L. and C.I.O. Units, a pamphlet states that the leadership of these organizations are conducting a "red baiting campaign in order to get the Communists out. Lewis, the leader of the C.I.O., is very active in this campaign. The Communist Party has had to support him, as he had prestige with the workers, but we should all realize that he is only an opportunist and had no use for any system except the kind that will give him power. The C.I.O. is a large union and Lewis and his henchmen are the dictators, but at the present time we cannot openly attack them without injuring the Party, so it is the duty of our members to stay in the Unions and advocate an anti-war policy."[10]

[⸮deletion: 1 line]

[⸮deletion: 1 paragraph: 9 lines]
[⸮deletion: 1 paragraph: 4 lines]

BAITING TRADES AND LABOUR CONGRESS
(Regina)

At a meeting of the Trades and Labour Congress at Regina a few days ago, William Stewart, delegate of the Hotel and Restaurant Employees and a number of the Communist Party, while under the influence of liquor set out deliberately to bait and badger A.E. Jameison and Percy Bengough, President and Secretary respectively, with the result that the meeting ended in an uproar and Jameison personally taking upon himself the opportunity to expel Stewart. It is hardly likely, however, that his expulsion will be effected. In view of the Communist Party efforts at this time to wreck the Trades and Labour Council with the view of substituting in its place the British Columbia Trades Congress, the expulsion of Stewart might have the effect of bringing the thing to a head. The Communist faction believe that with the added weight of C.I.O. Units which carry stronger left wing membership that they can impose their policy and break up the Jameison, Bengough and Showler machine of the T.L.C.[11]

GENERAL
JAPANESE STRESS LOYALTY TO CANADA
(Vancouver)

Recent arguments, both pro and con, have been advanced in Western Canadian newspapers regarding the Japanese in British Columbia.

In this connection, our attention has been drawn to the efforts of the Nisei (Japanese Canadian Citizens' League) in British Columbia to stress their loyalty to the British Empire. So far it is reported the second generation Japanese in this area have donated voluntary subscriptions amounting to slightly over $2,500 to the Federal Government for purposes of national defence. These monies have been collected from various Nisei organizations throughout the Province and do not include donations which have been subscribed to the first War Loan or the National Red Cross Society.

Due to the concern felt by local Japanese in connection with the trend of American-Japanese relations, the Nisei publication "The New Canadian", published an Editorial in its February 9 issue which is quoted in toto:

Canada and U.S.-Japanese Relations

Canada, and especially British Columbia, will observe with gravest concern the trend of American-Japanese relations. Facing upon the Pacific our Province has a vital interest in these relations, which, if not becoming worse, still remain in a highly explosive state.

From the distance of its prairie capital, the Winnipeg Free Press points out a very doubtful road for Canada and the Empire to follow in urging support for American [12] interests in the Far East. While our southern neighbour may have expressed its disapproval of Japan's action in the Far East, its own policy, as Bruce Hutchinson ably points out, "is not to save Asia from Japan but to save the Asiatic interests of this nation. It is in fact standing entirely upon its own rights, but not going to the rescue of China."

For Canada and the Empire to assist the United States in the Far East at this time is a course which no thinking Canadian, especially a British Columbian, would advise.

We have our hands full in Europe. Despite the apparent calm in the war, there is no doubt of the impending disaster that we must be prepared to face. We are pledged to stand alongside the Mother Country, to follow a course in Europe to its bitter end and final victory. To that end we must devote the entire energies and resources of a united Canada. The pulling of American chestnuts out of the China Fire is the least important task we have at hand.

The amicable and common sense settlement of the Asama Maru incident, acclaimed by the press both in London and Tokyo, provides the touchstone of Anglo-Japanese relations, and concomitantly, the touchstone of Canadian-Japanese relations.[13]

SECRET

INTELLIGENCE
BULLETIN

ROYAL CANADIAN MOUNTED POLICE
HEADQUARTERS, OTTAWA

WEEKLY SUMMARY
MARCH 4, 1940

CONTENTS

War Series
No. 20.

EDITORIAL

Three Communists Arrested

The arrest in Ottawa on February 24 of three Communists caught red-handed in the act of printing and distributing subversive literature has had the effect of shocking the people of Canada into a clearer realization of the presence of a powerful traitorous organization in their midst. It has also made evident that the Communist Party is not composed only of human derelicts, morons and "screw-balls" (as popularly believed) but is drawing its converts from almost every "respectable" class of society. The three arrested, for example, represented the federal Civil Service, the Canadian Army Service Force and the newspaper fraternity. These, however, were only more unfortunate, not more culpable, than the hundreds, perhaps thousands of other men and women who are working with a fervour worthy of a better cause to destroy our constitution, our government and our whole social structure. They are particularly numerous in youth organizations, in universities, in labour unions, in foreign nationality groups and in the ranks of the unemployed. Many individuals are unaware, of course, of the real motives and often criminal character of their leaders.

164

They are befuddled and subverted by pernicious tales of corruption and autocracy at home and of brutal British and French aggrandizement abroad. They believe that "peace-loving" Russia is the sole protector of humanity and the first Model State. The mesmerism of lies is as effective with Communists as it is with Nazis in Germany, resulting in both cases in moral and political idiocy.

It is plain that the forces of Democracy and individual freedom must look to their existence. "Turning the other cheek" is only inviting disaster. Half the war is in Europe. The other half is behind our lines in Canada and must be waged with equal resourcefulness and decision.

In a recent pamphlet the Communist Party of Canada charges: "The King Government and the main capitalist groups.....have wiped out your democratic rights and set up a ruthless, despotic regime". Such an imaginary picture exactly describes the hideous reality of a Communist Dictatorship.[1]

COMMUNISM
SABOTAGING THROUGH YOUTH CONGRESSES

Already the Canadian Youth Congress in conjunction with the Consiel de Juenesse (committee representing a number of French-Canadian youth organizations) are making plans to sponsor a Congress of Canadian Youth Organizations in Montreal during the first week of July. The main theme of this congress will be anti-conscription and anti-war. Because of its joint sponsorship this congress will replace the annual Canadian Youth Congress although its composition, purpose and control will be essentially the same.

The Y.C.L. is very satisfied with the results of proceedings at the Youth Congress held recently in the United States, particularly regarding the attitude that the congress adopted towards the Russo-Finnish question. It will be recalled that the resolution presented to the congress condemning Russia was not passed. It is hoped that this will discourage any display of sympathy for Finland at the forthcoming Canadian gathering. Dave Kashtan, National Secretary of the Y.C.L., remarked that it is well worth noting that the Y.M.C.A., Y.W.C.A. and the United Church Youth Group had so far done nothing for Finland.

The Y.C.L. intends to follow in a determined manner the controlling of election of delegates from mass youth organizations to the congress and to ensure that Y.C.L. members will be elected as delegates wherever possible to represent youth organizations. It is expected by the Y.C.L. that there will be a powerful C.P. block at the conference, that every precaution will be taken to make sure that it will be covered.

The majority of the delegates attending the congress from the Y.C.L. will represent the larger centres. The recent withdrawal of certain factions from participation in the Youth Congress has undoubtedly had a demoralizing effect throughout the country yet, at the same time, has left the field open to the subversive influence of the Y.C.L. and C.P. (An infusion of a sufficient number of healthy-minded youth into the congress might have the effect of completely frustrating Communist aims)[2]

The Young Communist League is exerting intense efforts to conclude the questionnaire campaign being conducted by the Youth Congress, in order to commence work to ensure a large Canadian youth delegation to the Montreal Congress. The Y.C.L. is anxious to get the support of the French-Canadian youth against conscription and the war and will make every effort to bring this congress to a successful conclusion from the point of view of numbers, concentrating on trade unions, Y.M.C.A., Y.W.C.A., student and United Church Groups (wherein the Y.C.L. exerts influence) in order to have French-English youth unanimity at the congress.

[✁deletion: 1 line]

[✁deletion: 1 paragraph: 11 lines][3]

SASKATCHEWAN UNION OF UNEMPLOYED

The seventh annual conference of the Saskatchewan Union of Unemployed commenced on February 20 with only seven locals represented and the delegates numbering 19. G. E. Davenport of Regina was appointed chairman of the first session and gave the opening address in which he stressed the need for unity of all unemployed in order to solve the various problems which arise from time to time. The organizer of the S.U.U., E.V. Mills, was the first person to submit his report, which dealt with standardization of relief, residential clauses regarding relief, amendment of the present Legislature governing the Province and the financial report.

It was decided at this first session that a delegation would meet members of the Provincial Government the following day to discuss the various issues raised at the conference.

It would appear that with 30 locals of the S.U.U. in existence and only seven sending representation this conference will not be very successful, and we are reliably informed that the Communist Party leadership in Regina are disgusted with the way the conference is turning out. Several of the more active participants in this conference are prominent in the Communist movement.

RISING COSTS AMONG UNEMPLOYED

The rising cost of living is being strongly felt by the unemployed on the West Coast and their discontent will be utilized to the utmost by the C.P. of C. For some three years the latter has shown little interest in either the single or married unemployed, but from now on fractions will be directed to concentrate on this phase of "agit-prop" and organization. Speakers will be sent out to conduct meetings along the lines of the old "block committees."[4]

COMMUNIST TACTICS AMONG THE MINERS

The Mine, Mill and Smelter Workers' International Union in the Timmins, Ontario area is comprised of three locals. For the past year or more there have scarcely been any Local Executive Board meetings, instead it has been customary to hold Joint Executive Board Meetings of all Local Executive Board members. One reason for this is that the poor attendance at Local Executive meetings made it necessary to combine all active members of all three boards into one in order to have a properly functioning body. As far as the C.P. of C. is concerned, however, the prime reason for the joint meetings lies in their early discovery that a loose directing body such as three distinct executives resulted in conflicting policy, as the members found it difficult to fashion a uniform policy as laid down by the Party.

However, in the Joint Executive Board their leader can hammer out the policy supported by the very talkative and active majority. They have a majority because every Party member turns out if at all possible, whilst the non-Communists attend in a sort of hit-and-miss fashion.

The Section meeting of the C.P. of C. Timmins Division always precedes any important Union meeting, so that plans can be made in advance.

All hope for building a strong Union at this point has resolved itself into the outcome of the present situation at Teck-Hughes Gold Mines, Kirkland Lake. Should any degree of success be achieved there, organizers will import a few highly trained C.P. of C. members as assistant organizers and endeavour to recruit the majority of foreign born miners and proceed to manufacture and create "incidents".

ILLEGAL TACTICS

The Communist Party will carry on its election campaign legally, if possible, but will not hesitate to use illegal methods and tactics where and when found necessary. They intend to justify their use of illegal tactics by pointing out that because of the Defence of Canada Regulations under the War Measures Act, civil liberties are so restricted as to render a democratic election impossible.[5]

SPLITTING THE C. C. F. VOTE

As a result of an uproar in the C.C.F. District Council over the nomination of Angus MacInnis in the Vancouver East Riding, Fergus McKean, [℀deletion: 1 line], grasped the opportunity to side-step his proposed Kootenay candidacy and inject himself into the Vancouver East contest. With no hope of winning the seat, the Communists will be very glad to contribute a split vote to the defeat of MacInnis who has so constantly fought the Party inside the outside the C.C.F.

[℀deletion: 1 paragraph: 7 lines]

DEMANDS OF CANADIAN SEAMEN'S UNION
(Halifax)

At a conference of the Canadian Seamen's Union held in Halifax a few days ago, it was decided that the Local of this organization send the following suggestions to its National President, Pat Sullivan [≫deletion: 2 lines] at Montreal.

(1) That demands be made for a higher standard of wages for seamen employed by the Canadian National Steamships, the increase to be not less than 50%, with a flexible margin to meet the rise and fall of the cost of living.

(2) A special grant for seamen to meet the extra cost of insurance.[6]

(3) Enforce the eight-hour day adopted by the International Convention.

(4) A flat war risk monthly grant of $25.00.

(5) A special insurance policy for losing life owing to the war.

LOCKPORT NOTES

Attempts will be made in the near future to call a meeting at Lockport, Nova Scotia, for the purpose of pressing upon the Cold Storage Companies the necessity of recognizing the Fish-handlers Union.

Receiving his proposed nomination as an Independent Labor Candidate at Lockport, N.S., J.A. (Pat) Sullivan [≫deletion: 2 lines] and President of the Canadian Seamen's Union, is encountering difficulties in this direction and apparently is making little headway.

R. Charles Murray, Secretary of the Canadian Seamen's Union of Nova Scotia and a [≫deletion: 1 line] is contemplating contesting a seat in the forthcoming Federal election in the Constituency of Shelbourne, N.S., as an Independent. He made a trip to Lockport this week before giving his decision to run as a candidate. At the present time he has no funds to sponsor his campaign and it is quite likely that resources will be provided by the Canadian Seamen's Union or the [≫deletion: 1 line][7]

UKRAINIANS STRUGGLE FOR NEW SOCIAL ORDER
(Toronto)

Toronto reports that the Ukrainian Labour Farmer Temple Association is excited over the prospect of other Ukrainian organizations holding a Congress, fearing this will be directed against the U.L.F.T.A.

A big meeting held by the Association the latter part of January was addressed by Alexander Melnychenko and Michael Dushnicky, [≫deletion: 1 line] The first spoke on the forthcoming Ukrainian National Congress in the U.S.A. to be held in the near future, asserting that the Ukrainian Nationals were planning to use this Congress for their own ends. He suggested that work for the liberation of the working class be continued, and said "As the Western Ukraine had been liberated, the time was not far off when other parts of the world would throw off the capitalist yoke and set up a better social system; Canada and the United States would be included." Michael Dushnicky gave a history of the progressive movement among the Ukrainians in Canada since its start in 1910, declaring that the movement in Canada was one with the Soviet Union. The U.L.F.T.A. has 86 halls and 165 units in the Dominions, he said.

Referring to the coming Congress, Dushnicky stated "Ukrainian reaction was attempting to consolidate its forces at the present time. Should this become a fact it would be a serious matter, because Ukrainian reaction would aim its first blow at the U.L.F.T.A."

He Promised that Bukowina and Bessarabia would be liberated in the same way as Western Ukraine. Although some of the Ukrainian population, after the war, would want to return to their homeland, for those who remained in Canada "it was necessary to continue the struggle for a new social order, not only in Canada, but in the whole world."

Questions were invited after the lecture. Several Nationalists in the audience took advantage of the opportunity and asked embarrassing questions, which however were answered satisfactorily as far as the general audience was concerned. To a question on the Russo-German pact, Melnychenko replied that he did not know why the pact had been concluded, but that their attitude towards Nazi-ism had not changed.[8]

[<deletion: 1 line]
[<deletion: 1 line]

[<deletion: 1 paragraph: 9 lines]

"AVOID A STRIKE"

Regarding the recent strike at the Coke Oven Department of the Dominion Steel and Coal Corporation, Sydney, N.S., information has been received to the effect that the International Union of the C.I.O. at Toronto has instructed the Leadership of the S.W.O.C. at Sydney to "lay off" in the interest of the C.I.O. in Canada and avoid a strike at the present time. The leadership have been further advised to forget their politics and fill the C.I.O. mill. It appears that John L. Lewis, International President of the C.I.O., is behind this move.

UNITED REFORM MOVEMENT

It has been decided that the main work of the Communist Party in Saskatchewan until after the election would be participation in the interests of the United Reform Movement. It is felt that this, coupled with a drive for subscriptions to the "Mid-West Clarion", Communist newspaper published at Winnipeg, is all that the general party membership can handle. Leaflets denouncing the war and attempting to cause disruption throughout the country will continue to make their appearance.[9]

GENERAL

TECHNOCRACY INCORPORATED—AN ENEMY OF
DEMOCRACY

(Another revolutionary organization, calling itself Technocracy Inc., is forcing itself upon the attention of Canada and the United States. As yet few people are aware of the insidious doctrines and blatantly militant technique of Technocracy. The following explanation seems to be in order).

On the surface Technocracy Incorporated appears to be a cold-blooded efficiency robot which reduces human and spiritual equations to a mechanical science wherein individuals become either regimented cogs in a soulless machine or else are consigned to the scrap heap.

A closer scrutiny, however, reveals Howard Scott, its director and leader, with headquarters at "Continental Headquarters, Technocracy Inc., 155 East 44th St., New York, N.Y.", obsessed by an entirely human (or rather, inhuman) ambition to emulate the "mad dogs" of Europe—ruthless usurpation of political power on this continent.

Technocracy makes its appeal to the classes rather than the masses—people with a smattering of learning and a craving for domination. However, it is prepared to enlist recruits from any and every subversive element, confident that, once under its influence, it can mold them into an inexorable juggernaut.

Scott recently made a tour of Canada, explaining his system and educating leaders to the methods of this new movement. In his wake there sprang up many small study groups whose propaganda has been so treasonable as to arouse strong protests from many loyal Canadians.

In outward form Technocracy Inc. suggests Arcand's "National Unity Party". Its adherents attend meetings dressed in uniforms of steel grey suits with grey shirts, dark blue ties and conspicuous red and white buttons in their lapels. They have their own peculiar salute and a military bearing.[10]

Politically, T.I. appears closely akin to Fascism. It condemns all political parties as working only for their respective interests, whereas it claims to represent the North American continent as a whole; it advocates the removal of international boundaries, the overthrow of the Price System, the abolition of money, and government by a selected group of scientists, or rather statisticians. "Adopt or perish" is one of their mottoes, unaccompanied by details as to how it is to be enforced. However, they appear to be ardent exponents of sterilization and the firing squad for all those who would oppose them. Their official literature (sold at all meetings) contains such passages as the following.

"The political governments of the United States and Canada are part and parcel of the Price System of this continent. They are the purveyors of scarcity, the merchandisers of national debt and the sowers of national dissolution. They are the ballyhooers of public confidence and the salesmen of sucker bait to their citizens. The political governments of the United States and Canada are the institutional blockades to social progress. They are the strong-arm squads of the merchant of debt and death."

"Technocracy Inc. charges the political administrations, the corporate enterprises, and the debt merchants of the United States and Canada with being in possession of the data and physical facts of the technological progression of this Continental Area. Technocracy Inc. charges these dominant interests with wilful suppression and distortion of the facts."

"It, in its greater patriotism of a New America, will present a clean, hard, bright design for living that will be the glory of all ages. And when the youth of America presents its ultimatum, let no minority, racial, religious, or economic, attempt to bar the highway to the New America; for if one does, the youth of this Continent will concede nothing short of that minority's annihilation."

A report on Technocracy from the Headquarters of the Mounted Police at Toronto says:

"At this present stage they are alleged to have cells in all the major cities in Canada and the U.S.A. and contact between the Canadian and U.S.A. groups is steadily maintained. The objective is to have their members placed in key positions [11] in industry and they claim to have achieved a certain success in this line already. They are reported to be working on government officials and to have contacts in the Army, Navy, Air Force and R.C.M.P. One of their successes is alleged to be in that they have their men on several Medical Boards."

Up to the present time, T. Inc. has confined itself to condemnation of the present system of government and economics and to the uttering of more or less veiled threats to possible enemies. It condemns war (circumspectly since September) but not on humanitarian grounds.

To sum up, Technocracy may be anything that any cold-blooded unprincipled leader wishes to make it. That it is evil, from a social and political point of view, there is no shadow of doubt. It is being promulgated as an instrument of autocracy for the regimentation of its followers and the enslavement of its opponents; it is the very antithesis of democracy, christianity and individual freedom; demands a complete break with the British Empire and, in short, is as potentially subversive as could well be imagined.

Reports from many centres intimate that large audiences attend Technocrat meetings (largely out of curiosity, it seems), and that small groups of ardent supporters continue the promulgation of its leader's doctrines among the receptive. At present it would seem that the longer established and numerically superior subversive elements will make it difficult for this comparative upstart to travel very far, but its presence should not be ignored nor its leaders permitted to overstep the legal mark with impunity.[12]

INTELLIGENCE
BULLETIN

ROYAL CANADIAN MOUNTED POLICE
HEADQUARTERS, OTTAWA

WEEKLY SUMMARY
MARCH 11, 1940

CONTENTS

War Series
No. 21.

EDITORIAL

Warning: Beware Communist Election Methods!

As Election Day draws near the picture of the united efforts of the Communist Party of Canada to take full advantage of the hustings and the polls to strengthen their cause by underhand and illegal methods becomes increasingly clear. Reports from Division Headquarters disclose how every political constituency throughout Canada is being examined by the Communist Party leaders for possible manipulation, if not actual representation,tationtationtation on polling day.

In those ridings where Red followers and sympathizers are numerous Communist candidates are openly running on the Communist Party ticket. In less favourable ridings every trick is being employed to defeat majorities by vote-splitting, spoiling ballots, rallying behind the more radical or disloyal nominees, and by propaganda calculated to destroy confidence in constitutional government.

A typical example of the working methods of these Red termites is contained in a report covering [⊱<deletion: 2 lines]

[⊱<deletion: 1 paragraph: 12 lines]

[⊱<deletion: 1 paragraph: 1 line]

[⊱<deletion: 1 paragraph: 2 lines][1][Page 2 is missing]

[⊱<deletion: 1 paragraph: 4 lines]

[⊱<deletion: 1 paragraph: 3 lines]

Similar meetings of Communist leaders are, of course, directing equally subversive campaigns in the other provinces—varying methods so as to take advantage of local problems—such as the conscription phantom in Quebec and poverty among fishermen in Nova Scotia (referred to in this issue). While the Communist Party may have few election victories to show for their efforts, the effect of their undermining of public confidence, fomenting suspicion and distrust of governments and destroying of national unity is far-reaching beyond calculation.[3]

COMMUNISM

COMMUNIST ELECTORATE RECEIVE INSTRUCTIONS

Definite election instructions have been issued by the Communist Party in conjunction with their recent nation-wide distribution of the "Manifesto" of Communist policy. Aggressive and illegal methods are boldly demanded of all Communist sympathizers.

To quote from these instructions:

The character of the election will determine the methods to be employed by the party in the election campaign. We must seek to employ to the maximum all legal possibilities offered by the election and the difficulties which will confront the Government during the campaign in suppressing our fight. At the same time, we cannot determine the CONTENT of our Campaign by the consideration of legal work, and must undertake to bring our agitation to the masses by illegal means...... Only the boldest and most militant election fight of the party will call forth the masses, forces of the workers and farmers, encouraging all anti-war forces to take up the fight, will create greater freedom of action for the party and the working class in the election campaign and following it.

Party Candidates, made known as COMMUNIST CANDIDATES, should be nominated in the constituency which offers the greatest advantages from the standpoint of developing the Party struggle....The campaign for the Communist candidates should be commenced by the above mentioned national election manifesto, and developed by local leaflets and other means of mass agitation. The candidate should not conduct his own work in such a way as to be arrested, the early stages of the propaganda for the candidate being conducted by illegal leaflets.

At each stage of the campaign, the district will have to determine on the basis of local circumstances, the legal activity, if possible, to be carried on by the candidate. If it appears that upon coming to the electoral [4] Officer for the nomination proceeding the candidate will be arrested, the general policy will be that the candidate should not appear and will therefore not be formally nominated. In such cases where the mass support has been developed strongly, it may be decided that the candidate should appear and even be arrested in order to further raise the level of the struggle.

In the cases where we have nominated candidates but the candidate has not qualified, because he would be arrested if he appeared for nomination, we should make the most powerful exposure of the anti-democratic character of the election during the days following nomination day and should call upon the people to mark the name of our candidate on their ballots.

In the case of Communists who have been nominated or who may be nominated because of positions as leading trade unionists as labor-progressive candidates—and every such opportunity should be taken advantage of—the campaign to be conducted by such candidates should be directed at the domestic aspects of the bourgeois policy, thus indirectly fighting the war itself. They should expose the profiteering, graft, lowered living standards, annulment of democratic rights, the poverty, suffering and ruin that the war will bring to Canada for the profit of the parasitic capitalists—UNLESS THE PEOPLE FIGHT BACK.

In all other constituencies we should use our campaign to call upon the people to write on their ballots, the word "Peace". The question will be raised again and again of whether or not there isn't some preferential choice between the candidates supporting the war. We must make clear to the people that to try to make a choice between grafters, thieves and murderers is impossible—that they should register their opposition to all of them and use their ballots to oppose the imperialist war.[5]

VICIOUS ATTACK ON CANADIAN UNITY
(QUEBEC)

A document entitled "Le Canada Francais et la Guerre", issued by the [?<deletion: 1 line] 'Stanley Ryerson', denounces Canada's and particularly Quebec's participation in the war. Every effort, it is apparent, is being made and will be made in the future to stir up dissension in that Province against the rest of Canada and Great Britain. The report declares:

"The principal problem, the only one which eliminates all the others and which the working class in Canada has to face is the following: Set an end to Canada's participation in this criminal and imperialist war. Our attitude must be a Leninist attitude: 'A revolutionary class in a reactionary war can only wish for the defeat of its own bourgeoisie.' Furthermore, declares comrade Buck:

"'While insisting on the fact that the imperialist combattants do not serve the interests of the working class and that a victory for one or the other group of imperialists means a victory for the reaction, the Communist Party raises also the question of the betrayal of the vital interests of Canada......Chamberlain's imperialist plan has not served the vital interests of the masses of the people of Canada and, during this war, one does not fight for any vital interest in Canada.'"

The report stresses that "the Canadian working class is facing new, difficult and revolutionary tasks....."Organize the united fight of the mass of the people in order to put an end to this imperialist war...." "In this fight, the role of the working class and of the masses of French-Canada, traditionally hostile to British imperialism, may be of decisive importance."

The second part of this report concerns French-Canada's attitude towards "the imperialist war", in which efforts are made to ferment distrust of the present Government. A repetition of previous propaganda is produced in other sections of this report. Under the title "Parti et Classes Dans la Guerre", Ryerson writes:[6]

"From the ideological viewpoint also, the nationalist groups carry the imprint of their origin by certain confusing tendencies which are also reactionary, mystic and fanatic; but all this is less important than the primordial fact that French-Canadian nationalism has really its justification in the present position of the people of Quebec: this nationalism expresses the inspiration of the French-Canadians for social and economic amelioration, for peace and independence from imperialism—all this, in the present situation, constitutes a revolutionary factor of the first importance."

"The only one, among all the political parties in Canada, the Communist party has taken a strong opposition attitude, irreducible to the imperialist war. It is the only organized force in the country which opposes war in placing itself on the side of the workers. It is the only party which unites the revolutionary fight against war with the nationalist, anti-imperialist fight of the people of French-Canada."

Ryerson concludes his mischievous appeal for Quebec's support of a Communist revolution with—

"French-Canada has entered this war against its wishes and full of mistrust. Its opposition to imperialism, directed by the working class and united with efforts of the Canadian workers in general, must play a deciding role in holding back the forces of imperialism, in putting a stop to our participation in the war of the profiteers. The war itself represents a paroxysm of the imperialist crisis. In exposing the masses to the most extreme suffering, to poverty, repression and to destruction; in giving arms to millions of workers; in throwing imperialism in the most dangerous, most desperate, most hazardous conflict, the bourgeoisie itself created the elements of a revolutionary crisis which may well lead to its own end."[7]

IN DEFENCE OF ARMY DESERTERS
(MONTREAL)

Reports concerning alleged desertions from the Canadian Active Service Forces are being received from Quebec Province. The most recent issue of "La Clarte Nouvelle" (French Communist publication and successor to "La Clarte" banned by the Secretary of State on October 5, 1939) contains an article defending such desertions which is calculated to fan dissension over the war issue in the Province. To quote in part:

"To go and become mutilated, crippled, killed on the other side of the Atlantic for the benefit of the shareholders of the International Nickel Co. They preferred to break the imperialist and profiteering discipline before being treated like human cattle. Let us compare the real patriotism so dear to these young deserters with the sweet hypocrisy, so sickening, of a Mackenzie King, puppet of Downing Street, who boasts openly in his speech of February 7 of the manner in which he had the Canadian people accept to fight for London. The manoeuvres of this old politician, the strongly servile servant of the rich, are called patriotism by those for whom patriotism is a low profiteering business in human lives; but those who revolt in the race to the slaughtering, who strike a blow for Canada and against the millionaires who betray us, those are patriots in the real and honest meaning of the word."[8]

[ℨ<deletion: 1 line]
[ℨ<deletion: 1 line]

[ℨ<deletion: 1 paragraph: 5 lines]
[ℨ<deletion: 1 paragraph: 3 lines]
[ℨ<deletion: 1 paragraph: 3 lines]

During a discussion between A. E. Smith [ℨ<deletion: 1 line] and members of the Regina Canadian Labour Defence League executive, the former made the statement: "Its too bad that the authorities won't take a little more concerted action against us, as we would then have something to agitate on. At the present time all we can do is keep rapping the Douglas Stewart case."

ARRESTS HAVE EFFECT

The news items in the daily press on the subject of the arrests of the Binder brothers and Saunders in Ottawa have had the effect of shaking Communist nerve. Not only some of the leaders, but many of the rank and filers, have hastily rid themselves of the federal election Manifesto. One unimportant party member at Vancouver promptly slapped his copies into the furnace as soon as he read the story in the "News Herald."[10]

ARE FISHERMEN AGAIN TO BE VICTIMIZED?
(LOCKPORT, N.S.)

As previously stated, [ℨ<deletion: 1 line] (including Pat Sullivan) are preparing fresh trouble for Lockport fishermen. This trouble has already started. The Yarmouth, Nova Scotia, "Telegram" describes the situation thus:

"Lockport, Feb. 22. With memories of the last struggle between the fish companies and executives of the Canadian Fishermen's Union still vivid in the minds of all residents of Lockport, there comes word the first conference of the Union will open here on March 4. The date was set recently in Upper Canada where it was also decided to hold it in the town which sprang into prominence because of the seven-week struggle between the two groups.

"The conference will be attended, it is reported, by national president Pat Sullivan, national secretary-treasurer J. S. Chapman, 1st vice-president D. Ferguson, and by the editor and publicity director, D. Sinclair, all of Montreal. It is expected representatives of 13 locals set up along the coast also will attend.

"The program includes the working out of a scheme to assist lobster fishermen who "at the present time are at the mercy fo the buyer", according to the announcement of the meeting.

"'Searchlight', official publication of the Union, contains an editorial blast against the two Lockport fish companies and against the Macdonald government. This has produced an unfavourable reaction among a large section of the population here, who feel they went through trouble before."[11]

SECRET

INTELLIGENCE
BULLETIN

ROYAL CANADIAN MOUNTED POLICE
HEADQUARTERS, OTTAWA

WEEKLY SUMMARY
MARCH 18, 1940

CONTENTS

War Series
No. 22.

EDITORIAL

Munitions of Lies

While Canadian Communists are courageous in their preaching of red revolution and the coming "dictatorship of the proletariat" they are cowardly when it comes to putting their dogmas into effect. The time is not ripe, they say, to turn words into bullets and manifestoes into murders, and in the meantime they can pursue the caution that is the better part of valour, while descending to every imaginable deceit and petty knavery in order to bedevil the population and their well-established ways.

Anything that smacks of decency or fair-play enrages your "honest" Communist. Any social or monetary reform fills him with despair. On the other hand, injustice, unemployment, profiteering, war are hailed with malicious glee as the culture on which his termites grow fat and kick. If there is no legitimate excuse for an industrial strike, he creates it. If employees still refuse to walk out he bullies and even kidnaps them. He infiltrates into responsible labour unions to destroy them. He fans racial and religious differences into suspicion and enmity. In short, there is no weak spot in our social structure that he won't exploit for his own nefarious ends. He even sought to turn the recent misunderstanding at St. Thomas into an anti-war strike. The "Sunday Worker", Communist daily

179

of New York, carried the following news item:

Canada to Probe 'Peace Strike' of Air Force Men

St. Thomas, Ont., March 9—Ontario authorities will begin an inquiry into the "peace walkout" of 300 men at the Royal Canadian Air Force Technical Training Center a month ago, Premier Hepburn announced today.

The Air Force men walked out of the Training Center in a spontaneous action, parading through the streets of St. Thomas in a demonstration against the war.[1]

At present full advantage is being taken of federal election activities to "educate" the voters. The latest trick is to steal voters' lists and use these for sending out the Manifesto "Withdraw Canada from the War" in envelopes stamped "Liberal Committee Rooms". Over 1000 pieces of such mail were seized between March 8-12 in the Toronto post office alone.

"The New Advance"

Acting under authority of a search warrant, Toronto city Detectives, under Detective Sergeant Mann, and assisted by a constable of this Force, searched the premises occupied by the "New Advance", situated at 21 Washington Street, for evidence in connection with the printing of the so-called "Election Manifesto" of the Communist Party of Canada. A number of documents, together with notes relating to the March edition of the "New Advance", were seized; these, after having been examined, were promptly returned to the premises from which they were removed.

This action brought forth a storm of protest from the Communist Camp. Mr. Kenneth Woodsworth, [?<deletion: 2 lines] saw fit to direct a letter of protest to the Prime Minister, the Minister of Justice and other Cabinet Ministers, in which he alleged that the "New Advance" is a publication designed to interest young people in the affairs of the nation; that it is non-partisan and non-sectarian; that its editorial board and advisory committee contain a number of outstanding youth leaders, young and old; that its circulation reaches young people in all types of organizations, churches, "Ys, students, trade unions, etc.

Whether Mr. Woodsworth acted in concert with the national executive of the Canadian Youth Congress, it is not known. It is important to note, however, that the Canadian Youth Congress came promptly to the assistance of the Communist cause—for it cannot be denied that the "New Advance" is the organ of the Young Communist League of Canada. The prompt action of Mr. Woodsworth again demonstrates the power wielded by the Communists in the Canadian Youth Congress, local youth councils and other youth organizations.[2]

COMMUNISM
Verdun Unemployed Strike for Relief Increase

Commencing on March 4, the Verdun Workers Union sponsored a strike of the Relief Workers at Verdun, P.Q., over the question of a general increase of relief allowances by 35%, 10% to be immediate. The City Council of Verdun unanimously voted in favour of the granting of the request and sent a delegation to Quebec to solicit permission to borrow in order to pay the 10% increase. Provincial authorities advised waiting until the end of March, when the agreement for relief is due for renewal between the Provincial and Federal Governments.

[><deletion: 1 line] include Jim Gauld, Bob Haddow, John Alexander and others. However, at the commencement of the strike, Party leaders requested the strikers to refrain from violence.

Napoleon St. Andre, [><deletion: 1 line] and president of the United Workers of Montreal, Cremazie Ward Section, which organization is closely affiliated with the Verdun Workers Union, is reputed to have made the following remarks in conversation with a friend:

"Our weekly meeting was cancelled last night, March 6th, due to the fact that our presence was required in Verdun, where the strikers marched on the City Hall during the evening. While this strike was not entirely organized by the party, we saw the possibility of taking full control of the situation, which was done with the help of our 150 comrades (20 from Cremazie) coming from all parts of the city. Strikes of this kind give us an excellent opportunity to create dissatisfaction in the ranks of the working class, and such a chance cannot be overlooked. A local of our association will shortly open in Verdun, and the best of results are a sure thing for us."[3]

[><deletion: 1 paragraph: 7 lines]

Present plans of the Communist Party call for a distribution of 10,000 appeals for public support, including the clergy and candidates in the forthcoming Federal Elections.

A sympathy strike of Plumbers and Steel Fitters in the employ of the City of Verdun is already effective. This was made possible through the efforts of Alex Gauld, [><deletion: 1 line] of the Local 144 of the United Association of Plumbers and Steam Fitters.

One leader of the strike, Peter Allen, president of the Verdun Workers Union, is a member of the delegation which proceeded to Quebec to confer with the Hon. T.D. Bouchard.

It is interesting to note that all the literature issued in relation to the strike was printed in the office of the Civil Liberties Union by several members of the Communist Party.

THE COMMUNIST ELECTION MANIFESTO

"The Federal election Manifesto", according to the Communist Party, "concretizes our line and tactics for the immediate period. It carries forward and elaborates our C.P. statement on the war, clearly analyzing the policies and tactics of the bourgeoisie, explains the differences in the war-camp and outlines the platform of our Party, the Party of the workers, farmers and people of Canada." Further, "The [4][✗blank]

Financing Dube

Booklets containing stamps valued at five, ten, twenty-five and fifty cents have been issued by the Communist Party of Montreal in order [5] to finance the election campaign of Evariste Dube in St. Mary's Ward. It is reported that there are 350 of these booklets in circulation, each booklet having a revenue of $6.75.

Illegal Votes for Dube

In order to impress Canadians in general by the number of votes on polling day, the chiefs of the Communist Party have arranged that all members as well as willing sympathizers of the Party of St. Mary's give the name of another member, non-resident, so that his name may be included on the list, therefore permitting him to cast a vote for the Party's candidate. Evariste Dube estimates that well over 300 names have been registered in this manner. He further states that "We must use the tactics employed by our foes, or be sunk."

Conventions Postponed

The Communist Party Leadership at Montreal state that due to the probable steps of the Government to declare the Party illegal, the various C.P. conventions will not take place this spring but will be postponed until a later date.[6]

NEWS FROM THE TORONTO FRONT

Subverting Youth Through its Congress

A Toronto and District Youth Congress is to be held on Sunday, March 17, in Carleton Street United Church at which delegates from youth organizations in Toronto and suburbs will be present. Questions to be dealt with at the congress will include Conscription, Civil Liberties, Work and Wages and Congress Organization.

The Young Communist League are attaching great importance to this congress as they intend to use it as a testing grounds for the National Youth Congress schedule for Montreal in July. Efforts will be made to condemn conscription and encourage the congress to sponsor action of youth against conscription; condemnation of the application of the War Measures Act except where military secrets are concerned; suppression of profiteering, and a demand for aid to unemployed youth.

The Young Communist League will endeavour to shelve discussion and action on the Finnish war, feeling that such an issue might isolate Communist and pro-Communist elements in the various youth groups.

Using the Unemployed

[✄deletion: 1 paragraph: 7 lines]
[✄deletion: 1 paragraph: 4 lines][7]

"Out of the Mouths of Babes"

The Ukrainian Labour Farmer Temple Association are spreading their anti-war propaganda (which challenges the Defence of Canada Regulations) through the medium of Childrens' recitations from their concert stages.

The following is a translation of such a Ukrainian recitation, entitled "When Peace Will Be":

"Capitalist reaction promises peace to the masses with the shedding of the workers' warm blood. Therefore, this is no peace but a simple lie and the murder of the masses. But the workers are glad and happy of the fact that the time is not far when a Day a great Day of Joy and Fear is approaching when the Workers are to make Peace for the world. In this way overthrowing reaction with its greedy system and false peace. The Day is approaching!"

Recitations of this nature are frequently given from the U.L.F.T.A. platforms.

Strike Unsatisfactory

The recently settled Coal Drivers', Helpers' and Truckmen's strike at Toronto has not completely satisfied the Communist Party, who were anxious to gain recognition of the Coal Handlers' Union as the sole bargaining agency with Toronto dealers. It is evident that Communist Party connections with the Union are confined mainly to foreign born workers who were unable to give the effective leadership the Communist Party desired.[8]

C.I.O. LOSES SAILORS' UNION
(Vancouver)

"The Sailors' Union of the Pacific", Vancouver, until recently a unit of the Maritime Federation of the Pacific, which was dominated by Harry Bridges and the C.I.O., is now asserting itself for affiliation with the A.F. of L.

A strange situation exists in the Vancouver and New Westminster District Trades & Labour Council in that the Inland Boatmen's Union which is the C.I.O. local, is also an affiliate. This brings locals of both the C.I.O. and the A.F. of L. under the same parent body. Expulsion of the I.B.U. could be effected by simply registering a formal protest on the Council chamber floor against dual memberships in the A.F. of L. However, the S.U.P. are reluctant to do this as they feel that the I.B.U. is losing out to their own organization and they hope eventually to absorb it. Thus they are determined not to introduce bitterness into the affair.

ORGANIZING THE MARRIED UNEMPLOYED
(Vancouver)

The Relief Project Workers' Union at Vancouver is arranging a mass meeting of all single unemployed as well as married unemployed in that city. Most of the single unemployed already belong to the ranks of the R.P.W.U. while the married unemployed have no organization of their own. It is believed that out of this mass meeting there will grow a more powerful organization, combining both forces.

It is the intention of the Organization Committee to draft a resolution for revision of the Municipal Assistance Act, and also to urge projects such as forest conservation, road surfacing and highway construction, to provide employment for both married and single individuals presently unemployed.

Included in this resolution will be an appeal for a better relief allowance for unemployed single and married men who, because of physical disability, cannot meet the rapidly rising living costs.[9][✂blank]

INSTRUCTING UKRAINIAN VOTERS

The Canadian Ukrainian Youth Federation branches throughout the Dominion are receiving directives from their Central Office of the Ukrainian Labour Farmer Temple Association regarding the stand to be taken in the forthcoming federal elections. The following immediate tasks are enumerated therein:-

(1) Circularization of a questionnaire dealing with youth problems must be made to all candidates in the locality where the branch is organized.[10]

(2) The C.U.Y.F. branches must organize open forums where nominate candidates in that locality are invited to speak, outlining their stand on the youth problems.

(3) The C.U.Y.F. must establish first voter organizations, the aim and object of which would be to encourage the youth to exercise their franchise for those candidates who are prepared to resist war and conscription. In this connection, the phrase "those candidates" will mean Communist Party candidates.[✂blank][11]

SECRET

INTELLIGENCE
BULLETIN

ROYAL CANADIAN MOUNTED POLICE
HEADQUARTERS, OTTAWA

WEEKLY SUMMARY
MARCH 26, 1940

CONTENTS

War Series
No. 23

EDITORIAL

"Clarion" Defies Law

"The Clarion" (describing itself as "Official Organ of the Communist Party of Canada Dedicated to the struggle to end the Imperialist war by united working class action in the interest of all the labouring people") was suppressed on November 21, 1939, by order of the Minister of Justice, under Section 39(a) of the Defence of Canada Regulations. It has been re-issued, under date February 24th, with the same name and editor, and carrying the explanation "Published twice per month, under conditions imposed by the King government in the Service of Reaction."

Unlike "The Canadian Tribune", (the Communist paper which posed as a legal successor to the deceased) this "Clarion" is simply a continuation of the old, bearing the issue number 1850 in chronological sequence to the issue banned, and bent on the replacement of Democracy by a Proletariat Dictatorship.

Its editorial, "The Voice of Our People", proudly boasts of being the voice of Lenin and Red Revolution. To quote in full:

    With this issue The Clarion enters a new phase of its service to the working-class movement. The phase of publication and distribution in conditions created by prohibition under Mackenzie King's vicious anti-working-class "War Measures Act". Under these conditions, equally as under the easier conditions which preceded them, The Clarion will speak out frankly and without fear or favor in defence of the interests of the working-class and the struggle for Socialism.

The situation in which the present imperialist war is being waged differs from that in which the war of 1914-18 was fought precisely in the measure that the revolutionary working-class movement is stronger and has a mighty socialist base and capitalism is weaker and unable to conceal, even superficially, the reactionary,[1] predatory, class character of the war.

While we shall continue, of course, to report upon all working-class activities it is obvious that our task now will be to comment upon news already known and give leadership to thought and action rather than to report events. In this task we shall be guided always by the brilliant teachings of Lenin on the relationship between imperialist war and social revolution. We shall strive, unremittingly, to deal with current events and working class problems and perspectives in a truly Leninist way.

The degree to which The Clarion will succeed in filling the role of "Iskra" in Canada will depend in no small measure upon efforts of those thousands of comrades who carry through the arduous and often dangerous task of distributing it and raising funds. To each of those loyal soldiers of the proletarian movement this editorial is a greeting and proud thanks. Between us we shall make our Clarion a mighty power for good in the working-class movement. A power that will outstrip any measures of repression that the capitalist class and its hired police may devise.

We are living in an explosive phase of "the epoch of wars, colonial revolts and proletarian revolutions". In guiding the workers of Canada through the struggles that this phase will bring The Clarion, as the voice of the Communist Party, will play a decisive part.

Labor's Answer

While "The Clarion" presumes to speak for the working man in "truly Leninist way", what does the Canadian Worker say? Another editorial appearing about the same date in "The Canadian Labor Press" ("A union paper published by union men in a union shop in Montreal") contains the following:[2]

Let us not fool ourselves that Communism in Canada is dead because of certain laws; rather has it been driven more underground but nevertheless more active than ever before and potentially more dangerous. It will come to you now in many guises and with the most friendly and unsuspicious approaches, so that one must ever be on the alert.....

We are all soldiers of Canada for the duration of the war and the first quality of a soldier is his unquestioning belief and loyalty to the Cause. Co-ordination and co-operation are vital; yet the Communists in Canada the enemy at home preach the opposite. They tell us we should overthrow this and we should overthrow that, we should have a revolution, in fact we should do everything but be peaceful, co-operative and understanding. Doesn't their very attitude suggest as to where their interests lie?

Some of the conditions that unions have to accept that are tainted with communism and become affiliated with the Red International of Labor Unions are as follows:-

1. Endorsement of the principle of revolutionary class struggle.
2. Application of these principles in its daily struggle with capitalism and the bourgeois state.
3. Recognition of the overthrow of capitalism through the social revolution and the establishment mentmentmentmentof the dictatorship of proletariat for the transition period.
4. Recognition and submission to the international proletarian discipline.[3]
5. Recognition and application of the decisions of the constituent congress of the Red International of Labor Unions.
6. United action with all the revolutionary organizations and the Communist Party of the country in all defensive and offensive activities against the bourgeoisie.

A close study of the foregoing should be enough to make a life long bitter enemy out of every red blooded Canadian Worker to anything that savors of Communism. If everyone realized the colossal gall of these unwanted disturbers in our midst, the Canadian Labor Press believes short shift would soon be made of this menace.[4]

GENERAL

ATTEMPTED SABOTAGE OF OIL CARGO

On January 16, 1940, three days after the S. S. "British Officer" had left Halifax in convoy, a fire broke out in the Chief Steward's cabin. The fire started with a whitish red flame of great intensity, but was brought under control in 15 minutes with the aid of a fire extinguisher. Pieces of what was obviously an incendiary bomb were found in the cabin afterwards. The case is being investigated by the Royal Canadian Mounted Police and the Federal Bureau of Investigation at Washington and the authorities in England.

The S. S. "British Officer", a British tanker, loaded a cargo of oil at Baton Rouge, Louisiana and cleared for London, England, on December

14, 1939. The same day she rammed a barge and grounded 15 miles South of Baton Rouge, resulting in considerable damage to the ship. The following day she was floated to Baton Rouge.

On December 18, the Master of the ship committed suicide by shooting himself at Baton Rouge and the Chief Officer assumed command. The reason for the Master's suicide is not apparent.

On December 19, the ship proceeded from Baton Rouge to New Orleans for repairs, which were effected in the Todd-Johnson Dry Dock, at Algiers, Louisiana, and returned to Baton Rouge to reload.

On December 27, the "British Officer" cleared Baton Rouge for London via Halifax. She arrived at Halifax on January 6, 1940, awaited convoy until January 14, and sailed the latter date for London.

Investigation shows that a fire pencil was placed aboard the ship before she arrived in Canadian waters, most likely at Baton Rouge.[5]

SERIOUS SPLIT IN DOUKHOBOUR RANKS
(British Columbia)

Less than a year after the demise of the Doukhobour leader, Peter P. Veregin, a Pretender has arisen to lay claim to the vacant "throne". Intimidation, forgery, bribery and corruption are preying upon ignorance and superstition to split the peace-loving Douks into two hostile camps. [6][✂blank][Page 7 is missing.]

COMMUNISM

"L'ECLAIREURE" RAVES AGAINST CONSCRIPTION
(Montreal)

The national executive of the Young Communist League of Canada have printed and are distributing a special issue of their official organ "L'Eclaireure". This special edition was published with a view to instructing French-Canadian youth in the Communist Party attitude towards the Federal elections.

In its entirety, it is an appeal to the youth of this country to take a firm stand against conscription. A leading article appearing on the front page and written by Evariste Dube, [✂deletion: 2 lines] Federal elections riding reads, in part, as follows:

> The youth of 1914 has sacrificed its life to enrich a gang of war profiteers. Our youth of 1940 must take advantage of this election campaign to show to the Government of warmongers that it does not want to participate in any manner at this slaughter, that it wants this war to stop and that our brothers who are already on the other side, be brought back.
>
> Youth of Ste. Marie Country, be the example of the French-Canadian youth in this election. Prove to the imperialist class that the French-Canadians are not ready to go and save the skin of these individuals and that if the imperialists want to fight, they can take the

arms and do so. As far as we are concerned, we have nothing to win in this imperialist war, war brings about misery, suffering and privations. Youth, prove that you are ready to united and claim the best conditions of life and work.

Embodied in an article headed "The Young Communist League Manifesto", a passage under sub-title "The Truth of the War" concludes as follows:[8]

The Canadian youth wishes to build up Canada and not to feed the foreign soil with its blood. It wants security and happiness, not monuments and cenotaphs. The young ones do not want to return to the country in onerous conditions such as cripples at the mercy of society and facing an unemployed life of hunger and misery.

The youth of the other countries are not the enemies of the Canadian youth. We have only one common enemy: the imperialist war mongers. Our enemy is in Canada, not in Europe. It is the multi-millionaire class and it is against this class that the Canadian youth must fight ardently.

The paragraph concluding the Manifesto reads:

Strengthen your fight against the conscription, for the civil liberties, against the profiteering, against the imperialist war. Ask for your superiors that they act in your interests and not in those of the war mongers. Build up your ranks, your committees and your management.

[☞<deletion: 1 line]

[☞<deletion: 1 paragraph: 9 lines][9]

THEY DOMINATE THE YOUTH CONGRESS
(Toronto)

A leaflet has made its appearance in Toronto concerning the forthcoming Youth Congress which will be held in July of this year. Distributed by the Young Communist League, the pamphlet outlines the purpose of the Youth Movement and urges the support of the various Youth groups. Paragraph seven headed "Does any Political Group Dominate the Congress or Councils?" is of particular interest:

No. The Congress and the National Continuations Committee are planned so as to be thoroughly representative of all types. Any bona fide organization has the right to two delegates and two votes and no more the Continuation Committee reflects this. A political group such as the Young Communist League which sends delegates from many districts is easily balanced by the Church and "Y" groups from all over the Dominion. Thus no single group can force its policy on the whole congress or on a local council.

The fact that the Y.C.L. is only allowed two delegates and two votes does not offer any hindrance to the Y.C.L. having as many delegates and votes as it can put in the field at the Congress, and being elected to the Congress as the representatives of other organizations or Youth groups. The contention that "no single group can force its policy on the whole congress or on a local council" is therefore absolutely incorrect, as past experience in the conduct of the Congress has proved.

COAL MINERS STRIKE

Coal miners at Mountain Park, Alberta struck on March 19. There are 375 men involved. Unpopularity of the pit boss is reported as the cause of the strike. Trouble may ensue when the hotel commences charging the miners cash for meals and beds.[10]

"MID-WEST CLARION" REAPPEARS
(Winnipeg)

With the arrest of John Weir, editor, [⸱<deletion: 2 lines] the "Mid-West Clarion" did not publish for the week ending March 9. However, the issue for Saturday March 16 embodies the previous week's issue and comes out as Volume 5, numbers 202 and 203. In the main the paper appeals to its former readers and "Democratic Canadians" to come to its aid.

Of particular interest is an item which appears on the first page regarding the arrested "Clarion" employees. (A reference is made to the seizure of the mailing list of the Russian language paper, "Kanadsky Gudok". This is a deliberate fabrication and it has been learned from a confidential source that some trepidation is being felt amongst those responsible for the publication thereof.)

[⸱<deletion: 1 paragraph: 3 lines]

JOINING DEFENCE LEAGUE

The Central Bureau of the Communist Party of Canada has issued instructions that each Party unit select one member to join a Canadian Labor Defence League branch. This would effectively link up the Party and the C.L.D.L. and at the same time prevent a wholesale influx of Party members into the said League. Great care is being taken to avoid giving the C.L.D.L. branches a "party face".[11]

ENEMY ALIENS

REGISTRATIONS, INTERNMENTS, RELEASES

Registrations:

        Total registrations to March 20, 1940 16,092

        Given exemption certificates 3,555

        Exeats granted to date 199

Internments:

        Total interned or detained since Sept. 4 405

        Released at once 3

        Released after appeal 93

        At present interned or detained 309

(The last figure includes one woman interned at Kingston Penitentiary and two men serving two years' sentences in Saskatchewan Penitentiary for escape from Kananaskis.)[12]

INTELLIGENCE
BULLETIN

ROYAL CANADIAN MOUNTED POLICE
HEADQUARTERS, OTTAWA

WEEKLY SUMMARY
APRIL 1, 1940

CONTENTS

War Series
No. 24.

EDITORIAL
KNOW THE FACTS!

"Is there any real danger from Communism?" asks the average Canadian. "Are you Police not just seeing red? Look at the Communist vote it couldn't elect one federal member! This isn't Russia!"

Such ignorance is bliss to the Communist Party of Canada. It is upon this very trait of the human mind that it depends for eventual victory. It is this ignorance that swallows the most blatant propaganda and lures it into actually protecting its destroyers.

It is true, the official membership of the Party in Canada is numerically small probably as small as the Bolshevist Party in Russia preceding the Revolution. Its defenders and sympathizers are many. Its organization is as strong (and as invisible) as a salmon net spread under water. Its strategy is dictated by Moscow's Political Bureau. Everything it knows, plans and does is by virtue of Ogpu Stalin's Secret Service, the most unscrupulous bunch of crooks the world has ever known.

Evidence of this is no longer confined to the Secret Police and their victims. Former USSR agents, press correspondents and others who know the true story of post-revolutionary Russia have published it to the world in all its horror. For the protection of Democracy, freedom and his own future welfare everyone should read it.

The most significant volume available to Canadians is "In Stalin's Secret Service" by W.G. Krivitsky, who, for fourteen years served in the Soviet Military Intelligence Department. Based upon first-hand knowledge by the one leading survivor of the Red Army purge, it makes clear as nothing else has the inside workings of the Soviet government. It is a story of electrifying import at a time when Russia, allied with Hitler's Germany, holds the key to the balance of power in Europe.[1]

Another "eye-opener" is "Assignment in Utopia" by Eugene Lyons. Here the former United Press correspondent in Moscow tells the dramatic story of his six years among the Soviets six years which saw the shattering of all his ideals in the face of the grim realities which surrounded him.

Scarcely a month passes without one or more magazines containing the experiences of refugees from Russian invaded areas or of those in America who have been victimized by the Red Octopus. And there are the findings of the Dies Committee at Washington as summarized recently in "Liberty". In fact there is so much evidence today on Russian Communism (or Stalinism) that there is no longer excuse for ignorance toward this homicidal mania, or for anyone asking "Is there any real danger?"[2]

LABOUR STRIKES

PAT SULLIVAN INSTIGATING SEAMEN'S STRIKE
(Montreal)

A dispute between the Canadian Seamen's Union and the Great Lakes shipping companies has arisen with the approach of the expiration of the present work agreement on March 31, 1940. John A. (Pat) Sullivan, [⪦deletion: 1 line] worker amongst labour unions, is busily engaged in formulating demands and a plan of action in event of the shipping companies refusing to accept the proposals of the C.S.U.

The Union will demand an increase of $15.00 per month for every rating as well as a change in the length of watches. A concerted effort will be made by the Union to gain control of hiring and firing of seamen. Should these demands be not entirely accepted by the shipping companies between now and April 15, Sullivan has instructed the seamen to prepare for strike duty.

The port of Montreal is not to be involved beyond the point of picketing both railroad depots to prevent men from being shipped to Western ports.

Well-known left-wing organizers of the C.S.U. are being posted amongst union locals of the various ports to be effected by the strike should it be called.

Sullivan has expressed his intention to show the companies that he means business and that he is prepared to "take the bull by the horns" and teach these companies that they cannot "play" with Pat Sullivan.

Conferences between officials of both sides of this dispute are still being conducted.[3]

STEEL WORKERS OF SYDNEY EXPECT STRIKE
(Sydney)

The 3,500 workers of Dominion Steel and Coal Corporation's Sydney plant are on the verge of striking for better wages and hours. For a month and a half Communist agitators have been urging the union to tie up the plant. A strike was called for March 21, but at the eleventh hour it was postponed pending the results from a board of conciliation and investigation set up under the requirements of the Industrial Disputes Investigation Act. This move was not initiated by the union.

The Halifax "Chronicle" of March 20 reports:

In reply to a telegram sent today (by the Union) saying that that body was not in favour of any procedure that might "cause a prolongation of the miserable wage condition" of steelworkers, the deputy minister of Labour answered that his department was ready to "immediately establish a board at once" and to "ask the board to act immediately to secure a settlement of all matters in dispute."

While it was no part of the plans of the Steelworkers' Union to have such a board set up they have accepted it with the understanding that the strike would not be called off but would be postponed pending the findings of the board members.

If negotiations fail and the strike occurs there is a possibility that 8,000 men in the coal mines will come out in sympathy, as they are under the same management as the steel workers.[4][Pages 5, 6, and 7 are missing.]

SABOTAGE

ATTEMPT TO DESTROY COTTON CARGO
(Halifax)

On January 25, 1940, the S.S. "Comedian" of the Harrison Line, Liverpool, England, loaded baled cotton at Mobile, Ala. On January 30 she proceeded to New Orleans, La., where she loaded more cotton and other cargo. On February 3 she sailed from New Orleans for Halifax to join a convoy.

Outside Halifax the "Comedian" was in collision with another vessel, and upon arriving at dock in Halifax on February 11, it was necessary to discharge her cargo of cotton.

A total of 11,085 bales of cotton were discharged into Shed 3 National Harbours Board, Halifax, between February 11 and 18. The bales were stored 7 tiers high.

On February 20, fire broke out in this cotton. A total of 5 bales caught fire; 4 of the bales ceased burning completely after the local firemen had extinguished the flames, but the fifth bale continued to smoulder and was thrown into the water of the harbour. The bales which caught fire were on the second tier of the pile, hence could not have been reached by fire from the outside.

After 24 hours' immersion the fifth bale was recovered, whereupon it burst into flames. Examination showed that the flames originated in its interior, and samples of the cotton at this point were submitted to the analyst. His examination revealed that the cotton has been saturated with oil—a type of petroleum hydro carbon, probably fuel oil. The presence of this oil undoubtedly led to spontaneous ignition of the cotton.

A thorough investigation was made by us at Halifax, as a result of which we are satisfied that the cotton was not tampered with subsequent to being unloaded from the "Comedian". In addition, we secured samples of the oils carried aboard the "Comedian" for lubrication purposes (this vessel is a coal burner) and found that they were dissimilar to the sample of oil extracted from the bale in question. This apparently eliminates any suggestion that the oil could have been placed in the cotton by a member of the crew of the ship— an unlikely act as, had the "Comedian" not been in collision, the fire would have broken out in the hold whilst the vessel was in mid-Atlantic and probably destroyed the ship.

According to the Master of the "Comedian", before being placed aboard at Mobile and New Orleans, the cotton was rebaled under police guard in special baling machines, which compress it so tightly that it is impossible to place a foreign substance in the interior of a bale, without boring a hole therein. For the reasons quoted above, it would appear that the oil was probably placed in the bale during the rebaling process at Mobile and New Orleans.[8]

COMMUNISM
COMMUNISTS POLL OVER 30,000 VOTES

The following figures to date were polled by C.P. candidates throughout the country in the recent Federal Election. It is interesting to note that
several of the "big guns" of the Communist Party, i.e., Tim Buck and
Stewart Smith, running in Hamilton East and Toronto-Spadina respectively, did not put in an appearance during the election campaign.

Montreal, St. Mary:	Evariste Dube		656
Cochrane, Ontario:	G.W. Teaple	[⁊<deletion: 1 line]	
	[⁊<deletion: 1 line]		3228
Hamilton East:	Tim Buck		695
Temiskaming, Que:	Thomas Church		3524
Toronto Broadview:	George Grube	[⁊<deletion: 1 line]	
	[⁊<deletion: 1 line]		2735
Toronto Spadina:	Stewart Smith		2720
Toronto Trinity:	Douglas Stewart		1052
Winnipeg North:	Leslie Morris		5260
MacKenzie, Sask:	Walter Wiggins		478
Prince Albert, Sask:	A.C. Campbell		178
Regina:	Jack Guest		603
Wood Mountain, Sask:		N.L. Buchanan [⁊<deletion: 1 line]	
	[⁊<deletion: 1 line]		4254
Yorkton, Sask:	T.G. McManus		384
Bow River, Alta:	Lawrence Anderson		867
Vegreville, Alta:	William Halina		2725
Vancouver East:	Fergus McKean		1286
	Total vote cast		30,645

[9]

TROUBLES IN MONTREAL DISTRICT BUREAU
Retort Discourteous

A wave of protest has been directed by the rank and file Communist
Party members against their Montreal District Bureau as a result of the
arrest of four comrades on the occasion of a raid conducted by the
Montreal City Police on the St. Catherine's committee rooms. The Party
heads are criticized for their lack of foresight which jeopardized the
freedom of the election campaign workers.

To this the District Bureau retorts:

An accusation of that sort cannot be made against anyone, and those
who fail to comply with the rules of the Party will be called before
a fraction of the Party and will be temporarily expelled from the
Party.

Looking for Funds

Failing to replenish the coffers of the Communist Party of Canada through more open and legitimate means, the Montreal District Bureau has instructed its leaders to hold their parties, socials, etc., in private houses rather than in public halls. This will eliminate rental fees and give greater opportunity of raising money through card games, bingo and the sale of beer at 30 cents per pint, which are not permitted in public halls.

CANADA'S C.I.O. ENDORSED BY LEWIS
(Windsor)

The regional director of the Committee of Industrial Organization at Windsor, Ont., announced at a regular meeting of the United Auto Workers' Local that the C.I.O. in Canada now has the "go sign" from John L. Lewis in connection with the merger of the C.I.O. and the All Canadian Congress of Labour (already reported in this bulletin). He added that five cents out of the per capita tax previously sent to Washington will now remain in Canada.[10]

The benefit which Local organizers hope to derive from this new arrangement is that under the colours of the A.C.C.L. they would be given "representation in Ottawa to do some lobbying the same as John L. Lewis has done in Washington."[blank][11]

INTELLIGENCE
BULLETIN

ROYAL CANADIAN MOUNTED POLICE
HEADQUARTERS, OTTAWA

WEEKLY SUMMARY
APRIL 8, 1940

CONTENTS

EDITORIAL

U.S. 84% with US

A poll of the United States Institute of Public Opinion (the "Gallup Poll") indicates an "overwhelming majority of Americans on the side of the Allies" and only 1 per cent favourable to Germany. This tide of favourable sentiment is steadily, inexorably rising despite all the desperate counter floods of Nazi-Comintern propaganda. However much the President attempts to maintain an official neutrality he himself finds irksome, some of his highest representatives risk their political heads by telling the truth. Mr. Cromwell, U.S. Minister to Ottawa, received only a mild rebuke for declaring that a victory for the Allies was necessary to the welfare of his country. The public press, movies and radio across the border are overwhelmingly sympathetic. A Canadian visitor to the United States is welcomed as during the last war, as though he were a hero.

The "New York Times", (always one of our staunchest supporters), recently printed a letter from Lawrence Hunt that exposed the hypocrisy of American "neutrality" in all its phases and the necessity and inevitability of open participation in the defence of our mutual ideals.

This letter, now reprinted in pamphlet form under the title "Pontius Pilate Still Lives", begins by riddling with ridicule and facts the commonest lies and arguments aimed to keep America out of the war, then turns to considering "some of the present pitfalls that constantly threaten our thinking":

"They're all alike." Who says so? Such strange bedfellows as Molotoff, the Soviet Minister of Foreign Affairs, Hugh Johnson and our milksop intellectuals who only yesterday were screaming at Chamberlain and Daladier for their "cowardly surrender" at Munich and their "betrayal" of Republican Spain. And to give point to their propaganda, they tar us with their brushes, Molotoff referring to our treatment of the Cubans and Johnson to the American Indians.

We can ignore the Communist bunch for the moment— they are part of the price we pay for the freedom we cherish. But the propaganda is vicious to the extent it helps us to fool ourselves. We know [1] better. Magna Carta, habeas corpus, the common law, William Shakespeare, the King James Bible, John Bunyan, Voltaire, Lafayette, the Rights of Man, Wordsworth and Bobby Burns—they are part of our heritage. They are not Prussian or Nazi or Communist.

The conquest of Austria, the ruins of Czecho-Slovakia, the massacre of the Poles, the attack on Finland, the torture of concentration camps, the bestial crimes against race and religion, purges, "blood baths", "Mein Kampf" and the Communist Manifesto—they are not English or French or American. No—we are not "all alike". We know all about that. But how long shall we let these propagandists help us delude ourselves?

Self-Delusion

Perhaps the loveliest self-delusion we are enjoying at the moment is the picture of America acting as a sweet holier-than-thou peacemaker when the war ends. We will be happy, comfortable and "disinterested". Our former associates will have gone through the hell of a war they desperately tried to avoid; they will be suffering, poor and tired out. Therefore we can do some more preaching, tell them what sort of peace they should make (not too harsh on the Germans, because they are "a proud race"), and how they must behave if they are to be like us.

Wait a minute. Suppose the Nazi-Communists win? Well, brothers and sisters, if that happens, we'll have to do an awful lot more than preach—far more than if we frankly and actively aided England and France now. It might be that we are counting a little too comfortably on the Maginot Line and the British Fleet. And, despite the peace-at-any-price propagandists, we do count on them.

If the Allies win without our aid, by what right will we have a voice

in the peace terms? What will have been America's contribution?
A few cheers, lots of "moral support" and goods for cash down.
Again, I say, don't let the propagandists fool us. Let's not fool our-
selves. We should at least be too adult for that.

The latest trick of the Pontius Pilate propagandists is to warn us
against propaganda. Apparently they assume that Americans are a
simple, childlike, almost moronic people who need nurses and
guards to keep them out of mischief. It is insidious stuff, which taken
in too large doses, is likely to cause moral impotence and intellectual sterility.[2]

Mr. Lawrence closes with the following admonishment and prophecy:

Seeking Belief

We are asked to shut our eyes to the most blazing truths, to avert
our gaze from the plain facts of our contemporary life, to stuff our
ears and to harden our hearts so that somehow, in some way, we can
escape from the tough realities of this world and, as a nation, evade
the tasks which nature, our moral traditions and the uncompromising forces of destiny have set for us to do.

This propaganda against propaganda makes many an average citizen throw up his hands and say, "What can I believe?" Well—you
can believe in yourself, your own common sense, your own decent
instincts, your own values and traditions which you cherish enough
to fight for. These peace-at-any price people who, consciously or
unconsciously, are giving daily aid and comfort to Comrades Hitler and Stalin will do some harm and create more confusion before
the courageous common sense of America says, "Enough—you're
a fake." They won't succeed, because we'll stop deceiving ourselves when the hour of decision is at hand.

The fashion of our present-day propagandists is to sneer at Uncle
Sam for acting in 1917 the role of the Good Samaritan. According
to these people, the Good Samaritan was a fool and a "sucker". He
actually inconvenienced himself in doing his share as a member of
the human family. There were no profits in what he did. But the
Levite was the "wise guy". He "minded his own business" and went
his own way. Didn't lose a nickel.

Perhaps Uncle Sam should do the same. I don't think he will. He
isn't that sort of a fellow. In due course he'll rub his eyes, stand up,
take off his coat, and do a man's job in a hard but worth-while.

Obviously the American people know what this war is about and what
is at stake. That is all we need to know.[3]

COMMUNISM
THE STRIKE MOVEMENT STRIKES AT DEMOCRACY
(Toronto)

"The strike movement acquires a great new significance. The war and the war regime gives to every strike at its inception in greater or less degree the character of a struggle against the war."

With this significant foreword the Central Political Bureau of the Communist Party of Canada begins its recent directives to the district bureaus of the Party throughout the Dominion. The district leaders are instructed to examine with utmost care the prospective developments of the strike struggles and to make the most energetic efforts to organize the fight of the workers for higher wages on the widest possible scale.

Another form of mass struggle to which the district leaders are instructed to give serious attention is the "mass demonstration". It is pointed out in the directives that due to the war "conditions have changed and the task of organizing militant fighting demonstrations for the demands of the people and against the suppression of democratic rights concerns us with special urgency".

Preparatory work for mass action is to be done through the medium of hundreds of small propaganda meetings and the distribution of leaflets to convince the masses of the position of the Communist Party, thus avoiding the problem of leading the mass action against the war oppression before the masses are ready, and so failing to seize the many favourable opportunities for the development of mass action. These particulars differ according to exact local situations:[4]

The Political Bureau feels, however, that the issue of the suppression of democratic rights is the one on which the masses particularly desire to take action.

Parades, complete with banners, considered the most effective form of mass demonstration, are to be organized wherever possible, and every opportunity to organize demonstrations on a united front basis with the initiative in the hands of some non-party organization (trade unions, women's groups, youth organizations, etc.) is to be fully utilized.

OSHAWA IRON STRIKE THREATENS TO SPREAD
(Oshawa)

Not the least significant of the several strikes now in progress or in preparation is that at the Ontario Malleable Iron Works, Oshawa, Ont. Although only approximately 175 men are involved there is a strong possibility that several other locals of the Steel Workers' Organizing Committee, of C.I.O. affiliation, may vote in favour of walkouts either on the basis of the demands of the Malleable Iron Workers for increased pay, holidays with pay and a closed shop, or in direct sympathy with the original strikers. A strong vote has already been taken by the employees of Fittings Limited of Oshawa and a walkout agreed upon.

Although the General Motors Corporation local of the United Auto Workers of America at Windsor, Ont. are closely watching developments of this strike and have promised the financial support of 2000 G.M.C. workers who have voluntarily agreed to pay $1.00 each toward the strikers' relief fund, at this moment it seems improbable that they will support it by a walkout, as they are apparently making good money at their plant and are about to commence work on war contracts.

The Malleable Iron strike was engineered by three well-know [⅜<deletion: 1 line] They are Richard Steele, Harry Hamburg and Jack Douglas.[5]

CANADIAN SEAMEN'S UNION MAY STRIKE
BEFORE APRIL 16

At a meeting of the Canadian Seamen's Union held in Toronto recently, J.A. (Pat) Sullivan, President of the C.S.U. and a prominent member of the Communist Party of Canada at Montreal, reported that negotiations are under way between the Union and the shipping companies for recognition of several major points—wages, overtime pay, etc.

It has previously been reported that the majority of these demands were too stringent and the shipping companies would not accept all the demands advanced. At this meeting Sullivan, however, stated that the shipping companies had agreed to most of the demands, but that until all points had been agreed upon the seamen would not move. He asserted that the Union is stronger today than it has ever been before, and that the seamen would probably have an opportunity to prove their strength before April 16. The Union Executive felt that the demands of the men were just and if the men would stand behind them they would get what they wanted, including recognition of the Union.

The Union has the lake shipping tied up at all ports as far as Montreal, Sullivan reported, and they have been promised the support of the Fishermen's Union in Nova Scotia. Members of the C.S.U. must stand by to see that the demands were met by the shipping companies before April 16, and if they were not granted it might be necessary to strike.

From the general trend of Sullivan's speech and the discussion amongst the men after the meeting was over, it appears evident that the strike, if called, will tie up the traffic on the lakes prior to the opening of navigation.

123 SOLDIERS VOTE COMMUNIST

As a result of the soldiers' vote only 123 ballots were added to the C.P. of C's total return of 30,000 odd, and in no way affected the political situation. Tim Buck (Hamilton East) polled 7 soldier votes, A.C. Campbell (Prince Albert) 3, Dube (Montreal) 10.[6][Page 7 is missing.]

COMMUNIST SUCCESS AT YOUTH CONGRESS
(Toronto)

The Young Communist League is greatly pleased with the result of the Toronto Youth Congress held on March 16, 1940. Every proposal initiated by the Y.C.L. delegation headed by Sam Walsh, and a steering committee of three was adopted by the Congress. It had been agreed beforehand that only two members of the delegation were to speak during congress discussions in order to avoid the appearance of Y.C.L. domination.

The Co-operative Commonwealth Youth Movement met with strong opposition from the Communist delegation when they introduced a proposal that the Toronto Youth Council should affiliate with their "No Conscription League", the Young Communists contending that the affiliation should be reversed so that the "No Conscription League" would be subsidiary to the Youth Council. This latter stand was adopted by the Congress.

The Congress set May 24 as an "Anti-Conscription Pledge Day", on which day it will endeavour to obtain pledges of opposition to conscription from leaders of political, religious and other such groups. The Y.C.L. is particularly enthused at the prospect of numerous large anti-conscription youth rallies to be held on May 24 in Toronto and vicinity.

POLICE TOO POLITE!
(Toronto)

Following the distribution of the Communist Party Election Manifesto in Toronto members of the Communist Party praised the politeness and correct conduct of the members of this Force in conducting searches. Such praise gave some concern to the leaders of the Party, who, fearing favourable reaction toward the R.C.M.P., issued instructions that Party members were to be on their guard against this form of guile.[8]

HOW TO ACT WHEN OUTLAWED

Information has been received to the effect that the Communist Party has recently issued to its branches another directive outlining their activities in the near future. In the main these instructions are similar to those that have been issued throughout the country. The opinion, it appears, is universal amongst the membership and particularly the leadership, that the Communist Party will shortly be "outlawed". In this connection we quote from the directive as follows:

The branches must discuss a plan of how they can work, if the Communist Party is outlawed, and all connection with the leadership is severed. The party may be outlawed within a very short time, and our leadership will have to stay under cover. The branches must be kept together, and devise ways and means of distributing anti-war leaflets and papers. The branches may have to write and print the articles, without any lead from our leadership, therefore we must put our literature and books away in a safe place, so we can get at it from time to time and copy articles written by Lenin and Stalin on the war. The branches may be unable to print more than one leaflet per month, but they must not get discouraged, and remember it is the steady drip of water that eats the rock away. It will be the constant work of our party that will finally destroy the rock of Capitalism and bring about the revolution.

If any of the members are arrested, they must not admit in the Court that they are Communist Party members. If the police have proof, that they were members at one time, the accused can say that they have dropped out some time ago. Never say anything detrimental to the Communist Party on the stand, but deny that you are doing any Communist Party work, or have any Communist Party connections.[9][Page 10 is missing.]

UKRAINIAN LABOUR FARMER TEMPLE ASSOCIATION

The U.L.F.T.A. is an organization of revolutionary Ukrainians politically subordinate to and controlled by the Communist Party of Canada. According to boasts of Communist leaders, the Ukrainian section is the largest, wealthiest and best organized subsidiary of the Communist Party of Canada; representing from 15 to 20% of the race, which dominates the majority. With headquarters at Winnipeg and 300 branches scattered throughout Canada, the U.L.F.T.A. possesses $500,000 worth of property in Winnipeg, a temple hall in Toronto worth over $100,000 and about 200 halls of lesser value. The combined assets of the organization run into several millions.

Besides its own integral organization, the U.L.F.T.A. subsidizes several powerful sections which are affiliated with it: "Workers' Aid Association", a Women's Section, a chain of "Workers' Co-operative Stores", "Ukrainian Youth Federation" and the "Society For the Liberation of Bessarabia and Bukovina", until recently called "Society for the Liberation of Western Ukraine".

Three newspapers are published by the U.L.F.T.A. for propaganda purposes; a daily, "Narodna Gazetta" (People's Gazette), with a circulation of 15,000; a weekly, "Farmerske Zytia" (Farmers Life), with a circulation of 8,000, and a monthly, "Boyova Molod" (Militant Youth), all published in Winnipeg.

Cancellation of the Temple's license on account of subversive activities has been recommended to the City Police Commission of Toronto by the Chief Constable.

GROWTH OF CANADIAN LABOUR DEFENCE LEAGUE
(C.L.D.L.)

Increased activity on the part of the Canadian Labour Defence League throughout the Dominion has been announced from Toronto. At a meeting held there recently members were instructed to communicate with members of Parliament and the Minister of Justice regarding sections 62 and 39A of the Defence of Canada Regulations. Speaking to this gathering F. Watts, [⊱deletion: 2 lines] stated that he was printing a leaflet which would be ready within a few days. He requested all branches to endeavour to get bondsmen to go bail for people who are expected to be arrested. He mentioned that up to the present time their task in this connection has been very difficult. 175 branches of the C.L.D.L. are already in Canada and more are being formed since the National President, A.E. Smith, went on tour.[11]

INTELLIGENCE
BULLETIN

ROYAL CANADIAN MOUNTED POLICE
HEADQUARTERS, OTTAWA

WEEKLY SUMMARY
APRIL 15, 1940

CONTENTS

War Series
No. 26.

EDITORIAL

The "New Significance" of Strikes

"The strike movement acquires a great new significance", asserts the Central Political Bureau of the Communist Party of Canada. Better wages and working conditions—the old grounds for agitation—are now seen only as a "legitimate" excuse for enlisting mass demonstrations calculated to retard our war efforts, stir up general unrest and destroy confidence in the democratic system of government.

An "honest" strike is both a legal and a popular weapon in the eyes of the public and therefore provides a magnificent "front" for dishonest ends.

Does the public know that there has been a marked increase of strikes since the second month of the war (as compared with the same 1938-39 period) and that many of these have been traced directly or indirectly to Communist instigation? This "many" includes, for instance, the Estevan Coal Strike, the Lockeport Fishermen's Strike, General Steel Wares

(Toronto) Strike, Verdun Unemployed Strike, and Malleable Iron Works (Oshawa) Strike; while at present Communist agitators have brought the workers of Dominion Steel and Coal (Sydney) of Algoma Steel and of the Great Lakes Shipping Companies to the verge of striking.

Last November we reported that the Communist Party were making every effort to increase their strength in trade unions in order to further industrial strikes, and quoted [≫deletion: 2 lines] as saying "We as Communists understand that to tie up industry at the present time is the best way for the workers to get their demands. The war machine needs what we produce."

While the majority of workers only want "their demands" it becomes increasingly obvious that the Communist leaders want far more than this: refusal of demands, strikes and eventually open revolution.

This is the "new significance".[1]

COMMUNISM

EXPELLING COMMUNISTS FROM LABOUR RANKS
(Vancouver, Montreal and Toronto)

The Vancouver and New Westminster District Trades and Labour Council have decided by a vote of 29 locals to 19 in favour of expulsion of Communists from its ranks. This action, taken on instructions received from the American Federation of Labour headquarters following the annual conference of the latter organization, caused perhaps the stormiest meeting in the history of the Council.

The total count on this issue in Vancouver was 2861 in favour and 1628 against, but it should not be assumed that the latter number are all supporters of the Communist cult. There are those who feel that it is better to let them "blow off their steam" and quietly lobby against them while preserving the traditions of British fair-play, and others who look upon the Council's meetings as hilarious entertainment which would be very flat without the Communists.

Identification of the Communists is left in the hands of the President, E. A. Jameison [≫deletion: 2 lines] are gleefully looking forward to examination of the "proofs" to be tendered against all faction leaders, hoping for loud publicity for the Party through the press reports and articles on their "discrimination and persecution".

Concurrent with the Vancouver and New Westminster District expulsion a similar decision was made by the Montreal Trades and Labour Council, where a special committee was selected to investigate whether any delegates were Communists. Should any be found they will be asked to withdraw from the Council.

[≫deletion: 1 paragraph: 3 lines][2]

[≫deletion: 1 paragraph: 12 lines]

In the same vein the Toronto District Trades and Labour Council recently decided by a vote of 76 locals to 47 that all C.I.O. locals within the Council be expelled. This move affects approximately 35 delegates representing about 5,000 members and includes all ladies' auxiliaries.

STRONG-ARM SQUADS TO BACK STRIKERS
(Montreal)

Indicating that the Canadian Seamen's Union are not expecting success in their negotiations with the Great Lakes Shipping Companies for better working conditions, before a strike is called, (as reported in last week's Bulletin) it has been learned that the Union headquarters in Montreal are preparing to send truckloads of men, comprising the so-called "strong-arm" squad, from Montreal to Prescott, Ont. on the morning of April 13. Another truckload setting out from Toronto is to meet them at Prescott where an attempt will be made to prevent crews from boarding the ships at present tied up there. "Strong-arm" action is scheduled for the following Monday morning.

It will be remembered that in previous cases of intimidation, the general mode of procedure was for the "strong-arm" squads to intimidate the seamen whilst Pat Sullivan, President of the Union, or one of his executives, while exhorting the men not to use violence at the same time do nothing to prevent it.[3][Page 4 is missing.]

PUBLIC DISAPPROVAL OF STRIKE AGITATION
(Halifax)

Continuous strike agitation by Communists instigated not for the improvement of working conditions but for the specific purpose of retarding our war efforts, is having its inevitable effects on public patience. The following editorial in the "Halifax Herald" of April 4 reflects the public's attitude:

Public Losing Sympathy

The public generally is sympathetic to unionism and is invariably ready to register that sympathy when working men seek better conditions, better hours and better wages. But arrogance in unionism is as distasteful as arrogance in the individual, and nothing will sever the sympathetic bond more quickly between labour and the public than arrogance as indicated by a disregard for public welfare.

A case in point is the numerous strikes or tie-ups resorted to by U.M.W. members who, without regard for the serious consequences involved, quit work for reasons that are often ridiculous and without justification.

A man doesn't get the shovel he wants, so fifty men refuse to go into the mine. Or someone disagrees with a decision of the mine superintendent, so a colliery is tied up.

Tactics of this sort are not worthy of the men involved who, more often than not, are the victims of vicious leaders whose only concern is their own personal advancement and who proceed on the theory that the best way for them to keep themselves in office is to keep trouble stirred up.

U.M.W. leaders would be wise to remember that there is a war in progress and that the vast majority of people are inclined to regard as traitorous anything that interferes with the efficient operation of industry. There must be no interruption with the war effort of this country, and men who take upon themselves either directly or indirectly the responsibility of causing trouble or permitting it to continue, have a lot to answer for.[5]

CIVIL LIBERTIES UNION SEEKS SUPPORT
(Montreal)

An interesting meeting took place recently in Montreal at which a few selected members of the French Committee of the Canadian Civil Liberties Union were present. The president, Hubert Desaulniers, outlined the course of action which the Union will adopt now that the "Government has been returned to power for another five years, charged with the specific mandate of continuing the war". Commenting on this point Desaulniers stated that:

"Our society has condemned the War Regulations, because it finds them unfit for a democratic country; furthermore, we see the danger of the War Regulations being enforced as never before. Therefore the society finds it urgent that propaganda be spread without delay among Canadian citizens. Our part as French-Canadians is to undertake this work in the Province of Quebec, and it is precisely for this reason that you have been invited here this afternoon to study the best way of doing this particular work.

"Our main task will be to start with the French booklet, just received and entitled 'Les Libertes Civiles en Temps de Guerre', of which 3,000 copies are available at the moment."

It was decided at the meeting that provincial government officials, as well as French-speaking members of Parliament, municipal officials, clergy, executive members of labour unions and labour groups, heads of universities and members of the Communist Party be given copies of this booklet for distribution and study purposes. These people will also receive other propaganda and a special letter urging them to co-operate with the society in its efforts to have the law in question repealed.

Similar methods of propaganda will be adopted by the English-speaking section of the Canadian Civil Liberties Union.[6]

FORMING AN ANTI-CONSCRIPTION LEAGUE
(Montreal)

Fear of conscription among the French-Canadian element in the Province of Quebec is to be capitalized by the Communist Party in the formation of an "Anti-Conscription League."

Henry Gagnon [⊱<deletion: 2 lines] Several outside organizations have been approached and have promised their full support. All Nationalist, Separatist, Fascist and such groups are to be welded into one united effort against the application of conscription.

An effort will be made to open Locals in almost every Ward in Montreal, from which the League will gradually expand its activities throughout the Province.

"A round table conference" is scheduled to take place soon. Each of the above organizations will be represented by at least two of its members. The Communist Party is determined to have at least ten members present who are not known as Communists. Only Henry Gagnon [⊱<deletion: 2 lines] The others will be representing outside organizations and will pretend not to know each other. In this manner the Communists hope to have members of their Party elected to all important committees and executive positions.

Should the attempt to weld these organizations into one group be successful it will create quite a formidable mass movement.

STRIKE FOR COLLECTIVE BARGAINING RIGHTS
(Oshawa)

Communist Party leaders consider the strike at the Ontario Malleable Iron Works at Oshawa of the greatest importance as a preparatory step to developing wide strike actions based on the demands for higher wages to meet the rising costs of living and for collective bargaining rights.[7]

In case the strike continues for any great length of time, collections and sympathy actions (resolutions to support) will be encouraged in other labour centres and circles in Ontario.

Communists attach particular importance to this strike as the first decisive walkout of steel workers affiliated with the C.I.O. in Ontario.

REVERSAL OF SEAWAY AND HIGHWAY POLICY

Communist Party leaders throughout the Dominion have been given notice of a complete reversal of policy adopted by the Central Bureau of their Party in regard to the St. Lawrence Seaway and the B.C.-Alaska Highway projects. Strongly advocating these projects before the war, the Party now looks upon the former as one through which "the predatory imperialists are preparing to seize the natural resources of the Canadian people in order to strengthen their war machinery and plans, and aided and abetted by the Kings, Hepburns and Duplessis, etc., each championing the demands of one or another of the Hydro-Electrical Power interests". The B.C.-Alaska Highway is opposed as an important avenue for an attack upon the Soviet Far East and a threat to involve Canada in the war policies of "American Imperialism on the Pacific."

Central Bureau directives assert:

"In particular the movement should take measures to arouse the railway units, seamen, longshoremen, etc, as well as the trade unions of the Maritimes, Quebec and Ontario and British Columbia against these projects."

On both of these issues district leaders are told to avoid the appearance of a mechanical reorientation.

"In the pre-war period our movement presented strong economic and defensive arguments well understood by the masses, as to why these projects should have been developed. It is not sufficient now just to say we are against them. We must and we can find equally as strong arguments, which the masses will understand with equal clarity, as to why these projects of the most powerful imperialist groups of monopoly capital must be blocked."[8]

"DER VEG" CALLS FOR "WORKERS' REVOLUTION"
(Toronto)

An article signed by J.B. Salsberg, [✂deletion: 2 lines] appearing in a recent issue of the Toronto Yiddish language newspaper "Der Veg" (successor to "Der Kamf") incites to a "struggle for freedom".

In Struggle You Shall Conquer Your Freedom, was an old though ever fresh slogan in the ranks of the oppressed. But, without a set goal, without militant knowledge, without theoretical knowledge could not be won the struggle for freedom.

So, our newspaper is not only a militant periodical in which are reflected all the phases of the struggle for the conquest of freedom but it also illuminates the road of the struggle and points the path that leads to the conquest of freedom.

Other articles are of a similar nature. A. Rivkinson praises Marxist-Leninist methods as "The Way Out":

The Zionist utopias are bankrupt. So is assimilation with other nationalities. The bourgeoisie is no more progressive than of yore, it has become aged and utterly reactionary. It is putrified through and through, broken and falling to pieces. The world lies in the hands of the degenerate petty bourgeoisie.

World problems must be approached with the Marxist-Leninist method. The victory of the working class in a sixth part of the globe gave a new approach to the national question. It shows the fundamental difference between freedom acquired in the former bourgeois revolutions and in the proletarian October revolution.

In contrast to any bourgeois revolution the workers' revolution sets forth as its task the attainment of not only political but universal emancipation. The workers' revolution sweeps away the medieval conditions in which subject races live.[9][Page 10 is missing.][✂blank]

ENEMY ALIENS "ARE WELL TREATED"
(New Orleans, La.)

That all Germans are not blinded by hate and the desire to malign everything British is sometimes shown from unexpected quarters. An intercepted letter, addressed by a German woman in New Orleans to her friend in Leipzig, Germany contains the following references to Canada's internment camps:

Mrs. Schulz wrote that the men have now been sent to another camp at Petawawa. Address, Internment Camp, Petawawa, Ontario. 46 men were freed, including: Reuter first, Kroll, Wannmann, Bratsch, Cibulka, Hausknacht, Pfalzer, Grassl, Gundermann. The Royal Mounted Police take care that the women in their need are not exploited as regards payment of rent and other claims which they may not now be able to pay. It is easier for the men than for the women, they are well treated and have enough to eat, which is not so easy for many women with children.[11]

<u>SECRET</u>

INTELLIGENCE
BULLETIN

ROYAL CANADIAN MOUNTED POLICE
HEADQUARTERS, OTTAWA

WEEKLY SUMMARY
APRIL 22, 1940

CONTENTS

War Series
No. 27

EDITORIAL

"CANADIAN TRIBUNE": HOW FAR?

"The Canadian Tribune", published weekly in Toronto, is decidedly "pink". One could scarcely expect it to be otherwise when it was organized by Communists as a "legal" resurrection of the (temporarily) deceased "Clarion". Everything about it is subtly anti-British and anti-war, with every fact distorted so as to put the Allies in an unfavourable light. For example, in its editorial, "The War Spreads", (issue of April 13) we read:

The War Spreads

The German occupation of Denmark and Norway was the logical outcome of events stemming from the Altmark incident of several weeks ago....

Judging by the dispatches from London and Paris the German action was received with no little satisfaction in what has lately become known as "spread the war" circles. Indeed there is reason to believe that had Germany not taken this bold action, the Scandinavian countries would probably have been subjected to some other form of pressure by the Allies.

For some months past there has been an incessant clamoring in cer-

213

tain British and French political circles for an "alternative front".
At first it was hoped that Finland might afford the opportunity for
such a flanking movement, but that hope was dashed with the signing of the Soviet-Finnish peace pact. From then on extreme pressure was placed on Norway to abandon her policy of neutrality and
co-operate with the Allies in halting the flow of war materials to
Germany through her waters.....
In any case "spread the war" advocates have realized their hopes
and the outlook for "innocent bystanders" is black indeed........
On the same date Toronto "Saturday Night" carried an editorial which
deals with the "Tribune" in the editor's suavely incisive and completely
decisive style. To quote in part:[1]

How Far Can It Go?

We find it extremely difficult, and we have no doubt that the
authorities find it equally difficult, to determine just how far the
Canadian Tribune's campaign can be carried on without offending
against the legitimate and necessary provisions of the Defence of
Canada Regulations. The country has just had an election, in which
it returned by an enormous majority the party supporting the Government which put Canada into the war. During that election there
may have been compelling reasons, in the very nature of our
democracy, for tolerating the candidacy and the arguments of persons who were desirous of stopping Canada's participation in the
war. The election is now over, and there is not the slightest prospect,
for several years to come, of changing either the make-up of the
new Parliament, or the determination to carry on the war which
animates the overwhelming majority of its members, and which was
obviously the reason why the Canadian people sent them to Parliament....
Their real object, which we take to be inspired by considerations
entirely foreign to the best interests of the Dominion, considerations
put forward by a foreign international organization which is at
present acting in the interest of German National Socialism, is to
render ineffective the war efforts of the Canadian people....
......As soon as Canada is no longer at war, it will be perfectly correct and proper for the Canadian Tribune and its supporters to
preach disarmament (local or universal), the abolition of private
property in the instruments of production, the establishment of com-
missars, the suppression of the capitalistic press, the erection of concentration camps for their political enemies, and all the other
incidentals of peace, freedom and happiness with which the Soviet
Republics are so plentifully provided. In the meantime they are
deliberately trying to damage the military effort of the Dominion,
and thereby to incur the risk of Canada becoming an appendage of

Germany instead of a member of the British Commonwealth of Nations. If Mr. Lapointe decides to ask the courts whether Canada has to tolerate such a periodical in war time, and the courts reply that it doesn't, our own sense of what is due to democracy and freedom will be in no wise affronted.[2]

COMMUNISM

COMMUNISTS REVIEW RESULT OF FEDERAL ELECTION
(Official Statement of Communist Party, Montreal Branch).

"The result of the Federal election which was carried through under conditions of war-dictatorship, conceals but in no way lessens the contradictions facing the imperialist bourgeoisie of Canada. While confirming the Liberal party in power as the main instrument of the Canadian imperialists in their conduct of the war, the vote itself is made up of the most contradictory trends and tendencies. Big business imperialists in Westmount supported King and Lapointe as the elements best fitted to serve the profiteering, reactionary, war-interests of Canadian imperialism. The French-Canadian masses and the majority of the people in the other Provinces, voted Liberal in their desire to express their opposition to Conscription (which the Liberals solemnly promised to avert) and to the policy of increasing involvement in the imperialist war (of which the Tories made themselves the cruder, more open advocates). By claiming to oppose Conscription, and to stand for "Moderate, limited participation," the Liberals secured a popular support which is an indirect reflection of the sentiment of the masses in regard to the war; while at the same time preparing a rude awakening for the people once they see the ruthless unfolding of the Government's war policy and its real imperialist aims.

"As the profound contradictions between the desires of the masses and the real content of the Liberal's policy comes into the open, as the war-offensive of reaction develops at home as well as abroad, a crisis will inevitably arise in the Liberal, majority camp. The bourgeoisie itself senses this, when it expresses its anxiety at the further crippling of the already decrepit Tory party, and the size of the majority representation in Parliament.

"It is clear that the Liberal 'Victory' is the direct outcome of the betrayal of the social-imperialist leaders of the Co-operative Commonwealth Federation who together with the leaders of the Social-Credit, and the Quebec Nationalists groups, climbed on the imperialist band-wagon and did everything possible to prevent the issue of participation in the war being brought before the [3] people as the only issue of significance. In this the C.C.F. leaders rendered a vital service to the imperialists; in this they made 'their contribution' to the continuance of the imperialist war which they openly glorified and supported.

"Only the Communist Party pointed to the real issue of war or peace, carrying on a revolutionary, anti-war campaign in defiance of the War Measures Act, intimidation, raids and arrests. The vote obtained by our candidates (reaching the high-point 5,200 for Comrade Morris in Winnipeg) was a conscious, revolutionary vote for the withdrawal of Canada from the War and the defeat of the imperialist bourgeoisie. On no account should the significance of the Communist vote be obscured or underestimated."

After giving particular attention to the Quebec situation, the statement concludes with the following significant paragraph:

"For the whole Party, the election must be simply a starting point for increased, more effective mass work. Systematic following-up and broadening of circles of contacts reached in the campaign, is to be accompanied by a clear orientation towards the decisive sections of the workers in industry, and towards the building of anti-war unity in joint with the broadest sections of the workers and petty-bourgeoisie of Quebec. Together with this, active and energetic recruiting of new, revolutionary combattants in the ranks of the Party of the working class, for the ending of the Imperialist war, for the defeat of reaction, and for Socialism."

STRIKE SUPPORT

Communist factions within subsidiary organizations are feverishly drumming up support for the various strikes now in progress and for the veritable wave of strikes they expect to come, particularly in the industries working on war contracts. In these latter, they point out, owners will try to break trade unions by invoking the War Measures Act.

Such "friendly" organizations as the Canadian Labour Defence League, Single Unemployed, etc. are being lined up to help strikers through donations of food, money and the services of trained pickets "who will do as ordered".[4]

REDS SEE "BRIGHT PROSPECTS" WITH TRADE UNIONS
(Toronto)

[≫<deletion: 1 paragraph: 4 lines]

Speaking to the gathering, Joe Gerschman stated that "Trade Unionists can see that the Unions will be forced to the left by the Government as the war goes on, and the time will come when the Trade Unions will be outlawed by the 'War Acts' which are being fed to the people of Canada piece-meal." He further stated that "it is the duty of the Communist Party to make the reactionary Trade Unionists see the truth. During the last three months the leading Trade Unionists have followed the line of the Communist Party and realize that the Defence of Canada Regulations and other war acts are the greatest danger to the Trade movement". Referring to the prosecution of the various members of the Party, Gerschman said that "this is merely the 'red herring' drawn across the trail to distract attention from the main issue which is to smash the Trade Unions under the pretext of 'red' leadership."

According to the speaker some of the Trade Unionists, notably in the Mine, Mill and Steel Workers' Organizing Committee, the Smelter Workers' Union and the Needle Workers Industrial Union, were beginning to see this.

The attitude adopted by the Communist Party is of considerable importance in that it reflects the policy to be adopted by the Party towards the Trade Unions—not in a new light, but confirming the line which the Communist Party could be expected to follow. A great deal of this may be due to wishful thinking on the part of the membership, however. At the same time whilst the unions may be forced to the left it may be anticipated that they will adopt a more militant policy than heretofore in a natural effort to establish themselves more firmly in industry and to increase their membership.[5]

DEADLOCK IN LAKE SHIPPING DISPUTE

In spite of the fact that the membership of the Canadian Seamen's Union voted confidence in their Executive headed by John A. (Pat) Sullivan, [≫deletion: 1 line] there have been strong indications since the outbreak of the strike on April 14 that almost 50 per cent of the seamen are critical of the Executive's action in calling a strike before asking for the introduction of a Conciliation Board by the Department of Labour, Ottawa.

The strike situation is still in deadlock and both sides appear to be adamant in their stand. The larger shipping companies of the Great Lakes are determined to man their boats and commence navigation as soon as ice conditions permit. They have agreed to pay a $5.00 per month raise in wages, but refuse to consider the addition of three men to the crew of each ship or the Union's demand for a closed shop with a Union representative on board each vessel.

The wage increase is apparently a minor consideration as far as the C.S.U. is concerned. It is worthy of note that since 1935 there have been annual increases in pay for all types of workers from porters to wheelsmen and oilers and today these men are receiving 50 per cent more than they were five years ago. The wages, even on last year's scale, compare favourably with good wages ashore.

The bone of contention seems to be the question of a closed shop and the employment of three additional men on each boat.

THE "CLARION" OUTLAW

The illegal Communist Party publication "The Clarion", in April 6 issue, continues its scurrilous attack on the Canadian Government and the war aims of the Allies. So far the location of the printing establishment responsible for this paper has evaded detection.[6]

FACTS REGARDING UKRAINIAN TEMPLE

The C.P. of C. has been greatly concerned over the question of a renewal of the licence for the Ukrainian Labour Farmer Temple Association Hall at 300 Bathurst, Toronto. While the Toronto Police Commission is deliberating as to whether or not a renewal will be permitted the Communists have been encouraging a campaign of "public spirited" citizens to protest against the Temple being closed.

Apart from the matter of precedent—which the Central Bureau of the Party feels will be applied to other left-wing halls—cancellation of the licence would mean cutting off an important source of the Party's income now obtained through the hall under various guises.

"Deliberation" over renewing the licence is not due to any doubt regarding the Temple's political complexion. The Communists themselves have given the facts in a book entitled "Lessons in Political Literacy", published by the Ukrainian Labour Farmer Mass Organizations (ULFTA) at Winnipeg in 1934, which acclaims their adherence to the revolutionary policies of Lenin and Stalin.

Under the sub-title "The Emerging of the Ukrainian Labour Farmer Mass Organizations" the author writes:

The function of such organizations which organized the Ukrainian workers and farmers in the field of cultural, educational and mutual aid activities and directed their organizing efforts for the benefit of the revolutionary labour movement, was carried out in Canada by the Ukrainian Labour Farmer Mass Organizations.

These organizations are:

1. THE UKRAINIAN LABOUR FARMER TEMPLE ASSOCIATION. (ULFTA). This organization was founded under the name of the "Ukrainian Labour Temple Association" (ULTA) on March 23, 1918, at Winnipeg, and not until the 5th Convention of the ULTA, held on February 6-9, 1924, was the name changed to the present form—the "Ukrainian Labour Farmer Temple Association".

2. THE WOMEN'S SECTION OF THE ULFTA. The ULFTA was instrumental in the organization of the Women's Section on the occasion of its 3rd Convention (July 2-6, 1922) when the following resolution was introduced: "A Women's Section of the ULFTA must be organized".[7]

3. THE YOUTH SECTION OF THE ULFTA. Its organization was decided upon by the 5th Convention of the ULFTA held in January, 1924.

4. THE JUNIOR YOUTH SECTION OF THE ULFTA. It was organized in July, 1931, at the 4th Convention of the Youth Section of the ULFTA.

5. THE WORKERS' AID ASSOCIATION. It was organized in Oc-

tober, 1922 by the initiative of the ULTA (now ULFTA).

6. THE SOCIETY IN AID OF WESTERN UKRAINE (TODOWYRNAZU) which was organized on March 1, 1931.

7. THE WORKERS' AND FARMERS' PUBLISHING AS-SOCIATION which was organized as a shareholding company and incorporated at Winnipeg on August 15, 1924.

In the section of the same Lesson, headed by the sub-title "THE WORKING CLASS CHARACTER OF THE ULFMO", the following is stated in part:

The class direction in the constitution of each Ukrainian Labour Farmer Mass Organization is therefore clearly defined as being for the benefit of the revolutionary labour movement and destitute farmers.

The historical turn of the organization to the path of the class struggle was firmly shaped during the joint 12th Convention of the ULFTA, the 7th Convention of the Workers Aid Association, and the 1st Convention of the TODOWYRNAZU held at Winnipeg in July 1931 under the following slogans:

Now we are taking the turn in a direction of the general revolutionary class struggle!

Long live the union of the proletariat with the destitute farmers in the struggle against capitalism!

Down with opportunism of the Left and of the Right!

Long live the strong welding of our organized fighting ranks![8]

The "Lessons" conclude with the following declaration:

The Ukrainian workingmen and workingwomen, the destitute farmers and their wives, living under the weight of bourgeois oppression and the ever-growing hardships and dissatisfaction with the rule of the bourgeoisie, are seeking a way out of their servile conditions as much as the whole working class and destitute farmers.

The one and only way out is by organizing the workers of Ukrainian nationality in the Ukrainian Labour Farmer Mass Organizations which, united with other revolutionary labour organizations and under the sole leadership of the Communist Party, will achieve the purpose of liberation of all workers by way of a proletarian revolution and establishment of dictatorship of the proletariat in its Soviet form of government.

"VERY SMART PIECE OF WORK"

The Salmon Purse Seiners' Union on the Pacific Coast, in its second annual convention held recently in Vancouver, passed a resolution oppressing Canada's participation in the present European conflict. George Miller, [⇾deletion: 1 line] is credited with this "very smart piece of work" by the district bureau of the Party. He is commended, not only for putting the resolution over, but also for getting a double column headline in the

"Vancouver Daily Province" over the story.

Miller's success was largely due to Fergus McKean, [⸰<deletion: 2 lines] in the recent federal election, who helped compile the resolution so that it would pass the meeting. There are many Roman Catholics among the Croatian, Dalmation and Yugo-Slav fishermen, and Party leaders of the district expressed satisfaction that these people were outwitted by Miller.[9]

SABOTAGE
GUARDING AGAINST A CANADA "BLITZKRIEG"

Danger to Canada of Nazi-Communist sabotage has been further impressed upon Canadians by a declaration of Martin Dies, chairman of the Congressional Committee on Un-American Activities, that he had obtained possession of a written Communist plan "to blitzkrieg the United States at the proper hour". A Washington report states:-

Dies told newsmen that the plan was obtained from Communist sources and contemplated paralyzing vital industries—such as utilities, communications, transport and steel—in addition to navy yards and airplane plants.

The chairman added that the blitzkrieg plan would be disclosed subsequently at a committee hearing and would show that "when the time is ripe the Communists and Nazis plan to do here what they have done in so many European countries."

Dies declared that Nazi Germany was co-operating with Soviet Russia in the undertaking. He asserted that the plan, "which we have in black and white", does not set a specific hour for quick seizure of the United States' vital spots.

Canada's Vulnerability

Thorough preparation against such an eventuality has been developing in Canada since September, 1938.

The "blitzkrieg" technique has been emphasized in counter-sabotage protection at our most vital "bottle-neck" points; particularly since September, 1939. Over sixteen hundred points were surveyed by the Civil Security Survey from coast to coast between September 1938, and August 1, 1939; and guard details planned where considered necessary by the field survey parties.[10]

These measures should not be interpreted as meaning that Canada is proof against a determined concerted plan to cripple our war effort through industrial sabotage. Constant vigilance is necessary on the part of all who have responsibility.

Vigilance against methods of indirect attack designed to circumvent guards is now considered particularly necessary.

For example the blitzkrieg technique might be attempted say, during the tourist season along these general lines:

Such targets selected as aluminum production, nickel production, industrial areas which depend on key power plants, zinc production, lead production, copper production, pig iron and steel, timber limits for forest fires, industrial cities for conflagration, Air Force training centres and others.

FASCISM

FASCIO PREPARING TO JOIN THE ENEMY

Tension is mounting here in Italian Fascist circles, particularly in Eastern Canada, where exists a profound belief that Italy will shortly enter the war on the side of Germany. Although still cautioning the rank-and-file to "keep quiet and work in silence", leaders of the Fascio fully anticipate the event and are making preparations toward that end. Some appear enthusiastic over the prospect of a war against Great Britain. To quote one of the foremost Fascist leaders in Montreal:

"I am very happy to know that Italy is getting ready to give a well-deserved lesson to Britain and France. We have been looking and preparing for this for a long time and now we are nearing the showdown."[11]

INTELLIGENCE
BULLETIN

ROYAL CANADIAN MOUNTED POLICE
HEADQUARTERS, OTTAWA

WEEKLY SUMMARY
APRIL 29, 1940

CONTENTS

War Series
No. 28.

EDITORIAL

The Sickle-Swastika

We are today in mortal combat with two powerful enemies. Although with one only it is a "declared" war with military action on land and sea, the other is supporting its ally with everything but fighting forces in their common ambition to destroy first the British Empire and eventually democracy throughout the world.

While this unholy alliance between former bitter enemies is kept hidden as far as possible innumerable symptoms of its presence keep coming to light. From the day that the Hitler-Stalin pact was signed the verbal assaults on one another ceased. Shortly afterwards the Moscow directed propaganda throughout the Communist world launched a peace-at-any-price campaign—on Hitler's terms. Here in Canada Nazis and Reds have pooled their hates against "the imperialist war" and in many instances have begun to fraternize. Our secret reports contain references to this friendship, and quote such Communist assertions as "Russia and Germany will one day make a military alliance and will divide Europe".

These signs are not peculiar to Canada. They crop up everywhere. Edmund Stevens, writing from Sweden for the Christian Science Monitor, reports:

A strange sidelight of the present situation in Oslo is the attitude of the Communist party toward the German occupation. The Communist newspaper Arbeideren continues to appear unhindered. Editorially it calls resistance to the Germans a "provocation" and appeals to the workers to co-operate with discipline with the German command. This contrasts with the other papers which, while they submit to the censorship, refrain from any editorial exhortations of this type.

The Communist Party's manifesto issued at Oslo puts full blame on the Allies for violation of Norwegian neutrality and demands that the Germans be left in peaceful occupation.[1]

To quote in part:

German troops have occupied several important points in our country, including Oslo. The German military authorities declare that the aim of the occupation is defense of the country and to prevent the possibility of its becoming transformed into a theatre of military operation.

The situation created in this connection depends on the strivings of the Anglo-French military bloc to extend the imperialist war and also to disarm Scandinavia—strivings the clearest expression of which is England's violation of Norwegian neutrality by the laying of mines along the Norwegian coast.

The Norwegian people, who never entertained hostile feelings towards other people, do not entertain them today, but are filled with an ardent desire to live and work in peace and freedom and do not want to be drawn into war.

From "Memorandum of Information on Foreign Affairs," published in London, is quoted the following significant remarks:

"The evidence before us has always shown that the signature of the Russo-German non-aggression pact marked the conclusion of a full and complete alliance secretly negotiated between April and August, 1939. A number of recent reports have gone far to confirm its existence. Refusal to recognise it is the height of folly and may prove dangerous. It would be as foolish as for Germany to refuse to recognise an alliance between Great Britain and France. Indeed, without recognition of the Russo-German alliance we shall find it hard, if not impossible, to plan our strategy....

One of the most significant events has been the transfer to Vienna of the European headquarters of the Comintern, which Germany is using for subversive work throughout the world, and especially in France. It is not only used for undermining morale, but also for espionage. Many people realize how deplorable it is for us to be in diplomatic relationship with the Soviet, which is at present engaged in the deliberate extermination of a [2] harmless people in Scandinavia, but too few yet recognise the practical dangers of this unhappy connection. Communist parties throughout the world receive their money and directions from the Russian missions abroad. There is scarcely an industry, a trade union or an even moderately left wing political party which is free of a Communist agent or member (whether they know it or not), who in turn has a connection direct or indirect with the regional Comintern organization. The Russian Government is consequently one of the best-informed in the world. Its diplomatic missions in many cases know every detail of labour organizations in the countries to which they are accredited, together with the productive capacity of key industries and many other details of supreme interest to a nation at war. At present Germany is deriving a very great deal of her extraordinarily accurate information about the position of the Allies through these sources and it is for this reason, amongst others, that the old Communism is proving such a useful instrument of policy and that Herr Hitler is only too pleased to have the Comintern at his disposal.

Not less important, however, is the birth of the new political creed to which we have referred. At present its importance is confined first to the development of relations between Russia and Germany, and, secondly, for internal propaganda purposes in both these countries. Very soon, however, it may have a wider significance and greater international importance."

The sooner this secret alliance is brought from under cover and understood as simply a part of a world-wide conspiracy against everything we hold dear the sooner we can take adequate measure to cope with it.[3]

COMMUNISM

LOYAL UKRAINIANS CONDEMN TEMPLE ASSOCIATION
(Toronto)

Since the Toronto branch of the Ukrainian Labour Farmer Temple Association were threatened with cancellation of their hall licence the Association have put on an outward semblance of respectability and are treading lightly from coast to coast.

In Vancouver, where they were fortunate enough to obtain a full page "approval" in the "Daily Province", they have shipped all doubtful books from their library to private homes for safe keeping and have even removed the pictures of Marx and Lenin from the walls. Seemingly that is all they think required to prove that there are no Communist ties to their organization.

Meanwhile, adding to the abundance of evidence already on hand against this organization, 22 Ukrainian lay and church groups representing 10,000 Ukrainians in Toronto, issued a brief to the press to show that "at least some of the supporters and apologists of the U.L.F.T.A. had to go a little out of their way to say what they did before the Police Commission and in their statements made to the Press."

The brief states that "most of the Ukrainians of Toronto do not (and they never did) regard the Association in question or the hall it controls as their cultural centre." It continues:

"The Ukrainians have found out by bitter experience that toleration by Moscow of the Ukrainian language, songs, dances, plays, concerts and costumes to a greater degree in Canada than it permits such things in the Ukraine is not out of any love or respect for Ukrainian culture or tradition, but simply because those things have been found a convenient means for attaining Moscow's ends.

"It is known, however, that even those innocent looking cultural things in Canada are spiced and flavoured in such a way that they are nothing else but a piece of Moscow [4] propaganda and a means of getting a grip upon the Canadians of Ukrainian descent......

"For anybody to come out with a statement that the Ukrainian Labour Farmer Temple Association of Toronto has no connection with Communism or Soviet Russia is just as futile and absurd as if they tried to prove that black is not black or white is not white."

It might be well for our "public spirited" citizens to take to heart the concluding remarks of the statement of these Ukrainian Canadians who are truly Canadian when, condemning Moscow control of the U.L.F.T.A., they say:

"Such food and fibre is not, to our understanding, the stuff desirable for building up a strong civilization or a Canadian nation, and no responsible Ukrainians in Canada, co-operating as they are with the Allies striving to win the war and to free the nations of Europe, including the Ukrainian people, will subscribe to the remote control work of the kind in this Dominion."

FINNS NEED COUNTER-PROPAGANDA
(Port Arthur, Ont.)

"The Finnish people are faced with a constant barrage of Left wing propaganda and I am of the opinion that if they could be divorced from this and instead given wholesome literature, economic, religious, and political, this kindly people would soon (with a little understanding), become a worthy Canadian people. The Finnish co-operatives sponsored among these people is an attempt to cultivate inter-communal life among themselves and to protect their economic standing as much as possible. The Finnish people are hungry for literature in their own language. This covers the Finnish people whose headquarters are at Port Arthur (Bush Workers, etc.)"

(From a confidential report on the Industrial Workers of the World).[5]

LAKE SHIPPING STRIKE TEMPORARILY LIFTED

The membership of the Canadian Seamen's Union on April 20 voted in favour of returning to work on the understanding that a $7.50 increase in wages was to become immediately effective and other points of the 1940 demands were to be arbitrated on.

With the strike temporarily lifted pending further arbitration, the men are determined to keep the picket lines intact, merely moving them from the docks on the ships, thereby enabling them to "work on" the non-union members employed by some of the shipping companies, at close quarters. Organizer Chapman of the Union instructed that action of this kind must be undertaken in such a way as not to cast a shadow on the Union. He added that it was, of course, unnecessary for him to tell the men how to take care of the "scabs".

[≫deletion: 1 paragraph: 15 lines][6]

LARGEST TRADE UNION EXPELS REDS
(Toronto)

After having expelled the C.I.O. locals from their ranks, the members of the Toronto District Trades and Labour Council, by a vote of 122 to 58, have moved to expel the entire Communist element.

In introducing the motion to oust the Communists, John Conlin of the Machinists' Movement read excerpts from the constitution of the Communist Party of Canada. He pointed out that this constitution ordered "Red" workers to work their way into trades and labour organizations and to endeavour to swing them over to the Communist Party.

This expulsion of the Communists means that the largest trade union body will be without Communist representation.

An amendment to the constitution was adopted with the object of preventing the Communists from getting back into the Council. In future all prospective members must take oath that they are not members of the Communist Party.

[≫deletion: 1 line]
[≫deletion: 1 line]

[≫deletion: 1 paragraph: 5 lines]
[≫deletion: 1 paragraph: 4 lines]
[≫deletion: 1 paragraph: 3 lines][7][Page 8 is missing.][≫blank]

LABOUR SQUELCHES MAY DAY AGITATION
(Vancouver)

Early plans of the C.P. of C. for elaborate parades on May Day have fallen through in most of the large cities of the Dominion. With the exception of Vancouver, May Day activities will be confined to the holding of mass meetings. In Vancouver the city authorities and the Parks Board have granted permission for the holding of the annual May Day parade and a meeting to be held at Lumberman's Arch in Stanley [9] Park as usual. The Committee in charge have issued a notice to the effect that Mayor Lyle Telford will be the main speaker at the meeting. Other speakers will be local trade union leaders.

May Day meetings will be based on agendas built up on criticism of the War Measures Act, wage levels, taxation and conscription.

Many trade union groups have flatly refused to enter into May Day activities unless they support Canada's war effort in their conduct. This unexpected turn of events is largely responsible for the abandoning of original Communist Party plans regarding the celebrations.

NAZI-COMMUNIST PLOT IN MEXICO

In conjunction with particulars of an investigation into a Nazi and Communist plot to foment an uprising in Mexico, released by the Dies Committee on un-American activities in the United States, a similar situation is found to exist in this country.

Reportedly started in Toronto, an organization has been set up to recruit Spanish War Veterans (former members of the McKenzie-Papineau Battalion) by the Communist Party of Canada. Recruiting officers are endeavouring to contact all former members with a view to dispatching them, early in May, to the United States. We are advised that Los Angeles is to be the focal point from where these veterans will proceed direct to Mexico.

Very few particulars concerning this matter are presently available but investigations are continuing and the situation is being closely watched. [10]

FASCISM

ROME CONTROLS ITALIAN VETERANS IN CANADA

Considerable pressure has been brought to bear recently upon the non-Fascist Italian War Veterans in Canada with a view to bringing them within the orbit of the Fascio. This pressure emanated from Rome and is consistent with a decree formulated by Signor Mussolini on December 8, 1939 which says, in effect, that all members of the National War Veterans' Association both in Italy and Abroad must join the ranks of the Fascist Party. This decree was published in the "Foglio di disposizioni", No. 29, December 8, 1939. The "Bollettino Italo Canadese" (Toronto) in its issue of December 8, 1939 featured the decree in the following terms: "The Duce has ordered that all war veterans be enrolled in the National Fascist Party".

In conformity with the wishes of Mussolini, special application forms were received by the Secretariat of the Fascio in this country. These forms fall into two categories; one, printed on pink paper, is intended for veterans who are already members of the Fascio and the other, printed on white paper, is meant for veterans who hold no membership in the Fascio and who had been called upon to enroll if they wished to retain their membership in the "Associazione Nazionale Combattenti" (National War Veterans' Association).

Thus, for instance, the forms referred to were distributed to members of the War Veterans' Association assembled in meeting at the Casa d'-Italia at Montreal on April 14. It transpired that all those attending were already members, with the exception of six. The latter were finally persuaded to fill in the forms and it is reported that as far as Montreal is concerned, almost the entire membership of the Veterans' Association is now enrolled in the Fascio.

The membership cards of the National War Veterans' Association, also sometimes referred to in Canada as the "Associazione Nazionale ex-Combattenti", come direct from Rome, each counter-signed by three members of the National directorate. Leaders of the Fascio have intimated [11] that unless the War Veterans join the Fascio they will be deprived of their standing as veterans and all the rights connected therewith, including pension privileges. The Italian War Veterans' Association of Canada must now be looked upon as an instrument of the Fascio controlled and directed from Rome through the Italian Consulate in Canada. The members of the Organization must, therefore, be regarded as "fighting soldiers" of Italian Fascism.

Italian Fascist activities, although conducted very secretly have become intensified. Agents of the O.V.R.A. (Opere Volontarie Repressione Anti-Fascisto) are known to be moved about the country contacting the Fascist leaders in the various localities. They move about very secretly. A meeting of O.V.R.A. leaders, presided over by the Royal Italian Consul at Montreal, Signor de Simone, took place in that city recently shrouded in utmost secrecy at which the International situation was discussed. It is known that two of the agents left Montreal immediately after the meeting and visited Ottawa, Toronto and other places in Ontario. The meeting in Montreal is said to have been attended by a special envoy from New York, whose visit has been kept a strict secret, even among the better informed members of the Fascio.

That Italy will become involved in conflict with Great Britain is looked upon in Fascist circles as inevitable. Recent information received from reliable sources would indicate that a number of the more prominent Fascist leaders are already preparing to flee the country should war break out.[12]

SECRET

INTELLIGENCE
BULLETIN

ROYAL CANADIAN MOUNTED POLICE
HEADQUARTERS, OTTAWA

WEEKLY SUMMARY
MAY 6, 1940

CONTENTS

War Series
No. 29.

EDITORIAL

THE PRESS ON ENEMIES WITHIN

Back in March, 1939 the Minister of Justice was quoted as saying in Parliament, "We are keeping a pretty careful watch over their (Communist) activities and we are prepared to protect Canadian laws and institutions." Since then Canada has become involved in war and the Press speaks in no uncertain terms on the subject of subversive activities "behind the lines".

To quote from a few editorials:

(1)   Brazen

Canada is at war with Nazism and it without sympathy for any country, party or element that aids and abets Nazism. This is what Russia is doing today. It is joined hand in glove with Germany in promoting aggression and browbeating weak, defenceless nations.

229

Do we want men in public office in Regina whose sympathies are
not with Canada and the British Empire and our allies in this war
but are with a country—Russia—that is regarded today as a jackal
among the nations?

Public office is a public trust, and notably so in this hour of
Canada's and the Empire's need. Is it not an insult to our Canadian
and British sentiment where persons of the type indicated should
ask for consideration at the hands of our citizens?

(Regina Leader-Post)

(2)   The Reds in Canada

In view of all the circumstances the right of free speech insisted
upon by the communists in Canada, even to the extent of condemning the government's war activities, is a peculiar demand. Communism in Russia presents no such privilege to the people either in
time of peace or war. Which means that these people who are
demanding free speech in this country in time of war, in order to
bring about communism here, really seek to institute a system of
government which would effectively abolish not only free speech
but individual opinion.

Russia and Germany are virtual allies at the present time. This
strange development furnishes the Canadian communists with a
situation which is difficult to explain. However, furnished with specious arguments from propaganda headquarters in Moscow, they
do their best.

(Calgary Herald)

(3)   Forestall the Reds

The time is long past for action by the Dominion government.
Manifestly the Federal Administration is the authority whose duty
it is to restrain the enemies within the gate from preaching the vicious doctrine and practising the slimy arts of Stalin.

Ottawa has ample evidence of the subversive activities of Canadian Reds, and Ottawa should outlaw them. If Section 98 cannot
be revived the sedition sections of the Criminal Code should be invoked. The vast majority of the Canadian people who are heart and
soul in the struggle against paganism are in no mood to tolerate the
machinations of "Reds" who would scuttle Canada as their masters
in Moscow scuttled Poland.

(Toronto Globe and Mail)

(4)   "Reds" Must Be Stopped

Abundant evidence has been forthcoming from Europe of the
treachery and intrigues of the Nazis and the Communists to convince Canada this is no time to trifle with the hirelings of Hitler and
Stalin. The struggle against the lustful dictators of the Third Reich

and the Soviet Republic is not going to be such a walkover for the Allies that we can afford to ignore [2] the conspirators in our midst. To give free rein to the subversive and treacherous elements who so brazenly carry on their propaganda is suicidal. In the light of events in Norway, Denmark, Poland and Czecho-Slovakia, we wonder what the authorities are thinking of when they tolerate the disruptive forces which seek to undermine Canadian industry.

(Globe and Mail)

(5)   Britain To Outlaw Reds?

Whether the British Government takes the step foreshadowed by the Daily Herald or prefers to follow some more moderate course, the Canadian Government and Parliament would do well to consider some action of their own for the restriction of Communistic activities in this country. Communist candidates fared badly in last month's general election but the fact that there were such candidates offering themselves for election to a war Parliament was sufficiently indicative of official indifference toward a political movement whose objective is the destruction of all the institutions and the repudiation of all the ideals which Canada is fighting to safeguard. Canadians want no "fifth column" in this country, whether it be Red or Nazi, and the Canadian Government has a responsibility in this regard at least equal to that which the British Government seems likely to recognize and exercise.

(Montreal Gazette)

(6)   No Trojan Horse For Canada!

In Canada we may well take the lesson of Norway to heart. The King Government was returned to power by the largest majority ever recorded in this country, and therefore it lies within the power of the Department of Justice to put an end to all subversive activities in the Dominion. It must not be forgotten too that while the strength of the Government forces was made apparent, the comparative weakness of those who are opposed to Canada's war effort was also in evidence. The conclusion therefore must be that it is the desire of the people of this country that the war be prosecuted to the limit, and that any obstacles to this objective must be removed.

(Saint John Telegraph-Journal)[3]

SABOTAGE

CANADA'S PECULIAR VULNERABILITY TO SABOTAGE

An alleged plot to sabotage the Boulder Dam in Colorado by floating timed high explosive mines down stream has been discussed in American newspapers. It serves as one of many warnings for Canada to take precautionary measures toward safeguarding its own strategic dams and power houses from enemy sabotage.

Canadian industry is dependent largely on some 20 hydro-electric power houses and is, therefore, peculiarly vulnerable to such forms of attack. Two such plants are responsible for the manufacture of 75 per cent of Britain's aluminum supply for aeroplanes. A similar situation exists in the manufacture of nickel, so that Canada's war efforts would be crippled and Britain's seriously hampered for possibly two years if many of these power houses were put out of action.

100,000 ITALIANS TO BE WATCHED

The increasing tension in Italy demands that precautionary measures be taken throughout Canada to forestall any possible acts of sabotage which might be committed by Fascists, of which there are many in the country, in the event of war between Italy and Canada. According to official figures there are nearly 100,000 people here of Italian origin. Many of these are active members of Fascist organizations whose loyalty is pledged to Rome. Significant is the fact that many of these members are naturalized British Subjects of long standing, it having come to our attention that some of them despite their 40 years in Canada and the fact that they have been naturalized upwards of a period of 30 years, are ardent supporters of Il Duce, and in addition to their moral support have subscribed financially to the support of the Fascist Party.

The Italian has a volatile nature and can be expected to go to any extreme on behalf of the Party to which he owes allegiance.[4]

SABOTAGING INDUSTRY THROUGH STRIKES

Several major industries, including iron and steel and Lake shipping, were brought last month to the verge of impotence through the influence of Communist agitators in their respective unions. At present the strikes are simply hanging fire (as compelled by law embodied in the Industrial Disputes Investigation Act) until the arbitrators have delivered their reports. Where the decision is unfavourable to the employees the latter will presumably abandon machines or ships, tieing up industry and commerce for prolonged periods and in utter disregard of, or more probably on account of, Canada's pressing war needs.

In most cases we know long in advance of Red plots for instituting strikes. For instance, "The Bulletin" of February 12 reported that leading Communists, including Pat Sullivan were making arrangements for a Seamen's strike on the Great Lakes this Spring!

The question in many minds is, are such strikes permissable either within or without the present range of law? The following editorial in the Montreal "Gazette" of April 26, discusses the matter:

Strike in Wartime

Although the threatened strike of automobile workers in Ontario appears to have been averted, the possibility of a serious disturbance

provided the Premier of Ontario with an opportunity of reaffirming
his position in regard to foreign interference in Canadian labour
problems, the automobile workers being affiliated with the C.I.O.
in the United States. Mr. Hepburn acquired some prestige on the occasion of a previous labour crisis in Oshawa, a prestige which he
capitalized in a subsequent provincial election. The prospect of a
peaceful settlement in the present instance precludes intervention
by the provincial government but the fact that a strike was threatened raises a question which is the concern of all governments in
Canada and upon which there ought to be a declaration of policy,
by the federal government particularly. There is a great deal to be
said for the Toronto Globe and Mail's contention that strikes and
lockouts should be prohibited in Canada for the duration of the
war,[5] as they are in Great Britain, and that differences between
employers and employees should be submitted promptly to conciliation and arbitration. Most certainly, the Dominion Government
should outlaw strikes and lockouts in war industries but, in order to
make the prohibition effective, the scope of the ban must be broad
enough to include a great many related industries and practically all
the so-called heavy industries. The more general the field covered
by such a federal decree the better the results will be. Either of two
methods may be adopted: the government may exercise its authority
under the War Measures Act, or, if this procedure is considered objectionable, it can easily persuade Parliament to put the necessary
teeth in the Industrial Disputes Investigation Act. At present the act
provides no means whereby the decisions of a conciliation board
can be enforced. The act itself, which covers disputes in the mining industry and certain others that are classed as public utilities, can
be broadened in its application to any extent that is deemed necessary. Prohibition of strikes and lockouts will impose no hardships
upon either labour or capital. There is nothing harsh or unjust in a
system of arbitration even where acceptance of the findings is made
obligatory.

THE HIGH COST OF "DEFENCE"
(Fort William)

[<deletion: 2 lines] has voiced the opinion of some of the members of
this association in the following statement:
"I know who makes trouble in Canada. The Communist Party scatter leaflets around and the police arrest the ones who scatter them,
and then the Canadian Labour Defence League come to the Ukrainian Labour Farmer Temple Association to get help in their
financial campaign."
It appears that the U.L.F.T.A. membership is not entirely pleased with
the idea of subscribing funds to the Canadian Labour Defence League.[6]

COMMUNISM

COUNTRY-WIDE STRIKES TO SLOW WAR EFFORTS
(Winnipeg)

The value of an "independent free newspaper", such as the "Mid-West Clarion", in

"Assisting and supporting the wage and strike struggles as experienced in the recent strike of the Canadian Seamen's Union on the Great Lakes, never losing sight of the possibility of instigating country-wide strikes leading up to a situation similar to that in 1919 (the Winnipeg general strike)"

was stressed recently by James Litterick, [⊱<deletion: 1 line] of Winnipeg.

In keeping with the policy of the Communist Party as regards the instigation of the country-wide strikes, the Party leaders in the Province of Saskatchewan are bringing pressure to bear on the C.I.O. Regional Director to hasten organization of the workers in the General Motors plant at Regina. These men are to be organized so that in the event of a strike in the Motors Plants in Eastern Canada, the Regina plant could be tied up as well. A Party faction of five men is already actively engaged within the plant laying the groundwork toward this end.

This country-wide strike movement is looked upon by some of the members of the Central Bureau of the Communist Party of Canada as the most effective means of opposing the present war.[7]

"VANCOUVER CLARION" MAKES SECRET APPEARANCE

A new monthly magazine called the "Vancouver Clarion" is being published in mimeograph form by the British Columbia District Bureau of the Communist Party of Canada. The introduction of this new monthly was undertaken by the leaders of the Party in anticipation of a ban being placed, in the near future, on the official organ, "The Advocate". If, and when, that occurs the new magazine will take its place and be published more frequently, probably every week.

This "Clarion", like its Toronto namesake, will disseminate forbidden propaganda designed to strike at conscription, the war effort and at the legislation calling for arbitration in industrial disputes. Issues will not appear on the street and only trusted Party members will receive copies. The cost of the magazine has been fixed at five cents to cover the expense of production.

It is believed that approximately 1,000 copies of the first "Vancouver Clarion" were printed but not all circulated, as some of the Party members who received their bundle of magazines for distribution destroyed them rather than run the risk of prosecution.

FALSE PROPAGANDA

The recent press announcement that Moscow had issued instructions to the Third International to support the country in which they reside in their anti-Nazi campaign is not being taken seriously by the Canadian Communists. They have issued a statement to the rank and file that this press announcement is nothing but false propaganda emanating from Great Britain.[9]

LABOUR'S "HOUSE-CLEANING" DIFFICULTIES
(Montreal)

The expulsion of C.I.O. locals from the Montreal Trades and Labour Council has struck a snag. On definite instructions of the American Federation of Labour the Typographical Unions must also be expelled because of their refusal to pay a special assessment levied by the A.F. of L. for the purpose of accumulating a fund with which to fight the C.I.O.

The delegates of the Typographical Union form one of the largest groups in the Council and their expulsion would cause the resignation of two of the executive officers who are Raoul Trepanier's supporters. As President of the Council, he is, therefore, unwilling to comply with the order and has so far refrained from taking action against both the C.I.O. delegates and the "Typos".

WORLD REVOLUTION WILL START IN EUROPE
(Montreal)

Evariste Dube [⊱deletion: 1 line] warned the unemployed of Montreal that we are still far from revolution in Canada. This statement was made on the occasion of an address in criticism of the proposed Bouchard plan of unemployed relief.

Enlarging on this, he informed his listeners that the working class was not yet sufficiently educated on the actual problems involved in a revolution, and that it would be silly to even suppose that the world revolution will start in Canada. Rather would the revolution start in Europe, later extending to the U.S.A. and finally entering Canada. The Communists of Canada, however, should prepare for the big day in order that they may be capable of handling the situation when the time arrives. He added that the Party seriously lacked imposing numbers and every member must lend full support to a concerted effort to recruit new members.[10]

WHY SHOULD RELIEF RECIPIENTS WORK!
(Montreal)

The relief plan as proposed by Paul Bouchard in the Province of Quebec, whereby relief recipients will be compelled to work for their allotment, has created quite a stir in Communist Party circles. They are determined to do everything possible to thwart Bouchard's efforts in this respect.

Communist Party representatives are very active in house to house canvassing for new members for the United Workers of Montreal. Thousands of propaganda leaflets are now in the making and will be spread among the labour clubs and mass organizations within the near future. Mass meetings to condemn the plan are scheduled for every Sunday. Advertisement of these meetings is undertaken solely by the Communist Party of Canada.

There is considerable talk of staging a march on the City of Quebec to prevent the relief plan being applied.

ANTI-CONSCRIPTION LEAGUE GROWS
(Montreal)

The "Anti-Conscription League" (previously reported in this bulletin as having been organized by Henry Gagnon, [≫<deletion: 2 lines] is growing rapidly. It will be remembered that committees were to be formed in all the Wards of the City of Montreal, after which the movement would be extended throughout the Province.

Having engaged the support of numerous outside organizations in their stand against conscription, the Communist Party have now instructed Gagnon to interview Fascist organizations with a view to inviting their support in the movement.[11]

GENERAL

"HINDUSTAN GADAR" FOR INDIAN REVOLUTION
(Vancouver)

This bitterly anti-British paper, published in San Francisco, is being received regularly through the mails in Vancouver and Victoria and distributed throughout Hindu districts. A recent issue contains the following excerpts:-

If you want freedom, make yourself fit for freedom.

If you want to be fit for freedom, become united and work together.

If you want to work together, give up partiality and envy, and learn to be one body as one person and act together.

The person who understands this understands that death is better than slavery.

The person who is afraid to die is a slave.

The English Government is now entangled in fighting with Germany, and subject nations must get up and obtain their freedom as our leaders planned.

England broke her promise in the last Great War, so do not let this precious time fly from hand.

Surely success in obtaining freedom should be at this time.

Act with unity.

The British Government deceives the Hindus many times with its promises, but do not be deceived this time.

A life of slavery is a life of shame.

A brave man does not live a life of shame.[12]

INTELLIGENCE BULLETIN

ROYAL CANADIAN MOUNTED POLICE HEADQUARTERS, OTTAWA

WEEKLY SUMMARY
MAY 13, 1940

CONTENTS

War Series
No. 30.

EDITORIAL
"FIFTH COLUMNS"

There are potential "Fifth Columns" in every country where there are Nazis or Communists. It is reliably reported that there are 100,000 Germans in the Netherlands and as many more in Belgium. The following Canadian Press dispatch from Paris throws light on the Yugoslavia situation:

Havas news agency in a dispatch from Ljubljana, Yugoslavia, said tonight that a "fifth column" of 9,000 Germans, including more than 2,500 Gestapo agents, is busy preparing the 500,000 members of the Yugoslav German minority for "der tag" of Hitler's coming.

According to information gathered by its correspondent, Havas said, the Gestapo—Nazi secret police—has 300 German-Yugoslav representatives in Slovenia, 800 in Croatia and 1,500 in Serbia. They are commanded by a Reichswehr officer.

In Yugoslavia, the dispatch said German "tourists" are charged with indoctrinating, organizing and finally recruiting the 500,000 Yugoslav Germans who, by virtue of Reich law, have simply to declare before a German consul that they consider themselves German citizens to be placed at the service of the greater Reich.

England has become so concerned over its peril from within that it is reviving the death penalty for those convicted of espionage and sabotage. We have read of Nazi "plantings" in Rumania, Turkey, Hungary, Norway, and even in South American republics. The Dies Committee has revealed the United States problem. What about Canada's?[1]

We have over 500,000 people of German birth or origin. Of these only a few hundred have been interned and a few thousand "investigated", despite the fact that a very large number are known to be in entire sympathy with Nazi aims and conquests. When we add to these the tens of thousands of Italians who secretly give allegiance to Mussolini and the Communists of every nationality who obey Stalin as a god, we must admit that we have all the human ingredients here for wholesale sabotage and even serious internal disturbances if and when the foreign dictators so desired. And despite these conditions a certain clamorous element is demanding repeal of the Defence of Canada Regulations.

We might well bear in mind these facts: Canada has been defined to Hitler as the last great "unpeopled" area of incalculable natural wealth only waiting to be developed by totalitarian efficiency; Germany is concentrating its attention first on the conquest of Europe as a necessary step to the invasion of Great Britain and the division of its Empire; the Russian Comintern is allied with Naziism in espionage and subversive activities here as elsewhere; the fanatical hatred of democracy and all that it represents has thrown every international law and every sense of decency into the discard and made any crime against us possible and even probable.

Very slowly but surely we are waking to the grim truth that we, in common with all other "free" nations, are fighting for our very existence—not only in Europe but within our own boundaries. Labour seems more alert than Capital to this. To quote from "The Labour Review" of the Canadian Federation of Labour:

It is not by the desire of Canadians that this is a "total" war: the decision to exterminate the British Commonwealth of Nations was made by Germany. We have no choice in the conditions of the conflict. If we are to meet the challenge we shall have to gird ourselves for the fight as France is doing. "France is engaged in a total war," said Premier Paul Reynaud the other day.

By definition the stake of this total war is a total stake. To vanquish is to save all. To fall is to lose all. That is the spirit of victory: we win all or we lose all. If Germany is not to triumph we must smash the network of spies and saboteurs which has been spread throughout Canada in the shape of a syndicalist movement among the industrial workers.[2]

SABOTAGE

INSIDIOUS METHODS OF SABOTAGE AND ESPIONAGE

Enemy sabotage is not confined to munition factories, troop transportation, wheat, metals and other heavy war industries. There is a long list of so-called minor commodities that, because of their smaller output and more modest capitalization, can be sabotaged by enemy agents with little difficulty and yet with serious results to the allies.

To describe two such cases that have come to our attention:

Cheese, it seems, is an ideal food for soldiers in wartime; it has highly concentrated food values and keeps fresh in storage for long periods. For these reasons England placed large orders in Canada for cheese; a commodity as vital as armaments.

Early this year a cheese maker found it difficult to buy rennet. Without rennet cheese cannot be made, and rennet is taken from calves bellies. Out of his difficulty and subsequent inquiries grew the industry's concern over the unreasonable shortage of this essential, and investigation revealed the startling fact that two companies in the United States had for some months been quietly buying up every available calfs belly in Canada. The Privy Council leaped to the breach with an Order prohibiting the export of calves bellies which was telegraphed to every Customs port in the country.

Under the guise of legitimate commerce our war effort had been menaced as effectively as by a corps of saboteurs. And the menace was only discovered when it already worked havoc. What influence was operating behind the United States companies?[3]

Another incident which draws our suspicion is that regarding one of the world's authorities on steel casting, a consulting engineer operating his own company at Salem, Ohio, with branches in Ontario, London and Paris. This engineer formerly worked for the German Herman Goering Works but now claims to have no German connections. He is consulted by armament manufacturers in Canada, England and France. In the course of his operations he learns details of the greatest importance regarding the possibilities of our plants.

Very recently his Ohio office instructed the Canadian office to submit copies of plant inspection reports in order that they might be transmitted to England and Germany!—Why Germany?—his excuse is that the instructions were a mistake in correspondence. Which may or may not be true.

These two samples are indicative of a wide and as yet unexplored realm for the operation of Intelligence. The war is being fought as well in the cheese factory as in the armament factory. A saboteur does not necessarily work with dynamite—it is more than likely his tools will be dollars purchasing rare and utterly essential products. Nor is it necessary that enemy spies will confine their efforts to convoys and purely military objectives; quite likely he will sit with his finger on the pulse of business and production in the office of an import and export agency perhaps having a direct wire to New York.

Arrangements are now being made for the co-ordination of officers of all Government Departments in defining every field and channel of probable enemy intrusion into our industrial and financial activities, so that effective steps can be taken to prevent such intrusion in future.[4]

FASCISM

ITALIAN COMMUNITY AT MONTREAL LOYAL TO IL DUCE

Addressing a meeting of the "Fronte Unico Morale Delle Instituzioni ed Associazioni Italiane di Montreal" (The United Moral Front of the Italia Institutions and Associations in Montreal) on April 17 at the Casa d'Italia, the Royal Italian Consul, Signor Paolo de Simone, under whose chairmanship the meeting was held, praised the Italian community of Montreal for the understanding and the sentiments they were showing in the "present political situation", adding "With their fundamental good sense the Italians (at Montreal) knew how to adhere strictly to orders given by Il Duce to the whole of his people".

The Consul also announced the names of the latest recipients of the "Stella del Merito al Lavoro" (Star of Merit for work done), praising them for their devotion to Fascism. He said that soon other Italians are to receive this honour from Rome and cited a number of individuals for their loyalty to Italy and the good patriotic work they had accomplished.

"Fronte Unico Morale Delle Instituzioni ed Associazioni Italiane di Montreal" is a federation of various Italian organizations in the city of Montreal organized by and under the positive control of the Fascio. It is significant to note that on most occasions the meetings of this "Front" organization are presided over by the Italian Consul who, as a rule, calls upon the various representatives or delegates to speak on behalf of their respective organizations. The sole purpose of this institution is to bring the Italian people within Fascist influence and domination. It is truly a Fascist instrument—an instrument of Rome—and because of the preponderance of trusted Fascio members on its Council it is able to control the vast majority of Italian nationals and people of Italian origin living in the city of Montreal.[5]

COMMUNISM

RED PARASITE ATTACHES TO ALL-CANADIAN CONGRESS
(Vancouver)

Communism, like a pernicious bush fire, is no sooner stamped out in one section than it blazes up with renewed strength in another. Having been smothered out of the A.F. of L. Trades and Labour Councils throughout Canada it is now boring underground from the international trade union front into the purely Canadian Trade Union front the All-Canadian Congress of Labour.

It seems that the executive of this Congress are providing the expelled Red Unions, with their international ramifications, with a respectable Canadian "front" behind which they can safely carry on their Fifth Column revolutionary activities.

[≻deletion: 1 paragraph: 3 lines]

[≻deletion: 1 paragraph: 15 lines][6][Pages 7 and 8 are missing.]

ONLY COMMUNISTS MARCHED ON MAY DAY

Celebration of May Day throughout the Dominion was limited this year to the Communist Party of Canada and its subsidiary organizations. The right wing Trades and Labour Unions refused to take part owing to the fact that Canada is at war.

No customary parades were held in any of the larger cities with the exception of Vancouver, where approximately 1100 persons marched under the banners of 16 organizations which were of strong Communist affiliation. There was a lack of enthusiasm displayed in this parade compared with post parades.

At mass meetings in all the larger centres of Canada speakers assailed conscription, Canada's participation in the war, the War Measures' Act, etc. Many leaflets were distributed both before and during the May Day celebrations by members of the Young Communist League and the C.P. of C. In every instance these meetings were poorly attended and little enthusiasm was shown.

The veterans of the Great War, in more than one centre, urged the municipal authorities to refuse to grant permits for a May Day parade, intimating that should one take place they would feel inclined to take the law into their own hands and disperse the marchers.

An amusing highlight of May Day, 1940 was provided in Vancouver when James Litterick, Communist M.L.A. of Manitoba Legislature and guest speaker at the parade, excelled himself in berating the Capitalist Powers, Canadian Government, Oil Combine and War Measures' Act, concluding with the change that there was a complete "Blackout" of democracy and free speech in this country! There were no interruptions.

LACK OF SUPPORT FOR "CANADIAN TRIBUNE"

The Communist Party is having considerable difficulty in raising money for the sustaining fund of their legal Party organ, the "Canadian Tribune". The main obstacles to the campaign established to build up this fund appear to be disruption of Party organization through recent arrests, resulting in poor contact between sections and District Committee and factional disagreements in some of the sections. Added to this is a general lack of enthusiasm on the part of members on behalf of this undertaking.[9]

QUARRELS IN TRADES AND LABOUR COUNCIL
(Winnipeg)

There is considerable discord among the membership of the Winnipeg Trades and Labour Council over the Executive's action in bringing before the general membership a resolution protesting the arrest of the three Communists connected with the "Mid-West Clarion"—the Winnipeg organ of the Communist Party of Canada. This, however, is only one of many quarrels which have occurred within this Council. The Executive are under the severe censorship of the rank and file because, during the last session of the Provincial Legislature, "they received nothing from the Government." This situation calls for a change in the political set-up of the Council.

INDISCRETION OF COMRADE GERVAIS
(Montreal)

Napoleon St. Andre, President of United Workers of Montreal, halted the speech made by E. Gervais before a mass meeting of this organization on May 1 in Montreal. Gervais, one of the Communist faction within the United Workers, was interrupted by his Party colleague after giving a vivid glimpse of the hidden Red hand within the organization.

The offending statement reads:

"This summer will see things our class never believed possible. The unemployed will come down the streets and avenge their honour in blood. Our emblem is the red star (most of you here know what I mean) and we must follow it, because it will lead us to success."[10]

GENERAL

DENMARK ANOTHER NAZI WORK-PRISON CAMP
(Kentville, N.S.)

How Canadian Danes view the invasion of their Fatherland is simply and graphically reflected in a recent article appearing in the "Danish Herald of Canada", published in Kentville, Nova Scotia.

THE FLAG DOWN

"With deep sorrow learned the Danes all over the world that our fatherland in the night between the 8th and 9th had taken down the flag which for more than 900 years was the sign for a free independent and ambitious nation, now living under the Pirate's Swastika sign, —the emblem for lies and Brutality.

"From a free and independent country, the eldest in Europe, Denmark changed in one night to a Nazi work-prison camp. 'How could it be helped'—Denmark came under 'Protection' of the pirate. What 'Protection' means have been shown in Czechoslovakia. The government decided this accompanied by the noise of German bombers over Copenhagen, with fantastic reason that by doing so it would save the country from the horrors of war. But as soon as Denmark was under German 'Protection' the Allies stated that Denmark could no longer be considered neutral or independent, but must be considered as the pirate's helper and would be dealt with as such.

"This is not the time to condemn the men who decided for our country. They apparently had no other choice, or at least they thought so. We must believe they did the best under the circumstances. We feel sorry for our people in Denmark who now must bear the burden."[11]

"In months, perhaps in years, will we be without any means of connection with our fatherland and unable to get in touch with our dear people there, and it will be unknown to us, the hardships and sufferings they will go through.

"As we suffer from not knowing, we must hope, that the present conditions soon must end, and that 'the robber' will get his well deserved punishment".

ENEMY ALIENS

REGISTRATIONS, INTERNMENTS, RELEASES

Registrations:

> Total registrations to April 30, 1940.................. 16581
> Exemption certificates issued.............................. 4295
> Exeats granted to date .... 222.

Internments:

> Total interned or detained since Sept. 4................. 405
> Released at once 3
> Released after appeal.. 136
> At present interned or detained .... 266.

(The last figure includes one woman interned at Kingston Penitentiary and two men serving two years' sentences in Saskatchewan Penitentiary for escape from Kananaskis.)[12]

INTELLIGENCE
BULLETIN

ROYAL CANADIAN MOUNTED POLICE
HEADQUARTERS, OTTAWA

WEEKLY SUMMARY
MAY 20, 1940

CONTENTS

War Series
No. 31.

SABOTAGE

"WE GERMANS THROUGHOUT THE WORLD."

The almost uncanny thoroughness of Germany's espionage system is continually coming to the attention of police authorities throughout the world. It would seem that there is scarcely a great munitions or chemical plant that has not been investigated and reported on by agents of the Gestapo with an eye to possible sabotage in time of war.[✂<blank][1][✂<blank]

This virtual enslavement by the Reich of all its "subjects" is continually being proclaimed by Nazi leaders. To quote Hermann Goering (Prussian Minister of the Interior):

"'We Germans throughout the world,' this is the text of our credo which expresses the unity of Germandom in its full magnitude. We, that is the racial comrades in the Homeland, the nearly one million German citizens living abroad and the many millions of persons of German blood living in Europe and overseas who must not be lost to German culture. The Third Reich is not required to prove the truth of this credo to anybody, for nationality is the cornerstone of the work and the power of the Reich. But I proclaim it here so that it may be heard and understood by the German people beyond our borders, not only by our German brethren abroad but by the whole world. Protection of German culture and German nationality is the foremost duty of the Reich."[2]

"We Germans throughout the world" is a term which expresses to Every German in the Reich the credo of unity with Germandom abroad. Everyone must do his share through unswerving devotion and sacrifice so that Germany may give to the Germans abroad what they are entitled to demand.

"WORDS THAT WON THE WAR"

The prolonged and bitter "War of Words" has finally culminated in "total war". But it should not be forgotten that "History's greatest battle" is only the effect of a cause which must persist, whatever the present outcome, until arbitrament by Force and the Gods of War is utterly destroyed from the face of the earth.

The first World War was a mere skirmish compared with the second, because it was largely military and economic. This second is a contest between two principles — Tyranny and Democracy, in both their political and spiritual sense — the former realizing that its ambitions are doomed to failure unless it can destroy its hereditary enemy. Thus nations divide not on the labels of "Haves" and "Have Nots" but on their beliefs in totalitarianism, vs. individualism, atheism vs. theocracy, nationalism vs. humanitarianism, and Stalin and Mussolini are potentially as much our enemy as is Hitler.

Canada's part in the war is not only to supply fighting personnel and war material but to sabotage our mental saboteurs wherever they exist. We have had plenty of grim warnings from other countries, so that the sneering remark "It can't happen here" simply smacks of enemy propaganda. We need to know that it can happen here and that in event of disasters in Europe it will happen here.

But arrest and punishment it not enough. We need to fight fire with fire by propaganda of the most effective kind. When the United States entered the war in 1917 George Creel headed a Committee on Public Information which "did its work so well that there was a burning eagerness to believe, to conform, to feel the exaltation of joining in a great and selfless enterprise" ("Words that Won the War" by James R. Mock and Cedric Larson). To quote from a review of this book in the Christian Science Monitor:[3]

A brief illustration of the technique of the Committee is sufficient to explain its wide influence. Through mimeographed press releases the Committee reached the smallest newspapers with authoritative reports that the poorer of these publishers had been unable to afford in pre-war days. All these reports were given the "right" twist somewhere between the sending and receiving points, in accordance with "voluntary" rules established by CPI. Patriotic advertising and patriotic themes even in regular commercial advertising, likewise were results of CPI endeavours. Even at State fairs the farm boys who were to be doughboys viewed family war exhibits under CPI sponsorship. Patriotic films and the Four-Minute Men in movie houses were CPI products. It must be about as easy today to escape from a concentration camp as it was to escape from the CPI in 1917.

Such propaganda constitutes in a very real sense "Munitions of War", and in its widest use the Dominion is contributing not only to its own security but to that of civilization "for the next 1,000 years."

THE COMMUNIST PARTY OUTLAWED

Since Mr. Justice Chevrier sentenced three Ottawa Communists for printing and distributing subversive literature and declared the Communist Party of Canada an illegal organization, people have been requesting further information:

1. Does the Judge's ruling apply to the Communist Party as a whole throughout Canada?
2. If it applies only to Ontario will it be necessary for each province to determine the legality of the Communist Party?
3. Can Communists be proceeded against by means of internment or must prosecution be instituted under Defence of Canada Regulations.

Rulings in the above connection are being awaited.[4][Pages 5 and 6 are missing.][✂blank]

MORE ANTI-WAR PAMPHLETS

It is understood that the Communist Party in Ontario and possibly throughout the Dominion intend to publish another pamphlet attacking participation in the war. In describing this leaflet, a prominent member of the Party has stated "If they (the authorities) think the first leaflet was bold they want to wait for a few days and there'll be one out that will blow them up. They'll want to shoot us then."[7][Page 8 is missing.]

"CLARION" INCREASES ITS STOP-THE-WAR EFFORTS
(Toronto)

Since "The Clarion" of Toronto was outlawed it has become more fanatic and more desperate in its efforts to withdraw Canada from the war before the Allies have succeeded "in directing it against the Soviet Union".

The issue of May 10 courts renewed co-operation with the C.C.F., reminding the Federation of its pacifist policy prior to the war, and asserting that only its leaders are barring the road to Socialism and unity with the Communist Party at the present time. It urges the C.C.F. members and supporters, despite their leaders, "to join the Communists in united action against the imperialist war, for peace and socialism."

In another article, headed "Fascist Strike-Breaker Heads Second Canadian Division", "The Clarion" rails at the appointment of Brigadier-General Odlum, charging that "the man who is appointed to command and order the slaughter and maiming of Canadians is a reactionary, Fascist, scab-herder, union-baiter, whose only desire is to safeguard the interest of the rich, and the welfare and, indeed, the very lives of the Canadian people are no concern of his."

Constituting another serious breach of the Defence of Canada Regulations is an article entitled "With the Troops", which enlarges upon rumours of discontent in the Canadian Forces. To quote:

"Although certain concessions have been wrung from the Government, responsible officers at the Exhibition Park admit that morale is not high among the men and that it is getting lower.

"The list of grievances has been partially rectified by sweeping changes emanating from Ottawa. Discontent was sufficiently rife during the winter and something just had to be done. Food is now much better. The question of family allowances is now being attended to also. The Department of National Defence was forced to break through its own bureaucracy and attend to this matter which was becoming a national scandal.[9]

"Further to thoroughly ingratiate themselves with the men the authorities are being very generous with leaves. It all adds up to the fact that the government is very anxious that nothing untoward should happen at the present time.

"Strangely, though, these methods are not working. There is a sullen, ominous discontent in the army, and the reflection of this feeling shows itself in the new petty crime wave which has been rising. Drunkenness is more pronounced; discipline is lax.

"There is a general desire to get out of the army, and this accounts for the fact that many devious ways are being used to achieve this. A great impetus was given this feeling by the extension of the war to Scandinavia. The men now fear that they will really be going to fight, and the long and short of it is that our boys just damn well don't want to get killed. They think that if they can get a crime record chalked up against them they will be kicked out of the army. If this method doesn't work they bank on others proving successful.

"The troops now in Toronto are mainly Black Watch of Montreal, the Royal Regiment and Engineers and Auxiliary Units. The general plan is that they will go to Camp Borden around May 24 for more intensive training. From there they will go to Petawawa for divisional exercises preparatory to leaving for overseas. It is planned to evacuate Exhibition Park completely.

"There is an urgent need for leadership among the soldiers. The problems of the soldiers must receive appreciative attention. Our party can do yeoman work in ending Canada's participation in the imperialist war if we give encouragement and leadership to the men who are being driven to fight for more profits for the millionaires."

"The Clarion", previously published in Toronto, is now being printed by the various districts of the Communist Party throughout the country. Editorials and news are prepared in Toronto and submitted to the various districts for printing and distribution. The Party have been taking every care in order to cover up this work and mail contacts are being closed guarded.[10]

"REFORMERS" SPLIT OVER BY-ELECTION CANDIDATE
(Saskatoon)

A definite split has occurred in the United Reform Movement of Saskatchewan as a result of a dispute which arose over the nomination of a candidate for the coming by-election in the Saskatoon constituency left vacant by the death of the Rev. W. G. Brown.

The Social Creditors and Conservatives are supporting the nomination of Rev. C. P. Bradley while the Communists who until now have been able to freely control the organization, are resolved to have [ℜ<deletion: 1 line], nominated for this candidacy. In addition to this the C.C.F. members indicated just as strong a determination to have Agnes Macphail, former M.P., fill the vacancy.

At present the Communist element have the support of the majority of the Zone Committees, with only four to take the stand against them.

[ℜ<deletion: 1 paragraph: 3 lines]

COMMUNIST ETHICS

Following up the resolution to expel all Communists from the ranks, the Toronto Trades and Labour Council is calling upon its members to state under oath whether or not they are members of the Communist Party of Canada. The Toronto District Bureau of the Party has instructed its member delegates to the Council to swear when challenged that they have no connection with the Party.

Justification of such procedure was suggested by a Bureau member in the question, "Could we not look upon our political ideas as our religious beliefs?"[11]

SECRET

INTELLIGENCE
BULLETIN

ROYAL CANADIAN MOUNTED POLICE
HEADQUARTERS, OTTAWA

WEEKLY SUMMARY
MAY 27, 1940

CONTENTS
The Enforcement of Defence of Canada Regulations

War Series
No. 32

THE ENFORCEMENT OF DEFENCE OF CANADA REGULA-
TIONS

The Defence of Canada Regulations form a part of the Federal laws of Canada which are today very much in the public mind. Unfortunately the uninformed public are inclined to place responsibility for the enforcement of the Regulations entirely upon the Federal Force, particularly with respect to the arrest and detention of enemy aliens and other persons suspected of treasonable or seditious acts or utterances. The responsibility in this regard rests with any Police Force whose duty it is to enforce the law in that particular district where an offence has been committed. The Provincial responsibility is outlined in Section 39B (1):

"A prosecution for an offence against either regulation 39 or 39A of these Regulations shall not be instituted except by or with the consent of, counsel representing the Attorney General of Canada or of the Province".

The above refers to the following Regulations:
"39.   No person shall
(a) spread reports or make statements intended or likely to cause disaffection to His Majesty or to interfere with the success of His

Majesty's forces or of the forces of any allied or associated powers or to prejudice His Majesty's relations with foreign powers:

(b) spread reports or make statements intended or likely to prejudice the recruiting, training, discipline, or administration of any of His Majesty's forces; or

(c) spread reports or make statements intended or likely to be prejudicial to the safety of the State or the efficient prosecution of the war".

"39A.   No person shall print, make, publish, issue, circulate or distribute any book, newspaper, periodical, pamphlet, picture, paper, circular, card, letter, writing, print, publication or document of any kind containing any material, report or statement.[1]

(a) intended or likely to cause disaffection to His Majesty or to interfere with the success of His Majesty's forces or of the forces of any allied or associated power, or to prejudice His Majesty's relations with foreign powers:

(b) intended or likely to prejudice the recruiting, training, discipline or administration of any of His Majesty's forces; or

(c) intended or likely to be prejudicial to the safety of the State or the efficient prosecution of the war".

It is true that in the majority of cases prosecuted under these Regulations action has been taken by the local City or Provincial Police in co-operation with members of the R.C.M. Police.

The question of internment is governed by the Provisions of Regulation 21 which reads as follows:

"21. (1)   The Minister of Justice, if satisfied, that with a view to preventing any particular person, from acting in any manner prejudicial to the public safety or the safety of the State it is necessary so to do, may, notwithstanding anything in these Regulations, make an order:

(a) prohibiting or restricting the possession or use by that person or any specified articles;

(b) imposing upon him such restrictions as may be specified in the order in respect of his employment or business, in respect of his movements or place of residence, in respect of his association or communication with other persons, or in respect of his activities in relation to the dissemination of news or the propagation of opinions;

(c) directing that he be detained in such place, and under such conditions, as the Minister of Justice may from time to time determine;

and any person shall, while detained by virtue of an order made under this paragraph, be deemed to be in legal custody.

(2)   If any person is in any place or area in contravention of an order made under this Regulation, or fails to leave any place or area in accordance with the requirements of such an order, then, without prejudice to any proceedings which may be [2] taken against him, he may be removed from that place or area by any constable or by any person acting on behalf of His Majesty."

Shortly before the outbreak of hostilities, being the latter party of August, 1939, when war with Germany was almost a certainty, an Inter-Departmental Committee was appointed by the Minister consisting of Mr. Norman A. Robertson, Department of External Affairs, Chairman, Mr. J.F. MacNeill, K.C., Department of Justice, Superintendent E. W. Bavin, R.C.M.Police. It was the duty of this committee to inquire into the evidence available against dangerous enemy aliens and other persons listed by the R.C.M.Police whose liberty was considered to be a danger to the State. The evidence in each case was examined by this committee and the names of those recommended to be interned were submitted to the Minister for action under the above Regulations.

Following the internment under the Minister's Order the person so interned has the right to object against the Minister's Order and this objection is placed before an Advisory Committee as provided under Regulation 22. The Advisory Committee so appointed consisted of: Judge F. Smiley, Chairman, W.P.J. O'Meara, K.C., Secretary of State Department, J. Fortier, Department of Transport.

Regulations 24 and 25 deal with enemy aliens and the power under these Regulations rests in the first place with the Registrar General of Alien Enemies and his Registrars appointed throughout the Dominion. It provides, in part:

" (2)   All enemy aliens who:
   (a) are members of enemy armed forces and who attempt to leave Canada;
   (b) attempt to leave Canada, and in regard to whom there is reasonable ground to believe that their attempted departure is with a view to assisting the enemy;
   (c) are engaged or who attempt to engage in espionage or acts of a hostile nature, or who give or who attempt to give information to the enemy, or who assist or attempt to assist the enemy, or who are on reasonable grounds suspected of doing or attempting to do any of the said acts;
shall be arrested and detained.[3]

Persons so interned under this Regulations may appeal to the Tribunal appointed by the Minister of Justice in accordance with the provisions of Regulations 26. After hearing any cases appealed the Tribunal makes recommendation to the Minister of Justice for final decision as to the appellant's release or detention. A total number of 405 persons were interned and a total of 166 were released on the recommendation of the Advisory Committee under Regulation 22 or the Tribunal under Regulation 26.

NAZI-COMMUNISM
COMMUNIST INTERNATIONAL DEFENDS NAZI CAUSE

Definite proof of the close alliance between Hitler and Stalin is contained in the May Day Manifesto of the Communist International. This manifesto absolves Germany absolutely from any blame for the outbreak of the present conflict. The Nazi invasion of the Scandinavian countries is explained as an act of self-defence against the aggressive democratic countries and is defined: "As an answer to the gross breach of the neutrality violated by England and France in Scandinavia, Germany sent its troops to Denmark and had occupied strategical positions in Norway."

The Comintern manifesto condemns Japan for its aggression in China and speaks of the struggle of Japan on the one hand and England, supported by the United States, on the other for the possession of the Dutch East Indies. The Communist International, hitherto so concerned over the National freedom of all people and nations, has not a single word to say for the Czechs, Austrians, Poles, Danes and Norwegians. Instead it devotes considerable space to the internal situation in France and England. It deals extensively with the persecution of "revolutionary workers" in these countries and the suffering of the labouring class and forced labour. There is only a short sentence devoted to the internal [4] situation in Germany in which it is claimed that "peace is the wish of the German farmers and workers". Nothing is said about the concentration camps in Germany and the persecution of the Jews. This is important. Those who have followed the activities of the Communist Parties in Europe and have read their Press see in the Comintern line a close relationship between Berlin and Moscow, a new phase of co-operation, not only between the foreign offices of the two countries but also between the official Soviet Press and the propaganda machine abroad.

Additional evidence of this turn in Soviet-German relations is contained in an article by Walter Albricht, an accredited and responsible head of the Central Committee of the German Communist Party, now living in Moscow. Albricht, of course, does not come out in open defence of the Nazi regime, but gives much space to the "Deutsche Volk"— the German People. He asserts that the German people want peace and friendly relations with the Soviet Union. He further asserts that the German people are being endangered by the "English-French warmongers". The inference to be drawn is clear: German people want peace; the peace policy of the German people is in danger. He admits that there are differences of opinion between the German "reactionaries" and the German people, but as to the main question, the question of resistance to the "British and French aggressors", he says there is no difference of opinion among the Germans; that there is full harmony between the German people and the Fuehrer including the Communists, and that this also applies to the friendly relations with the Soviet Union. Regarding England and France he has a totally different story to tell:

"Quite different is the situation in England and France. Despite the fact of the normally functioning democracy in England and the temporarily bridled democratic regime in France, the Governments of England and France do not express at all the wishes and needs of the people. What started the war? English big business and finance sought in this way a way out from decaying capitalism". The present struggle, he maintains, is one of "English capitalism, English imperialism, French capitalism, French imperialism versus German people".

Arguing against Hilferding's thesis that the war alone will sweep away the Hitler regime, this spokesman of the Communist International condemns such a belief as insane and criminal. Says he, "To accept Hilferding's war policy is criminal because a victory by England would mean that the greatest reactionary force of the war—England—would dictate to a lesser reactionary power—Germany."[5]

Discussing the tasks confronting the Communist Parties in the world, Albricht declares the Soviet people and the German people have a common interest in frustrating the English war plans. The Soviet people and the German labouring class desire the immediate end of the war in the interests of the working masses. Instead of the devilish plan of England, the Comintern has its own plan for Germany. By peaceful commerce with the Soviet Union and with the East, Germany cannot only supply itself with the products required but will also become self-sufficient and secure.

Most significant is the fact that there is not a word about the overthrow of the Hitler regime in Albricht's article; nothing about the liquidation of Nazism; nothing about the fate of the nations now under Nazi Domination. But even more significant is Albricht's demand to suppress the internal enemy in Germany, the Thyssens, etc. In this connection he states "He who intrigues at the present time against the German and Russian people is an enemy of the working class and helps English imperialism". He even calls upon the German workers to ferret out these enemies of the people and hand them over to the Gestapo.

"IT IS NO TIME FOR HALF MEASURES"
(Toronto)

Brigadier-General D.C. Draper, Chief Constable of Toronto Police Department, on May 14 issued an urgent plea to Canadians to be more awake to the gravity of the present situation and to utilize their every resource, moral, mental and material, in order that freedom and democracy shall not perish from the earth. As a step to this end he recommends more drastic suppression of subversive elements.

To quote in part:

We need to awake to the seriousness of the situation. It is not time for half measures, no time for disguising the real issue. Britain is engaged in a life and death struggle with a relentless and a crafty foe, so that we can continue to live peacefully in this land of present peace. Let Britain and France fail—which God forbid—and our peace and our lives and our possessions here will be worth what Poland's were—and no more. Do you imagine, in such a case, a country so [6] rich in potential wealth as Canada would be safe from the foul cupidity and merciless greed of a triumphant tyrant?

Just think of it for a moment. Think of your children's day and generation. Do we want them to be free in a free country, or broken on the torture-wheel of a Nazi occupation of Canada? This is a war to a finish. At its end, either the freedom we cherish will endure, or the savage creed of a godless autocracy will sweep freedom, religion, justice and happiness into the limbo of forgotten things.

In Canada for the past few years there has been a great deal of haphazard wishful-thinking concerning the activities of the Communist, Nazi, Fascist totalitarianism.

In this crisis I feel a compelling influence to place before you the following recommendations for immediate action on the part of the Federal Government of Canada:

1. To outlaw all subversive organizations.
2. To order a nation-wise system of registration in person, and card identification, of all foreign-born adults.
3. To cause the internment of all foreign elements and known Communists who are active in obstructing, directly or indirectly, by whatever means, Canada's War Effort, as described in Section 39 and 39(a) of the Defence of Canada Regulations.
4. That Section 62 s.s. 5(b) and (c) be amended to read that the procedure for Appeal be direct to the Minister of Justice within 10 days of the date of decision of the Court.

A number of Communist papers and pamphlets have been issued of late which urge the Canadian workers to follow Stalin and learn from him the art of overthrowing the capitalist system; also they have succeeded in a number of instances in causing [7] strikes in industrial establishments where war equipment and materials are in course of manufacture. Is it worse to wreck the Government than to wreck the industries which enable us to wage war against the savages of Europe who would wreck the Empire?

Another plank in the Communist programme, which no doubt is in direct sympathy with the Nazi organizations, is the campaign for the abolition of the Defence of Canada Regulations, and they are bending every effort towards this end. In my opinion, these Regulations should be strengthened as herein recommended, rather than relaxed. All Canadians should be awake to the dangers of these subversive organizations in our midst, who will neither assist us in winning the war or obtaining peace, and who certainly will not help to rebuild this country after peace has been finally attained.

As you know, Communist members have been recently forced from the various labour organizations into which they have been "boring in" during the past few years. Also various organizations throughout the country, to as far west as Vancouver, are now advocating the disfranchisement of all members of subversive groups...

Since the beginning of this year the Government of France has outlawed the Communist Party, and many of its leaders in that country have been sent to jail or to concentration camps, and press despatches would indicate that some similar action has now been taken in Britain. While several individual Communists have been arrested in Canada and some convicted and sentenced to varying terms for offences against the Defence of Canada Regulations, much more extensive action is necessary to properly restrain these enemies within our country.

As evidence of the destructive efforts of these enemies, the latest leaflet, sent through the mail to members of the Active Service Forces and of the Non-Permanent Militia, and issued over the imprint of "The Political Committee, Communist Party of Canada", contains the following:

"To really defend Canada and your own rights it is your duty to cleave to the side of the working class, to fight against the capitalist warmongers who brought on this war. Your enemies are not the German people;[8] the German working class will deal with the madman Hitler and win their freedom. They, not Chamberlain who built up Hitler, will smash the Nazi dictatorship.

YOUR ENEMIES ARE AT HOME! THEY ARE "OUR OWN" CAPITALISTS WHO FIGURED ON BARTERING AWAY YOUR LIVES FOR PROFITABLE WAR CONTRACTS FROM THE ENGLISH AND FRENCH IMPERIALISTS.

LONG LIVE THE FRATERNAL UNITY OF THE WORKERS OF THE WORLD.

THE IMPERIALISTS HAVE STARTED THIS WAR. THEY HAVE HURLED HUMANITY INTO CARNAGE AND DE-STRUCTION FOR THE SECOND TIME IN THIS GENERA-TION. IT IS UP TO THE SOLDIERS, THE SAILORS, THE AIRMEN, THE WORKERS AND FARMERS, UNITED BY THE COMMON BOND OF CLASS INTERESTS, TO END THE CAPITALIST SYSTEM THAT BREEDS NOTHING

BUT CRISIS, POVERTY AND WAR, TO ESTABLISH A SOCIALIST CANADA WHICH WILL MEAN PEACE, SECURITY AND HAPPINESS FOR OUR PEOPLE. JOIN THE COMMUNIST PARTY OF CANADA!!"

The tactics outlined above as being used by the Communist Party during this war are essentially the same as those employed since the formation of the Party in Canada in 1922, and not alone in Canada and the United States, but in all other countries of the world, with the object of causing internal strife and revolutions in all nations.

What is true of the Communist is also true of the Nazi and Fascist who, while probably more subtle in their methods, nevertheless have as their major objective the disruption of Canada's war effort. The duplicity of the German, as evidenced by the many recent acts carried out by Germany under the direction of Hitler in direct violation of her pledged word, should be ample assurance that the majority of Germans who have come to Canada since the last war, and particularly since the rise of the Nazi regime, and who have taken out naturalization papers, have done so as a means of facilitating and furthering acts of espionage and the promotion of Nazi doctrines in Canada.[9]

Let us all awake to a true realization of our responsibilities. Let us now resolve solemnly that all the resources which we, as Canadians, can command, shall be used to support Britain and her Allies in this war. As the oldest Son of the Empire, let us try to emulate the unconquerable spirit of the people of England, and to determine in our hearts that no effort shall be too great, no endeavour too immense, for us to undertake as a British Dominion. Britain is looking to Canada at this grave crisis in her history for the greatest measure of help she has ever been called upon to give. Let us see to it that Canada responds—fully—completely—unreservedly, whole-heartedly. For only so shall the Peace that is Canada's remain a peace perpetuated for posterity.[10]

COMMUNISM

THE RED HAND PULLS ANTI-CONSCRIPTION STRINGS
(Montreal)

The Communist Party of Canada is progressing with its organization of the Anti-Conscription League, as previously reported in this Bulletin. With the movement well under way, Henry Gagnon, [⅋<deletion: 2 lines] outlines the party policy with the latter organization briefly as follows:

"In organizing such a movement we must have the full support of all those who do not share our Communist ideas, may they be Liberals, Conservatives, C.C.F., Nationalist, Separatist, Fascist, etc. Therefore, we must in no way hurt the feelings of those who, while being against conscription, favour to some extent Canada's war attitude against Germany.

It is also very important that our supporters do not become aware that we are Communists. To assure this our speakers must use the utmost care to refrain from using anti-Imperialist talk, slang words like "Britishers", "Capitalists", "Downing street agents", etc.

Our plan is to hold mass meetings in public halls at least twice a month this summer. Our own hall is not to be used for anti-Conscription League Mass meetings because it is known for what it is by the police, which is enough for us. We will organize anti-Conscription League cells to work as the ones in the Party at present. These cells will meet every week to hear the contents of a report as prepared by the heads of the movement and will then act according to the instructions contained. No monthly fees will be asked of the members. Other means to get money must be found. Later this summer a general executive will be chosen. Propaganda will be distributed by way of printed circulars, or by painting slogans on fences, etc., as well as the posting of hand lettered bills.[11]

Our Communist attitude must become one resembling Nationalism, as this one seems to be the most popular in this Province. Another reason for us favouring Nationalism is that the Catholic clergy holds it in high favour. As all priests are against conscription we intend to write them individually, interest them in the importance of our movement and then ask for their financial help."

PERIL TO LABOUR THROUGH EXTERNAL CONTROL

In compliance with the dictates of the Russian Comintern, the Communists of Canada are focussing their energy on the stirring up of dissatisfaction among the industrial workers. This is unquestionably the most effective and safest weapon in their determined struggle against the Allied war effort. Whereas, for instance, the risk in spreading anti-war propaganda is great they can organize strikes in key industries with impunity by working under cover of legitimate labour unions and denying under oath that they have any connections with the Communist Party of Canada.

The majority of trade union members are not "red" nor do they sympathize with the aims of that organization, but experience shows that C.P. members of any trade union are the most militant and energetic in furthering the legitimate aims of the union and thus gain a disproportionate influence in that union.

Particularly obnoxious to legitimate unions and threatening to Canada are those Communists who operate through international trade unions the controlling heads of which, being resident in the United States, are beyond Canadian jurisdiction.

It is true that trades and labour councils of American affiliation in all the Canadian industrial centres have passed resolutions refusing representation tationtationtationon the councils to delegates who are members of the C.P. of C., but the Communist Party is not greatly concerned over this ruling because they feel that its enforcement can be overcome with the assistance of left wing sympathizers sitting on the executives of the councils. Failing this, their members are expected to take the oath required and still remain in the Party.[12]

Canadian C.I.O. unions are, one by one, transferring their affiliation to the All-Canadian Congress of Labour—supposedly autonomous Canadian trade union federation—as previously reported in this Bulletin. This plan has been "worked out" in discussions with the C.I.O. heads in the U.S.A. and had to be approved in each instance by them. The outcome is quite obvious when one considers the effect of this addition of 65,000 Canadian C.I.O. members to the 30,855 members of the A.C.C. of L.

Another serious "disease" among labour unions having external affiliations is exploitation by dishonest leaders. The most recent example of this is the case of Ben Gold, [⊱deletion: 1 line] of the International Fur Workers Union, and his ten lieutenants who were convicted on an Anti-Trust Act charge as a result of trying to maintain a monopoly in the fur trade by a "reign of terror" marked by kidnappings, stabbings and murder. [⊱deletion: 3 lines] while touring our Dominion carrying out the plots as concocted by Gold. Furthermore, it must be pointed out that although Gold is dictating the policy of an industry which is not a "key industry", he instructs his Canadian organizer (in a recent letter outlining the policy to be applied against the employers in Winnipeg) not to lose sight of the fact that "the employers must realize that the war situation created a shortage of labour and brought more business. Under these circumstances they would not like to face another strike situation". Similar interferences may well be expected from the headquarters of the other international unions whose Canadian members are engaged in producing war supplies.

Bad as this situation may be in times of peace it is a definite hazard while Canada is at war. It means that Canadian industries are vulnerable to sabotage from external influences at a time when their unfaltering service is most essential to Canada's war effort.[13]

"UNITED WORKERS" RESENT COMMUNIST LEADERSHIP
(Montreal)

The United Workers of Montreal are at present undergoing reorganization as a result of dissension which has arisen between the Executives of the various wards of this group and the Communist Party of Canada. The Communist Party District Bureau at Montreal had informed the United Workers of the appointment of three members who were to assume leadership of three different wards of their organization. The United Workers objected to the appointment of the three men who, in their estimation, were considered ineligible for such positions.

In addition to the dissension over the appointment of the three Communist leaders to the leadership of the United Workers, the latter organization has passed a resolution that no funds collected would be shared with the Communist Party of Canada unless they could be spared after local expenses had been met.

FIFTH COLUMN FEARS A SIXTH COLUMN
(Vancouver)

The establishment of a "Sixth Column" by the veterans of the Great War in British Columbia has filled the Communist Party leaders there with apprehension. This organization is designed to combat "Fifth Column" activities.

The Party Bureau members fear greater personal danger from groups of the "Sixth Column", loosely organized and undisciplined as it is, than from the Government. Curiously enough the branch of the Government they would prefer to have in control is the R.C.M.Police, reasoning that this Force would not act without instructions from Ottawa, which takes time for thought and provides opportunity for evasive manoeuvres. Furthermore, such orders would be carried out "to the letter with dignity and restraint", whereas the ex-service men would adopt "strong-arm" methods. The Party leadership in the West Coast Province has expressed thankfulness of the ample time provided them by the "passing of the buck" between Federal and Provincial Governments over the banning of the Party, which is giving them time to destroy all incriminating documents, bury literature for safekeeping and prepare underground channels of communication.[14]

COMMUNIST EQUIVOCATION

Anticipating arrests in their ranks and the enforcement of the ban placed upon their organization, leaders of the Communist Party of Canada are preparing to voice a loud protest through the trade unions declaring the ban is directed against labour and trade unionism rather than against the Communists.

A special supplement of the "Toronto Clarion", underground organ of the Toronto district of the Communist Party of Canada deals with the adopted defence, and reads in part as follows:

"They outlawed the Communist Party because they want to stem the rising tide of demands for wage increases.

"They want the Communist Party out of the way NOW because they are plotting to smash and outlaw the trade unions and other labour organizations later."[15]

SECRET

NO PLACE FOR SIXTH COLUMNS

Police forces are swamped with a flood of complaints regarding alleged subversive activities. Switch-boards are jammed with messages to the same effect. A well meaning but ill-informed public, particularly veterans and their organizations, are letting their imagination run riot. Old incidents, second-hand gossip, a German-sounding name, a Teutonic haircut, almost anything now assumes a sinister aspect and immediate and drastic action is demanded by the police.

The Right Honourable the Minister of Justice, as well as senior police officers, have issued statements to the press, pointing out to the public that all this is merely hampering the police and is in fact liable to create the very effect desired by the enemy—confusion.

Reports received from police posts throughout the country indicate that peace officers are facing the situation with good common sense. Nevertheless, much valuable time is being wasted. Consideration is being given to enlisting the co-operation of the Press in an effort to abate the nuisance.[1][Page 2 is missing.]

SIXTH COLUMNS

AGITATION AGAINST GERMAN-SPEAKING PEOPLE
(Vancouver)

Fifth column hysteria in British Columbia is fostering feeling of resentment among loyal citizens of German birth or extraction and may create the very conditions that are now largely imaginary in that province.

It is reported that:

Conditions remain quiet in German circles but a spirit of bitterness has now been aroused among those who have heretofore strictly followed their Lutheran or Baptist Churches and taken no part in Nazi propaganda, feeling they have been unjustly branded as 5th columnists.

A picture of the German-speaking situation in the Pacific Coast Province is drawn by an observer as follows:

"1. THERE IS NO ORGANIZED FIFTH COLUMN IN THE PROVINCE OF BRITISH COLUMBIA.

2. THERE IS A FAIR AMOUNT OF MATERIAL FOR SUCH A MOVEMENT.

3. THERE IS, AT PRESENT, NO LEADERSHIP FOR SUCH A MOVEMENT.

4. A STRONG LEADER COULD, WITHOUT DOUBT, GATHER THESE FORCES AND BECOME A THREAT.

"Material for a fifth column is found not only among German-speaking people but outside of this class as well. Our analysis produced the following results: Nazis and Nazi sympathizers; Technocrats; National Unity Party followers, Communists and disgruntled and dissatisfied citizens.[3]

"To our knowledge, there is no timber for strong leadership to be found among German-speaking people in Vancouver or in the Provinces of B.C. For possible leadership we should look among the English-speaking people to take the lead. (We class Italians with Nazi sympathizers or National Unity Party.)

"We have pointed out on more than one occasion that it is our contention not more than TEN PERCENT of all German-speaking people, West of Ontario, are of ENEMY birth. The other ninety percent are bewildered and dumbfounded why they should be put in the same class as enemy aliens. It is pointed out that our local newspapers condemned in no uncertain terms the treatment of the minorities in Germany. Now they foster and promote class hatred, the very thing for which we are fighting Hitlerism. To escape persecution is the reason given for migration to Canada, to enjoy the much heralded freedom under British justice. It is pointed out that on the whole these people are an industrious, thrifty and peace loving people. They are law abiding, all they ask is that they be given an equal chance at making a living with other people of the Dominion, and to be left in peace. The result of this blacklisting of Germans all over the country is not a healthy one. It is quite reasonable to suggest that, if the supposed friends are turning their backs on them, then in the end they will have to turn to the enemy for salvation. We do not wish to appear as alarmists, but it is only natural that one reaps what he sows.

"We suggest that a difference be made between Germans of enemy birth and German-speaking Germans born in other countries. If our papers would hold out the hand of friendship to the latter class, we feel the response would be cordial. To make and hold friends is not by brow-beating methods, but by kindness. This is our observation at this time."[4]

PERSECUTION OF RACIAL MINORITIES

"Persons of present enemy origin suspected of Nazi activities have been interned. Persons of potential enemy origin are known and are being closely watched.

"The overwhelming majority of foreign-born citizens are passionately anti-Nazi.

"Any cessation of labor or diversion of effort to deal with matters that are and can only be handled by the police would be helping the enemy.

"Any persecution of racial minorities in this country is unworthy of our people and foreign to our traditions and our national spirit." (Minister of Justice)

The imperative need of strictest Government supervision of war-time law enforcement, in order to prevent such injustice, is strikingly portrayed in the following letter from a German-born citizen addressed to the Commissioner, R.C.M.Police:

Dear Sir:

Police Chief ------- has advised me to seek your aid and counsel in the matter of a very unpleasant local situation. He is hoping, as much as I am, that if I lay the facts of my case before you, you may be able to help us with a problem that is involving a large percentage of the foreign-born people in the district.

I am of German birth, and this morning I was forced by malicious gossip and rumour to resign my position as assistant manger of the ----- Hotel. As far as local authorities are concerned, my record is clear, but obviously this is not enough. My resignation was not motivated so much by a fear of what the unwholesome talk would do to me as by the fact that the hotel and its manager would continue to suffer as long as I continued as an employee. So serious has the situation become that Mr. ----- has been threatened by over-zealous patriots who accuse him of championing a Nazi spy.[5]

Conditions are just as bad for my wife—a Canadian girl from sound, loyal English stock. My problem is this: What can I do to prove to the people who are so willing to believe every obvious and incredible lie about me that I am a loyal and patriotic Canadian citizen?

My record is briefly this:

I was born in Plauen, Saxony, on November 15, 1904. My father was Julius Willy Geigenmiller, and my mother an Englishwoman, Florence Gee. My father's business interests were in England, where he lived for many years, and I received some of my education there, living with my English relatives.

The situation abroad was so desperate that I decided to emigrate and in July, 1928, I came to Canada. At that time, a campaign was conducted in Europe to encourage emigration to this country. In the period since I arrived in Montreal, I have never belonged to a German or German-Canadian organization of any kind, and I have deliberately avoided fraternising with other German-born people. I can honestly say that I have tried, to the very best of my ability, to be a good Canadian citizen.

My naturalization papers were completed in August, 1933, and my registration number is 108449, Series A. In 1937, I was called back to Germany by my father's failing health, and he has died since that time.

Since the outbreak of war I have not communicated, or attempted to communicate with anyone in Germany, and I have no desire to be anything but a good Canadian. When I had a long talk with him today, Chief------ informed me that rumours are being spread not only about people of German birth, but also about anyone of foreign birth and even born Canadians with German names.

I am well-known in the hotel business, and I know it will be impossible for me to hold a job anywhere else under the circumstances. My status seems that of a man without a country, because people still refuse to look on me as a Canada, and I am no longer a German.[6]

If it is possible for me to enlist for active service, I would be glad to do so, and I believe I am in good physical condition. If this is closed to me, what is to happen to me, and thousands of others like me who are being forced from jobs to nothing for the crime of being born in Europe? We would welcome a system of closer police surveillance.

Surely, in time, the feeling of loyalty to Canada of these foreign-born citizens who are being hounded into the streets will be replaced by one of embitterment. What can we hope for in a country that we are only too glad to call our own?

I know that you must be flooded with requests for information at this time, but I would appreciate an answer, if it was at all possible.

Sincerely,

----------[7]

FASCISM

"MUSSOLINI COMES BEFORE ALL"
(Vancouver)

Italian Fascists throughout Canada know exactly where they stand in the event of Italy entering the war against the Allies. The Fascist oath (according to reliable information) is as follows:

"That I will defend Fascism and Mussolini even with my own blood. Mussolini comes before all."

In the meantime such Italians may be said to be "good citizens" as they for the most part comply with the Fascist principle that before one can be a good Italian and loyal Fascist he must be a good subject of the country of adoption.

It is reported from Vancouver that:

The viewpoint generally accepted among the Italians is that it is good business to become naturalized and obtain full benefits of citizenship, but in event of Italy going to war against the country of their adoption, then Italy and Mussolini come first.

Apart from the general excitement and growing spirit of bitterness in these tense times, the people of the Italian Colony—including the Fascist element—are behaving very well, and giving no real cause for complaint. The Fascist element believe the day is now close at hand when they will be considered enemies in Canada, but until war is actually declared, apart from confidential Fascist boosting talk among themselves, they are living within the law until the call comes.[8]

COMMUNISM

READY TO CONTROL YOUTH CONGRESS
(Montreal)

Provincial Youth Councils throughout the Dominion are holding conferences during the month of June in preparation for the fifth Canadian Youth Congress which is to be held at Montreal on June 5, 6 and 7.

The Young Communist League is exerting its full effort in an attempt to obtain a strong representation at the Montreal Congress. Although they do not expect to be able to control the Congress this year they are determined to prevent the Congress from going on record as supporting the war.

The Congress agenda this year includes (1) Youth Training and Scholarships, (2) Jobs, (3) Conscription, (4) Higher Wages, (5) Help for Young

Farmers, (6) Health.

Since the beginning of 1940 there have been waves of requests to the Department of Labour, Ottawa, for conciliation boards as provided for under the Industrial Disputes Act. The introduction of these conciliation boards is considered very desirable by the Communist Party trade union leaders as it has been learned that with these boards operating on a "give and take" basis the Union is fairly certain of some concession, however small, thereby strengthening the prestige of the Union. This helps towards an increased membership and ultimately the influence of the Communist Party is strengthened because its members within the trade union concerned having taken the initiative in the dispute receive the credit for the gains.[9]

RALLYING AGAINST SIXTH COLUMN ACTION

Recent Communist Party directives to its various branches stress the need for education of all members on the developments of the "Sixth Column", "British Allied League" and other national organizations. Attention is also directed to the imminence of national registration of the Canadian population.

With reference to the organizations combatting Fifth Column activities in this country, the directives state as follows:

"The party must take the offensive against the nationalist organizations. Stickers and leaflets should be put out by every branch, bearing the slogans "No Private Armies", "No Vigilantes", "No Storm Troopers", etc. We must get busy on this issue at once and conduct a vigorous campaign against these organizations, in order to protect the C.P. and ourselves. Every member must be responsible for putting up a number of stickers weekly. Resolutions must be passed in trade unions and organizations to offset mob violence."

A campaign as outlined above would no doubt tend to aggravate the situation rather than discourage the organizations who are taking up the fight against the subversive elements.

LOSING FAITH IN REVOLUTION IN GERMANY
(Vancouver)

Stories of war sabotage, particularly on railroads, by Communists in Germany are losing credit with their brothers in Canada. Executive members of the C.P. on the West Coast are beginning to suspect that the German Communist is one with the German people in their ambition to destroy the British and French Empires. A recent article by Walter Ulbricht of the Central Committee of the Communist Party of Germany, printed as a front [10] page story in the Party's B.C. organ "The Advocate", contributes to this local enlightenment. The writer declares—

"The revolutionary workers and progressive forces in Germany, who are, at the cost of great sacrifice, fighting against terror and reaction, do not wish to exchange the present regime for a regime of national and social oppression by British Imperialism and German big capitalists who are subservient to Britain."

This statement has somewhat destroyed the faith of Canadian Communists in the idea that a revolution within Germany was imminent and would stop the German armed forces from actual assault on the British Isles. These people had believed that Communists in Germany were steadily working for the overthrow of Hitler, sabotaging war work wherever possible and were ready to revolt as soon as a rising revolutionary situation was apparent throughout the British Commonwealth.

Despite this awakening amongst our C.P. officials, they will no doubt continue to fashion their policy by directives emanating from Moscow.

CIVIL LIBERTIES UNION RUIN THEIR CAUSE
(Montreal)

While the recent convention held by the Canadian Civil Liberties Union in Montreal was a striking example of the effectiveness of Communist Party tactics in attaining results, even the Communists must admit it was a collosal blunder. The convention was too obviously "packed" — at least 85% of the 150 delegates being Communists—and reaction from the loyal elements has all but wrecked the Union.

Sponsored by various organizations with Communistic leanings, the Convention brought about 500 persons from all parts of Canada to discuss such subjects as Censorship, Rights of labour and employer, Law and Civil Liberty, Rights of minorities, Rights of aliens.[11]

The main resolution (adopted by a unanimous vote) was a strong protest against curtailment of civil liberties and constitutional rights and uncontrolled power of the Government to rule by Order in Council under the Defence of Canada Regulations, War Measures Act and the Censorship Regulations. It demanded that a halt be called to the formation of Sixth Columns, that the aforementioned statutes be amended by the Government to restrict and protect the rights of the people and The People of Canada were urged to support the action of the Conference, to organize themselves in a movement to regain their rights and to assist in the defence of those prosecuted for defending their rights and liberties.

Two speakers at this meeting aroused stormy anger by daring to defend liberty at the expense of traitors. As confidentially reported:

    (a) H. Larocque of the Pan Canadian Union proposed the annulment of the Main Resolution, stating "many people wish Tim Buck to remain at liberty", (loud cheers by the gathering) "but if this is the feeling of this conference then we have the Fifth Column right here in this hall" (booed and hissed by the audience).

    (b) Lou Golden of the Toronto Civil Liberties Association made a motion to bar Nazis, Fascists and Communists from any or-

ganization working for Civil Liberties. He also made a motion
to amend the Main Resolution in various ways, but was badly
shouted down, and R.L. Calder, K.C., Montreal, interjected "I
trust the meeting will treat the amendment with the contempt it
deserves". Mr. Golden also started a discussion with, "Is everyone in favour of winning the War?" This was greeted with
silence, then a few hesitant "No's" were heard. The question was
then called irrelevant and buried under further discussion.

The balance of the speakers were favourably received, most of them
speaking on and in favour of the main resolution. On a motion that the
outlawing of the Communist Party be condemned, R.L. Calder, K.C. advised that "it would be wise to leave this motion aside the trust the Courts
of the land and find out whether [12] they are trustworthy. Furthermore,
that by condemning Section 62 it means we are condemning the outlawing of all or any organization whatsoever."

Private discussions were held during the Convention, which were attended only by special delegates, members of the Communist Party. All
present at these discussions were as one in their rejoicing over the success
of the Nazi offensive, as they regard Great Britain as the main obstacle to
the destruction of capitalism. They voiced the opinion that before either
side can destroy the other the Soviet Union will act, and that the workers
will rebel as soon as they have suffered enough and the necessary revolutionary conditions are created. It is expected that conscription in Canada
will cause a revolutionary situation in Quebec of which they hope to take
the fullest advantage.

As this Conference was given much publicity in the local newspapers
and revealed the complete domination of the Union by the Communist
Party, it has undoubtedly weakened the C.C.L.U. (which the Communist
Party regard as the only remaining legal organization completely under
its control) by arousing public reaction against it and causing many
prominent citizens to withdraw their support.

Since the Conference the Communist Party has informed the Union
that in return for their continued support it will be necessary for the Union
to stop Jean Charles Harvey, editor of "Le Jour" and executive member
of the Union, writing articles against the Party and on danger from Fifth
Columns. To this is added a recommendation that should Harvey refuse
to comply with this request he be expelled from the Union.

[✂deletion: 1 paragraph: 4 lines][13]

INTELLIGENCE
BULLETIN

ROYAL CANADIAN MOUNTED POLICE
HEADQUARTERS, OTTAWA

JUNE 24, 1940

CONTENTS

War Series
No. 34.

"BRITISH ISLES ONLY?"

It was essential that the country should appreciate the urgent grave situation facing Canada and that not an hour should be lost, declared Premier Mackenzie King in Parliament on June 18.

"We've been watching and saying after France, probably the British Isles will be attacked," he said. "Are you sure it will be the British Isles only?"

He did not wish to speak words of defeatism. He believed in ultimate victory but it would be "a very long and sorrowful time before that was reached."

The enemy was not likely to pick and choose between parts of the British commonwealth. The enemy knew the part Canada was playing, how dependent Britain was on Canada for food and munitions.

As certain as that day follows night, the enemy would do its utmost to see that aid was stopped from Canada and other parts of the Empire.

FOREIGN ELEMENTS

MINERS DEMAND EXPULSION OF ENEMY ALIENS
(Minto, N.B.)

A "trouble spot" has occurred at Minto, N.B. due to the presence of Italians among the employees of the Miramichi Lumber Co.

On June 10 these employees, numbering about 300, held a mass meeting and passed the following resolution:

"That the Company be notified that unless action is taken regarding German and Italian born aliens, whether naturalized or not, who have up until now shown apparently more loyalty to the land of their birth than their adoption and whom we believe if they are not now engaged in subversive activities would be if given the opportunity; That unless each man's loyalty is proved beyond doubt, that we will refuse to go down in the pit with them Friday morning.

Sgd. Wm. Walkcr, Chairman
Arthur Ouellette, Secretary."

The resolution was forwarded to the Minister of Justice and Labour by [⊱deletion: 2 lines] They employ about 11 Italians and 6 Germans.

It is reported that Horace Pettigrove, Fair Wage Officer, and the Deputy Attorney General are aware of the situation and have advised Mr. Taylor that everything necessary was being done and there was no cause for uneasiness.[2]

HOW INJUSTICE PLAYS INTO ENEMY'S HANDS
(Toronto)

Although there are pro-Nazis and pro-Fascists still at large the public should not lose sight of the fact that the majority of Canadian citizens of German and Italian origin are definitely pro-British and that unfounded suspicion and persecution of such must inevitably weaken their loyalty and further the cause of the enemy.

The enemy are perhaps more conscious of this than we are, as the following report from Toronto suggests:

Local Nazi sympathizers are displaying some satisfaction in the fact that, due to the general feeling of the public against all Germans, those Germans who were not in favour of Hitlerism are nevertheless being discriminated against just as much as the others.

The Nazis feel that this attitude of the public will cause those Germans who were previously against them to change their views. I have myself noticed that this is actually happening in a number of cases who were definitely anti-Nazi a short time ago; some of them are now saying that they would not assist in any way in the rounding up of Nazis and are even expressing sympathy for those who have been interned.

Many Germans feel that injustice is being done them by the general anti-German drive which started recently. No only Germans feel this way but also other nationalities such as Italians, Ukrainians, Hungarians, Jugo-Slavs and others. They fear that the resentment against Germans will spread to others not of British stock.

So much for the German element. A similar situation is forming among those of Italian origin, despite many proofs of loyalty from Italian-Canadian groups. Indeed, in their desire to destroy Fascism in Canada they sometimes show a tendency to go to the other extreme as shown by a recent report from Vancouver:

At the meeting at Hastings Auditorium on the evening of the 10th instant about 250 persons were present, and the meeting was under the chairmanship of Mr. Angelo Branca, assisted by Marino Culos as a secretary.[3]

A resolution was passed condemning Italy and Mussolini for entering the war on the German side; a copy of this resolution is to be sent to Prime Minister King; one to Prime Minister Pattullo, and one to Mayor Telford.

The aim of this organization (called the Italian Canadian War Vigilante) is to sponsor a registration of all Italians in Vancouver and probably British Columbia, whether Canadian citizens or not.

In a resolution of the Italian veterans of the last war, Mr. Charles Penway and Mr. Tony Rita also condemned the Italian Government for the declaration of war.

Most of the Italian business men, according to Mr. Branca, have agreed to contribute $5.00 per month toward the war cause. A charge of one dollar is made for each one becoming a member of the above association. Their aim is to combat "Fifth Column" activities amongst the Italians. According to my viewpoint, it is on the same basis as the so-called Anti-Nazi "Sixth Column", and it will prove to be more of a menace than a help since three members will be elected at a later meeting to scout and report on "fifth columners", and that's where some trouble may develop. I personally think if things are left to the police we would have no trouble about sabotage of our industries by Fascist sympathisers, because now they are all scared stiff since hearing of those arrested, and have shut up like clams.[4]

LABOUR UNREST

"TROUBLE LOOMING AHEAD FOR AUTOMOTIVE INDUSTRY"
(Windsor)

There was a flare-up at the plant of the General Motors of Canada in Windsor last week which resulted in twenty-seven of the workers deliberately walking out of the plant at noon with the intention of not returning until the next morning. Reliable information is that this action resulted from an extra half hour's lunch period, necessitated by certain production problems over which the management had no control. To make it worse, according to the best information available, there was not even a grievance submitted to the management. What it amounted to was a deliberate strike participated in by non-union as well as union members and appears as a thoroughly irresponsible action. Union Leaders, including Regional Director Burt, admit privately that the men are in the wrong, but unfortunately, Burt, as well as the other leaders obviously feel that they must inject the union into the picture and work for the individuals regardless of the individuals' membership or non-membership in the union and regardless of how heavily the responsibility should be placed upon the shoulders of the individuals involved.

Labour unions in the United States, particularly the C.I.O., already have indicated strongly that they are planning to take full advantage of the opportunity afforded by the re-armament and national defense program to agitate in order that the employers grant them additional concessions. According to the progress that the C.I.O. is making, there is evidence that trouble is looming ahead for employers in the automotive industry. They also have made open announcements of their intentions to completely unionize the aircraft industry, and will not co-operate in the defense program but instead will utilize all its resources and economic power to press for higher wages and reduced hours. It is reliably reported that the C.I.O. contemplates using every means at its command to prevent what it terms any encroachment on the gains organized labor has made.

Regardless of the public statements to lead the public to believe that the Canadian C.I.O. affiliates have been granted autonomy, this is only for official and public consumption in Canada and does not give a true state of affairs. There has been to a degree an infiltration of the ideas and methods used by the C.I.O. in the United States into the Canadian affiliates.[5]

ORGANIZING NEW TRADE UNION CENTRE
(Regina)

Leaders of the Communist-controlled Committee for Industrial Organization in Canada continue their efforts to entice all dissatisfied trade unions and unorganized groups of workers into their fold. The latest step in this direction is the drafting of a constitution for a new trade union centre. Such draft constitution was prepared by the C.I.O. officials in the United States and will be used as a basis for discussion at a National Congress being called for this Autumn in some Eastern Canadian centre and expected to be attended by 100,000 people—including 65,000 from the C.I.O.; 30,000 from the All-Canadian Congress of Labour, and the remainder from Catholic syndicates in Quebec and other non-affiliated unions. The merger of these trade unions will be the all-important issue before the Congress. We are advised from Regina that:

The main objective of this trade union centre will be to organize the unorganized in the basic war industries, such as Trail, Flin Flon and other metal mines. This, of course, is following a line as discussed by Leslie Morris, [❧deletion: 2 lines] in defeating the war aims of British Imperialism by fomenting strikes and labour trouble in the industrial field.

MANY UNIONS RETURNING TO A. F. OF L.
(Toronto)

The International Ladies Garment Workers Union in conference on June 5, by a vote of 640 to 12, decided to go back into the ranks of the American Federation of Labor. The action, opposed by a small amount of Communist delegates, caused a demonstration of approval throughout the assembly hall.

At the opening of the Convention David Dubinsky, President of the Union, indicated that he did not favour affiliation with the A. F. of L. The Convention, however, received assurance from William Green, President of the A.F. of L., that the Executive Council (A. F. of L.) would recommend abolishing of the assessment at the last Convention in September and instead would levy a tax for organizing activities. This promise paved the way for the Union's return.

The International Ladies Garment Workers Union was one of the leading unions instrumental in the formation of the Committee of Industrial Organizations and was suspended by the A. F. of L. in 1936.[6]

The Convention also went on record in favour of cleaning the Union's ranks of all notorious and active Communists, and instructions will be issued to the numerous workers in the U.S.A. and Canada accordingly.

Attempts to rejoin the A. F. of L. are being made by other Unions in Canada including the International Typographers Union, and certain Trades and Labour Councils have taken the initiative in a movement to rid the A. F. of L. of the Communist element.

[❧deletion: 1 paragraph: 6 lines]

At this meeting of the Council a letter was read from the Street Railwaymen's Union endorsing the attitude taken by President Jamieson in regard to the suspension of certain unions. The Union also sent three new delegates to the Council, all of whom are known to be anti-Communists.

MRS. NEILSON, M.P. ADDRESSES
UNEMPLOYED ASSOCIATION
(Toronto)

A meeting was held by the Unemployed Single Men's Association in Toronto on June 11, attended by 500 people, including Mrs. Dorise W. Neilson, M.P., Ken Woodsworth, Secretary of the Canadian Youth Congress, J.K. Bell, Secretary of the Unemployed Single Men's Association, and other well known radicals.

Although it was noticed that few of the Red element were present, and the meeting was opened by singing the National Anthem, the opinions expressed were distinctly subversive in tone.

J.K. Bell spoke on conditions prevalent amongst the single unemployed in Canada today how they were roaming the country looking for work and how after attempting to join the Army, and being turned down as unfit, were left to wander with no thought of their welfare. He commented upon the police picking up the men passing out the leaflets (cries of "shame") and contended that the unemployed today wanted jobs and not conscription. He suggested that the people petition the Government to start work programs for the unemployed youth of this country.[7]

Ken Woodsworth, following the same trend as Bell, condemned the members of Parliament for their lack of nerve in not speaking up for the youth, stating "Only one member of Parliament had the nerve to get up and speak for the youth".

Mrs. Neilson was very well received by the meeting. Our confidential report refers to her comments as follows:

"Mrs. Neilson opened by stating the East meets West and rapped the Government for conditions and suffering of the farmers and the poor of the East. She went on to say that the Government voted $700,000,000 for war and $750,000,000 for something else but could not find a cent to relieve suffering and gave statements of contracts given to Ford and General Motors for $400,000,000 each. She stated that the rich will get richer and the poor poorer and that the war bonds were only something to make the bankers rich. She commented upon the mess the men had made in the running of Parliament and called upon the women to organize for better conditions. She quoted a Chinese proverb regarding buying a loaf of bread with a yen and a rose with the other and stated that the $100,000 voted for flowers, etc. at Ottawa would have been better spent on starving people. She quoted Dr. Weir of B.C. regarding the health of young men joining the Army and she also stated that poverty was one of the worst subversive elements in Canada, that the people were 100% loyal but she could not say the same for the Government. She went on to say that the war taxes would affect the working class with regard to clothing, food, etc. and that men were being fattened up before going to war while new life at home was not getting a fair deal. In closing she called on women to organize and carry on the war that was at home."[8]

LEADERSHIP NOT WORRIED

The outlawing of the Communist Party has given its Toronto members and sympathizers a "good scare" for the time being. The leadership however are not worried, as they insist that the longer the War lasts the worse conditions will become for the small taxpayer and the proletariat and the better for the Red Revolution. It won't be long now, they promise, before strikes and trouble can be expected from coast to coast.[9]

COMMUNISM
"ALL-RED" NATIONAL YOUTH CONGRESS
(Montreal)

Another National Youth Congress will be held under auspices of Montreal Youth Council in Montreal the first week in July. This Congress promises to be largely comprised of delegates from subversive organizations, including the Young Communist League, Young Communists, United Workers, Anti-Conscription League, Canadian Civil Liberties Union (Communist controlled Montreal section) and Youth Councils.

At a Youth Parliament Session held in Montreal on June 1 and 2 a resolution of loyalty to the Government had been defeated by a majority vote, with the result that the Y. M. C. A., the Young Men's Hebrew Association, the Young Women's Hebrew Association and the Co-operative Commonwealth Youth Movement had withdrawn their delegates from the Session and the Montreal Junior Board of Trade had publicly announced in the press its denial of affiliation with the Montreal Youth Council and strongly condemned the Council for its past activities.

Despite public reaction and the severing of other Youth organizations from the Montreal Youth Council, this body is determined to hold the National Youth Congress next month, unless prevented by the Police. Therefore it can be presumed that this Congress will be wholly controlled by the left wing elements.[10]

DISORGANIZATION IN SASKATCHEWAN PARTY RANKS
(Regina)

The Communist Party of Canada in the Province of Saskatchewan appears to be seriously disorganized as a result of the outlawing of the Party and other left wing organizations and the arrests of Clifford Peet and Gladys McDonald, leading Communists.

Organizers are contacting local leaders and members, instructing them that under no circumstances are they to correspond with the District Bureaus at Regina and Saskatoon. Owing to the seizure of mailing lists when Peet and McDonald were arrested, the Party leaders fear that the authorities will take steps to check all the mail from those named on the lists. Efforts are being made, but with little or no response from country points, to raise funds for the defence of those arrested.

A. C. Campbell, leader of the Saskatchewan Party, recently visited Winnipeg and stated that no one would attend meetings of any kind. It would appear that he was advised to return to Saskatchewan immediately and notify the Party leaders to stay under cover for at least six months, if necessary.

Some anxiety is noted in connection with the evidence which may be given at the trials of Peet and McDonald, and it is understood that if documents are produced or evidence forthcoming dealing with the ramifications of the C.P. of C. in Saskatchewan the whole leadership will be disowned by the Central Committee and an underground organization promoted from Toronto.

T. H. Newlove has been retained to conduct the defence of Peet and McDonald, and it is believed that he has some contact of a confidential nature in the Attorney General's Dept. in Regina.

It is of interest to add that the C.P. of C. are reported to have a complete list of the license number, names and body colors etc. of all R.C.M.P. cars operating in Saskatchewan.[11]

<u>SECRET</u>

INTELLIGENCE
BULLETIN

ROYAL CANADIAN MOUNTED POLICE
HEADQUARTERS, OTTAWA

JULY 15, 1940

CONTENTS
"First Line of Defence"

War Series
No. 35.

<u>COMMENTS</u>
"FIRST LINE OF DEFENCE"

"Those who regard the British Isles as the last outpost of the Continent are wrong. It is, of course, nothing of the sort. These islands do not represent the geographical and political extremity of Europe; they are not the last corner of a continent in which the remnants of a well-nigh shattered European civilization now repose. They are rather the first line of defence of a great world system, made up of an Imperial Commonwealth, and the freedom-loving countries of the new world. He who attempts to invade these shores dare not, and must not, regard his expedition as one rounding off a series of European conquests, but rather as the beginning of a great and terrible adventure which offers not the slightest prospect of final success, against an Imperial system, and great continents possessed of illimitable man-power and resources. They command the oceans and

276

spirited peoples who do not know defeat, and if necessary will blockade the whole continent of Europe so that Germany and her allies would perish in their very triumphs. Military success on the Continent is one thing; sometimes in the past we have failed to prevent it. Conquest of the world is another; no one has yet achieved it."

From "Memorandum of Information
on Foreign Affairs."

QUEEN VICTORIA WAS NOT INTERESTED

Notice recently placed in the vestibule of Greenwich Police Court, London:-

"By listening to or reporting rumours of calamity you help the enemy. Follow the example of Queen Victoria who, at the age of 80, in the black days of the Boer War, said, 'There is no depression in this house, and we are not interested in the possibility of defeat—it does not exist'."[1]

NAZIISM

SYMPATHY FOR INTERNED TRAITORS!

(The following letter should be an object lesson to thousands of enemy dupes who oppose the law to their own destruction.)

Ste. Rose du Lac, Man.,
June 24, 1940.

"Hon. Ernest Lapointe
Minister of Justice
Ottawa.

(Or to whom it may concern)

Shortly after the war broke out, a Mr. Leo Shebbler of Ste. Rose, was interned for reasons no one here knew at the time. A few months later his wife came around with a petition to have him released, thinking as we did that he was a good citizen and being moved by the tears and pleadings of his wife to have him come home, and provide for his family as he was previously doing, a number of people and I signed the petition. Whether the petition had anything to do with his release or not I don't know, but I do know that I and everyone else who signed the petition would like to see him interned again.

Since his return he treats everyone with contempt, even the police, he refuses to work, is showing a very mean disposition, and is a member of some Nazi Organization, and in the opinion of the police, is a dangerous man to have at large. I hope you will issue orders to have him sent back to the internment camp for the duration of the war.

Yours truly,

(Note: Ordered re-interned by Minister of Justice)[2]

INCREASING BITTERNESS AMONG GERMANS
(From a confidential report) (Toronto)

"The internment of suspected Italians and some Germans has a sobering influence on the German element here. At the present time there are no gatherings at private homes to celebrate Hitler's victories, and Nazi propagandists who have previously been pretty active, prefer to stay in the background for the time being.

As more and more Germans-naturalized and unnaturalized—are being put out of work throughout the city and articles appear in local newspapers urging Canadian families to discharge all German domestic servants, bitterness and anti-British feeling are steadily increasing amongst the German element. With no hope to secure employment, many of them are prepared and quite willing to go to internment camps, especially as they believe that the war will soon be over and that they will be indemnified after the war.

Most of those German nationals who have applied for naturalization as British subjects but have not received their citizen papers as yet are now not interested in getting them. Germans, whether naturalized or not, and even those who try to be good Canadians, are now morally isolated, harmed in their material interests by an often-unrelenting boycott, unable to secure employment, suspected of being fifth columnists and forced by war regulations to register with the registrar of enemy aliens, so that Canadian citizen papers are now practically useless, they contend.

Germans here greatly appreciate the attitude of the Federal Government towards so-called sixth columnists and are thankful that serious disorders which inevitably occur in times of great stress when emotional hysteria takes the place of reason have been prevented. They point proudly to the fact that in the present war no acts of sabotage have been committed or attempted by Germans as yet and in their own interest they are anxious to see that no sabotage will ever be committed by a German fanatic in this country.[3]

ITALIANS
ITALIAN NATIONALS IN CANADA

The number of Italian nationals in Canada, as determined by Canadian law, is estimated, on the basis of the available information, at about 8,000 at the end of 1939. This estimate is arrived at by taking the number of persons declaring themselves as Italian nationals at the census of 1931, adding the immigrants of the period between June 1, 1931, and December 31, 1939, who stated on entering the country that they were of Italian nationality, and deducting the number of former Italian subjects who have been naturalized between the same dates, as obtained from the records of the Secretary of State, and also making a reasonable allowance for deaths.

Now, at the census of 1931, 17,087 persons described themselves as of Italian nationality; between the date of the census and the end of 1939, 2,604 immigrants of Italian nationality entered the Dominion but in the same period 10,981 persons of former Italian nationality became naturalized Canadian citizens. This would give us a total of 8,710 Italian nationals in the Dominion at December 31, 1939, provided that there had been no deaths of Italian nationals and no emigration of Italian nationals during the period. No figures of deaths are available by nationalities and no figures of emigrants are available, but a reasonable allowance for the former would reduce the number of Italian nationals in Canada at the close of 1939 to about 8,000.

DISTRUST OF ITALIANS IN MINING AREA
(Michel, B.C.)

Following the Italian declaration of War the English speaking miners in the Michel district did not wish to go underground with the Italian miners owing to the possibility of sabotage. There are approximately 200 Italian miners employed at the Michel Mine, and the feeling between the two factions (English and Italian) was very strained. The company officials called a meeting on June 10 when all the miners were informed by Mr. B. Collison, the manager, that if they stopped work now they were no better than Fifth Columnists. After some discussion the English speaking miners decided to continue work.

Reports indicate that conditions are now quiet.[4]

COMMUNISM
"VICTORY FOR THE WORKING CLASS"
(Montreal)

Communist literature of the most fanatically destructive type continues to be privately mimeographed and distributed by "Literature Agents" of Branches. A copy of a recent bulletin edited and published by the Educational Committee of District 2 of the Communist Party was forwarded from Montreal. Its three closely-printed double sheets seek to arouse "the masses" into revolting against the Imperialist War and turning the Dominion over to the "strength and impregnability of Bolshevik leadership" (Comrade Lenin). To quote in part:

For Bolshevik Understanding of the War and our Tasks.

The fact that the imperialist war has entered a new stage of ferocious intensity that "our own" imperialists have been suffering defeats, and that reaction is going to frenzied extremes in its attacks on the working class—all of this puts to the sharpest test the revolutionary firmness and understanding of every Communist.

It is at times like this that the bourgeoisie, along with its violence and fascist repression, exerts the full pressure of chauvinism, of capitalist deception and hysteria, in an attempt to wipe out the influence of the class-conscious vanguard of the workers, to defeat the strike and anti-conscription and other struggles of the working people, and to harness the masses to the war-machine of imperialism. Just because of this, the sharpening and deepening of our Marxist, Leninist, Stalinlist understanding of the War and our tasks, is today a vitally important, immediate responsibility of each one of us. In this, our most precious weapons, steeled and tested to invincibility in the fires of war and revolution, are the teachings of Lenin on the struggle against imperialist war, for Socialism, and the wise, bolshevik leadership of Stalin, and of Dimitrov and our World-Party of Communism. Their teachings are no set of dead, abstract formulas, but rich, concentrated experience,[5] living leadership, which learned till it is a living part of us, can give our work the quality of Bolshevism, and guarantee our victory....

For a class-conscious worker, the only interest is in a victory for the working class, to put an end once and for all to the slaughter and blood-drunk tyranny that will otherwise continue for decades, in an unending nightmare. And if the achievement of that victory demands that in each belligerent country the workers carry forward the class struggle against their own bourgeoisie, for its defeat and overthrow—then, clearly, the test of revolutionary class-consciousness and proletarian internationalism will be in the refusal to be brow-beaten and stampeded into 'class-peace', (submission to the bourgeoisie, abandonment of struggle), and in courageous, unflinching adherence to the revolutionary fight for Socialism !......

This imperialist war is the product of imperialism as a whole, imperialism which is "a world system of colonial oppression and of the financial strangulation of the over-whelming majority of the people of the world by a handful of 'advanced' countries" —and which on another occasion Lenin described as one "bloody lump."....

The class character of the present war is determined by the rule of monopoly capital in the belligerent countries, monopoly capital in extreme stages of decay, of counter-revolutionary frenzy; the war is an exploding of the insoluble contradictions of the system of imperialism as a whole, contradictions which the English and French imperialists had sought for years to divert against the stronghold of the rising world-system of Socialism, the U.S.S.R. In the bloody fiasco of those attempts, imperialism is engaged in the mutual destruction of its parts (Anglo-French-American imperialism vs. German imperialism), using as always the masses of workers as its cannonfodder.......

In Canada, the contradictions of imperialism run sharp and deep; and today, our work to lead the Canadian working class forward on the path to the socialist revolution requires tireless leadership to the struggles in industry, among the unemployed, the youth, the women, and, of crucial importance, the struggle against conscription, the struggle for national equality of the French-Canadian people![6]

In this, we shall remember the words of Comrade Stalin: "Contacts with the masses, the strengthening of these contacts, readiness to listen to the voices of the masses — in this lie the strength and impregnability of Bolshevik leadership."

HOPES OF GERMAN CANADIAN PEOPLE'S LEAGUE
(Deutsch-Kanadische Volksbund)
(Toronto)

[℀deletion: 1 paragraph: 3 lines]

Most members are sure that after Hitler has harassed or invaded the British Isles, thereby further exhausting Germany's war machine and at the same time thoroughly stirring up the labour element there, the Soviet Union will make stronger and stronger demands on Germany, bringing these demands to a point where Hitler will have to turn against the Soviets. Then, it is said, the German Army will be no match for the Red Army. The left element in Germany, which has been ordered inactive so far as the war against "British and French Imperialism is concerned", combined with thousands of Nazis tired of war and disillusioned, will at that time come into play as Dimitroff's "Trojan Horse" inside the German forces and make the Soviet invasion of Germany a walk-over appearing in the Netherlands, Belgium, France and the British Isles in the role of the true liberators from Imperialism, Naziism and Fascism.[7]

THE FIFTH CANADIAN YOUTH CONGRESS
(Montreal)

The Fifth Canadian Youth Congress was duly held in Montreal on July 5-8. Mayor Houde delivered a short address, stating that the Defence of Canada Regulations prevented him from saying what he would like to say on certain subjects. He urged them to persevere in their spirit of tolerance and good-will and closed his remarks by stating that there were many eyes turned upon them. Mayor Houde was widely cheered.

Nine affiliated groups withdrew from the Congress during the opening proceedings when those present failed to adopt a clear-cut resolution to support the Federal government in its war effort:

The Montreal Presbytery of the United Church.
The Montreal Y.W.C.A.
The 20th Century Young Liberal Women's Association.
The National Council of the Y.W.C.A.
The Greater Winnipeg Young Liberals.
St. Andrews United Church.
The South Winnipeg Young Liberals

International Millinery Workers Union Local 49.

The loyalty resolution which was finally adopted by the Congress was as follows:

"At the time when Canada is at war, we wish to reaffirm our allegiance to the democratic traditions of our country and of the British Commonwealth of Nations, freedom of speech, press and assembly, the right of trade unions to organize and the rights of minorities."

A report was adopted demanding that the Militia Act be struck from the statutes because of the fact that it still contained the provision respecting the conscription of men for overseas service. A report was also adopted demanding that the interned trade union leaders, Sydney Sarkin, Pat Sullivan and Kent Rowley be granted trials. A suggestion was made to have the words "and Communism" added to a report dealing with Fascism as a threat to democracy, but this was turned down by a very large majority.

It is quite apparent that the Canadian Youth Congress is calculated to undermine the morale of the younger generation in Canada, to [8] inculcate an entirely wrong impression of responsibility of citizenship and to discount the traditions and principles for which this country is now at war.

It is of interest to add that all those who withdrew claimed that the Congress was not representative and did not express the true opinion of Canadian youth.

CLEANSING PROCESS IN TRADE UNIONS
(Vancouver, B.C.)

It will be recalled that last May 17, Vancouver trade unions were suspended for failure to remove Communist representatives from the Council, and that this action was taken by C. Hughes, representative of the American Federation of Labor.

Subsequently some of the suspended unions held a meeting and voiced their opinion that the reason for the expulsions was a pretext and not in accord with the resolutions of the American Federation of Labor. The action of the Vancouver and New Westminister District Trades and Labor Council was condemned as being arbitrary and dictatorial. A month later however, after further consideration a total of 11 of the suspended Unions had made application for reaffiliation.

In contrast to these the Bricklayers' and Masons' Union, Local No. 1 decided unanimously against reaffiliation with the Council, thus breaking a connection of over 50 years' standing. At the same time the Union announced that they were not a Communist organization and probably had not one Red in their ranks.[9][Page 10 is missing.]

GENERAL
WHY "JEHOVAH'S WITNESSES" HAVE BEEN BANNED
(Saskatchewan)

The International Bible Students Association is a world wide organization which has been in existence since 1897. It is under the control of an American named Judge Rutherford, who for years has been attacking our churches and our political organizations claiming that they are betrayers of the common people.

Until the Spring of 1939 this organization was regarded as politically harmless, most of its members being looked upon as merely religious fanatics. Since that time the "Witnesses of Jehovah" have displayed a stiffening attitude, decidedly opposed to British policy.

Little groups have been organized throughout the provinces. They receive literature and records from the Watchtower Bible and Tract Society, Inc., of Brooklyn, New York, which is the American branch of the international association. The "Witnesses" travel around their district, usually in pairs, distributing their literature, playing gramophone records of speeches of Judge Rutherford, and preaching to anyone who will listen to them. They do not sell the literature, but make it clear that donations are very acceptable and necessary to carry on their work. They display a very religious attitude at all time and are very persistent in expounding the views of Judge Rutherford.

It is not known as yet, whether or not the organization has any headquarters in this Province, or who might be in control of their activities. From recent seizures it has been noted that "Witnesses" who have been subjected to court action are advised to communicate with the Legal Desk of the Watchtower and Tract Society, 40 Irwin Avenue, Toronto 5, Ontario.

Among reports on file we note: On May 28, 1939, a large meeting held in the City of Prince Albert by these people was addressed by one J. D. Ferguson, of Toronto. At this meeting, a pamphlet "Fascism of Freedom" was distributed. This piece of literature stresses the need for protecting the freedom and civil liberties of the people. The Roman Catholics and other religious denominations are bitterly attacked for conspiring to introduce dictatorial methods in America. In one place in the pamphlet the following passage appears: "At Ottawa, Canada the Coliseum was engaged for this convention of Christians (Jehovah's Witnesses). Ten days later notice was served on Jehovah's Witnesses [11] by the Board of Control that the use of the Coliseum is granted subject to there being no utterances made against any church or religious denomination of those connected with churches or religious denominations." This is what they mean by restriction of freedom.

Another incident of note occurred at Wakaw, Sask., on August 5, 1939, when about 130 of these people held a parade on the streets of the town carrying placards bearing the words "Religion is a racket and a snare."

A recent report concerning the Hillmond District in this Province indicates that many persons of German origin, who have been active in the Nazi movement, are now taking part in the work of the Jehovah's Witnesses. Obviously, they feel that they might cause a diversion for the authorities under the cloak of religion, or that they might at least cause some embarrassment.

Among the cases that have resulted in convictions in this Province since the outbreak of war is that against Einar A. Anderson, of Big River, Sask., who made statements during September last to a man about to join the army, which were intended or likely to discourage him from doing so. There were such remarks as "You should think twice before you take a step like that, if you do, it will mean eternal damnation." and "He who lives by the sword shall die by the sword." He defaulted in payment of a fine imposed against him and served 60 days in goal.

[℘<deletion: 1 paragraph: 4 lines]

"Civilized nations are preparing for war, which means that the picked young men of the race will soon be brutally, coldly and deliberately dragged from their loved ones by the gold-braided general staffs, and marched into the slaughtering pen."

He also defaulted in payment of a fine imposed and served a term in gaol.

[℘<deletion: 1 paragraph: 5 lines][12][℘<deletion: 3 lines]

[℘<deletion: 1 paragraph: 3 lines]

[℘<deletion: 1 paragraph: 4 lines]

There are clear indications that the "Witnesses of Jehovah" are becoming much more active in this country and that they are being spurred on by the Association itself. While their numbers seem to be quite limited, it is possible for them to bring into existence a very undesirable influence, an influence which is both defeatist and pacifist, and which is definitely opposed to our British policy.

The general policy of this association, although preparing their propaganda from the Bible, is definitely aimed at stirring up animosity toward the churches and the authorities. Such a policy, cannot be regarded as anything but subversive at this critical period through which our Empire is passing.

(On July 4 "Jehovah's Witnesses" were declared an illegal organization by Order in Council.)[13]

AN AMERICAN VIEWPOINT

(Taken from a Copyright editorial, United Business Service, June 22-1940).

<u>Airplanes And Guns are not Enough:</u>

The transition from a peacetime to a wartime economy, which we discussed on this page last week, will involve something more than the stimulation of aircraft production, a bigger steel output, and more ships. We must not only prepare materially for a war which we may "inherit" from the French and British (in addition to the standing menace that this country faces on the Pacific side) but prepare out minds and wills to face new and stringent conditions of life.

It is a hard thing to say in the hour of their bitterness, but lack of sufficient aircraft is not the only reason for the military disasters suffered by France and Britain. Behind that lie conceit a fatuous confidence in their own invincibility, smug satisfaction with their victory of 25 years ago, unwillingness of people and rulers to make sacrifices, or to adjust their viewpoint to changing circumstances. So they failed to prepare adequately in spite of ample warnings.

As a people we suffer from the same self deceiving softness. We once thought we could abolish liquor by voting. We should have learned something from the results of that "noble experiment". We thought we could borrow and spend our way out of depression into prosperity. It seemed so much easier than the path of hard work and sound economics. The President has told the people that we can prepare for war without sacrificing our living standards, and the women need not give up cosmetics. This last is a small thing, but the German women did it several years ago.

And that is the root of our trouble we don't want to give up anything. Labor unions are unwilling to modify wage hour standards. We shrink from compulsory military training, but it would do our boys a world of good. Only our poor boys go into the CCC, but in Germany every boy poor or rich must serve six months in the CCC (Arbeitsdienst). We play politics a game of getting jobs, bonuses, or other gratuities out of the public treasury. Inefficiency even corruption in office is tolerated with a shrug of the shoulders. Public indifference and political collusion prevent the effective suppression of crime.[14]

We must purge ourselves of this easy going softness. Our whole national life needs tuning up in every department. THAT IS THE MOST IMPORTANT ELEMENT IN PREPAREDNESS.

FOREIGN SEAMEN PREVENT CONVOY'S SAILING

Many seamen of foreign nationality have left their ships in the harbours of Quebec and Halifax, refusing to sail to the British Isles or the continent. It is reported that their number is increasing at a serious rate. At present the striking sailors are being held in the Immigration sheds along the water-fronts, but such accommodation is limited and other provisions may have to be made for the sailors' detention.

It is of paramount importance that the shipping of supplies, munitions, etc. to Great Britain should be maintained at all costs. Police have been instructed to assist the immigration officials in every way possible to solve this vital problem.[15]

SECRET

INTELLIGENCE
BULLETIN

ROYAL CANADIAN MOUNTED POLICE
HEADQUARTERS, OTTAWA

AUGUST 26, 1940

CONTENTS

War Series
No. 36

[Pages 1 and 2 are missing]

"UNION MEMBERSHIP NOW A NATIONAL DUTY
(Windsor, Ont.)

Communist audacity and duplicity are strikingly exemplified in the latest effort of the Committee for Industrial Organization to beguile labor into its ranks.

To the end that the industrial capacity of Canada, requisite to the successful prosecution of the war, might be utilized to the fullest possible extent in the present crisis, the Government on June 19 approved certain principles to make for the fuller co-operation between employers and employees, and to prevent the possibility of Canada's war effort being hampered by any serious labour trouble.

Apparently inspired by this Order-in-Council, a four-page leaflet, designated as "Pamphlet Vol. 510", was immediately published and distributed by the Canadian C.I.O. and the Steel Workers' Organizing Committee, containing such remarks as:

"Join Now! Your Government Expect YOU To Organize."
"Any employer who stands in your way is guilty of a treasonable and unpatriotic act of non-co-operation with the Government and blocks a truly effectual war effort."

<u>"Union Membership Is Not Only a Personal Advantage.....It Is Now a National Duty."</u>

Clause 9 of this Order-in-Council reads as follows:

"That workers, in the exercise of their right to organize, should use neither coercion nor intimidation of any kind to influence any person to join their organization."

This seems to be plain and understandable, yet the Pamphlet [3] No. 510 goes far beyond the bounds of reasonable persuasion and deep into the realms of intimidation and coercion and fully demonstrates the extremes to which the C.I.O. will go in its desire to gain power, to say nothing of its continuous efforts to infringe upon management's rights to run their own business. In addition, it demonstrates the advantage the C.I.O. obviously insists upon taking of the good intentions of the Government by attempting to claim that the Government expects our workers to join the Union.

WAR BUDGET a "COLOSSAL SWINDLE"
(Toronto)

A so-called "educational bulletin" has been issued by the Communist Party of Canada, containing their views of the last federal budget. To quote in part:

"The bill appropriating 700 million dollars for this year's war expenditures is a colossal swindle of the common people of Canada....

"Large as it is, Canada's total war expenditure could be covered without drawing one cent from the already over-taxed and underpaid workers and farmers by taking a small part of the accumulated surpluses of the capitalists and by taxing their incomes.

"The despicable traitors who lead the CCF are proving their value to the bourgeoisie by covering up the war appropriations swindle with progressive phrases. The dictatorial control of labor in England and New Zealand, established with the aid of the Labor leaders, is hailed by Millard as "socialism", and Coldwell openly demands that similar measures be taken in Canada.

"Masquerading as 'conscription of wealth and industry and labor' these measures are actually used [4] by the monopoly capitalists to assume dictatorial control over the working class and of the whole economic structure, so as to ensure the maximum profits from the war, and to crush all opposition ot their policies. Similar measures are being planned for Canada. Every move in this direction is hailed by the CCF spokesmen.

"All the forces of the progressive movement must be thrown into the urgent task of exposing these facts to the masses of people. In this way the working class can most effectively answer the 'fifth column' propaganda of the bourgeoisie. When the masses begin to understand the full implications of the war appropriation swindle, they will see that the real enemy at home is the capitalist class and its government. Canadian capitalism has proved its bitter hostility to the true interests of our country. Today the capitalists stand revealed as greedy exploiters who are bent on ruining the Canadian people for their profits."

INTERNMENTS PROVING MOST EFFECTIVE

Reports reaching this office indicate that the internment of leading Communists has had a disconcerting effect upon the Party members generally, although it is noticed that the Party itself is still active, particularly in connection with the printing and distribution of subversive literature.

Under ordinary circumstances, it is quite evident that members of the Communist Party would prefer to be prosecuted through the courts and so become martyrs to the cause through the publicity that would result from court proceedings. Under present circumstances, however, they have no guarantee that they will be prosecuted, and it is noticeable that the leaders fear internment because of the quiet way in which their activities are definitely stopped.[5]

EJECTING RED FROM TRADE UNIONS
(Vancouver)

Previous reference has been made in the Bulletin under the heading "Cleansing Process in Trade Unions — Vancouver, British Columbia" to the suspension of various Vancouver trade unions from the Vancouver and New Westminster District Trades and Labour Council for failure to remove Communist representatives.

At a recent meeting of the Council, a recommendation to reject the names of nine Trade Union members representing five affiliated locals was passed by a vote of fifty-one to twenty-six. [≿<deletion: 3 lines]

Thirty other delegates, representing some eleven unions were accepted.

It is understood that the local Communist Party leaders have expressed chagrin at their failure to deceive [≿<deletion: 1 line] on the credentials of their nine members rejected. Under the circumstances it is understood that they will now devote most of their energies toward furthering Communist propaganda in the Committee for Industrial Organization, the Housewives' League and the Youth Councils.

26 TONS OF TRACTS!(Vancouver)

Some idea of the lengths to which Jehovah's Witnesses were intending to go in propagandising their subversive tenets was recently brought to light when members of the Vancouver city police and R.C.M. Police raided three buildings occupied by the organization. It was estimated that the literature seized weighed over 26 tons![6]

"WHERE DO YOU STAND?"

(Quoted from a front-page editorial by Mrs. Dorise Nielsen, M.P., published in "The Canadian Tribune" of July 27.)

You know as well as I that these last months have brought startling changes to Canadian life. We have witnessed our democratic forces and traditions receive blows which have for the time being laid them low. The impact and force of the blows have temporarily stunned us and the very real presence of reaction standing over us, armed with enormous powers, constitutes no mean menace.

Now is the time to show of what stuff we are made. Are we to cringe and cower? Are we to grovel and whine, yet lie inert and take the count? Not I. As I write, I know your reply will be the same as mine. Together, we will say NO.

You and I am speaking to every individual reader of the Tribune must realize one thing. You are the sinews. You are the bone and muscle. You are the mind of democracy. It is your ideals, your hopes, your love of freedom, and your demand for justice which reaction hates and would destroy.

The great body of democratic thought in this country must rise and, with confidence, assert itself, to banish and defeat the enemies of the people. Then it is for you and I to help in every way to arouse this great body of public opinion by every means possible and with great speed. One of our best aids in this wonderful work is the Tribune. A newspaper circulation is like the blood stream flowing through the body of the public. The Canadian Tribune brings to each one of us the truth, and it brings information to encourage and instruct......

Sincerely yours,
(Sgd.) D. W. Nielsen.[7]

CIVIL DEFENCE

NAZI GATHERINGS CONSIDERED A MENACE

It has come to our attention during the past three months that Germans and others who contribute in thought and deed to Nazi ideology and its aims have been gathering in various homes ostensibly for the purpose of celebrating family weddings and other similar anniversaries, but in reality to listen to German broadcasts and to discuss and celebrate the successes of German arms on the European continent. These gatherings have given rise to feelings of apprehension among the loyal residents of the districts concerned and many complaints have been received in this connection. While such complaints have been founded more on suspicion than evidence and do not give us grounds to warrant arbitrary action strict surveillance has been maintained in districts where the population is predominantly German or of German origin.

It is considered that a definite danger exists in allowing people whose aims and ideals are diametrically opposed to those of this country to gather together in large numbers without supervision, and it is considered desirable that such meetings be prohibited. To this end, it has been requested that the necessary legislation be enacted to give the police power to supervise any such gatherings and if necessary to disperse them.[8]

A NEW CONCEPTION OF POLICE
BASED ON URGENT NEEDS

(By E. F. Rogers, in "Police Chronicle and Constabulary World", London.)

In the days before the war, it was frequently contended and admitted that the continual output of modern legislation had stretched the manpower of the Police Service to the utmost limit. Yet during the past nine months, it has been proved that, far from being an already fully occupied body, the Police must be regarded as the first line of Civil Home Defence: which, incidentally, for the first time in our history has become as important, and vital to the welfare of the nation as foreign service.

Consequently, the time has come for an entirely new conception of police duty based on the imperative needs of the moment, in which the police should have ample powers to take appropriate action in the event of enemy invasion or treasonable activities by Fifth Columnists.

To Cope with New Developments.

A few weeks ago the publication of such a suggestion would have been regarded as a fantastic joke, but the most horrible lesson which emerges from the mad welter of blood and suffering which now covers Europe, is that there is no limit to what our enemies may attempt. That being so it is obvious that to attempt to carry on the defence of the country along pre-war standards of decency and civilized conduct is positively suicidal.

What is required, indeed, what is absolutely essential if the horror and carnage which has already ravaged so many peace-loving countries is not to be repeated here, is the immediate imposition of legislation by which the police and kindred defence organizations shall have unlimited freedom of action in coping with whatever new developments may arise in the conduct of this most peculiar of all wars.

It has been said with some truth that by the recent Defence legislation the British people have placed their rights and liberties in pawn until the defeat of Hitlerism enables them to be restored. The fact that, in the very stronghold of free speech and action, the Legislature has thought fit to take this step is sufficient justification for the introduction of the most drastic measures and for the [9] subordination of all other considerations to the one supreme duty of making the greatest possible contribution to the defence of the country.

GREATER SUPERVISION

Many aliens have been interned and a few self-confessed pro-Nazis have been arrested; but there are still many others at liberty masquerading under British names and with carefully cultivated speech about the country. The only effective method of combating their potential activities is by the immediate introduction of a system of supervision which will bring every possible traitor under supervision.

Every railway station should have an investigation officer who should have power to require every traveller to furnish proof of his bona-fides; the Roman defensive tactics of walled cities must be revived and the entrance to every town and village should be guarded day and night; every strategic point on road, rail, river and canal junctions, munition works, police stations, power-houses, water tanks docks, etc., should be under armed guard if they are not already so.

Above all, the present ridiculous system of so-called identification by cards which can be duplicated by the thousand by any jobbing printer should be disregarded. What is wanted is an entirely new issue of cards printed upon some material which will be far more difficult to duplicate, and provision should be made for the insertion of photographs, fingerprints and full particulars of all employment for, say, the past three years.

SABOTAGING OUR TOURIST TRADE

The United States' license plates — hitherto out-numbering Canadian plates on every highway — have dwindled this summer to a small minority.

For the rumor-mongers have been having a field day at the expense of Canada's tourist trade from the U.S. One of the strongest subversive efforts of our enemies has been to scare and worry Americans who would ordinarily spend some part of their summer here. Here are some of the rumors:

That gasoline is 75 cents a gallon in Canada;

That food is scarce;

That cars are being confiscated for war purposes;

That border restrictions are so severe that American tourists [10] coming into Canada can't get back home;

That you need a passport to get into Canada;

That Canada is again adopting prohibition — curbing sales of beer, wine and liquor as a war measure;

That people with German sounding names are liable to be arrested and questioned.

INTELLIGENCE
BULLETIN

ROYAL CANADIAN MOUNTED POLICE
HEADQUARTERS, OTTAWA

SEPTEMBER 30, 1940

CONTENTS

War Series
No. 37

LABOUR UNREST

BIRTH OF CANADIAN CONGRESS OF LABOUR

The merger, on Sept. 9, of two powerful Canadian labour organizations—the All-Canadian Congress of Labour and the Congress of Industrial Organizations—has a significance transcending merely the Canadian labour guild and directly affecting the social and political life of the Dominion. Whether or not this effect will prove injurious remains to be seen.

According to the presidential address of A. R. Mosher of the A.C.C., greater unity among workers means greater national efficiency and productivity during ear days and better economic conditions afterwards. On the other hand the C.I.O. has international affiliation; embraces many insurgent unions under Communist control and is covertly antagonistic to the war and democratic government.

It is obvious that the A.C.C. is confident of remaining the parent stock of this new hybrid and of absorbing or at least nullifying the injurious effects of the social irreconcilables. It is equally plain that the C.I.O. has temporarily sunk its identity under a new front, "The Canadian Congress of Labour", in the conviction that it will eventually oust the old A.C.C. leaders and weld the new Congress into a powerful revolutionary machine.

Throughout the four days' convention (the tenth) of the All-Canadian Congress, the regular officers presided and the C.I.O. union delegates were little more than "guests", although permitted to speak and to vote on resolutions and amendments to the constitution. Consequently the meetings were controlled with dictatorial despatch and ingenuity despite loud protests from Red Zealots. The last business on the agenda, however, namely the election of officers for the new Congress gave the C.I.O. a chance to show their numerical strength by placing four members on the seven-man Executive Board. For president they nominated Nigel Morgan of British Columbia, delegate of the International Wood Workers of America (C.I.O.), but Mosher (president of the A.C.C. since its inception 13 years ago, and president of the Canadian Brotherhood of Railway Employees and Transport Workers since its inception 32 years ago) was elected with a substantial majority. Norman Dowd,[1] Ottawa, member of the Canadian Brotherhood of Railroad Engineers, was also retained in his office (secretary-treasurer)[><deletion: 2 lines], and M. M. Maclean, Ottawa, C.B.R.E., also remains on the Executive. The new members of the Executive are Patrick B. Conroy, Calgary, vice-president of District 18 of the United Mine Workers, a C.I.O. affiliate vice-president; C.H. Millard, C.I.O. regional director; Silby Barrett, U.M.W.; and Saul Spivak, Toronto, Amalgamated Clothing Workers.

A significant incident was the announcement of Charles Beattie, president of the Canadian Association of Railwaymen and vice-president of the former A.C.C. of L., that he had received instructions to withdraw members of his organization from the Congress, as "We prefer a purely national organization".

More than 60 resolutions were submitted to the convention. The first five originated from the Canadian Brotherhood of Railway Employees and Other Transport Workers and were evidently designed to stamp the proceedings from the start as eminently loyal and lawful. Resolution No. 4, condemning the forces of Naziism, Fascism and Communism and declaring the Congress "unalterably opposed to the doctrines of all groups which are subversive to our free democratic institutions and that the chartered and affiliated unions of the Congress be urged to refuse membership to any person known to be a member of or closely associated with such subversive groups", brought the first serious clash among the 224 delegates. R. F. Wright and Joe Black of Toronto and Nigel Morgan of Vancouver demanded deletion of the word "Communism", while Murray Cotterell, Joe Wall and M. M. Maclean successfully defended its inclusion. The resolution was carried with deletion of the words "or closely associated with" (such subversive groups.)

Another row was precipitated when President Mosher read a telegram from the Canadian Seamens Union, urging the Congress to raise its "powerful voice" against the internment of Pat Sullivan and J. S. Chapman (president and secretary respectively of the Union) and demand their trial or immediate release. C. S. Jackson, (C.I.O.) was particularly violent in his denunciation of the Defence of Canada Regulations, of the Government's "discrimination and intimidation" of union workers and of "this Imperialist War". Nigel Morgan, Wm. Logia and several more spoke in the same vein. Joe Wall rose to say that if the members knew the true reasons why Sullivan and Chapman were interned they would not waste time in their defence. He promised to enlighten any delegates who cared to meet him in the hall afterwards. This brought angry shouts and demands for plain speaking but the President finally restored order.

Resolution 16 embodied similar sentiments regarding Sullivan and Chapman and brought about similar repercussions. It read:[2]

"Whereas in the past many of the leaders in Canadian life have openly expressed admiration for Hitler, Mussolini, and for Fascism, and have spoken favourably in support of such a system for Canada; and

[ᴂ<deletion: 1 paragraph: 4 lines]

"Be it therefore resolved that this Convention protest against the policy of arresting such opponents of Fascism, and allowing freedom for those people who favour and support Fascism, and who, under cover of fighting Fascism abroad, would institute Fascism in Canada."

Another distinctly subversive resolution (No. 28), submitted by the National Union of Domestic and Industrial Gas Workers, Toronto, declared that "the war emergency is being used in a manner opposed to the cause we are fighting for, by outlawing the right to strike and by interning persons fighting for labour's rights without public trial," and demanded:

1. The repeal of the Defense of Canada Regulations.
2. The release of P.J. Sullivan and other labor leaders now interned.
3. That no working class body be outlawed because their platform does not conform with the views of the present government.
4. That this Convention instruct its officers and all affiliated bodies to give the greatest publicity to this resolution and lend full support to the labor victims of these injustices.

Reviewing the convention as a whole, the four-days sessions were carried through with comparatively little friction and no serious rift as between the merging bodies. This was due largely to the President's shrewdly dominating personality and carefully laid plans, which continually crushed C.I.O. protests as "out of order" or else referred them to

a committee for "further consideration". In brief, this merger was obviously framed and railroaded through by the "higher ups" without [3] taking
the rank and file into their confidence.

The future destiny of the Canadian Congress of Labour is hard to
predict. It already claims a membership of over 100,000 and has instructed
the incoming Executive to attempt "a complete consolidation of Canadian
labour" by exploring the possibility of a merger with the Trades and
Labour Congress of Canada with its 150,000 and to accept international
as well as national unions into its fold. Its power for good or evil will
depend upon the element that gains control. Mosher, Dowd and Maclean
of the old A.C.C. are undoubtedly "on the spot", with a minority vote in
the Executive and with Nigel Morgan and a group of radical leaders plotting either their overthrow or their conversion to Communism.

"HOW TO BAG GERMAN PLANES"
(As suggested in a letter from a Vancouver Pole)

Dear Sir:

When I was young in Poland all my chums and older people wanted
to go to America or Canada. They had no money for the ship ticket yet
they were willing to work hard many years, even to risk their life, just for
a fare to Canada. I believe German people would do anything if they could
come to Canada to live.

Why not promise that any German pilot who lands his aeroplane on
English soil shall get free fare to Canada, where he will be treated as a
friend, get citizen papers, free land. There are lots of Czecho-Slovakians,
Austrians and other nationals who will gladly land their planes in England
just to run away from the war and enjoy living in Canada. I am sure Hitler cant fight this........ I believe we can bag many German planes in this
way.

(Signed)

Sylvester Borushko.[4]

COMMUNISM

MAYOR HOUDE: FRIEND OF COMMUNISTS
(Montreal)

In view of Camilien Houde's internment for opposing registration,
remarks made by Mrs. Phil. Cuttler, [⸱<deletion: 2 lines], at a recent meeting of the league at her home in Montreal, are highly significant.

Mrs. Cuttler said that she was sorry for the Party and the League over
the internment of Mayor Houde because when he was attending the Youth
Congress "he had stated that he knew what we taught and that we knew
what he was thinking. The leaders of the Congress personally asked
Mayor Houde what he was thinking and he answered that he wanted to
become leader of an anti-conscription and anti-registration movement. He
did not say it publicly because the Congress was to be held shortly after

that."

Mrs. Cuttler said further: "He promised a grant of $200, but was interned before making it. He knew he would be interned so he organized a committee who will continue his work, and some leaders of the Communist Party and the Young Communist League worked with that Committee. Before his interment Mayor Houde had 200,000 circular printed against conscription and registration and King and Lapointe promises during the elections. These copies are printed but are not paid for. The league and the party will cooperate to pay the expenses. The league will obtain 25,000 copies."

Mrs. Cuttler expressed sorrow for Houde "because he would have started the revolution and we would have continued it, and he could not have stopped it. But all is not finished; we are going to work hard. The men will join the army and work within its ranks and the women will do the hard part of it."

LOYALTY RALLY BY FRENCH CANADIANS
(Montreal)

At a gathering, on August 13, of over 2500 people of the St. James Market district of Montreal, the loyalty of French-Canadians to the King [5] to Canada and to the Defence of Canada Regulations was strikingly registered.

Because it had been reported that members of the Communist Party of Canada and of the National Unity Party would be present to break up the meeting and thus create the impression that there was a strong anti-loyal faction, a strong detachment of Montreal City Police were on hand to preserve order. A few of Camilien Houde's supporters attempted to start trouble when the last speaker, Gustave Duperron, president of the Unemployed Association, addressed the audience, but this was immediately quelled, and at this stage the gathering sang "O Canada" and "God Save the King".

[✂deletion: 1 line]
[✂deletion: 1 line]

[✂deletion: 1 paragraph: 4 lines]
[✂deletion: 1 paragraph: 5 lines]
[✂deletion: 1 paragraph: 3 lines][6]

NAZIISM

HITLER WOULD LIKE CANADA

Translated from "The Day", Yiddish daily paper published at New York. Preface: Der Deutscher Bund, the German-American Bund and other Fascist organizations are Hitler's instruments in the New World.
Hitler spoke on January 30, 1940. Said he:
"Canada is a pantry full of food. But it is a closed pantry; they let no one

come in. One can find there all sorts of treasures, but heavy locks hand on the doors."

Special envoy mentioned by Hitler, F. J. Brockhaus, well-known Nazi journalist, explorer and spy. This Brockhaus has travelled through the United States several times from shore to shore. He has also travelled through the other Americas, and lately has expressed his opinion in a book, printed in Hamburg, later translated into English under the title, "Between the United States and the North Pole."

In his book Brockhaus pokes fun at the United States, "which calls itself America. The United States are as much America as New England or North Dakota are America."

Hitler used the same language as his spy. He said:

"Parts of Latin America are nearer to Europe than the United States. The United States, however, want to hold themselves big, hence they call themselves America."

Hitler's agent, Herr Brockhaus, says in his book that the individualism in the United States begins to decay, because lately there has developed such discontent. The same, he declared, was true of Canada.

Herr Brockhaus also states that the United States, together with Canada, take up a huge stretch of land, and that Canada is rich in all raw materials, but is sparsely populated. Hitler repeated that with even more Nazi impudence:[7]

"Canada", said Hitler, "is a pantry filled with all the good things but a few million people, who just happened to come earlier, have hung heavy locks on this pantry. We, however, are waging a war of those who have nothing against those who have too much.

"Canada and also the United States are like those bad sons who will not acknowledge their own father. Not they, the privileged ones, built up the land—it was the Germans who did so—it was they who there (in America) had labored with their sweat, cultivated the land, and made it what it now is."

Brockhaus in his book develops the thought that—"It is difficult to predict how large a part of the riches of Canada and the United States would be secured by the Germans right up to the North Pole. But we can now do only one thing, keep our eyes open and remember that we now live in a period when everything is possible."

Think you this impudence enough? But not enough for Hitler. He talked on furiously.

"We now wage a war against those who have too much, and not they but the Germans are entitled to the greater part of America." And he went on:

"The world must now look with open eyes. The world must forget that which has been, and now have in mind that which is now."

"The Day" then declares, the Nazis are now armed with all the facts and in all detail. Brockhaus went through the United States five times right up to the North Pole; he even went to Finland. He explored the land, the possibilities and riches, but also the people, and he came to the conclusion that, "The people of the United States and those of Canada are as different and far apart from one another as the British and Americans are apart in thought." He recognizes no such things as Americans, less than that, that there are such people as Canadians.

"In Canada", states Brockhaus (see Andre Siegfried's book on land and people) "there are British people who came here earlier than the others, and have hence seized the reins in their hands. But there are also Frenchmen, Canadian Frenchmen—they are not Aryans—they have, it is true, European blood. There is no such thing as pure Americans, and there will never be Canadians as such.

"The deeper one goes into the land one sees there are no Canadian people as such. There are those who cannot say a word of English or American."[8]

The Nazi spy tells his brethren, those of German blood, "They should not sit in the New World with folded hands, but should explore everything in the New World which can be of use to the Nazis."

Hitler, in his speech, indicated he has had enough exploration and espionage.

"The time has come to break the locks on the Canadian pantry, and to carry out from there all the good things which are there stored away."

Concludes the writer in "The Day":

"Hitler looks with watery eyes on the New World."

GERMAN FEAR STRONGER THAN LOYALTY
(Regina)

Although many of our German Canadians are antagonistic to Hitler and all that he represents, they are mesmerised with the dread of his eventual conquest of Canada and the vengeance he will wreak on those who might now oppose him.

This attitude of mind is continually coming to light when individuals suspected of being connected with subversive activities are being questioned by police officials. One officer reports as follows:

During the course of a recent conversation with a prominent German Canadian who was bemoaning the fact re. Registration and at the same time trying to demonstrate his loyalty, he was asked the question. "Have you Germans or persons such as yourself in positions of authority made any public attempt to demonstrate your loyalty to the Crown?" To this the good citizen made the following reply, "Oh no, we would be afraid to do this in case Hitler was to hear of it and then our treatment by the conqueror would be far worse than your own."[9]

SABOTAGE

PROTECTION AGAINST SABOTAGE

Since the outbreak of war, the policy of federal and provincial governments has been to assume responsibility for the security of all publicly owned buildings and developments and to leave the protection of privately owned property to its respective managements. Until recently this policy has proved in a large degree satisfactory to all concerned.

At the same time the R.C.M.P. assumed the somewhat onerous task of carrying out an intensive search for major weaknesses in our industrial armour and of educating and advising private owners as to the most effective means of removing those weaknesses.

In the course of such work over 1900 vital points in all provinces have been surveyed and the managements of key industries such as nickel, aluminum, lead and zinc have been advised as to the utmost necessity of maintaining adequate protection from possible sabotage of their hydroelectric power plants.

The results have been highly satisfactory as regards the arousing of industry to its deplorable state of insecurity in a world rife with fifth columnists and saboteurs. On the other hand, many owners are showing reluctance toward applying protective measures because of the expense involved, and claim that the Government should at least stand the cost of the special guards required.

Although up to the present there has not occurred any major catastrophe due to saboteurs the possibility of serious impairment of our war efforts from such a cause is always imminent, and nothing can be left to half-measures or chance.

SPECIAL DETENTION FOR STRIKING SEAMEN

The serious threat to our shipments of war material caused by striking seamen on convoy ships, has been met by an Order in Council authorizing the internment of such strikers in special jails and camps for an indefinite [10] period or until they decide to return to their duties.

Early in the summer it was brought to the attention of Authorities in Ottawa that an increasing number of seamen of foreign nationality aboard Atlantic freighters were either deserting their ships upon arrival or else remaining on board and refusing to work. While some made low wages a pretense for their conduct, it was obvious that their real motives were fear of the enemy and indifference or disloyalty to the allied cause. By July 12, it was reported that the situation was becoming acute. Several ships laden with vital war supplies had been prevented from sailing with the convoys. As a temporary measure, the strikers were confined in the Immigration Detention Sheds, but as such accommodation was an inducement rather than a deterrent to mutiny, sterner disciplinary measures were required.

During August and early September the situation grew considerably worse, with Belgian, Polish, Greek, Norwegian and other foreign sailors sabotaging our war efforts by tying up cargo boats. Ordinary internment being considered insufficient punishment for such an offense, it was recommended, after consultation with Immigration and other departments of government and with provincial governments of Quebec and Nova Scotia, that such strikers be dealt with by a special tribunal and sent to special imprisonment camps.

On Sept. 12, Order in Council 4751 was passed authorizing the detention of any alien seaman who deserts his ship or refuses to sail on such ship or refuses to perform his regular duties on board. The Order provides for detention for the duration of the war, or "until he is ready and willing and actually proceeds to serve on a ship sailing from Canada" during which time "he may be employed on such labor" as the Minister may determine.[11]

INTELLIGENCE
BULLETIN

ROYAL CANADIAN MOUNTED POLICE
HEADQUARTERS, OTTAWA

NOVEMBER 11, 1940

CONTENTS

Nazism:
    Corrupting Sudeten Settlers
    Nazism in High Circles
    War Profiteering In Germany
    [≫deletion: 1 line]
    Extracts from Private Letters
Japanese:
    Our Japanese Await Events
Communism:
    Problems of Party Organization
    Women Leaders to Take Over

War Series
No. 38

NAZISM
CORRUPTING SUDETEN SETTLERS
(St. Walburg, Sask.)

Despite internment of many enemy aliens and registration of thousands of German birth or origin, pro-Nazis continue their insidious plotting on Hitler's behalf. The following report gives a vivid glimpse of their methods in certain small towns in northern Saskatchewan:

The atmosphere of hate in Goodsoil and Flat Valley is fiendish. The leaders are daily fostering discontent and hatred against the Canadian Government. The growing up boys are being educated by their parents to despise the Government and flag and look to the German nation to rectify their troubles. Fully 90% are dissatisfied and only listen to the LO: PM news which comes from "Salt Lake City". As Von Massow said: "It is the German truth put in the English tongues for diplomacy sake." They are converting the Sudeten colony to their cause by showing them how Hitler has always kept his word to the people whilst the Canadian Government has always let them down. They use the line that the railway did not come through, no prices for all farm products on top of high delivery costs. 60% of those talked to all claim they will return to Europe as soon as the war is over. There are five large trucks at Goodsoil and one at Golden Ridge and from observation these always have from six to ten Germans in them whichever way they seem to travel. Two were observed carrying men from Pierceland, Monday, Wednesday and Friday. These have high sides on and are covered by tarpaulin so exact number of men inside are not visible. I was told a meeting place was at "Blue-Bell" on the Meadow Lake-Goodsoil road.[1] [Page 2 is missing.]

NAZISM IN HIGH CIRCLES
(Regina, Sask.)

Professor Watson Kirkconnel, formerly of Manitoba University, now associated with Dalhousie, on the eve of his departure from Winnipeg recently gave an address on the subject of the non-English groups living in this country. Now Professor Kirkconnel has made a reputation for himself in the literary world based largely upon his sympathetic studies of the New Canadian and his problems of adjustment to a none too friendly environment. While favorably disposed towards all who are genuinely loyal to the land that has given them shelter and a chance to be somebody, the noted Canadian scholar has little use for the enemy within, and this is what he has to say of the nazi press and its devotees:

"While the ratio of penetration of the German Nazi press is smaller than that of the Italian Fascist press, it nevertheless suggests a circle of Nazi fifth column sympathizers, ominously much wider than the 500 individuals thus far interned at Petawawa and Kananaskis. To those who know the facts, the dimensions of this pro-Nazi group and the intimacy of its contacts with high circles in our national life are really alarming."

Professor Kirkconnel estimates the number of readers which formerly subscribed to the 'Deutsche Zeitung fur Canada' as having been around 7,600.[3]

WAR PROFITEERING IN GERMANY
(Quoted from United States foreign-language press)

The "Neue Volks-Zeitung" (New People's Journal), published in German in New York, gave a survey of war profits in the Third Reich in its issue of October 5. The article stated that since 1937, German stock companies have not needed to include all their gains in their financial statements and that since the outbreak of the war the financial statements no longer appear in the press, but are sent to the "Reichsanzeiger" (The Gazette) which is not published. Finally, the financial statements themselves can be "prettied up" at will for they are not subject to inspection any more.

Typical examples included the I.G. Farben (International Chemical Industry) which estimated the value of its plants and machinery at 432 million Rm. on January 1, 1937. In the two years preceding the war the capital was increased by 173 million Rm. and 243 million Rm. were written off—so that the amortization was over a third of the capital assets; the Klockner, Hoesch & Hanich Works in the Ruhr which increased their capital assets by 192 million Rm. between 1933 and 1939 and wrote 216 million Rm. off; the Heinrich Lanz Mannhein Machine Works, with a capital of 7 million Rm., which increased its plant by 4.2 million Rm. and wrote off 4.3 million Rm. in a single year, declaring only a 4% dividend, a fact which was used by the Nazi authorities to prove to the Mannhein workers how small were the profits made by the German war industry. Meanwhile, the actual earnings of the Heinrich Lanz Co. were stated to be at least 60% per annum and these were duly invested.

The taxes on industry are high, but the profits in war industries have been so fantastic that taxes have been easily met, idle industries subsidized and tremendous gains re-invested. Although the Bureau of Statistics (now a branch of the Ministry of Propaganda) published a decrease of 5.4% on the profits made by German industries in 1938, the "Frankfurter Zeitung" estimated an increase of 13% over 1937 and a further increase of 12% in 1939 over 1938.[4]

Further, German Big Business demanded that the increases in income tax introduced at the outbreak of war be rescinded and Hitler once more yielded. The increased taxation was side-tracked. In the meantime the Nazis are increasing their pressure on salaries paid to German workmen and employees.

"Grow rich, ye barons of industry, bank, and a stock-market"—That is the slogan of unmasked National Socialism, according to this article.[✴blank][5] [Page 6 is missing.]

EXTRACTS FROM PRIVATE LETTERS.

A letter to Canada written in Denmark and smuggled into Sweden for posting says of the Danish attitude towards the Germans in Denmark: "We don't see the German soldiers. No, we just look right through them, and it's getting on their nerves." The writer refers to British bombing raids: "There are British bombers over Denmark every night especially. Nyborg Fredericia and Aalborg aerodromes have received a severe shellacking on bombs. Even here in Bogense (Fyen) have the British bombers been, the last time was 2 a.m., so in the cellar we go not losing any time. The British seem to know where the benzine tanks are hidden and they sure made a mess of Kiel. We could both hear and see them, also Flensberg got it . . . The people in Denmark figure the British bombers coming over as their own and wish them good luck on their journey. The bitterness here is high, but we hope and wait, patience is necessary and we have it: the Police are having a hard time at the Danish-German border as everybody from Germany is trying to cross."

Speaking of Portuguese opinion of the Axis powers, in a letter from

Portugal to Montreal, dated September 20, the sender writes: "So far as the masses of the people are concerned, the Hun is more and more unpopular every day. Forty Hun lorries came through the Oporto a few weeks back to fetch soap, so they said, but they took food and petrol as well I believe, and the drivers were hissed by the crowds and villagers around, and there were cries of 'Viva Inglaterra'".[7]

JAPANESE
OUR JAPANESE AWAIT EVENTS
(Vancouver)

The Japanese "problem" in Canada is at present more conspicuous by its absence than by anything else. Japanese leaders, from the beginning of the war, have been openly advising their race to mind their own business pursuits and remain loyal to the land of their adoption.

Last June the Japanese Consul at Vancouver, Mr. Nakauchi, made a tour of Japanese settlements in British Columbia, addressing gatherings on the topic "Guide to Japanese residents in Canada in relationship with the European War", in which he stressed the necessity of Japanese in B.C., particularly the Nisei, of "living as Canadians". Although he made references to the Sino-Japanese War and the establishment of a new order in Asia, it was believed that he did this in order to placate the older Japanese who, though few in number, are still, and will always be, "Japanese".

That same month a report from Vancouver stated:

Amongst the Vancouver Japanese, and particularly the Nisei, nothing but loyalty to Canada is expressed both by word and action. They have subscribed generously to the Red Cross Fund, have purchased quite heavily war bonds, and their women are very busily engaged in speeding up voluntary production of clothing and comforts for the European refugees, to send to England. One of the leading Japanese women in this City at a recent meeting said:

"We are making a special appeal to our Red Cross Workers. Our unit, with thousands of other units across Canada must rally to the emergency call from London, England. In our comfortable homes far from the battlefields of Europe we cannot fully realise the terror and destruction, the hunger and privations of the millions of civilians who have been driven by bombs out of home and country, but as women you can appreciate [8] the urgency of this appeal . . . . we do not ask the impossible, but bring in your garments as quickly as possible to the office of the Nippon Club, your group leaders or myself. Members of the Japanese-Canadian Unit, the Empire needs you."

An extract from a recent issue of a local Japanese newspaper dealing with the Nisei effort in connection with Canada's part in this war stated "Many Japanese are anxious to fight in this war. They only await the opportunity to enlist. The Japanese in British Columbia are definitely patriotic to the Allied Cause."

At the same time it must not be overlooked that about 75 per cent of the Japanese born in this country are registered with the Consulate in Vancouver. This registration makes them subjects of Japan, and they are considered as such by the Government of Japan to whom they owe allegiance. This is verified by the fact that their Government recently published an edict whereby those Canadian born not registered in Japan must obtain Canadian passports when travelling to that country. For those who are "registered" the Canadian certificate of birth is sufficient. Several hundreds of these Canadian-born Japanese travel to Japan annually and out of these the percentage obtaining Canadian passports is indeed small.[9]

COMMUNISM
"PROBLEMS OF PARTY ORGANIZATION"

(Excerpts from "The Monthly Review" of August, 1940—an official and illegal organ of the Communist Party—give interesting insight into the Party's present struggles and ambitions under adverse conditions.)

The new situation created by the Imperialist War confronts the Communist Party of Canada with tremendous responsibilities and a series of new, complex problems. We are the only party that has characterized this war for what it is—a criminal, imperialist war: the only party which strives to mobilize and organize the Canadian people in opposition to the war. . . . Our party bases itself upon the scientific teachings of Marxism-Leninism . . . .

We study Marxism-Leninism, not as a dogma, but as a guide to action. To fulfill the great tasks before our party—we must master the art of concretely applying the principles of Marxism-Leninism in the given situation that confronts us . . . .

We have fought, and continue fighting, to become a party of a new type, a genuine Bolshevik Party, able to organize and lead the Canadian working class and it s allies forward in the struggle against this imperialist war, forward to the fulfillment of their historic mission . . .

The organizational policy of our party is determined by its tasks and aims . . . . Our tasks are to arouse, mobilize and organize the Canadian working people in the struggle against the imperialist war, for peace, for the rights and interests of the people. Our aim is to win the majority of the working class, to rally the masses of Canada around the working class, in the struggle for socialism . . . . The bourgeoisie has been compelled to cast aside its "democratic" mask, to throw away the kid-gloves, to rule by the most unbridled methods of police-military dictatorship. Concentration camps, the death penalty are the weapons taken up against the Canadian working class by [10] Mackenzie King, Holt, Coldwell and the rest of the war camp.

Our party is faced with the urgent task of organizing its work on a basis that will guarantee that we will meet the new, sharpening situation, that no matter what the bourgeoisie will do, our party will continue to fulfill its duties to the workers and common people of Canada, and will continue to grow . . . .

The failure to draw the political organizational conclusions from the above principles and facts of life are responsible for the amateurish methods of party work and the slowness in reorganizing the party on a "war footing". Once the politics of the problem are understood we can acquire experience . . . .

Some comrades until recently suffered from illusions, and in practice held up and hindered the reorganization of the party. They underestimated the sharpening political situation and "argued" that we were failing to take advantage of all possibilities for wide, legal mass work, insinuating that the measures being taken to create and strengthen the "underground" apparatus signified the acceptance of "voluntary illegality". These are dangerous "theories" and can find no place in the party. The heavy blows of the bourgeoisie in the recent period settled the question, also serving as serious reminders that we must continue along the path of applying Marxist-Leninist organizational principles, and eradicate all remaining weaknesses and illusions . . . .

Our party is not a conspiratorial clique. We are the vanguard party of the Canadian workers. It is the bourgeoisie which tramples upon legality and tears to shreds the established constitutional liberties of the people. Democracy and legality have become impediments in the path of the warmongering Canadian bourgeoisie and are destroyed by them. They are unable to rule in the old way. They are afraid that the people will utilize the limited, pre-war democratic forms in their own interests; hence they enacted the War Measures Act to rule in a naked, vicious, dictatorial fashion.

Under such conditions, a working class party, if it be a serious party determined to do its duty, must answer the bourgeoisie by reorganizing it, by combining legal and illegal work to guarantee that the struggle for the interests of the working class will go forward.

"Entrench the party deeply among the masses!" That was the advice given us by Lenin. At all costs, at all times, the Communist Party must maintain and continually strengthen its roots and connections among the masses. Separation from the masses, from the Mother Earth [11] of Communism, would be fatal for our party. To guarantee that this will never happen we have taken measures, and will do everything that is necessary to protect the party membership, organization and cadres from the terror and violence of the capitalist state . . . .

To fulfill our vanguard role, to be able to adequately combine legal and illegal work, it is necessary to pay more attention to another basic question—that of the party and its relationship to other forms of working class organization.

"The Party is not merely an organized detachment, but the highest of all forms of organization of the working class, and it is its mission to guide all other organizations of the working class . . . . the party is an embodiment of the connection of the vanguard of the working class with the working class millions" . . . .

As a decisive political task we must improve and raise the quality of the mass work of our comrades in the trade unions, in all the mass popular organizations of the workers and their allies. The raising of the Socialist class consciousness of the workers, the spreading of Marxist-Leninist teachings among the masses—that is decisive in the present period. It is essential to strengthen the ranks of the workers, to fit them for the difficult struggles of today and the bigger battles tomorrow, decisive too for the building up of the ranks of the party which is a key task of the day for the working class movement.

At the outbreak of war the party took a number of very important organizational measures to bring our forces on to a proper "war footing". Political discussions on the new situation, the new policies and tactics, the new organizational problems were held from the top to bottom of the party. To guarantee the functioning of the party, to provide all possible safeguards for its membership and sympathizers, its organizations and its cadres, we revamped our entire organizational setup. Forms and methods of organization which correspond to the tasks and political situation of the pre-war days did not suit the new war situation. Our party in pre-war days had ten provincial and regional committees. We increased the number of districts. Now our district committees have much smaller areas to look after. The party branches were reorganized. The large mass branches, built up in the pre-war days, were done away with. The number of party branches has been greatly increased. They are relatively small, flexible bodies today. A reorganization of the party section committees was carried through in all districts to broaden the leadership, to give greater political assistance to the branches and the mass work. The work of the Central Committee and the Political Bureau was reorganized. Experience shows that these measures were timely and correct . . . .[12]

The conditions of imperialist war demand even more political attention and guidance from the leading committees and cadres to the party branches, the closer study of their work, achievements and problems. For the activity of our party branches, and each individual comrade, assumes greater political importance than ever before. The pre-war methods of work—the holding of mass meetings, the spreading of the "Clarion" and legal literature, the house-to-house canvassing—these activities formerly carried through by the branches are no longer possible. The appearance of outstanding national and district leaders of the party before big audiences, the utilization of the C.B.C. and privately-owned stations, these are also banned today. This does not mean that, in conditions of illegality as imposed upon us by the King government, leading party figures will not find ways and means to speak to the masses. We have found, and will find ways to do this. But it does add emphasis to the work of our party branches, to the work down below among the workers, on the job, in the trade unions, in the working class neighbourhoods, in the barracks and camps . . . .

Our branches will develop only if they tackle live political jobs, the current problems of the masses in their factory, union or locality, if their work is activity that contributes to the strengthening of the struggle and consciousness of the working class. Our branches must pay more, not less, attention to the current needs, moods and sentiments of the masses, must react faster than ever to anything and everything that is agitating or affecting the masses. Our branches must be encouraged and inspired to develop their own initiative, to become active political bodies which influence the life and struggles of the people . . . .

The most effective base of a party branch is the factory, mine or mill, the places of proletarian work. In the reorganization of the party we must do everything possible to maintain and strengthen our bases in the factories, mines and mills, in the big industrial enterprises. "Face to the industries, to the factories, mines and mills!"—that is the slogan of the party. We must entrench our Party deeper and deeper among the proletariat of the main industries, we must do more than ever to strengthen the struggle for their demands, to build up their trade unions, to raise their class consciousness and fighting ability. Our section and district committees must devote their concentrated attention upon these branches of our party, upon these sections of the Canadian proletariat. . . .

Our party has already sustained severe blows and some of our best comrades are languishing in prisons and concentration camps, the victims of the ferocious King-Holt-Coldwell war camp. We will learn [13] from the lessons of the past ten months and strive to prove this in practice.

OUTLAWING REDS

Sacramento, Cal., Sept. 22 (AP).—A bill to outlaw the Communist Party in California was passed last night by the State Assembly. The vote was 66 to 3. Approval by the Senate and signature of the Governor are necessary to make the measure effective.

"WITNESSES" SUPPRESSED

Auckland, New Zealand, Oct. 24.—(C.P. Cable)—An order was published in the official gazette today suppressing the religious sect, Jehovah's Witnesses.

WOMEN LEADERS TO TAKE OVER

A change has been noted in the policy followed by the Communist

Party of Canada, in that in some districts preparations are being made for women to take over the leadership of District Committees. There appears to be a twofold reason for this: first, that women are less likely to come under suspicion; secondly, that the Party would not lose responsible leadership and become disorganized if the leader were interned.[14]

INTELLIGENCE
BULLETIN

ROYAL CANADIAN MOUNTED POLICE
HEADQUARTERS, OTTAWA

DECEMBER 23, 1940

CONTENTS

War Series
No. 39

NAZISM

NAZIS PREPARED FOR UPRISING
(Toronto)

The activities of the Underground Nazi Organization in Toronto continue at irregular intervals, with meetings being called by the group supervisor when so directed by the leaders.

At a recent (typical) gathering the usual discussion on the current situation took place and members were warned that if they are arrested they must not divulge anything regarding these groups.

In so far as the situation in Canada is concerned, the group was instructed, by the medium of discussion, and by unanimous decision, that members must support any subversive uprising no matter what party or political faction might be the instigator. If the C.P. of C. started such an uprising they must support it because the C.P. is considered by them to have considerable strength and potentialities for hindering Canada's war effort.

Not only are the meetings being held by the men but the women are active in an unorganized way in bolstering the spirits of their menfolk.

The spirit that pervades these people may be illustrated best by the following remark that was made by the wife of one of the interned men:— "I am not sorry that my husband is in. At least I know what he is there for."

Through careful and discreet discussion with a large number of Germans in this city, it is estimated that 8 out of 10 with whom contact was made believe that Hitler will win the war. Further, many Germans who prior to the war took no part in politics and were not affiliated with any of the pro-Nazi movements have changed their views, and it is estimated that 5 out of 10 of such Germans are now pro-Nazi.[1]

All these people have full confidence in "der Fuehrer" and are loyal to the Nazi idea and German regime. Their attitude was revealed during a discussion over the consequences of the possible defeat of Germany. The unanimous opinion was that the German and Italian people would rather perish than lose the war. This applies equally to Reich Germans and those born in Austria and the Balkan States.

JEWS DOING THEIR SHARE
(Regina)

(Despite anti-Semitism in Saskatchewan, instigated by Nazi Agents, Jews continue to enlist. To quote from a recent report:)

While there has always been a certain amount of anti-Semitism in Regina and Saskatchewan, as elsewhere, the recent outburst expressed itself thus:

"It's a capitalist war; a Jewish war; the Jews are not enlisting, but let other people fight their war."

Nothing could be more revealing as to the source of such defeatist propaganda. We are sure the "Deutscher Bund" was not dissolved, but went underground, and their sinister activities are going on in a more subtle manner. The fact is, as the military authorities at Ottawa know full well, Jewish-Canadians are enlisting away out of proportion to their quota of population.

As for the "capitalist" war, it takes capital to fight a war. The Jewish community as such has subscribed generously, away out of proportion, not because they consider it a "Jewish" war, but because they understand the clear-cut issue of decency versus brute force much better than people who take their freedom too much for granted.

A Leader-Post reporter, Harold Colter, informs a fellow-reporter, Harold Hyman, that there has been quite a lot of talk down-town about the alleged failure of Jews to enlist. The Leader-Post editorial helped to quieten the Klu-Kluckers for a time. A definite statement by the military authorities would do more to convince the Canadian community, sullenly suspicious of anyone who is not English, Scotch or Irish, that Canadians of Jewish faith are doing their part.[2]

The press, too, might credit the Jewish community with the fact that a special room has been set aside in the Talmud Torah, Jewish community centre, for Red Cross work, and English speaking Christian Canadians are using that room as though it were their own.

FASCISM

WESTERN FASCISTS ARE CHASTENED
(Vancouver)

The Italian attitude of mind has undergone a profound change since last summer, due to the arrest of all Fascio members, to the increasing United States sympathy with the Empire and to the continuous disasters to Mussolini's forces on land and sea. All this has had a most chastening effect on temperaments vastly different from those of the bull-headed Germans—stilling their boastings and, in many cases, causing them to avoid the public.

In reference to those arrested and later released unconditionally or on parole when found not to be active members of the Fascio, these have been kept under quiet surveillance and their general conduct is giving no ground for complaint.

The relatives of the interned men now appear resigned to the fact that neither money, lawyers or influence will release the internees who were members of the Fascio in good standing at the outbreak of war with Italy. They admit that if internment is justified, that it is only right that all members should be interned and that if one is favoured by release then all should be released. They would naturally like to see their interned men released, but so long as no favouritism is shown we will have a minimum of trouble from these relatives to contend with.[3]

FRANCE

QUEBEC AND THE VICHY GOVERNMENT
(Montreal)

(This delicate problem is briefly reviewed in the following confidential report.)

It appears time that very careful consideration should be given to (a) The attitude of Canada towards

(i)   France in general
(ii)   The Vichy Government
(iii)   The DeGaulle Committee

and (b) The position of French Canada in the picture and the place which French Canadians can take in solving the problem confronting us.

With regard to (b) it would appear that four different opinions exist:[⚹blank][4][Page 5 is missing.]

COMMUNISM
NEW CANADIAN SOCIALIST STATE

A Party Directive, under the heading "A Political Letter on our Present Tasks", is important as a statement of the present views and policy of the Communist Party of Canada. The "letter" opens with:

"In the course of organizing and leading militant struggles of the workers and farmers for their immediate demands, it is our task to carry on the most wide-spread and concrete revolutionary propaganda under the slogan: An Independent Socialist Canada!"

Enlarging upon this subject, it advises all members to struggle against C.C.F. and reactionary trade union officials. It attacks so-called British labour traitors and the Tory ruling class, referring to the British Government as the most despotic Government in the world.

It contends that the network of finance, trade and industry, with British capitalists, places Canada in most imminent danger; that the British bourgeoisie made peace with Hitler to maintain class domination, and that the Canadian bourgeoisie have now been incorporated into the United States imperialist system under the disguise of a "Defence Union".

It is especially important, it declares, to expose the sordid "Victory" propaganda of the Churchill-Chamberlain-Attlee Government, echoed in Canada by King and the bourgeoisie; that the real strategic plan of British imperialism is to hide the appalling cost to the British masses until the revolutionary socialist working classes of the continent are able to revolt against the bourgeoisie and Nazi power and then to step in at the opportune moment to dictate terms to their German and Italian rivals, as the price for crushing the Socialist Revolution. The only path of deliverance for Europe will be the revolutionary socialist workers and standing behind them the Soviet Union.

In dealing with the struggle for an independent Socialist Canada, it calls for the exposure of the anti-Socialist character of the [6] policy of the big bourgeoisie and, in opposition to this policy, working class aid for the socialist revolution in Europe. According to the letter, the only way out for the Canadian masses is to follow the following program:

(a) Form a new Canadian Socialist State.
(b) Nationalization and amalgamation of banks, large scale industries and railways under the control of the new State.
(c) Immediate raising of living standards.
(d) The new State would be freed of foreign ties with capitalists, and foreign relations would be determined solely on the best interest of Canadian people.
(e) The French Canadians granted the right to self-determination, even up to separation.

IN DEFENCE OF JEHOVAH WITNESSES

Members of the Communist Party, who may have religious connections, are instructed to do everything possible to aid Jehovah's Witnesses in presenting their cases to the court and public, as a defense of religious freedom. It is likely that the Communist Party will follow a plan of writing to newspapers criticizing the prosecution of Jehovah's Witnesses. In this way the C.P. hope to secure support from religious-minded people into obstructing government action.[7]

ANOTHER BLAST FROM THE CLARION
(Toronto)

A recent issue of "The Toronto Clarion", published by the Toronto Committee of the Communist Party of Canada, contained a special supplement dated November 7, entitled "The Birth of Socialism", which states that the collapse of armed intervention did not halt the efforts of the Capitalist States to destroy the new Socialist Society, that the Soviets were refused loans and trade agreements, that they were subjected to an illegal blockade, and that spies and wreckers were in the country to sabotage industry and impede industrialization.

To quote:

"The rulers of the capitalists states instituted a well-financed anti-Soviet propaganda campaign, in order to conceal the truth from the masses under their domination.

"The presses poured forth thousands of books, news-papers and magazines devoted to lies and slanders against the Soviets. Anti-Soviet lecturers toured every capitalist country. Every newspaper office became a lie factory, wherein were manufactured the most weird and wonderful accounts of imaginary Soviet 'famines', 'starvation', 'mass purges', and so on.

"In Canada this propaganda campaign has been carried on for 23 years. The result is that many Canadians know no more about what is going on within Soviet Russia than they do about life on Mars.

"They have been pumped so full of anti-Soviet propaganda that they often accept the vicious lie which compares the free, prosperous Socialist State with the brutal Nazi dictatorship."

The article concludes in a statement that an independent Socialist Canada is the only solution to the problems facing the Canadian people; that the lesson of 23 years of working-class power (U.S.S.R.), shows that [8] only a Party of a new type can unite and lead the masses in a successful struggle for power, and to constantly build the Communist Party of Canada is therefore part of the struggle for Socialism.

The Communist Party also distributed a short, two-page "Anniversary Manifesto", which covered the ground dealt with by the supplement to the Clarion, and this also stressed the need for an "Independent Socialist

Canada"—the new slogan decided upon by the C.P. of C.

DISLOYALTY AMONG SCHOOL CHILDREN

Members of the Jehovah Witnesses in Ontario and the Prairie Provinces have apparently instructed their children in an anti-British attitude. To date this has consisted in refusal to participate in patriotic exercises. In Hamilton, Ontario 25 children have been barred from the schools following their actions against such exercises. In Edmonton, Alberta the City Police are investigating four children who refused to salute the flag following an order by the School Board for regular patriotic exercises. From Saskatchewan come numerous reports of failures to participate in saluting of the flag and singing of the national Anthem in the smaller schools.

While this movement was obviously instituted by the Johovah Witnesses there is no doubt that the children themselves have recruited sympathizers from among malcontents. It is also noted that there is no predominant nationality among the culprits, at least so far as can be judged from the names of those reported.[9]

U.S. REDS SEVER CONNECTIONS WITH COMINTERN

The Communist Party of the United States, at a special Convention held in New York recently, voted to dissolve all affiliations with the Communist International and all other foreign organizations. This action was taken for the specific purpose of removing the party from the terms of the so-called Voorhis Act which will become effective in January, 1941 and which will require groups under foreign control to register with the Department of Justice.[✖blank][10]

UKRAINIANS

ARE UKRAINIAN NATIONALISTS LOYAL TO CANADA?

The Ukrainian Nationalist movement in Canada is of the European origin and is much older than Italian Fascism or German Nazism. It was organized underground by patriots of the defeated Ukrainian armies in the struggle for Ukraine's independence against the Soviet Union and Poland. A secret Ukrainian Military Organization (the UMO) was formed by Col. Evhen Konovaletz in order to perpetuate the struggle by means of terrorism, as ruthless as that of the Comitadjis of the Balkan nations against the Turks. Assassinations of Polish high officials and even of the pro-Polish Ukrainians followed. State and private property has been raided and destroyed, often resulting in punitive action being taken by the Government of Poland against the innocent Ukrainian peasants in reprisal. These acts of terrorism were directed by leaders of the UMO from Germany, Czecho-Slovakia, Austria and Lithuania where they enjoyed the safety of political refugees.

In 1929, Col. Konovaletz reorganized the UMO into a world-wide Ukrainian Nationalist Movement, known henceforth as the "Organization of

Ukrainian Nationalists" (the OUN). Retaining the old aims and somewhat reforming the methods, the OUN movement gradually spread throughout Ukrainian society in all countries where Ukrainians lived. Many former generals and other officers of the Ukrainian and Russian armies, diplomats, intellectuals, etc. scattered throughout Continental Europe joined the OUN, forming a Supreme Leadership of the OUN, with headquarters in Berlin, and with Col. Konovaletz as the Leader. A book by Dr. D. Dontsov, a Ukrainian savant and editor of Lwow, entitled "Nationalism", was readily accepted as ideological basis for the reorganized Ukrainian Nationalist movement. Certain features of Italian corporate philosophy have been appropriated in that book and in the movement, some slogans of which are: "The nation above everything!" "Liberty through Nationalist revolution!" Thus the OUN proceeded to organize its sections in all parts of the world, including Canada.

The Ukrainian Nationalist movement as a political force in Canada begins with the organization of the "Ukrainian War Veterans Association"[11] in 1928, in Winnipeg, by veterans of the Ukrainian wars, many of whom have been members of the UMO, who came to Canada to escape apprehension by Polish authorities. [✂deletion: 2 lines] Dr. Ivan Gulay, O. Wasylishin, W. Kossar, W. Hultay, M. Sharyk, and a dozen others. Some of the above mentioned continue as leaders of the Ukrainian Nationalist Federation (the UNO) and in the recently united Ukrainian Canadian Committee. The leadership of the OUN and political ideology was accepted by the Ukrainian veterans' association for its own, and within a short time 16 branches of the organization were formed in the Dominion. And needless to say, the appearance of the Ukrainian Nationalist Organization on a Canadian scene was met with hostile opposition from all organized Ukrainian groups in Canada.

In the face of growing hostility and the evident failure of making any headway here, the leaders of the UWVA have decided to set up an organization that would offer a wider scope of activities and remove the restrictions as to membership qualification existing in the Veterans' association. Thus, in 1932 the Ukrainian Nationalist Federation of Canada (the UNO) was organized, with headquarters in Saskatoon, where the present organ of the UNO, the New Pathway, was being published and also where the headquarters of the UWVA had been moved from Winnipeg in 1934. Hence the leaders of the UWVA have also become the leaders of the newly formed UNO, and the supreme leadership of the OUN and its ideology became the part and parcel of the UWO. Although the existing Ukrainian organizations persisted in their opposition to the UNO, the Nationalists succeeded in building a successful organization, somewhat fashioned after the Communist ULFTA, and with branches in all Ukrainian Canadian communities. The Veterans' association was incorporated as an autonomous section and charged with the task of inspiring militant spirit in the ranks of the UNO. Having been established in 1930 as a Nationalist publication by a [⊱deletion: 1 line], M. Pohorecky, and several other Nationalists, the New Pathway (Nowy Shlah) was accepted as the organ of the UNO, aiding the new organization in its development into a redoubtable movement in Canada.

In the meantime Hitler came to power in Germany and the OUN leaders simply hitched their vehicle to the Nazi machine in a hope that one day the Fuehrer would crush the Soviet Union and thus aid them in the reconstruction of the Ukraine along the totalitarian lines, with Konovaletz emerging as dictator. Consequently the whole movement found itself entangled in the Nazi machine. By own choice or force of circumstances the leaders were enlisted into the services of the Nazi Gestapo, the Intelligence and Propaganda departments, including the leader Konovaletz. Konovaletz was reported having been also in the service of the Soviet G.P.U., and on this account was assassinated two years ago in Rotterdam [12] under mysterious circumstances. The Nationalists claim that an agent of the G.P.U. named Valuke murdered their leader, while a Detroit journalist, Adler, advanced an opinion that it was the Gestapo that ordered his death. It is therefore interesting to note that Konovaletz had visited Canada in 1929, reportedly on the invitation of Wasyl Swystun, then the president of the Ukrainian Self-Reliance League and now a nominal leader of the UNO, in a futile endeavour to link this patriotic Canadian organization with the OUN.

Another prominent leader of the OUN, who is reported to have been in the service of the German Gestapo and the Soviet G.P.U., is O. Hrybiwsky-Senyk. As liaison officer of the OUN, he made many visits to Canada and the United States on a secret mission to the Canadian UNO and the ODWU in the United States. Col. Roman Sushko, Gen. Victor Kurmanovich, both serving in the German army at present, Gen. N. Kapustiansky, and perhaps other representatives of the OUN have also visited Canada at the invitation of the UNO and made public appearances. A close link between the OUN in Europe and the UNO in Canada has been maintained, large sums of Canadian money steadily flowing into the OUN treasury while to the UNO executive in Saskatoon came orders and directives from the supreme leadership of the OUN in Berlin, Vienna, Prague and Rome.

Prior to this war the UNO has therefore reflected the policies and the sentiments of the OUN in all their activities and press organs. On this score the UNO was branded as a pro-Nazi group by most of the Ukrainian organizations in Canada. However, when the present hostilities broke out the UNO leaders were among the first to declare unconditional loyalty to Canada and the British cause. Having been somewhat disillusioned in Hitler on account of the Carpatho-Ukraine incident, the Nazi Germany was declared as vicious a foe of the Ukrainians as the Soviets are, and this attitude is maintained by the UNO to the present moment. In fact, the UNO is at present more outspokenly anti-Nazi and pro-British than appear to be those Ukrainian organizations whose loyalty has never been questioned and who were in conflict with the UNO for years because of its pro-Nazi sympathy. It is also a component part of the Ukrainian Canadian Committee which unites all legitimate Ukrainian organizations in Canada in the task of aiding the war effort of Canada. Whether its loyalty is sincere or not remains to be proved.

The fusion of opposing Ukrainian organizations was accomplished but recently through efforts of Prof. Simpson of Saskatoon and Capt. Tracy Philipps, representing the British Council of Education. Previous to November 15, there existed two opposing Ukrainian "representative committees" in Canada: the "Representative Committee" formed by the UNO and the Ukrainian Catholic Church lay society, the Brotherhood of Ukrain-[13]-ian Catholics; and the "Ukrainian Central Committee", uniting the Ukrainian Self-Reliance League and its affiliated sections, the Ukrainian Hetman Organization and the Ukrainian United Organizations. The effort to form a united committee soon after the war started had failed due to the fact that some of the above stated organizations frankly refused to identify themselves with the UNO because of its pro-Nazi tendencies in the past. Meanwhile the UNO leaders have secretly patched up their differences with the leaders of the Catholic Church and formed with the BUC the above "representative committee", with an imposing advisory board comprised of Prof. Watson Kirkconnell, J. T. Thorson, M.P., R.K. Finlayson, and Prof. Simpson. Rev. Dr. W. Kushnir, secretary of Bishop Ladyka, became president of the Committee.

Now in the united Ukrainian Canadian Committee the UNO has retained its dominant position by fact of the apparent support of the Ukrainian Catholic Church, whose representatives together with those of the UNO have been placed in the executive positions. It will be seen therefore that having entrenched itself so firmly in the life of Ukrainian Canadians it would be difficult to impugn the Nationalist UNO without disrupting the whole structure of Ukrainian Canadians.

The strange affinity between the Ukrainian Catholic Church and the Nationalist movement in Canada and in the United States, which is of recent date, may be variously interpreted. Until about two years ago the Nationalists have been ardent supporters of the Ukrainian Orthodox Church, while the Ukrainian Catholic Church supported the Hetman Royalist movement. However, with the ascendance of Col. Melnyk to leadership of the OUN, the Catholic Church is seen as making a sudden about face. It is explained that it is due to the fact that the supreme leader of the OUN is an ardent Catholic and former administrative assistant in the Ukrainian Catholic Church for the Metropolitan Sheptycky, who might have evolved some plan or compromise with the Catholic Church with regard to the conversion of the Orthodox Ukraine. On the other hand, the most prominent leaders of the Catholic Church in the United States and Canada as well as many priests of the Church are ardent Nationalists. In Canada, Rev. Dr. W. Kushnir is reported as being a follower of the late Col. Konovaletz and friend of the present leader, Col. Melnyk. In the United States, Auxiliary Bishop Ivan Buchko is a declared Nationalist who has already earned for himself a name for his anti-British declarations. There may be other forces at work among the Ukrainians which ferment inexplicable factors in these political orientations and re-alignments.

   At their best, the Ukrainian Nationalists in Canada may be regarded with a big question mark.[14]

INTELLIGENCE
BULLETIN

ROYAL CANADIAN MOUNTED POLICE
HEADQUARTERS, OTTAWA

FEBRUARY 17, 1941

CONTENTS

War Series
No. 40

NAZISM

NAZI SYMPATHIZERS STILL BOASTFUL
(Vancouver)

The following reports can be considered an accurate portrayal of conditions along our West Coast at the present time, wherein it is noted that those Germans who were wavering as to which side to take are now leaning more towards loyalty to this country. On the other side, despite Italian reverses, the local Nazis are supremely confident of an ultimate Hitler victory, more contemptuous of the Italians, regard recent British victories in the east as a small sideshow which will fade into insignificance when their Fuehrer decides to go into action against Britain.

"The general attitude of the local German element is at present quiet but decidedly there are two entirely different ways of thinking. On the one side we see the influence of the latest victories in Albania and more recently in Libya in that these are really welcomed with joy by the loyal Germans who are as anxious to see a British Empire victory as are any other British subjects. The attitude of the other side is just as hostile as ever. I have spoken to several of our Nazi friends, asking for their explanation of the inactivity of

Hitler towards Italy. The answer in general terms is always that Germany, through the wisdom of Hitler, knows what she is doing, that Mussolini is not much good anyway, that Great Britain, with 2 ounces of butter weekly, will soon be starved out and that the Fuehrer knows exactly when and where he will play his hand. Everyone of these people, as I have pointed out before, is a fanatic, they do not care now much destruction is caused or how much blood is shed; Hitler will triumph and rule the world."

"With the stiffening of British opposition the Nazi cause is losing more and more sympathizers. As time goes on, more people become employed, which is also a contributing factor in making people more satisfied. Many of the former sympathizers are now heard to remark that Canada is the best place to live in after all is said and done and, although our [1] system may have its faults, it is not too bad compared with what is being said about German workers compelled to put in 60 to 70 hours a week.

"The partnership of Italy and Germany never was very popular with the Germans here. It was considered a necessary evil to counteract the British-French pact. It has been rumored that, in Germany, people only cheered Italian visitors because they were forced to or because they wanted to please the Fuehrer. Since the Italians are meeting with reverses, it is pointed out that not much was expected of them and it only goes to show how much superior the German nation is to all other nations. Besides, Great Britain is throwing her whole weight and that of the Empire against Italy, both in Egypt and Greece. This will, of course, only weaken Britain all the more and when the day of reckoning comes, when the Fuehrer gives the word, Britain will not be able to stand up against the far superior German race and its soldiers.

"Again, it is pointed out that the affair in Egypt and Greece is only a sideshow. The real issue will take place on British soil. The dividing of the British Empire will take place at the Peace Table and not in Africa or Greece.

"However, the masses have gained new respect for Britain and have taken courage to oppose the sympathizers of Germany. In short, the masses have something to point to which are facts and not merely suppositions or promises.

"The old, dyed-in-the-wool Nazi sympathizers brand all the favourable news from the war theatre as just so much British propaganda to bolster up the spirit of the people knowing that Britain is on its last legs. This class always did and always will call all news in our favour British or Jewish propaganda or outright lies.

"On the whole, we are pleased to report that the tide in German circles is turning more and more in our favour. We predict that if

the war lasts another year there [2] will be very few Nazi sympathizers found at large. If the tide once begins to turn in Britain's
favour against the Germans then we believe we shall have only a
mere handful of this specie amongst us who will cling to Nazism.

We still believe that our border should be kept under surveillance. If any trouble arises here we look for it coming from the
South. The brains and plotting will be done there."[3]

FASCISM

ITALIAN COLONY CONTINUES DEPRESSED
(Vancouver)

It is reported that the Italian Colony is depressed and very careful not
to attract notice by word or deed. Some take the defeats of the Italian Army
much to heart and many believe that Italy will soon be out of the war.

The most bitter man in the Colony at present is the lawyer Angelo Branca, who "cannot understand how a great patriot like himself could be
defeated in the December Municipal Election, when he stood for re-elec-
tion on the Parks Board". It is believed he regrets having taken such a conspicuous stand in the political affairs of the Italian Colony and will give
no more trouble.

An increase in church attendance is now noticeable, and over the
holiday season Father Bortignon had packed congregations at the Sacred
Heart. Bortignon's former arrogant manner has completely changed for
the better. As Chaplain of the Ex-Combattenti, Bortignon was certainly
pro-Fascist, but today it is difficult to draw a pro-Fascist whisper from
him, all his apparent dealings with his congregation being strictly orthodox.

Among the relatives of interned men, gossiping and hoping for their
release are still prevalent. However, the assistance of Angelo Branca or
other lawyers is being ignored in their appeals for clemency for their interned men, it being now well recognized no lawyer can act in these
cases.[4]

COMMUNISM

KRIVITSKY IS DEAD!

Walter G. Krivitsky, formerly in control of the USSR Secret Service
for Western Europe, who dared to revolt against the murder ring and fled
with his family to America, is dead. He knew the Ogpu would eventually get him, as they got Trotsky and hundreds of others who have attempted
to escape the death sentence.

For a time he took refuge in Montreal under an assumed name, feeling
that he was safer in Canada than in the United States. He informed us that
he and Trotsky were marked men and said, after Trotsky's death, that he
would be the next. When the Dies' Committee investigating Un-American
activities asked him to give evidence he ignored the risk and went to

Washington.

During his four years' respite from death he succeeded in doing more than any other living person in exposing the unspeakable curse of the international Communist system. Through articles in the "Saturday Evening Post", through his "best selling" book "In Stalin's Secret Service" and through his public testifying Krivitsky made the world fearfully familiar with the methods of the most ruthless band of cut-throats known to history.[5]

ANOTHER POLITICAL LETTER

(A copy of this latest Communist directive was seized in Regina. It originated from the Centre (Toronto) with orders to be copied and distributed amongst all members of the District Executive Committee and Branch Leadership.)

Dear Friends:

The alliance line, expressed in the slogan, "an independent Socialist Canada", and elaborated in our August letter, demands the development of the most widespread revolutionary propaganda to explain to the workers and farmers the only way out of the present war catastrophe. This is our basic task, which must be coupled at every step with the development of the immediate economic struggles against the home plunder program of the Canadian bourgeoisie. But this must not be understood to mean that we have abandoned immediate agitational work, have ceased to concern ourselves with influencing the immediate course of political events, that we are indifferent to the growing ferment and criss-cross currents within the war camp from the standpoint of our tactical line. On the contrary, our basic line provides the groundwork on which we can correctly develop our immediate agitational work, profoundly influencing the daily course of events, correctly orientating on each phase of the growing crisis of bourgeois politics, and draw close to and influence the mass currents which are forming at this stage, as yet without having in large part broken loose from the war camp.

It is the task of every alliance organization, and especially of the district leading committees to use the alliance line, embodied in our August letter, as a guide to practical daily public agitation in the rapidly changing, turbulent situation . . . . .

The fight against the King government must show how at every turn this government has pretended to cater to the desires of the people, only to betray them. It is necessary to emphasize over and over again how King concealed his preparations to throw the country into war under pretensions of defending and representing Canada's independence, how he belied all his solemn promises by plunging the country into war, making a farce of his so-called Canadian "nationhood" by going through the motions of a separate declaration of war. We must show that King performed the same policy of deceit on the issues of conscription. The smelly record of the King governments of the past must be dug up by our agitation. The [6] Beauharnois scandals, the grafting of the federal and provincial liberal organizations, the whole rotten record of Liberal leg rolling and bureaucratic grafting must be used to point up the money-making scramble of the contractors and profiteers today, who are being protected by the King administration and plunging the country into a vast indebtedness as a result. The materials published in the Monthly Review and in other documents relating to the last budget should be used to the full in this connection.

We must show that King now is planning new treacheries. After supplying Japan for years with the means of war, he is planning at the behest of his Washington masters to plunge the country into war in the Pacific and to step up his deceitful training plan to full war-time conscription.

The developments of the next period will further shake the influence of social-reformist war propaganda among the workers and the base of the King government among the western farmers and in French Canada. Our purpose must be to put on foot such a powerful agitation among the masses as will help to raise the struggle to sufficient strength to hinder the government to the utmost in its plans to overcome the impasse of its war policy, to prevent it from taking masses with it in support of deeper involvement in war, to hinder and block its effort to find a way out.

Guided by the development of the situation and the development of strike movements and anti-government sentiment among the masses we must develop our fight for an Independent Socialist Canada more and more as an actual struggle to influence the course of events, to impede deeper involvement in the war, to help extricate the country from the growing catastrophe proving to the people that we are not merely propagandists for a final way out, but are concerned to save the nation from each new and greater danger that besets us.

In this struggle the new form of the people's front tactic consists in approaching the broadest masses in each district on the basis of the immediate platform of struggle against the capitalist profiteers and grafters, who are turning the so-called "war effort" into an orgy of profit-taking for themselves. To this immediate platform to economic and civil liberty demands which was embodied in the federal election manifesto, must now be added the fight against any involvement in war in the Pacific, against any extension of the military training plan into conscription for expeditionary service.

Political Bureau.[7]

DISLOYALTY AND DISRUPTION CONTINUE

Although the Communist Party of Canada had been outlawed and many of its leaders interned, it continues its relentless warfare against our political and social structure. New mimeographed editions of the "Clarion" appear at irregular intervals to be circulated through underground channels. Moscow directives will reach Red agents in Canada and are slavishly obeyed to the letter. Foreign speaking groups and large industrial plants continue to provide the most fertile soil for sowing seeds of disloyalty and disruption. Evidence of the progress of this hidden war accumulates in our secret files. The need of more actively combatting this enemy's propaganda is stressed by one conversant with the facts. He writes:

It is in the light of Comintern instructions from Moscow that one must read the news of 15th December, 1940 that "The British Minister of Labour (Bevin) at Glasgow sharply warned Russia against attempting to interfere in the internal wartime affairs of the British peoples".

Meanwhile, the western Dictators are having to 'change direction Left'.

(a) Hitler is posing himself as a Leader of the Workers of the World whom he fears. He is calling upon them to unite against the white-collared pluto-Democracies. Here, too, the Hitler-Stalin pact works, spasmodically.

(b) Meanwhile, Mussolini and the small pro-German clique are trying to deflect popular anger by swearing to Italian workers, among whom are many revolutionaries in Black Shirts, that he will "shoot the bourgeois-classes, as food hoarders".

(c) Within the Russian empire, Stalin's hand is desperately weak. The Comintern abroad is one of his few remaining tricks.

(d) At a moment when our war industrialization must be increased and when Labour (for working it) is of vital importance, we simply cannot afford to lack sympathy or to make mistakes. It is also essential to understand the objectives, the psychology and the world-machinery of the Communist International.

Something we can hope for (and it is a great deal) is to succeed in detaching the mass of the politically uninformed dupes from the hard [8] core of religiously convinced Communists. The latter are directed from Moscow, now in connivance with Berlin, to saw the roots and destroy the branches of the civilization of all the English-speaking peoples.

"LABOUR CLUBS" SPREAD COMMUNISM
(Montreal)

In the City of Montreal the Communist Party have opened a few so-called labour clubs for the unemployed and others who wish to meet their friends and discuss various problems. All executive members except one will be elected at large so as not to arouse suspicion. No weekly meetings will be held and the clubs will be used exclusively for recreation purposes. The Party's representative in each executive is to report on the activities of his respective local.

The Party members expect a good deal from these clubs. Various societies and movements will be asked to provide programs and to address meetings. As there are quite a few independent labour clubs in the Province of Quebec, the Party have in view the possibility of forming a federation of all or many of these clubs.[9]

"THE DAY" EXPOSES "DAILY WORKER"

(The following is a full translation of a front-page article in "Der Tog" ("The Day"), Yiddish language newspaper, of New York, of January 13, 1941).

CLARENCE HATHAWAY, FORMER EDITOR OF "THE DAILY WORKER", U.S.A., EXPELLED FROM COMMUNIST PARTY; "FREIHEIT" PRETENDS TO BE NO MORE A COMMUNIST NEWSPAPER, OBVIOUSLY TO CATCH NAIVE READERS.

In the official organ of the Communist Party, "The Daily Worker", it was announced that Clarence A. Hathaway, who was for ten years the Editor of "The Daily Worker" and who was counted one of the three principal leaders of the Communist Party, was yesterday formally expelled from the Communist Party. No precise reasons were given. It was only reported that Hathaway was actually expelled from the party as long ago as October 10th, but the Party gave him three months to whitewash himself from the charges brought against him. As he failed to prove it he was formally expelled from the Party of which he himself, from 1919, was one of its builders and organizers, and up to late one of its principal leaders.

The charges against him were that he did not personally and politically comply with the obligations of the Party and that he has thereby harmed the prestige of the Party. It was also announced that it was since July last that he was no more the Editor of "The Daily Worker".

The "Morgen-Freiheit" which up to this late date was known as the official organ of the American Communist Party, Jewish Section, published in its edition of last Saturday a formal announcement which is intended to say that it is no more a Communist newspaper.

The announcement that "The Morgen-Freiheit" is no more the official organ of the Communist Party was embodied in a report on a conference which, it is stated, the Communist Party convened and which was composed of its trusted Jewish Communist leaders. It is stated in the report of the "Morgen-Freiheit" that at this conference Israel Amter, Chairman of the New York State Committee of the Communist Party, declared as follows:-

"Amter stressed the importance of helping the 'Morgen-Freiheit' in its circulation and in its financial drive, for though the 'Morgen-Freiheit' is not a Communist newspaper it is the only progressive, anti-war and pro-Soviet Jewish Daily".[10]

According to the same report in the "Freiheit" Amter concluded his speech with an appeal for continued activities by the Communist Party to organize the Jewish masses.

All well-informed circles close to the Communist Party considered all this as a trick by the Communists to catch naive Jewish readers. It is also important to connect this with what appears in "The Daily Worker".

"The Daily Worker" which was up to now the official English organ of the Communist Party, had already some time ago officially declared that it is no more the official organ of the Party. It was then explained by the same informed non-Communist circles that the "Daily Worker" had made such declaration because of the new Federal law whereby all organizations which may be considered as controlled by organizations abroad must register with the State Department of the United States.[11]

SLOVAK POLITICAL ORGANIZATION IN CANADA

(Compiled from different reliable documents at the Translation Office, R.C.M. Police Headquarters.)

Background

Many people by habit or by ignorance confuse the Czechs with the Slovaks. Though both are of parent Slavic race they never fail to stress their ethnographical, linguistic and, most particularly, religious differences—the Czechs being mainly Lutheran Protestants and the Slovaks Roman Catholics.

Because there are different organizations in Canada which are called Czecho-Slovak, many people who think they know things Czecho-Slovakian confuse the two and refer to Slovaks when they mean Czechs.

Number of Slovaks

According to "L'udovy Kalendar" ("The People's Calendar") of 1939, there are about 40,000 Slovaks in Canada. The great majority of them came to Canada after 1926. These Slovaks were mostly young unskilled labourers with no other purpose than to earn a better living than was afforded in their home country. They were employed in the lumber camps in British Columbia, on farms as labourers, in the coal, gold and other metal mines and foundry works.

It is further shown that up to 1929, the first year of the great depression, the bulk of these Slovak workers did not belong to any political organization. A number of them might have belonged to a Slovak mutual benefit society which at the time was politically innocuous. A very insignificant number belonged to political organizations and to the Communist Party prior to 1930.

First Slovak Organizations

The first organized group of Slovaks in Canada, according to an article in the above mentioned Calendar, was the "Slovenska [12] Robotnicka Podporna Spolka" ("The Slovak Workers' Aid Organization"). This organization had existed in the United States for some time and a branch

(Branch 96) was organized in Toronto about 1930. It was the first Slovak organization with a strong radical tinge. While of no great consequence at first, it had become the breeding place for a stronger, purely political organization, led by the Communist Party of Canada, the SKS.

The SKS

"Slovenska Kulturna Sdruzenia" (Slovak Cultural Association"). In the Communist phraseology it was called "A Language Mass Organization". Such mass organizations were established here and in other countries of other nationalities. Thus there was a Russian mass organization, a Ukrainian mass organization, etc. Most of them were called "cultural organizations" or "cultural clubs". This was the Slovak cultural association which educated its members for Leninism and a dictatorship of the workers.

"Hlas L'Udu" ("Voice of the People")

This was the mouthpiece of the SKS. It was banned with other papers under the Defence of Canada Regulations.

It may be said that the "Hlas L'Udu" was one of the most aggressive of such foreign language papers published in Canada. It was bitterly anti-British. Certain non-Communist Slovak elements seem to have supported "Hlas L'Udu" because of its anti-Czech and therefore anti-British character.

"Jiskra" ("The Spark") must not be confused with the "Hlas L'Udu". The "Jiskra" was the mouthpiece of the Czechs and not of the Slovaks, yet the Slovaks helped in the establishment and in the existence of the "Jiskra". While there are about 40,000 Slovaks in Canada there are only 10,000 Czechs and the "Jiskra" was but a tiny, mimeographed sheet. However, it was doing a great deal of harm.

Origin of SKS

All the leaders of SKS in Canada stress the fact that it was the years of economic depression, beginning with 1929, that gave impetus to the organization of SKS in 1930. It is stated that the Slovaks in Canada, suffering from dire distress, not familiar with the language of the country, felt somewhat abandoned and helpless.[13]

Methods of Communist Propaganda

SKS operated and still operates by means of the proven system of camouflaged subsidiaries. These subsidiaries are: choirs, dramatic circles, orchestras, schools for children and for training of leaders, youth organizations and, above all, workers' sport circles. All these organizations are paraded as non-partisan or even non-political, but the plays that the dramatic circles represent are radical; the spirit in all the organizations is radical; they are headed and guided by proven Communists, and they subscribe to every activity started by the Communists. The Communists can thus claim that they are supported by non-political organizations. All the above-mentioned subsidiary organizations are still in operation and active.

The first quarters of SKS in Toronto, at 334 Queen Street West, became the center of Slovak radical activities. Branches now exist in numerous towns and cities throughout the Dominion.

[⊰deletion: 1 line]

[⊰deletion: 1 paragraph: 4 lines]

The N.V.P.S.

These initials stand for "Neodvisla Vzojomna Podporna Sdruzenja" ("The Independent Mutual Aid Association"). This is a powerful Czecho-Slovak mutual benefit society. However, as Slovaks are in the majority there and dominate it, it may be considered an almost purely Slovak organization.

"Kanadska Slovenska Liga"
("The Canadian Slovak League")

While the above-mentioned SKS was the organization of the Slovak pro-Communists and Communists, the "Canadian Slovak League" was the organization of the Slovak nationalists.[14]

Czech Slovak Strife

In order to state the aims and character of this league we must go back to the political and social conditions in Czecho-Slovakia prior to its dismemberment and occupation by Hitler.

It will be recalled that Czecho-Slovakia was established as an independent State by the Treaty of Versailles. During the Great War of 1914-1918, the Czechs who lived in the two provinces, Bohemia and Moravia, under Austrian domination, formed unofficial legions which they called "Sokols" ("Hawks"), and fought successfully and in many cases most victoriously on the side of the Allies. When the two provinces of Bohemia and Moravia were established as a Czech independent State the large province of Slovakia was added thereto, and together they formed the Czecho-Slovak Republic. It was the Czechs who dominated the country and formed the government. Under the Treaty of Versailles the Slovaks were granted certain rights and a measure of home rule in their own province. But since the inception, and particularly in the latter years, prior to the dismemberment of Czecho-Slovakia, the Slovaks constantly and bitterly complained against being slighted by the Czechs. Some of the differences between the Czechs and Slovaks were deep-rooted, such as the religious issues. The Slovaks wanted not a laic State but a Catholic State. The Czechs thought that religious matters must not be mixed with State affairs. The Slovaks felt themselves oppressed by the Czechs and yearned for a full measure of autonomy.

The Loyal Czecho-Slovak Association

"Narodna Sdruzenia Slovakov, Cechov A Karpatorusov ("The People's Association of Slovaks, Czechs and Karpatho-Russians"). This is the name of the Czecho-Slovak organization in Canada which promoted the "Odboy" here. It should be noted that there were but very few Slovaks in this organization, though the name includes them.

The "Odboy" or "The War Efforts" on the side of Britain (which is the actual meaning of the "Odboy") was fiercely attacked from three sides. First, by the nationalist Slovaks—unofficially led by the Canadian Slovak League. Second, by SKS, the Slovak pro-Communist Party. Third, in a lesser degree, by the Czech pro-Communists, centered around "Jiskra". This struggle, despite the War Measures Act, is still carried on against the "Odboy", and echoes of it can be found weekly in the official organ of the N.S. SCK., "The Nova Vlast ("New Homeland").[15]

"Odboy" ("Defence")

The word "Odboy" has since become a by-word and a sacred word. It is the term given to the Czecho-Slovak National action for the restoration of independent Czecho-Slovakia. Secret "Odboy" organizations were organized in Czecho-Slovakia. They are headed, instructed and advised by Benes who lives in London, England.

An "Odboy" was organized in Canada. It was promoted and led by Dr. Pavlisk, the Czecho-Slovak Consul General in Canada, with the help of the N.S. SCK.

The "Odboy" is raising men and money in Czecho-Slovakia and abroad for new Czecho-Slovak legions to fight on the side of Britain against Hitlerism in general and for the restoration of Czecho-Slovakia in particular.

Internal Struggle for Domination

As stated above, The Independent Mutual Aid Association is a powerful organization dominated by a Slovak majority. Two Slovak organizations fiercely compete in it for power: SKS and Canadian Slovak League seek to use the organization in support of its own policies—policies of an independent Slovakia under Hitler and against the "Odboy", (that is, against our own war efforts). As the majority of the members of N.V.P.S. are working people, SKS has made a strong headway.

Occasionally, SKS and the Canadian Slovak League, though mortal enemies (as the first are Communists and atheists, while the second are strong Catholics and nationalists), nevertheless unite in action against the "Odboy" and against the N.S. SCK which is largely a Czech and not a Slovak organization.

Independent-minded Slovaks

It must be remembered that there is a small number of Slovaks, mem-

331 of the N.V.P.S., or who do not belong to any organization and who

bers of the N.V.P.S., or who do not belong to any organization and who either support the "Odboy" or are altogether neutral. Amongst the latter are many Slovaks who have become thoroughly Canadianized.

It is significant that, when registration of all enemy aliens was imposed by the government and Czecho-Slovaks were permitted special exemptions, only the Czechs took advantage of these, the Slovak nationalists of the Canadian Slovak League brand preferring to be treated as aliens rather than to be expected to support the "Odboy".[16]

SECRET

INTELLIGENCE
BULLETIN

ROYAL CANADIAN MOUNTED POLICE
HEADQUARTERS, OTTAWA

MARCH 20, 1941

CONTENTS

General:
  Why Canadian Tribune Was Suspended
  Police Investigation of Nielsen Propaganda
  Internees have Four-Fold Trial
Communism:
  "Western Farmer" Endorsed by Reds
  An Independent People's Government
  New Communist Paper Sent Students
  Clarion Raves at "More Dictatorship"
  Sabotaging our Tourist Traffic
  Fate of Russian National Church
  "Out of the Night"

War Series
No. 41

GENERAL
WHY "CANADIAN TRIBUNE" WAS SUSPENDED

The recent suspension for a period of three weeks of "The Canadian Tribune" aroused in some quarters criticism for unjust interference with the "freedom of the press". The recommendation for such action against the "Tribune" was made by the Press Censorship in the belief that this weekly paper published in Toronto and circulated throughout Canada was contravening Section 39A of the Defence of Canada Regulations.

The "Tribune" first appeared January 20, 1940, ten months after the "Daily Clarion" (Communist paper) was declared illegal. Long before its appearance the Police were aware of the intention of certain people previously connected with the "Clarion" to fill the vacancy with a publication which, while remaining within the letter of the law, would perpetuate the traditions and policies of the defunct paper.

At present innuendo is the chief weapon of the "Tribune". There is little in the average issue which is definitely anti-British. It is rather in the clever headlines, the well-edited excerpts from reputable papers, that it insinuates against our system. In this its editorial policy is more or less identical with that of the "Clarion" until about 1938.

332

The parallel between the two goes further. Distribution of the "Tribune" is, for the most part, by local agents who are all known Communists. There are no subscription drives but there are constant "sustaining fund" drives carried on by affiliates of the Party still within the pale of the law. It is further interesting to note that a few weeks before the first issue of the "Tribune" appeared all subscribers to the "Clarion" were contacted by circular letter for subscription to the new paper.

[⊰deletion: 1 paragraph: 4 lines][1]

[⊰deletion: 1 paragraph: 4 lines]

R.A.C. Ballantyne is the executive secretary of the Civil Liberties Union, Montreal Branch, [⊰deletion: 3 lines]

From its first issue one of the "Tribune's" primary policies has been criticism of the Defence of Canada Regulations in their application to Communists and so-called Union Leaders. In this connection, Mrs. Nielsen's Point No. 9 in her Ten Point Program, "Release of Trade Unionists and other anti-Fascists Now Interned", has been given considerable prominence by the "Tribune". Mrs. Nielsen's platform gives every indication of being dictated by the politically wise. The "Tribune" on the other hand has a well-developed policy developed long before Mrs. Nielsen became front-page news. It would seem, therefore, that their ideology has a common source C.P. of C.

Suspension of the "Tribune" was not the result of any one misdemeanour but rather of an accumulation of petty offenses on the border-line of legality that tended to discourage faith in democracy and retard our war efforts. The editors had previously been warned to be more moderate in their manner of expressing their views but, despite this, in recent weeks they published several items that were distinctly subversive in tone and so brought about the three weeks' suspension ruling of the Government.[2]

POLICE INVESTIGATION OF NIELSEN PROPAGANDA

Last August Mrs. Dorise Nielsen, M.P., published a leaflet entitled "Why I Opposed the Budget". As the contents were suspected of contravening the Defence of Canada Regulations and the leaflets were being utilized by Communists for the furtherance of their anti-British ends, they were seized and examined. They contained the following passages:

"I am writing to you, the Canadian people, because it is the only way I can reach you. I feel that if you know the truth you will lift your voice with mine in protest, especially against the injustice of this war budget. Mine is only one voice, but yours is the voice of millions.

"You have been told by press and radio that this budget was patriotic, that it ensured equality of sacrifice and equal participation in the war effort. That is a lie, and this war budget is instead the greatest hoax ever perpetrated on the nation. This budget means greater poverty, suffering and misery for the Canadian people, while at the same time it ensures further profits for the few. It means that the Canadian people, who are now suffering greatly, will be compelled to finance this war, besides giving their sons. It means that those who now own and control vast wealth will continue to build up even greater reserves, by way of war contracts, and also ensure for themselves interest upon loans they will issue to the government...

"Besides sacrificing our sons, we are to bear a burden of taxation and debt which will drag us down to a degree of misery such as we have never yet experienced. It cannot be patriotic to support this. It is not loyal to allow such treatment of our people, for we are not a poor, impoverished nation. We are wealthy, and these sacrifices we are asked to make are unnecessary and uncalled for. Our government is doing today just as it did during the Great Depression. It is acting as the Charlie McCarthy of the big business Bergen; it is protecting the wealthy at the expense of the nation.[3]

"Besides some of our men giving their lives, others will have to work in the mines, in the factories, in the fields, their labour regimented by the enormous powers of conscription taken by the government. Our women are to see their dollars grow smaller and smaller in value and, with despair and growing anxiety, realize that they can no longer feed and clothe their families. Our children are to suffer from malnutrition and lack of medical care, their little pale faces bearing mute testimony to our nation's indifference.

"To that we are doomed unless, in loyalty to Canada, to our people and their future, we raise our voices in one great effort to protest against this injustice...

Dorise W. Nielsen, M.P."

Subsequently, a pamphlet (containing 47 pages) was published by the Canadian Tribune Publishing Company of Toronto. This contains the speeches made by Mrs. Nielsen in the House of Commons; in addition, the first issue contained the wording of the leaflet "Why I Opposed the Budget" under the heading "Open Letter to Canadians", with the exception that where the leaflet contained the following passage:-

"That is a lie and this war budget is instead the greatest hoax ever perpetrated on the nation",

the "Open Letter to Canadians" contained:-

"That is untrue". (The remaining words were omitted)

[✂ deletion: 1 paragraph: 5 lines]

The leaflets were seized and the matter duly referred to the Attorney General's Department for a decision; no action being contemplated,

[✂ deletion: 1 line][4]

[✂ deletion: 1 paragraph: 4 lines]

[✂ deletion: 1 paragraph: 14 lines]

The matter was subsequently referred to the Attorney General's Department of Saskatchewan who requested that this Force conduct an investigation for the purpose of ascertaining whether, or not, there was sufficient evidence available to prove publication of the leaflet, as there appeared to be grounds for instituting a prosecution under Regulation 39A, D.O.C.R.; following this, an investigation was conducted respecting the circumstances surrounding the publication, etc., of the leaflet which in no way differed from other inquiries of a similar nature.

The Union label on the leaflet indicated that it was printed by the Eveready Printing Company of Toronto but in view of the fact that the pamphlet also contained the wording of the leaflet, with the change already referred to, and that same was published by the Canadian Tribune Publishing Company, it was necessary to search the premises of both these businesses on October 26 under authority of a search warrant issued under the provisions of the Defence of Canada Regulations.[5]

At the premises of the Eveready Printing Company, approximately 50 pieces of correspondence were seized, a perusal of which established that [≈<deletion: 1 line] ordered the printing and distribution of approximately 115,000 copies of the leaflet and that after repeated requests, [≈<deletion: 1 line] subsequently issued a cheque for the sum of $98.38 being the unpaid balance less $15, which had, for some unknown reason been paid by [≈<deletion: 2 lines]

At the premises of the Canadian Tribune Publishing Company, a few proofs and five copies of the pamphlet were seized but, following examination and reference to the Attorney General of Saskatchewan, they were returned to [≈<deletion: 1 line] on November 25.

Details of the investigation were duly submitted to the Attorney of Saskatchewan, following which instructions were received to return the leaflets, etc., to the persons from whom they were obtained and this action was followed.[6]

INTERNEES HAVE FOUR-FOLD TRIAL

Recent criticism in Parliament that under the present set-up people can be railroaded into internment camps without reasonable evidence of their guilt and without a chance to refute the charges laid against them, was answered by Mr. Lapointe, Minister of Justice. He explained that the suspect is protected by four separate tribunals.

1. Before he is recommended for internment the police have investigated his activities and gathered all pertinent evidence obtainable.
2. Such particulars are submitted to Crown Counsel especially appointed for the duty, who examines the suspect on basis of police reports and recommends internment or otherwise.
3. If the case is considered sound it is then set before an examining committee (Mr. Norman Robertson, now acting Under-

Secretary of State for External Affairs) and Mr. J. F. MacNeil
(Justice Department) who, if the facts warrant it, submit them to
the Minister of Justice for an order for internment.
4. The Minister decides whether to issue the order or not. If the man
is a British Subject he has the right to object to internment. Such
objection is heard by an advisory committee appointed under
Section 22 of the Defence of Canada Regulations as the proper
authority to act in the matter. The committee sends its recommendation to the Minister of Justice who must then use his discretion.[7]

COMMUNISM
"WESTERN FARMER" ENDORSED BY REDS.

"The Western Farmer"—a new weekly newspaper bearing the slogan
"Save the Family Farm"—made its first appearance in Saskatoon, Sask.
last October. Its publishing committee are Dorise W. Nielsen, M.P.,
Minerva Cooper and H. G. Miller [꒒deletion: 2 lines] Henry Mills,
Robert Paul and F. G. Gudmundson. Miller is the managing editor.

The "Western Farmer" would seem to be the fulfillment of a long
cherished desire on the part of the Communist Party for an independent
farm sheet through which they might promulgate their doctrines. Certainly the views of the C.P. of C., as expressed elsewhere by its individual
members both by word and print, are appearing weekly in "The Western
Farmer".

Communist leaders are urging their followers to support it as they
would their own press when not banned, by subscribing to and reading it
faithfully. One leader declares:

"The drive for the "Western Farmer" must be regarded as our
main task in the coming month. Nothing can be allowed to interfere
with its success. This paper can become the most powerful organizer and agitator for the farmers. It will be the medium for leading and developing the farm struggle. Through it the farmers of the
West will work out the form of organization best united to their
needs.

"The paper is not our Paper or our organ. It is a mass farm paper
which reflects the immediate needs of the farmers and which will
set them on the path of struggle against the effects of capitalism and
war. As such it deserves our best effort.

"The leading committee holds every member responsible to do
his utmost to make the apparatus a success. Make your plan now
for immediate response to the Drive Appeal and spare no effort until
the paper is firmly based in the farm homes."[8]

AN "INDEPENDENT PEOPLE'S GOVERNMENT"
Communists continue to issue "political letters championing their

latest scheme for the overthrow of democracy in Canada. The term "People's Party" crops up in the speeches of radicals all over the English-speaking world and was particularly prominent at the "People's Convention" in London, Eng. last January when a massed gathering of Reds repudiated the war and the Churchill Government.

To quote briefly from the latest "letter" (secretly circulated):-

We propose a movement, uniting the working class, the youth, the Western farmers and the French-Canadian people for an Independent People's Government, a genuine Canada First Government, to save the country from being hurtled over the precipice. The chief tasks of such a government which create the basis for immediate unity, would be three:

1.   To give Canada an independent voice, free from blind, profit-seeking subservience to the war policy of other governments, to prevent the futile spreading of the war, to protect Canada's youth and manpower from futile sacrifice through "blank check" commitments to other governments.

2.   To save Canada from being plunged into war in the Pacific at the behest of the USA.

3.   To put an end to the orgy of war-profits and war-graft and save the nation from the economic ruin towards which it is now heading.

Favorable conditions for the development of a genuine mass movement for this immediate program and an independent people's government are coming into being. To hold its mass base in Quebec and Western Canada, the King government was compelled to make out-and-out pledges against conscription for overseas service, against committing Canada's manpower to the British government. This demonstrated not only that for the time being US imperialism was not interested in a large-scale Canadian expeditionary force to Europe, but also the tremendous force of the Canadian [9] people's opposition to commitment of Canada's manpower to the British government. In moving now towards total conscription, towards the preparation of a large-scale expeditionary force, the King government faces the critical problem of a shake-up in Liberal-Tory party relations, and the shifting of the government mass base primarily to the British chauvinist-Tory party base. In the face of a powerful agitational drive and exposure of their conspiracy against the Canadian masses, this cannot fail to create serious difficulties and profound disturbances for the bourgeoisie. With the strengthening of the strike movement for higher wages to meet rising living costs, the growth of the new farm movement in the west, the deepening resentment of the Quebec masses and the increasing evidence from the European war itself, of the futile death awaiting Canada's youth there, it becomes increasingly a practical possibility to develop a united people's mass movement strong enough to block the present disastrous road of government policy, to prevent further sending of our youth to certain death in Europe, and to turn the tide of events through the struggle for an independent peoples' government.

"NEW COMMUNIST PAPER SENT AMONG STUDENTS."
(extract from the Montreal of Feb. 13.)

Apparently shifting their battle ground from McGill University where they distributed the "Red Martlet", the Young Communists of Quebec yesterday distributed another pamphlet, "The Red Triangle", to students of Sir George Williams College.

Copies of the pamphlet, attacking the Dominion's "Call to Arms" and charging that "Canada's students are not cannon fodder in an imperialistic war", were forwarded to the R. C. M. Police by the students who received them.

"The Red Triangle" is the latest move by the "Reds" in Montreal, it was learned yesterday. Almost every day, from hidden presses, new attacks on democracy are launched.[10]

"CLARION" RAVES AT "MORE DICTATORSHIP"

Canadian Communists pretend to see in the Dominion-Provincial conference on the Rowell-Sirois Report just another attempt by the Federal Government to gain more dictatorial power for the prosecution of a "capitalist war". While the Royal Commission had been originally appointed for improving social conditions the findings, asserts "The Clarion", are now being used for the destruction of democracy.

To quote from the latest mimeographed issue of this outlawed sheet:-

In short, the Conference was the first open indication in this war of the growing difficulty of Capitalist rule in Canada. MacKenzie King's first attempt to get centralized powers to persecute the war more fervently for his class failed miserably, and will now give place to arbitrary actions (similar to the rule by order-in-council in the case of civil liberties, about which, significantly, there is no talk of "provincial vs. federal authority") to enforce the war monopoly's policies in the field of finance. On the other hand, trouble can be expected when this is done. While the federal Liberal machine, obeying the dictates of London and Washington, moves to harsher and harsher class rule, some of the provincial opportunists who sense the possibility of furthering their sectional capitalist interests by exploiting the rising movements of the rural masses, will move against the King regime. All the evil fruits of national disunity, of semi-colonialism, of British versus American imperialist interest, of sectional capitalist disputes, of the frustration of Canadian independence which has become the hallmark of the British North America Act, will ripen in the coming months.

The question of democratic rights, economic reforms, complete autonomy for Quebec, an independent foreign policy in line with the national interests of the Canadian people—these are all focal points of the struggle for the control of our own destiny, against the financial oligarchy which in peacetime brazenly refused to introduce a national system of social legislation, and now in wartime attempts to gain increased federal powers to place even greater war burdens on the backs of the people.[11]

The conclusion to be drawn is that the promising people's movements which are developing in multifarious ways and forms are the guarantee that the struggle against the financial oligarchy and for Canadian independence will be carried on in this war. The people's movements must be taken out of the hands of Hepburn and Aberhart. The opportunism of these men must be exposed. The drive of Ottawa for increased central powers must be shown to be what it is and what it holds for the people: more dictatorship to reduce living standards to pay for the capitalist war.

Only an independent Canadian people's government, based on the Western and Ontario farmers, on the specially oppressed Quebec people, on the industrial workers, can solve the problems of the Canadian people at this moment, and stop the mad drive of the big business government to increased participation in war, to starvation and to national ruin. And only such a government could deal, in conference with the provinces, with the democratic requirements of all parts of Canada and oppose the program of big business.

CORRECTION

In "Intelligence Bulletin" No. 39, under the title "Quebec and the Vichy Government", we quoted from a confidential report that intimated that M. Louis Francoeur of Quebec was broadcasting views on the present French situation that were out of harmony with those held by Premier Godbout, and that his remarks "would appear to encourage the totalitarian section of the groups supporting Vichy".

We have since been advised that our informant misinterpreted statements attributed to M. Francoeur, and that in fact M. Francoeur [≥<deletion: 1 line][12]

SABOTAGING OUR TOURIST TRAFFIC

Organized sabotage of our American tourist traffic by the Communist Party of Canada has long been suspected. Rumours calculated to discourage American tourists from crossing our border were undoubtedly responsible for a serious decrease in the number of such visitors last summer and efforts were made to trace the rumours to their source. Last month definite evidence of sabotage came to hand in the form of circular of a defamatory nature. One of these, signed "Jack Canuck, Jr." and couched in familiar Communist parlance and addressed to "American Youth", contained the following assertions:-

"...No less than 150 labor leaders who worked for peace and freedom have been interned in these camps for the 'duration' without trial or hearing."... "Truth is outlawed in Canada. We can't get authentic news. Some 50 of our Canadian newspapers have been banned. More than 200 foreign publications, many of them American, are not permitted entry into Canada." ..."In Canada, the Mounties represent fear and oppression." ..."You see, the war has changed Canada. Under the War Measure Act, the state more and more assumes a dictatorial pattern. Freedom of speech, press, and assembly in short our civil liberties have been destroyed. Under our very eyes we see the beautiful Maple Leaf, the symbol of Canada 'from sea to sea' being transformed into a horrible swastika. Yes, even embryo storm troopers like the 'Legion of Frontiersmen', Civic Protection Committees appear on the scene to assist the RCMP IN THEIR NEFARIOUS WORK. Naturally you ask what kind of government have you got in Canada?" ..."Our country is being ruined by the war. Canada's best sons are being sacrificed. The war is rapidly breeding fascism in Canada. We are learning from experience that the only hope for our country and for peace is to rid ourselves of our profiteers, would-be dictators, grafters, and war makers who prevent the Canadian people from reaching a full nationhood. Amongst young and old the spirit of true Canadianism lives and the fight goes forward for a free, independent Canada, a free people's government. This is the only hope for Canada."[13]

FATE OF RUSSIAN NATIONAL CHURCH

(The following are a few facts about the history and development of the Russian Greek-Orthodox Church since the October Revolution and the advent to power of the Bolshevists in Russia.)

During and after the October Revolution, the Bolshevist Party in Russia was violently anti-religious, particularly against the Russian national church which is the Greek-Orthodox Church. It may be noted that the source of the hatred of the Bolshevists against their national church was not so much in their objection to religion in general as to the fact that up to the revolution the Russian Church was in full and complete alliance with Czarism in the suppression of radicalism in Russia.

The highest ecclesiastical office of the Russian Church is that of Patriarch. Under him are Metropolitans. The Patriarch corresponds to the Pope in the Roman Catholic Church and the Metropolitan to the Cardinal. After the October Revolution and Metropolitan of the Russian Church was thrown in prison and subsequently liquidated. Other high prelates of the Church had the same fate. It was then that ancient local churches were converted into museums, workers' clubs and stables.

But religion as a creed could not be stamped out. Many of the faithful kept on congregating and worshipping in the fields and the woods, on river sides and in private homes. As the years passed a form of church organization under the abnormal conditions was getting established by itself. When the Russian Bolshevist authorities realized that religion cannot be stamped out by violence they resorted to anti-religious propaganda and State control.

First a thorough purge was made in the church. The remnant of the ancient Clergy that was loyal to Czarism was liquidated. A new Metropolitan was appointed by the Soviet Union Government with a nominal status, formally though not actually similar to the status that a Metropolitan held under the Czars. Even the Holy Synod was re-established, but under the same conditions as the Metropolitan, that is completely subservient to the State.[14]

Following the Russian October revolution millions of Russians, including many of the upper strata, formed communities in Japan, Manchukio, China, United States, Canada and many countries in Europe, including Serbia and Bulgaria where the national church is the same as Russia's.

The overwhelming majority of the Russian Clergy in the Russian communities abroad did not recognize the Russian Synod and Metropolitan set up at home by the Bolshevist Government, but established temporarily a dissident Russian Greek-Orthodox Church with headquarters in Yugo-Slavia. Some of the bitterest adversaries of Russian Bolshevism, including the former White Guards and modern Fascists, were the promoters and leaders of this dissident church. For a time it was hoped that Bolshevism would be overthrown and the authority of the Russian national church restored in Russia. But the temporary Russian Church abroad has now taken on a form of permanency.

Thus there are today two Russian national Greek-Orthodox churches. Very few Russian communities or individuals abroad recognize the Russian home Church. If there is anywhere abroad a Russian Parish recognizing the Russian home church, it may be assumed that it is not sincerely religious, but is using religious prercgatives only in order to carry on Soviet propaganda.

[≈<deletion: 1 paragraph: 5 lines][15]

"OUT OF THE NIGHT"

No one who has read "Out of the Night" by a former secret agent of the USSR can hold any lingering doubt regarding the unmitigated cruelty and bestiality of Communism and Nazism in their true colours. Therefore everyone should read it—not for pleasure, but for the better protection of democracy.

In a letter, printed in Toronto "Globe and Mail", Mr. Joseph Sedgwick, K.C., reviews the book and brings its lesson home to Canada.

He states in part:-

The most significant and revealing book to be published in many a year, Jan Valtin's "Out of the Night", has so pointed a message for the democracies that it deserves intensive study by all interested in the preservation of free institutions—and it has a special lesson for Canada, where many of our people have been prone to dismiss Fascism and Communism as alien faiths incapable of growth on our soil.

Valtin makes clear what those of us who have studied Communism have always contended, namely, that Fascism and Nazism are movements that grew up to combat the original terror of the Communists. Force begets force to oppose it, and the campaign of murder, arson, sabotage and organized brutality of the Communist factions in Europe called into being the other equally brutal philosophies of Fascism and Nazism. In the clash of these two forces democracy in Europe perished and the stage was set for the present conflict. Indeed, it would appear that for years Stalin was working to eliminate free institutions, even if in so doing he brought to power Fascist government, it being obvious that he feared democracy, which in its essence was opposed to his and similar tyrannies, and preferred a totalitarian government similar to his own, however it may be called, knowing that tyrants could get together, but that no agreement was possible between a tyrant and a free people. The Nazi-Russian pact and the war which sprang from it are the answer. Throughout Valtin's book he quotes the consistent order from Moscow: "Don't bother about the Nazis—our true foes are the Social Democrats." No different is the present Moscow-inspired Communist attitude, which supports Hitler and heaps abuse on what it calls the "imperialist" powers—Britain and the United States.[16]

The lesson for us is that all subversive movements must be stamped out in future as soon as they are recognized. It is not a denial of freedom to deny to the enemies of freedom the right to agitate for its abolition. In a word, democracy has not merely the right but the duty to protect itself from its enemies, to prohibit their propaganda, and to smash their organizations.

Valtin, in his career as a Red terrorist, was under the direction of the R.I.L.U., controlled from Moscow. This same R.I.L.U. issued its orders to Buck, Ewen and other Canadian Communist leaders—orders not unlike those given to Valtin. This Colonel Price showed in 1932 when he published a pamphlet, "Agents of Revolution", containing actual copies of letters of direction from R.I.L.U. headquarters in Russia to our Canadian Communists...

Now, as a war measure, Communism has again been outlawed. It should be outlawed in war and peace, and one can only pray that our public men will never again encourage or permit the growth of this cancer on our body politic. If they do, it may well destroy us as it destroyed the democratic Germany of the Weimar Constitution.

Joseph Sedgwick.[17]

INTELLIGENCE
BULLETIN

ROYAL CANADIAN MOUNTED POLICE
HEADQUARTERS, OTTAWA

APRIL 7, 1941

CONTENTS

EXCERPTS AND SUMMARIES FROM
COMMUNIST PROPAGANDA LEAF-
LETS RECENTLY SEIZED THROUGH-
OUT CANADA BY POLICE.

War Series
No. 42

FOREWORD
COMMUNISTS' "SECRET WEAPON"

Communists in Canada and the United States are stepping up their under-cover war on democracy by showering the continent with written propaganda. Scarcely a day passes without a mimeographed sheet or pamphlet falling into Police hands. The contents are largely variations of the familiar theme songs, "Stop the Imperialist War" and "An Independent Socialist Government".

Youth is urged to resist conscription; labor unions to stage strikes; farmers to make exorbitant demands on governments; the "middle classes" to protest against corruption and Fascism in high places—and all this with only one end in view: disorganization and demoralization of society so that it can the better be destroyed by revolution.

Arguments and methods are similar to those employed in other countries—revealing an international "ring" directed from Moscow. A "People's Front" really means enslavement of the people by a group of misanthropes; "Socialism" really means government by secret police; "Liberty" means the destruction of political, economic and religious freedom. Because the Government knows all this, Communism has been outlawed in Canada and 89 Communists have been interned. However, those still at large continue their campaigning with such slanders and lies as these quoted at random from their leaflets.[1]

"THE KITCHENER COMMUNIST"

(Sensational headings distinguish this second issue of the leaflet produced by the Kitchener Section of the Communist Party of

344

Canada).

ACT NOW FOR HIGHER WAGES

Higher Living Cost Must Be   Full Support To Goodrich
Met By Higher Wages To   Workers' Demand For
Avoid Poverty   Wages!

BILL WALSH ANTI-FASCIST
COMMUNIST LEADER JAILED
Demand The Release Of Bill Walsh!

HELP DIG THE GRAVE OF CAPITALISM AND WAR!

JOIN THE COMMUNIST PARTY!

LET THE RANK AND FILE TAKE OVER

PASS THE KITCHENER COMMUNIST ON TO YOUR FRIENDS

HELP SPREAD THE TRUTH!!!!

Halt Speed-up!

DON'T BUY THE WORTHLESS SCRAPS OF

PAPER (War Certificates) THEY WILL

NEVER SURVIVE TO REPAY!

IS THIS FIGHTING FOR LABOR?

"VOLUNTARY" SAVINGS

FIGHT THE PROFITEERS BY DEMANDING HIGHER WAGES![2]

"THE TORONTO CLARION"

(The following front-page letter appears in "The Official Organ of The Toronto Committee Of The Communist Party Of Canada").

OUR PAPER

To our readers:

The Toronto Clarion is the voice of the Communist Party in our city. It has appeared illegally ever since the King war dictatorship banned the publication of the Clarion Weekly. It will continue to appear, despite all difficulties and dangers, until such time as the working class smashes that ban, and wins back the right to publish its own legal press.

Our paper is one of the most powerful group of newspapers in the world today the illegal Communist Press, published in every part of Canada, in Great Britain and in its subject colonies, in Germany and the nations groaning under the Nazi yoke, in Spain, Italy and every country where the dictatorship of capitalism has forced the revolutionary movement underground.

These papers do not have the limitless financial backing or the mass circulations of the capitalist press. But they possess one asset which no capitalist paper can boast of they tell the truth.

Our paper tells the truth about this criminal imperialist war. That is why it must be published illegally. That is why it is hated and feared by those in authority. That is why it is eagerly welcomed and read by thousands of Toronto workers. That is why its circulation is steadily growing larger.

Use the Clarion! Read it carefully from cover to cover. Pass it on to your friends and shopmates. See to it that every single copy has a wide circulation.[3]

Contribute to the Clarion! Send us letters, articles, stories of what is happening in your factory, your barracks, or your neighborhood. Let us work together to overcome the weaknesses of our paper, to make it a better propagandist and a better organizer for the cause of peace and socialism.

The Editors

"INFLATION—DOES IT MATTER?"

This is a hectographed circular distributed by the St. Andrews Section of the Communist Party of Canada, Montreal. It deals with the raising of funds for war purposes, either by taxation, reduction in social services, savings, or inflation.

The last paragraph reads:

"But whichever course is followed, it is the people who pay and pay and pay for a war which is not of their choosing. There is no difference between the aims of King and Hepburn, since those whom they represent are raking in the profits as the war spreads from Europe to Asia; there is only a difference in tactics. The question before the Canadian people is not one of inflation or no-inflation, it is of getting rid of all those who put profits before human lives, of establishing a People's Government which will represent the workers and farmers, the French Canadian people and the middle class, at whose expense the pockets of the monopolists are bulging."[4]

"THE BIG PUSH IS ON"

This is another mimeographed leaflet of the Toronto and District Young Communist League, written for the "education" of the undergraduate. It asserts that engineer students are being rushed into industries as a source of cheap labour, that campus life has become like the life of a military camp, that open forums, debates, etc. are eliminated. It arraigns "the big war push" as solemn pledges broken and will of the Canadian people betrayed; while, in the interests of the big "shots" of industry and finance, the lives and careers of students are being put on the block.

In conclusion:

"Students can learn the 'real meaning of democracy' only by car-

rying on a united struggle against the curtailment of education, a-
gainst regimentation on the campus; and, together with the workers,
farmers and middle class, by fighting for a truly democratic government, for an Independent People's Government."

"POOR SENATOR MEIGHEN IS SURPRISED AT YOU!"

This is a one-page mimeographed leaflet distributed by Group C4,
Central Section, Toronto Young Communist League, referring to an alleged statement made by Senator Meighen on January 22—"The capitalistic way of life is just the way of rewarding man's toil". Under "The
capitalistic way of life", four headings are quoted, namely, unemployment, low wages, starvation relief and war.

It also attacks the "anti-labour" Defence of Canada Regulations, conscription and secret treaties with the United States as constituting immediate danger of Canada becoming embroiled in a war with Japan, and
closes with an appeal to the working class to unite with the youth, western
farmers and French Canadians for an Independent People's Government.[5]

"STUDENT BEACON"

Under "Books or Barracks" this three-paged mimeographed leaflet issued by the Toronto District Young Communist League warns that to
secure support of students for the War Effort, government propaganda has
painted a vivid picture of life under Hitler and the fate of German universities. But what about Canadian Colleges?

"Look around you, to your own campus for example. You have
doubtless read in the Varsity the bare announcement that the Mc-
Lennan Laboratory is being used to train naval recruits, and you
have seen them on the campus. But do you realize what this must
mean to the students who use this building and have to put up with
the resulting overcrowding and curtailment of facilities. Students
work hard raising money to go to school and train for scientific research; this means little to our federal military administrators."

It quotes as other examples the requisitioning of sections of the Ontario Agricultural College and the University of British Columbia, and
even residences of the University of Manitoba. It advises students to

"Discuss this situation amongst your classmates; form committees
to circulate petitions demanding that the military forces be withdrawn from university buildings, and stationed at the homes of the
wealthy if no other accommodation is available.

"Students will be conscripted and sent overseas, therefore as students demand the conscription of wealth to pay for this rich man's
war."

The rest of the leaflet includes excerpts from an address by Theodore
Dreiser under the heading, "The United States Must Not Be Bled For Im-

perial Britain."[6]

"WHO ARE THE COMMUNISTS?"

This four-paged mimeographed leaflet has an introductory note:
"We offer no apologies for this unsolicited letter. The customary
channels used in the interchange of ideas having been denied us we
adopt this unorthodox method. The interchange must, for obvious
reasons, remain one sided this is our loss."

The circular contends that the Communist Party was declared illegal
in indecent haste and that the Government has done its best to spread the
"agents of Hitler" story. It argues that not only the Communists but others
are of the opinion that the Communist Party and the people of the U.S.S.R.
compose a most powerful enemy of Fascism and that because of this belief
the Communists count the people of Russia and their Communist Party
as their friends and, in accordance with the dictates of common sense,
maintain a close alliance and collaboration with them. It contends that this
collaboration does not take the form of "orders from Moscow" and that
this claim is quite preposterous, because it would be in direct opposition
to the most basic principles of the Communists and the structure of their
Parties.

It describes the Communists as simply "ordinary people", not a "disturbing element", and following in the footsteps of previous reformers—
Christians, Lutherans, Roundheads, Robespierre, the Spanish people, etc.
It appeals to the middle class to become allies, stating that "the creative
tasks of these two great classes will be made immeasurably easier and
more rapid if the middle class with its technical and intellectual skills takes
its place with all other freedom loving peoples and marches with them
across the frontiers of a new society."

(Signed)
"The Communist Party of Canada
January, 1941."[7]

"MR. KING! MR. CHURCHILL! WHAT ARE YOUR WAR AIMS?"

This circular was distributed by the Communist Party of Canada, St.
Henry Section, Montreal, P.Q., during the early part of February. It contends that the basic features of Hitlerism are being put into operation in
Canada and Great Britain, and quotes the following as so-called facts:
"In his recent appeal to the Italian people, Mr. Churchill made no
call for an anti-fascist revolution. He actually praised Mussolini's
past record, but arrogantly called for Mussolini's overthrow for his
action in fighting against Great Britain. Mr. Churchill is no enemy
of fascism. Are Churchill and King against aggression?"

It declares that concentration camps are filled with anti-Fascists, while
notorious Fascists are harboured, decorated and financed.

"The war aims of Messrs. King and Churchill are to provide graves for the working class youth and gravy for the war profiteers. Under the mask of 'all out for the war effort', fascism is being established in Canada. In contrast with Spain, where the people forged the weapon of a People's Government, with which to fight fascism, we are being robbed of democracy and sold into fascist slavery."

The circular closes with an appeal to the people to unite and by struggle to form a New Independent People's Government.[8]

"1940—A REVIEW."

This is a nine-page printed eulogy of the Soviet's foreign policy which allows it to seize lands and yet remain outside the imperialist war. It boasts that as a result of "enlargements", including Bessarabia, Northern Bukovina, the Baltic countries of Latvia, Estonia and Lithuania and the Western Ukraine, the USSR can now speak in the powerful voice of 193,000,000 people.

It contends that "the successes fo the foreign policy of the Soviet Union are all the more significant in that we achieved them all by peaceful means, and in that the peaceful settlement of the questions both of the Baltic countries and Bessarabia was achieved with the active co-operation and support of the broad masses of the people of these countries...."

Under the heading, "Nazi Weaknesses", the "Review" mentions the shortage caused by the British blockade and that "despite denials, Germany is also getting to feel the effect of the consistent R.A.F. bombing of industrial establishments, docks, and railway lines, especially in Western Germany".

In dealing with "U.S. imperialism", it explains that following the defeat in Europe, the British were forced to come to terms either with German or American capital, and that Churchill chose the latter course. "Canada's role" is to support an Independent People's Government to save itself from being plunged into war in the Pacific at the behest of the USA, and to put an end to war-profits and save the nation from economic ruin.

It applauds the "People's Convention" which was held in London, England, on January 12, and in closing refers to the New Social Order—World Socialism.[9]

"SAVE! .. OR ELSE!"

(A circular under the above heading and opposing the War Savings Campaign has been distributed from two points in Montreal: the St. Lawrence and St. George Section and the St. Henry Section of the Communist Party of Canada.)

"It is to force the low-income groups to bear a still greater share of the costs of this mass slaughter for imperialist expansion and profits. It is to drive still lower the meagre living standards of the Canadian people. It is to complete the transformation of our national economy to war economy to an economy based on the production of 'Guns,

Not Butter'".

The circular supports conscription of profits and says that the Excess Profit Tax is an absolute fraud, that the Government borrows money from Big Business and then hands it back in the form of gifts for plant extensions and profitable war contracts. As regards the War Savings Campaign, it says, "We are told in Nazi fashion 'Save... or else'".

It concludes with: "Make a stand now! Don't be bullied! Protest! Organize! The rich must pay the costs of THEIR war!"

"THE PEOPLE DEMAND PUBLIC TRIAL OF THE MASCIOLIS"

A circular under the above heading, distributed by the Northern Ontario Committee, Communist Party of Canada, attacks the release of the Mascioli brothers while an anti-Fascist named Joe Billings is still interned. It charges the government of "whitewashing" the Masciolis at the request of the Hollinger interests instead of putting them on open trial; and demands that Joe Billings should have a trial to prove "that Joe Billings has been interned without a trial because he fought for the workers as a loyal Canadian would against fascism and all that finance capital represents!"

(Note: Billings is a Communist interned under the Defence of Canada Regulations).[10]

"REPEAL THE FOUR MONTH SERVICE!"

A one page mimeographed leaflet distributed by the Toronto Committees of the Communist Party and Young Communist League, says in part:

"Our warnings have been only too justified. The King Government has broken every promise it made....."

"Now the 'Big Push' is on. The King Government is declaring 'total war' on Canadian youth. The training period has been increased to four months. The last two months are going to be served with the active service forces. In that way, they expect to 'turn on the heat', to break down the resistance of the conscripts. We warn you that if the Canadian people allow this new, cynical betrayal to take place, that the next step will surely be conscription for overseas service, despite all King's promises.

"The truth is that Mr. King is preparing to send 500,000 Canadian boys to their death in Europe, Africa and Asia.

The circular urges unite protests to force "the repeal of the four month service."

"PARADISE FOR PROFITEERS"
(The Clarion)

This is an eight page mimeographed pamphlet of the District Committee of the Communist Party, circularized in the St. Catharines, Ontario District. It carries the usual polemics against capitalism and describes Canada as a paradise for profiteers, where our youth are "wanted for profit". It mentions "new attacks" upon the workers and urges them to demand higher wages, and closes with the usual appeal for the people to unite in the struggle for an Independent People's Government.[11]

"TOTAL WAR"

(From an anti-conscription circular issued by the Toronto Committee, Communist Party of Canada).

It asserts that the Government has assumed power to conscript labour, manpower and industry; that conscription is designed for overseas service and that all denials are deliberate lies; that manpower is conscripted by the pegging of wages at levels which mean continued poverty; that the right to strike has been taken away and that trade unions face destruction. It contends that the farmer has been conscripted by Government price fixing and that democracy itself is conscripted by the abolishment of freedom of speech, press and assembly. Income has been conscripted by higher taxes, higher prices and forced loans, "But Not One Dollar of Wealth has been Conscripted".

In conclusion, the circular urges Canadians

"Build a Powerful People's Movement to:

Fight Against Profiteering and Increased Living Costs!

Fight Against Conscription of Manpower!

Demand Complete Conscription of Wealth!

Demand Restoration of Civil Liberties!

Demand the Right of Workers to Strike and Organize for Higher Wages!

Demand an Independent "Canada First" Foreign Policy, Which Will Not Pledge Canada to Fight Anyone Else's Battles![12]

"SIR WALTER CITRINE DOES NOT SPEAK FOR BRITISH LABOR."

(From leaflet issued by Quebec Provincial Committee, C.P. of C., on this "knighted labour leader").

"Sir Walter advised Canadian labor to give up all its rights in order to 'achieve victory'; he promises the return of these rights after the war. Despite his title and many initials that follow his name, we can refer to him only as a dangerous liar. The capitalist class has surrendered nothing. Profits and more profits is their share f the war. Labor, on the other hand, is being subjected to anti-strike laws, wage pegging legislation, increased hours of work, so-called voluntary loans, and other measures that will lead to a rapid deterioration in the conditions of the working class unless there is immediate action to put an end to this situation.

"The workers must act to protect their rights and to improve their conditions at a time when profits are at their highest. They must not heed the advice of the Canadian editions of Sir Walter Citrine, the

Moores, the Trepaniers, the Millards and other such labor leaders."

"THUMBS DOWN"

(Circular distributed by North Saskatchewan Committee, C.P. of C., in Saskatoon attacks the War Savings Campaign.)

"Of course, you will be rewarded with a 'Thumbs Up' button even though you will have a distinctly 'down-in-the-mouth' feeling when you consider what this deduction from your pay means"....

"The 'TIGHTEN YOUR BELTS' policy of the King Government does not apply to these profiteers and grafters who plunged our country into war for the sake of greater profits. BEHOLD THEIR 'PAY-TRIOTISM' while the Canadian people are asked to pay for the war in HUNGER, POVERTY AND DEATH!

"'THUMBS DOWN! on the out-and-out robbery of the small earnings of the people. THE PROFITEERS AND GRAFTERS WANTED THIS WAR. LET THEM PAY FOR IT!'"[13]

SECRET

INTELLIGENCE
BULLETIN

ROYAL CANADIAN MOUNTED POLICE
HEADQUARTERS, OTTAWA

MAY 28, 1941

CONTENTS

Nazism:

War Series
No. 43

NAZISM

NAZI ACTIVITIES IN BRITISH COLUMBIA

(The following confidential survey of the above subject indicates that German agitation is progressing along Communist lines seeking to demoralize and sabotage labour with specious arguments and lies.)

"A check-up reveals that the nazi sympathizers still hope for a German victory. It is pointed out that the cause of the working man is at stake; Hitler is the champion of the working man and his cause is a just cause. It is argued that conditions throughout the world cannot become better or improve as long as English nobility, in collusion with the Jews, keep sweat shops and slavery flourishing; U.S.A. government is controlled and directed by Jews and England. In the end, all this will avail Great Britain nothing because the stage is set for the workingman to take his place in world affairs. Hitler and the German people are hailed as the great liberators.

"It is further alleged that the workers of English and non-German origin are beginning to see the light in Canada and the U.S.A., hence all the

353

strikes across the border and the reluctancy of Canadian workers to co-operate to the full in the prosecution of the war. We are told that the worker knows that, should Great Britain win the war, then privation and starvation with unemployment following cessation of hostilities will cause untold hardship upon the workingman. On the other hand, should Hitler win the war, order will come out of chaos the world over. All workers will have employment and the upper class will have to work for a living instead of living off the toil and sweat of the workers.

"It appears that the above philosophy is the latest propaganda material used at the present. This is nothing less than fifth column activity. It is the old trick of the Nazi, viz., to undermine the home front, especially the production front. If this can be accomplished, it is conquest without bloodshed. By picturing the future for the workingman as rosy, by appealing to selfishness, to everything that one holds [1] dear, family, good home, social life, etc; all these things one can enjoy provided one has an earning capacity and an income; all this is promised by victory of Hitler.

"On the other hand, the picture is changed should Hitler lose. The propagandist will picture the future in its darkest form. The present position will not be secure under the old Democratic system. Has not the past taught that depression follows every war under such a system. What then will become of the home! The mortgage company will get it. What about the family! Will they have an equal chance with the members of the white collar class? Again, what has history taught in this respect. If one has money to educate one's children, they have an opportunity to earn a living. If not, then the boys will be chased from one city to another, deteriorate and become loafers, etc. Look what conditions prevailed in Germany before Hitler's rise to power and look what the Nazi did for the worker! For the common people in Germany! Everyone works, good wages are being paid, everybody has plenty and a good standard of living prevails, etc., etc.

"Forces are at work using the above described propaganda. These forces are not always of German origin. There is only one difference between Hitler and Stalin. The former still recognizes private ownership as long as it serves his purpose, whilst the latter does not recognize private ownership. In ideology and principle there is no difference between Nazism and Communism."[2]

COMMUNISM
FLOOD OF LIES CONTINUES

The red blight of Communism continues its insidiously destructive work through underground channels. No matter how many whispering campaigns are broken up, or how many scurrilous leaflets are seized and destroyed, fresh propaganda takes their place.

Although the lies have one aim the complete overthrow of our social system they vary in methods and points of attack. The term "Imperialist War" is largely supplanted by "Capitalist War". Instead of urging the proletariat to fight for Communism or Socialism, the goal now is "Peoples' Party".

They still believe that the weakest link in our democratic armor is the labour union. So, despite continuous rebuffs, they continue to worm their way into labor's inner councils, where they foment discontent until it breaks out in strikes.

In a recent leaflet, called "The Young Steel Worker," they commence their incitement to trouble by charging:

"In most of the big steel plants young workers are deliberately discriminated against. The older workers get poor enough wages, but young men and women get much less unless the workers, old and young, are united in a strong fighting union, like in General Steel Wares."

In their "Eight-Point Program" they declare:

"Strike action is necessary, above all things. The full burden of the war budget will be felt even more heavily as time passes. It is the stated policy of the government to cut consumers' goods down to the minimum, to limit the necessities of life, to inflate the currency by these 'indirect' means, in order to gear the [3] economy of the country for the production of vast supplies of the destructive engines of war. Inevitably, then, the workers in industry are feeling the pinch as their real wages decline much faster than their nominal wages increase through the phoney system of 'war bonuses'."

And in another pamphlet they acclaim "A Peoples' Movement to End This":

"Despite the R.C.M.P. Gestapo, the Communist Party brings home these truths. The situation will grow worse, and not better. The Canadian people must create a United Peoples' Movement of workers, farmers, small business men, professionals and all who feel the load of misery and injustice."[4]

"FARMERS' UNION" SPONSORED BY REDS

It is reliably reported that the Communist Party of Canada is organizing a new Farmers' Union in Calgary, Alberta with the purpose of bringing the farmers of the southern portion of the province into [≥<deletion: 1 line] C.A. Nolan, of Redland, Alberta [≥<deletion: 2 lines] although he is completely unaware of the real sponsors of the union.

For the northern part of the province it is intended to organize a branch of the Farmers' Union who will push the movement through the United Farmers of Canada.

Lional Edwards, [≥<deletion: 2 lines] is said to have stated that when the United Farmers of Alberta met in Calgary last January many of the farmers expressed dissatisfaction with the laisser-faire attitude of its

leaders and demanded a more active and militant organization.

The Farmers' Union intends to be actively militant, along Communist lines, at the same time taking every care to disguise its connections with the C.P. of C. For instance, it will become more closely associated with those labour unions whose demands are similar, in contrast with the U.F.A.'s allegiance with the Industrialists.

In brief, the Communists are looking forward to two powerful drives on the farmers of Alberta by the Farmers' Union in the south, and by an aggressive "boring from within" in the north. The first is already well under way.[5]

MAY DAY CELEBRATIONS A FIZZLE

May Day celebrations by would-be revolutionists were conspicuous by their absence this year. Instead of public parades displaying red banners and threatening slogans, the outlawed Communist Party of Canada confined themselves to secret hide-outs and their secret weapon, the hand-turned printing press.

Even the bombardment of lies, prepared for the occasion, was less violent than the authorities expected. The main assault on democracy was labelled "May Day Manifesto" and might have been written by Hitler himself with a view to blitzkrieging our war efforts and inducing us into suing for a separate peace.

Under the title "The Way Out of War", it asserts in part:

"Only the overthrow of the ruling classes can bring peace to the peoples of the imperialist world..... For it is a lie that this is a war against fascism! It is a lie that the defeat of Germany by Britain and the Dominions will benefit the people. It is a cheap lie that we are fighting for 'democracy'.

"The victory of the ruling classes of either side will mean horrors in future for the workers and farmers .... The fight lies in Canada, against our own reactionaries who have gagged the workers' organizations, crushed their free press, interned and jailed their courageous leaders; against the corrupt financiers and industrialists who are using the opportunity the war affords them to fasten a Canadian Fascist regime on the necks of the masses!....

"Under the war dictatorship of the biggest capitalists our country is heading for disaster! In the interests of declining British imperialism, Ottawa demands ever fresh sacrifices from our people...... This must not be! Every trade unionist must fight this plot, must fight for the right to strike, for higher wages, for the release of trade union leaders from the clutches of the RCMP....... Every young Canadian must refuse to be conscripted for foreign wars, must refuse meekly to accept the dictates of the ruthless military dictatorship which is being established in Canada!"[6]

The leaflet lauded the Soviet Union as a land of peace and Socialism, and an ever present reminder to the workers of all lands that the people can seize government and run their own factories, mines, banks, etc. In the meantime, while working for an independent peoples' government, Canadian workers should demand the repeal of the War Measures Act and release of imprisoned trade unionists and Communists.

The Manifesto was distributed at Montreal and Val D'Or, Quebec; Timmins, Kirkland Lake and Fort William, Ontario; Winnipeg, Manitoba; Regina and Saskatoon, Saskatchewan; Calgary, Lethbridge and Coleman, Alberta and Vancouver, British Columbia. While the distribution methods were cunningly conceived, some leaflets were seized and their distributors arrested.

In Montreal four large red flags bearing the sickle and hammer as well as the maple leaf were placed at various conspicuous points. Two crudely made red flags were also found at the entrance of the Montreal High School, and painted on the school steps were the words "scholarship and not bullets". In Montreal a few circulars entitled "Oppose King's Blitzkrieg on your Lives" were left on the roof of a high building where the wind could scatter them to the streets below, and in other parts of the city a small number of the Manifesto were written in Ukrainian and distributed through the mails. In Saskatoon a circular headed "Free Press" and demanding retention of democratic rights and freedom of the press, were found. Altogether, the quantity of literature distributed was comparatively small.[7]

"CANADIAN YOUTH—Oppose King's Blitzkrieg On Your Lives."

This two-page leaflet, distributed by the Young Communist League of Toronto, attacks conscription as a manoeuvre to split the ranks of youth and to lull them into a false sense of security, and as merely a prelude to the mass shipment of Canadian youth overseas. It closes with:

"Conscripts: Organize your democratic committees in the camps to protect your conditions. Don't knuckle under the regimentation plans of the brass-hats!

"Soldiers: Unite with the conscripts in the struggle for improved conditions. Don't let the brass-hats use you to help regiment the conscripts! Join with the working people of Canda in the struggle against King's 'Blitzkrieg' against the Canadian people!

"Working Youth: Demand an investigation into the conditions in the camps and the immediate improvement in medical attention. Help the boys fight for free transportation!"[8]

A LETTER FROM RUSSIA

(When a Montreal Communist was recently apprehended for internment, letters from Russia in his possession disclosed terrible conditions among the peasants of that country. A literal translation of one letter is quoted below:)

"To my beloved Sister, Brother in Law and Nieces:-

About our Health, Thank God, for the future should'nt get worse.

My dear Sister, your money I received. I wondered why I didn't get any letters, when I received the $8.00 we were all nearly dead. We were all starving that we ate potato peelings that someone else used to throw out. So you can imagine that death would have been much easier but one cannot kill himself.

When I received the $8.00 from you we all came to life again. We bought some food.

I wanted to write you to thank you and I did not have your address so I sent Uncle Itzel a letter for you but did not get an answer. I also wrote a few letters to the old address and received no reply. Therefore I beg you, my dear Sister to take an interest in me and write me a letter with your correct address. I beg you to answer me and don't forget your fond Sister. We are all in great misfortune also I know you are not so well to do yourself. If you were in more wealth you would not have waited so long to send us money and as you did'nt want to send us empty letters but thank God you did send us money but please send us a letter and tell us what you are all doing.[9]

You certainly saved us from a sure death and we are still alive.

Since then we have received $5.00 more, My dear Sister no one can help me as much as you. Even God himself. We prayed to God to help us in one way or another, but he did'nt until you had mercy on us.

I beg you for the future not to forget us. My dear Sister I should call you Mother instead, You did more than a Mother could do.

Please dear Sister send me a letter and write me what you and your children and Leizer are doing.

Write me where your children are working. Please write soon and I will write soon telling you all about myself.[10]

SOVIET UNION CONSCRIPTS LABOUR

The denial by the Soviet Union and by Communists everywhere that there that there is forced labour in the Soviet Union, is refuted by no less an authority than "Pravda", official organ of the Soviet Union Communist Party. In a front-page article, entitled "The Call To Labour Service Successfully Completed", it deals at length with the conscription of labour under an order issued by the Presidium of the Supreme Soviet State Council under Stalin's signature. It is shown in this article that workers have been conscripted for the various industries, railroads and farms in the same way as for the different units of the army. The workers were classified according to their physical and mental abilities for the different classes of work.

First the new conscripts are put in training centres for a certain period. Following the training period they are shifted to the various industries. There is no indication as to how long the term of service is. It therefore must be assumed that it is indefinite.

Much pride is shown to be taken in this plan of conscription of labour. It is termed "a high standard of Bolshevist activization". It is made to believe with pride that only in the country of Socialism such a plan could be achieved. The workers are told that it is a revolutionary act of a high calibre which no Capitalist country could carry out.[11]

GENERAL
"FREE ITALY" PROPOSED

An Italian connected with "Il Mondo", New York (an Italian-language monthly), writing to London (England), suggests the creation of a "Free Italy" corps similar to de Gaulle's for France. "As you know, there are four million Italians in the United States and we are sure that the creation of a corps parallel to General de Gaulle's Free France could recruit them in large numbers. It would be desirable to set up this recruiting in Canada. But of course we should need the authorization and the support of the Government in London.

"I have talked this over with Max Ascoli of the Mazzini Society and with Alberto Tarchiani and being a former army officer myself, I am willing to work to organize the recruiting with the certainty of obtaining not inexperienced men but thousands of veterans of the last War now in this country."

MALAYA BANS "WITNESSES"

The Watch Tower Society ("Jehovah's Witnesses") and their publications have been suppressed throughout the Government of the Straits Settlements. Information supplied by R.C.M. Police Intelligence proved "very useful" in furthering such action, writes the Deputy Inspector-General of Police from Singapore, Straits Settlements.[12]

ISOLATIONIST GROUPS IN U.S.

A British journalist attached to the new British Press Service in New York summarizes the chief groups of Isolationists, in the U.S.A. Although the movement for aid to Britain is widespread the writer maintains that since the Presidential election "Munichism has been growing like a weed" and fears that appeasers, of both the Right and Left, will make the most of their opportunities if Italy is defeated.

[≯<deletion: 1 paragraph: 12 lines]

While Wall Street is said to be pro-British by tradition, many manufacturers, fearing social revolution, are prepared to forego big immediate profits resulting from the war in order to hold on to what they already have.

Appeasers of the Left include [∻deletion: 1 line] like Quincy Howe, [∻deletion: 1 line] who are organizing a "march on Washington" through the National Maritime Union which they dominate, to protest against financial aid and sale of ships to Britain.

Although the present target of these anti-interventionists is the William Allen White Committee which in the writer's opinion is "crumbling to pieces, having over-played its hand", the real political enemy is Roosevelt. Having failed in the election they are trying a roundabout method of attack.[13]

INTELLIGENCE
BULLETIN

ROYAL CANADIAN MOUNTED POLICE
HEADQUARTERS, OTTAWA

JUNE 19, 1941

CONTENTS

War Series
No. 44

COMMUNISM

SABOTAGING WAR INDUSTRY BY STRIKES

Factory Labour is considered at this time of national emergency to provide the one really vulnerable point of attack in our political structure. The Defence of Canada Regulations and the thorough manner on which they are being enforced have made revolutionary propaganda by the usual channels of mass meetings, printed matter, new "front" organizations, extremely dangerous. On the other hand, infiltration into legitimate labour unions affiliated with the Trades and Labour Congress, the Canadian Congress of Labour or the Congress of Industrial Organization, where influence can be directed toward stirring up grievances to the striking point, is a comparatively easy matter.

With the factories full and working overtime, conditions for organization could scarcely be better. Workers and Management alike realize that war production must proceed at all cost, and Communists (working in the name of Labour Organization and "fair demands") intend to force up these costs so high that Management will refuse to pay them and the Workers will walk out thus sabotaging our defence of democracy both here and abroad.

It should be borne in mind that such strikes represent minority rule. There are only a few Communist agitators in any factory, but these

361

workers who will take possession of a mass meeting and by threats, promises and misrepresentation sway the majority to militant action. The fact that such action has been largely successful in recent months has had the effect of inflating the influence and the demands of the agitators and the Communist Party as a whole.

Monthly reports from our R.C.M. Police Divisions disclose many instances of these Communist-inspired strikes and preparations for strikes.

"O" Division (Western Ontario) reports eight strikes in Ontario during April, most of which could be traced directly or indirectly to illegal sources. To quote:-

Communist Party of Canada

C.P. of C. activities during April have been directed mostly to activity in the Trade Union field. Insofar as unit [1] work and organization work of the Party are concerned, it appears to be almost at a standstill. This is accounted for by the lack of direct contact between the centre and the rank and file. The Party leadership apparently realizes the danger of allowing members who have been even moderately prominent as functionaries of the Provincial and City Committees to make direct contact with the Units. As a consequence, the rank and file members are dependent for direction and instruction on their Unit Secretary and Organizer....

C.P. Activity in Trade Unions

As referred to briefly above, the C.P. is concentrating its efforts in the Trade Union field. During the month of April eight strikes were reported in this Divisional area and while the majority may be characterized as of minor individual importance, it should be borne in mind that the C.P. is exerting its efforts to make the industrial population of Canada strike-conscious, and indications are that these strikes are the precursors of an epidemic to which the C.P. will bend every effort to exploit to the full advantage. In these activities the C.I.O. Unions, which are now affiliated with the Canadian Congress of Labour, afford the best scope.

Strikes during the month of April:

Exolon Abrasives Plant, Thorold, Ont.—One hundred men went on strike on March 26th as a result of a demand for increase of pay. The plant is a non-Union one and by noon of April 1st work was resumed after an agreement had been reached.

Schofield Knitting Mills, Oshawa, Ont.—Eighty employees engaged at these mills struck work for a wage increase and recognition of the Textile Workers' Union on April 7th. The strike was declared illegal by the Federal Government on April 8th, but despite this the workers did not return to work until April 16th when negotiations were entered upon. Alex. Welch, Ontario representative ativeof the Textile Workers' Union, and [✁deletion: 1 line] took a prominent part in the negotiations, which are still proceeding.[2]

Canadian Seamen's Union—As the result of five Steamship Companies' failure to comply with the suggestion put forward by the Arbitration Board that the C.S.U. be recognized as the sole bargaining agency between the employees and employers, approximately 750 seamen were reported to have struck work on April 11th. The five dissenting Companies did not appear to experience much difficulty in raising crews and many of the strikers have returned to work in defiance of Union orders. This partial strike of seamen is still in progress insofar as the five Shipping Companies are concerned. Dewar Ferguson, acting President of the C.S.U., [ᵃ<deletion: 1 line]

Fruit and Produce Drivers' and Helpers' Union, Toronto—On April 9th about 156 members of this Union went on strike for better conditions and higher wages. This is an A.F. of L. Union and during the progress of the strike the Brotherhood of Teamsters, Chauffeurs, Stablemen and Helpers endeavoured to negotiate with the employers. Their efforts were not attended with any success and although no agreement between the Fruit Produce Drivers' Union and the employers has been reached to date, the men returned to work on April 11th. M.H. Nichols, [ᵃ<deletion: 1 line] acted on behalf of the Teamsters, Chauffeurs, Stablemen and Helpers.

Defence Industries Limited, Nobel, Ont.—Thirty-eight men struck work on April 10th at this plant, but a settlement was reached on April 11th. The strike was not the result of Union activities but of a spontaneous nature.

Ontario Sand Company, Brougham, Ontario—On April 23rd 103 truck drivers employed by this Company struck work for an increase of pay. The strike lasted until April 30th when an agreement was reached. This was a partial strike as half of the men involved continued working throughout its duration.

National Steel Car Corporation, Hamilton, Ont.—On April 27th about 2,500 employees of this firm went on strike demanding Union recognition, and the reinstatement of the President of this Branch of the S.W.O.C. who had been dismissed by the management. The management refused to [3] reinstate Tanner (the man referred to) after the recommendation of the Conciliation Board, as a result of which the Federal Government installed a Controller in the plant on April 30th. Tanner was then reinstated. On that date the men returned to work and negotiations are still proceeding.

Goderich Salt Company, Goderich, Ont.—Thirty-five employees of this firm struck work on April 5th demanding better conditions. A settlement was reached and the men returned to work on April 10th.

During May the number of strikes in Ontario had increased to 14, while June's strikes have already started.[4]

NO COMMUNISM IN CAPE BRETON STRIKES

When so many strikes throughout Canada can be traced directly to Communist manipulation it is gratifying to know that the recent strikes in the Cape Breton coal fields were the result of only the usual maladjustments as between management and labour and have been, or are being, settled without "red" influence of any sort.

Following a strike in one colliery the men have returned to work on a "curtailment" basis as a protest against their officers accepting the findings of the Government Conciliation Board without first referring them back to the workers. The political loyalty of the miners (United Mine Workers of America), can not be questioned.

Now that the coal mining industry has been declared an "essential service" within the provisions of the Defence of Canada Regulations, conditions generally should improve.[6]

[≫deletion: 1 line]

[≫deletion: 1 paragraph: 8 lines]

MASS LANGUAGE ORGANIZATIONS

The activity of the these organizations has followed the Party line and it has been reported that small Unit meetings of the members continue to be held in private house.

The Independent Mutual Benefit Federation (I.M.B.F.) is quite obviously being used by the Mass Language Organizations for absorbing membership and for raising money by means of socials, dances, picnics etc. There is no indication that the money raised is for requirements or needs of the I.M.B.F. and it is presumed that at least a portion of that money is used for Communist Party purposes.[7]

ANNIE BULLER CONVICTED ON THREE CHARGES
(Winnipeg)

Annie S. Buller, a leading Communist of Manitoba and publisher of the "Mid-West Clarion", appeared for trial in Winnipeg City Police Court on May 20, 1941 and was convicted on three charges under the Defence of Canada Regulations and sent to gaol for two years.

The first charge was that she "did unlawfully make, print, publish, issue, circulate or distribute a certain edition of a newspaper, periodical or publication known as Mid-West Clarion bearing date the 17th day of February A.D. 1940, containing material, reports or statements intended or likely to be prejudicial to the efficient prosecution of the war, contrary to regulation 39A of the Defence of Canada Regulations."

At the conclusion of the evidence for the prosecution, the Court ruled that a prima facie case had been established and the accused took the witness stand. Under cross examination she admitted that she was Business and Circulation Manager of the Mid-West Clarion and had come from Toronto to Winnipeg to organize the paper in 1937. She denied having written any of the material contained in the issue of the Mid-West Clarion dated February 17th, 1940 as she was away from the city at that time on business which she later admitted was for the purpose of collecting funds for the Mid-West Clarion to enable it to carry on. However, she stated that she did not disassociate herself from anything which that issue contained and did not consider anything in it subversive. She stated that after reading it and in the light of later events, that if she had been writing the articles referred to by the prosecution as being subversive, she would have enlarged upon them and made them stronger and that she agreed with everything it contained.

A further charge against Annie Buller in connection with the issue of the Mid-West Clarion of February 24th, 1941 was heard at this time.

Accused was found guilty on the second charge and sentenced to 12 months concurrent.

A total of 12 charges in connection with the Mid-West Clarion had been laid against this accused together with John Vievirsky alias Wywiorski alias Weir, William Arnold Tuomi, and John Magnus Clark. Fol-[8]lowing the verdict of Guilty having been rendered on the first two counts and sentence being passed, Mr. Moffat, Crown Attorney, entered a Stay of Proceedings in each of the other ten charges against Miss Buller.

A further charge against Annie Buller of continuing to be a member of an illegal organization, of which she was found guilty and sentenced to 12 months consecutive with the first 12 months, was disposed of the same day.

On May 30 Jock McNeil, [≫deletion: 1 line] was convicted and sentenced to twelve months. This conviction is being appealed and he is at present at liberty on bail.[9]

YOUTH CONGRESS SHOWS "RED" CONTROL
(Toronto)

Over 200 members of Youth Councils of Ontario and Quebec met in Toronto May 24-25 to register their grievances against present social conditions.

The conference took the form of a Trial, in which the prisoner at the bar (presumably the Government) had no defendants and all witnesses (including the jury) were accusers. Several members of the General Steel Workers' Union (C.I.O.) were there to give evidence against, while Miss Helen Simon, International Fellowship Secretary of the American Youth Congress, was present on Sunday to show how the same "injustices" were in operation across the border.

In short, this conference disclosed again that Youth Councils exist for one specific purpose; namely, the spread of Communist doctrines among

Canadian youth. All the familiar Communist charges against the war, capitalism, conscription, taxation and internments were voiced by the delegates, while the need of organizing young workers in every industry for the "ultimate triumph of the Canadian people" was particularly stressed.

The following preamble, a typical Communistic proclamation, reflects the tone of the conference:-

"At this time of crisis when the attention of Canadians is drawn to the fight for freedom and justice in the international sphere, we call upon all Canadian Youth to stand as a bulwark for a democratic way of life for all peoples and to protect Canada against threats from abroad and the menace of Hitlerism within.

"Who are the Canadian Hitlers against whom Canada's youth must defend their country? They are those who are engaged in piling up profits for themselves, in keeping most of the people poor with low wages and high taxes, in fighting against trade unionism and in denying the liberties of a free people. They cry against 'subversive elements' among the people in order to turn the spotlight of public indignation away from themselves. They pose as fighters against Hitlerism, as 'patriots' while they crucify democracy in Canada. [10]

"It is they who raise loudest the cry for conscription for overseas service and conscription of labour in the factories and it is in their interests to force conscription on the Canadian people. They hope by this regimentation to raise the profits and trade the lives of our Youth for war contracts. In the name of Democracy, these traitors seek every means of regimenting and goose-stepping the Canadian people. Theirs is no loyalty to Canada, but only to their private profits. On the other hand we believe that the vast majority of the Canadian people are not primarily interested in private profits, but are truly concerned with the immediate and future welfare of the Canadian people. We as young people take our stand with them.

"As young Canadians, we say that our fight for democracy and justice begins in the country that we love most of all, in our own Canada.

"We will not rest until all the enemies within and without—the enemies that preserve poverty, insecurity, and violation of liberty, have been destroyed.

"We declare our unshakable faith in the ultimate triumph of the Canadian people, in their struggle for freedom and economic and political justice. This is our loyalty to and our faith in Canada!"

Dewar Ferguson (C.S.U.) presented Mr. Bowers (same union) who described how first the ship owners and then the Conciliation Board had tried to break up the Seamen's Union by discrimination and intimidation, and had finally succeeded in having four of their leaders interned.

Ferguson continued the story of how the "Conciliation Board had held us up nine months" and how "although the Board were unanimously agreed that we had the right to organize, two companies resisted and took in scab labour. And they have police protection so get away with it."

Ferguson contended that Regulation 21 (D.O.C.R.) should be repealed and claimed that Pat Sullivan could not secure a trial or his release under Habeas Corpus. Further, that the appeal judge had said that undoubtedly many innocent people in Canada were interned upon representations made by informers who were unreliable.

Ferguson expressed the opinion that Parliament could not overrule Habeas Corpus, adding that at the present time Canada was being ruled by a [11] military class, saying, "This is how democracy is taken from us, like in Germany." The speaker maintained that if (Pat) Sullivan had only been a seaman he would not have been interned but that this was done because he was head of a union. He urged that protests be entered against such proceedings and criticized Order-in-Council, P.C. 2385 of April 4th entitled "The Merchant Seamen Order of 1941", mentioning that it listed 268 Committees of Investigation who had the power of taking off a ship and interning anyone who is accused of being an agitator. He mentioned that 200 of the 268 Committees of Investigation were members of the Royal Canadian Mounted Police and that Youth should see that this legislation was wiped off the statute books.

Councils representing school and university students, religious bodies, farms, factories, civil liberties, education and training, Y.W.C.A., Y.M.C.A., etc. voiced complaints of working conditions and prescribed remedies.

Robert Ward and Red. Taylor of Steel Workers' Union contrasted conditions in their plants before organization with those after and urged greater efforts toward organizing in other shops. Ward said, "We are snooping 'round here and there and making them organize as much as possible... We are trying to put this across among young people— Only by voicing their opinions are they able to combat conditions prevalent at this time."

Miss Wright (General Steel Workers' Organizer) also told of great advances made in wages, working conditions and treatment by bosses since they had become a strong union.

It was unanimously decided that Youth Councils should co-operate with the youth in trade unions in the extension of organization, and assist unions to obtain all their demands.

Miss Geraldine Shuster (Students' Council) advocated students' government in secondary schools. The students would appoint representatives to co-operate with teachers on arranging suitable study courses, methods of teaching and all other school problems. Other girls enlarged upon the subject.

It was decided in caucus that the Youth Congress and Councils should investigate the Schofield Woollen strike conditions; also that congratulations be sent to the workers of Acme Screw and Gear Company on their splendid victory. Conscription for over-seas service was condemned at every opportunity.[12]

A young girl, Christine Smith, spoke nearly 15 minutes against conscription. She urged that the public are being fooled by the four months' training plan, that after four months the soldiers in training never come out unless they are unfit and stated that it apparently takes a lot of the unfit business to return them to civilian life. She said that it's "Forced Conscription" and stated that our poor young people are all going to the slaughter house and that we stand by doing nothing to stop it.

Among those present were Ken Woodsworth, (Secretary C.Y. Congress), Bob Ward (Chairman), Bernard Muller (Editor "New Advance") and Dewar Ferguson, (Canadian Seamen's Union).[13]

STEEL WORKERS URGE STRIKE ACTION

Communist concentration on Trade Unions as effective channels for sabotaging our war industry is revealed again in the second issue of "The Young Steel Worker". This Communist-inspired paper carries the familiar attacks on increased taxes, war loans and war savings plans, and urges all youths to resist such measures by joining Trade Unions and instigating unauthorized and even illegal strikes.

To quote:

"Through unity and STRIKE ACTIONS, over the head of the Millard Clique, you can carry on a successful fight for HIGHER WAGES and to MAKE THE RICH PAY FOR THEIR WAR!"

(By "Millard Clique" the writer refers to C.H. Millard and the Steel Workers' Organizing Committee.)

"THE PRACTITIONERS"

(An Editorial in Winnipeg Free Press reviews the Communist technique in operation in Great Britain and points out that similar methods are functioning here despite the illegality of the Communist Party).

To quote in part:-

Innocent Canadians learning of these facts for the first time would be likely to express their astonishment that these conditions are permitted to exist, and then go on to rejoice that we order these things better in Canada where the Communist party has been outlawed. But the grounds for self-satisfaction on this score are not as firm as some may think. It is true that the Communist party is outlawed in Canada and that membership in it is denied except in the case of the odd person here and there who courts a holiday in jail. But though the Communists have gone into retreat, we still have with us the

Communist technique and its practitioners.[14]
These practitioners follow their British exemplars at a discreet distance, it is true. Like them, they have no time or willingness to discuss the issue of the war or to place the responsibility for it where it belongs. One might infer from listening to their bleatings that the Government of Canada, in collusion with the Government of Great Britain, had brought on the war in the interests of "privileged classes"—in order to get power further to oppress, enslave and rob the down-trodden poor. Millionaires are popping up in the world of business like dandelions on the average Winnipeg lawn after a warm spring rain. All our public men, who are in positions of authority and responsibility, are the stooges of scheming scoundrels who are trying to steal the world and hide it in their pockets. And this drivel goes on endlessly, whiningly, or truculently. It can be heard openly in Parliament and upon election hustings; it can be read in publications that sail as near as they dare to the wind; it finds expression, as in England, in subversive activities under thin disguises such as "People's Convention," "People's Movement," and so forth. These are the tactics and the methods which we have described as "the Communist technique". Of course, it is not being operated in Canada by Communists. But a dunghill by any other name would smell as vile.[15]

GENERAL

YOUNG DOUKHOBOURS REFUSE WAR SERVICES
(Regina, Sask.)

Large meetings have been held by Doukhobours in the Blaine Lake, Verigin, Pelly and Kamsack districts at different times during the month for the purpose of deciding whether those Doukhobours subject to the National War Services Regulations should accept a proposal made by the Board at Blaine Lake on April 24th, 1941 that they should work on public projects in lieu of military training.

Prior to the conference held at Calgary, Alberta on May 7, 1941 delegates were appointed at the various meetings held in the districts mentioned in the preceding paragraph. However, it is very significant that all the delegates elected were opposed to the young Doukhobours accepting work or training. From the reports available apparently no progress was made at the conference in the way of definitely deciding whether or not the proposals of the Board should be accepted.

To date the majority of the Doukhobours are against accepting the Board's proposals, but are awaiting the decision of the Doukhobours in British Columbia before expressing any definite intentions.

[⊱<deletion: 1 paragraph: 3 lines]

The matter was discussed with the Attorney-General of Saskatchewan, who was satisfied that the situation was serious and expressed the opinion that no leniency should be shown to those Doukhobours who endeavour by any means to defy the rulings and requests of the National War Services Board. It has since been decided that those in the 21-year-old class would be subject to call for work on public projects.

As a result of statements made by Nick Shukin and Nick Dergousoff, Doukhobours of the Buchanan district, Saskatchewan, on May 13th and 23rd respectively, these men have been convicted under the Defence of Canada Regulations.[16]

SECRET

INTELLIGENCE
BULLETIN

ROYAL CANADIAN MOUNTED POLICE
HEADQUARTERS, OTTAWA

JULY 19, 1941

CONTENTS

Communism:
General:

War Series
No. 45

COMMUNISM

WILL COMMUNISTS FIGHT FOR DEMOCRACY?

With Germany forcing Russia into a mutual protection alliance with the Democracies, the Communist Party of Canada is, for the second time since the war started, thrown into a state of utter confusion.

Originally, it will be recalled, this was a "War for Democracy". After Stalin's pact with Hitler it became an "Imperialist War". Now that Hitler is again the common enemy the war will have to be given a new label and the domestic war against "capitalism" waged with new slogans and tactics. Industrial strikes aimed at slowing up production of war machinery and tirades against recruiting and conscription will have to cease if Communists wish to escape the unforgivable sin of assisting Stalin's enemies.

A few reports from the Communist Party field begin to show the new order.

[⊰deletion: 1 paragraph: 1 line]

[⊰deletion: 1 paragraph: 14 lines]
[⊰deletion: 1 paragraph: 3 lines]
[⊰deletion: 1 paragraph: 4 lines][1]

371

"FOR RELEASE OF LABOUR PRISONERS"
(Winnipeg)

"Committee for Release of Labour Prisoners" have been formed under Communist direction in several cities throughout Canada. The aim of these committees seems to be the waging of a "nuisance" campaign of criticism against the Government, until it is forced to release all Communists and repeal Section 21, D.O.C.R.

A 32-page pamphlet entitled "They Fought For Freedom", printed in Winnipeg, is being hawked around by sympathizers at five cents per copy. It contains a commendatory foreword by Mrs. Doris Nielsen, M.P. After recounting the trip to Ottawa of 15 wives and a number of children of interned "labour leaders" and the disappointing results of their hearings with Mr. Lapointe and the Special House Committee, the pamphlet strikes out with the usual Red propaganda on "dictatorial methods" of government, "suppressing the common people", the "beginnings of Fascism", the "political police, the R.C.M.P. have now full power to terrorize the population", and the building up of "a mighty People's Movement". (This article is signed by Norman Penner of Winnipeg). Biographical sketches and pictures of a few internees round out the appeal.

A typical picture of one of these committees in action is given by the Officer Commanding "D" Division (Winnipeg). To quote:

A letter to the Editor of the Winnipeg Free Press and published on June 21, 1941, and signed "Committee for the Release of Labour Prisoners" per Norman Penner, criticizes the Government for allowing Regulation 21 D.O.C.R. to remain, this despite protests from widely diversified sections of the populace, also as to the tribunal which determines appeals in such cases and the fact that despite such tribunal the Minister of Justice in the final analysis is the sole judge as to whether or not an internee should or should not be released.

An open air meeting under the auspices of the Committee for the Release of Labour Prisoners was held on the evening of June 30 at which the release of interned labour leaders was advocated. Norman Penner read the resolution, Wm. Kardash, M.L.A. elect and M.J. Forkin spoke.[2]

An appeal is being made to the Prime Minister by means of postcards in an effort to effect release of the internees. This postcard reads as follows:

To the RIGHT HON. W. L. MacKENZIE KING
Prime Minister of Canada,
Ottawa, Ont.

As a Canadian citizen I most vigorously protest against the internment and detention by your government of anti-fascist labour leaders. I believe that your policy subverts and undermines our basic democratic rights and therefore I demand that you immediately issue orders for the unconditional release of all anti-fascist prisoners.

(Name)   (Address)

M. J. Forkin has been nominated as a candidate to contest the Ward 3 seat in the City Council. This election was occasioned through the disqualification of Jacob Penner (interned). Wm. Kardash, M.L.A. elect is to act as campaign manager and Forkin has stated that one of the chief planks of his platform is a request for liberation of Mr. Penner and other Communists or former Communists from internment.

It would appear that the present activity of this Committee is due to the turn of events in Russia, which they hope will favour their appeal at this time. Generally speaking the Communists feel that they have a safe approach to our loyal citizenry and will gain their sympathy now through Russia's entry into the war.[3]

ONTARIO'S JUNE STRIKE WAVE
(Toronto)

The Ontario strike wave of May extended into June and expanded considerably. The former C.I.O. Unions that became affiliated with the Canadian Congress of Labour, through Communists within the Union, have carried on an intense organizational campaign throughout the Province in industries producing war materials. An outstanding feature of these strikes is to be found in the fact that among the Organizers representing the Unions affected are such [✂<deletion: 2 lines] as Harry Hunter, Harry Hamburg, Alec. Welch, Mike Fenwick, Arthur Williams and George Harris, to say nothing of C. S. Jackson who has now been interned.

The arrest of C.S. Jackson, organizer for the United Electrical and Radio Machinists' Union, came to them as a surprise, and has caused considerable trepidation as to their own safety in the minds of Communist sympathizers who have taken an active part in Trade Union activity and who are afraid that their connection with the Party has become known to the police.

[✂<deletion: 1 paragraph: 5 lines][4]

ORGANIZING FOR POTENTIAL STRIKES

Information received from our Hamilton Detachment indicates that the National Steel Car Company employees at that point are considering taking further strike action as they are not altogether satisfied with the Conciliation Board setup at the time of the previous strike at this plant.

It will be recalled that the Government put in a manager of this plant when it was decided that the Company could not see their way to comply with the Conciliation Board's finding.

For over two months there has been serious dissension between the Cape Breton coal miners and their local U.M.W.A. officers as a result of the latter having accepted the rulings of the Government Conciliation Board without first referring them back to the workers. The workers, who have been pursuing a "slow-down" policy, are now threatening to go out on strike.

When Silby Barrett, International Board member for the U.M.W.A., urged the men to abandon their "slow-down" policy and obey their officers the men retorted by demanding the dismissal of the entire District Executive Board, including Barrett. John L. Lewis has ordered the Union members to be guided by Barrett, but if they refuse there may be serious trouble in the Glace Bay area.

As stated before, Communism is playing little or no part in the dissension.[5]

PEOPLE'S MOVEMENT ACTIVE IN WEST
(Edmonton, Alberta)

The People's Party sponsored by the Communist Party of Canada (see "Bulletin" No. 41) is steadily spreading throughout the Prairie Provinces and is particularly active in Alberta through its People's Movement Committee. In the recent Federal by-election campaign it fought hard, if unsuccessfully, for the election of A. A. MacLeod (Editor "Canadian Tribune"), [≻deletion: 1 line], supported by Mrs. Dorise Nielsen, M.P. and William Kardash, M.L.A..

After the election, the People's Movement Committee held several organization meetings to decide upon the future action to be taken. It was considered that as the name of the organization was now well impressed upon the public mind, it should be followed up with an intensive campaign to build the movement into a province-wide organization and thence into at least a Western Canadian movement. After considerable discussion at a meeting held on June 3 at which Mrs. Doris Nielsen, A.A. MacLeod, Mel Doig were present, it was decided to call a Western conference to be held in Edmonton as soon as possible for the organization of the People's Movement Committee in all the Western provinces.

The new organization will function along the lines of the illegal Canadian League for Peace and Democracy. The campaign committee rooms will be retained as long as possible as the Headquarters of the People's Movement Committee, a library is to be established and special attention is to be given to drawing all trade unions into the movement. So far in Edmonton, the Hotel and Restaurant Employees Alliance, the Barbers Union, and the various packing plants' employees unions have promised their support to the new organization. In addition to trade unions, all left-wing organizations and the membership of those organizations that have been banned are to be approached with a view to having them take out actual membership or affiliate with this new body. Among the organizations that supported A. A. MacLeod in his campaign and which is likely to take part in the new People's Movement is the illegal organiza-

tion, Technocracy Inc. The ex-members of this Association were canvass-
ed by a member of the Communist Party and promised in all cases to support the People's Movement Committee candidate, A.A. MacLeod, in the
election. Already ex-members of the Ukrainian Labour Farmer Temple
Ass'n are holding house socials, etc., under the guise of the P.M.C. and it
is felt that they have been prompted in this by the sympathy shown to this
outlawed organization by A. A. MacLeod and other People's Movement
Committee speakers.[6]

The policy to be followed by the P.M.C. with respect to the Social
Credit and C.C.F. parties was outlined by A. A. MacLeod before he left
Edmonton. He advised that it would not be good political strategy to openly oppose the Social Credit and C.C.F. bodies because these organizations
were of a left nature and commanded a large following that would be useful to the P.M.C. if they could ever gain control. Therefore, he suggested
that the leadership of the P.M.C. quietly endeavour to influence the membership of the two farmer organizations into the P.M.C. and thus put the
leadership of both the Social Credit and C.C.F. Parties in a position where
they could not very well oppose affiliation with the P.M.C.

A point of interest with regard to the control of the P.M.C. was ascertained when [⊰deletion: 1 line] Harry G. Swanson and James A. Mac-
Pherson, stated during a conversation with other Communists that the
People's Movement Committee "takes its orders from the East", apparently meaning the National Executive Committee of the Communist Party in
Toronto or wherever it happens to now be located. Furthermore, they
stated that it was the policy of the Communist Party to keep Communists
from being openly identified with the P.M.C. so as not to give it a Communistic character.[7][Pages 8 to 12 are missing.]

MILITANT STRIKE ACTION DEMANDED

Government authorities, if not the general public, have long known the
plans of the Communist Party to hasten the proletariat revolution through
encouraging militant strike action in every industry. In Canada, since the
outlawing of the Party, their organizers have had to work entirely under
cover of legitimate trade unions, but their power for evil has been none
the less effective for that. Strike after strike has been traced directly to
C.I.O. organizers who are members of the Communist Party. Thanks to
the police authority granted under the Defence of Canada Regulations, a
few of these enemies of Society have been dealt with, but many more,
relying for immunity upon their trade union membership cards and upon
public influence manipulated through dupe "front" leagues and associations, remain at large to sow dissension and retard our war efforts.

A "Trade Union Letter", written and disseminated with great secrecy
in Vancouver by these revolutionists, is particularly interesting because
of its specific instructions on ways and means of developing "strike struggles". Most significant is its reference to "the danger of duration agree-

ments" and "increases in basic rates of pay". Although this "letter applies mainly to the British Columbia field the same tactics are being followed everywhere.

To quote in full:

Trade Union Letter

B.C. is at present observing the most important upsurge in the working class movement since the outbreak of the war. To date thousands of workers have received increases amounting to tens of thousands of dollars. Among these are: loggers in various camps, carpenters and other building trades workers, pulp and paper workers, civic employees, and many others.

This upsurge indicates the extent to which the working class of B.C. are re-acting to the new industrial activity and to the rising cost of living. This movement has arisen spontaneously out of the growing needs of the workers.

The present wave has by no means reached its height. Some important sections of workers are now moving into position to demand increases. Among the most outstanding of these are: the railroaders, sections of [13] shipyard workers, street railwaymen, some building trades, civic employees, foundry workers, steel workers, etc.

The pressure of objective conditions is also having a deep affect on unorganized workers, who are now clamoring for organization. The first opening in mining has already been made through the union vote in Bralorne. In lumber and saw mills the workers are prepared for organization, but in lumber the union is being bucked by the boss loggers association, with the result that there is little consolidation of the organization, and in sawmills practically a new start has to be made. In the maritime industry the desire for organization is stronger at present than at any time since the defeat of the Longshoremen's strike. This is reflected by the genuine movement from below among the seamen for unity of the two main seamen's organizations.

What have the workers gained from their demands? In all cases where workers asked for increases they won certain concessions. However, the trend of present agreements is far from satisfactory. The agreements between employer and employees have been characterized by three main features:

1. In many cases duration agreements have been signed. (shipyards, etc.)

2. In many cases the workers have been granted a cost of living bonus rather than an increase in the basic rate of pay.

3. In practically no new places since the war broke out has there been union recognition on the part of any employer.

How are we to explain the fact that labour, in some instances, gained only small increases in the basic rate of pay—and in many instances received a cost of living bonus? How are we to explain the fact that workers have not secured recognition of their unions? The answer to these questions lies in an understanding of the main features of the present surge.

What is the main feature of the present wage movement? The most outstanding feature is the lack of militancy in the movement. With the exception of few small isolated actions no militant struggles have taken place.[14]

How are we to explain the lack of militancy and struggle among the workers? There are a number of factors which must be analyzed before any consideration can be given to the tactics necessary to quickly improve the situation.

1. The first and most fundamental reason for the lack of militancy and weakness in the sweep of the movement, is to be found in the fact that the basic sections of the B.C. proletariat the loggers, miners, and marine industries, have not to any extent entered the struggle. In all three of these basic industries there exists strong sentiment for struggle but it is not crystallized or organized. In the main, these industries are unorganized. The fact must impress itself upon each revolutionary worker that so long as these industries remain unorganized, and so long as they are not in the position to play their role in the labour struggles, that of the vanguard, the B.C. labour movement, will be incapable of widely effective working class action.

2. The second most important reason which has effectively tied labour's hands, is the encirclement of labour by Federal and Provincial orders and laws. The movement has not yet gained sufficient strength and militancy to break through this encirclement, although to some extent these orders and laws have been exposed.

3. The third most important reason is the reformist trade union leadership who hate and fear the workers' struggle and seek to collaborate with the bosses. They hide from the workers the fact that through militant struggle the workers could break through the capitalist front and receive basic wage increases, union recognition and better working conditions. These reformist leaders constantly warn the workers that they must under all circumstances observe the government anti-labour laws, and thus they help to prevent militant action.

4. The fourth most important reason is the failure of our Alliance to effectively play its vanguard role in leading the workers' struggles, giving conscious direction to it and raising it to higher levels through the application of truly revolutionary trade union tactics. The Alliance is isolated from many important sections of workers.

But even in many places where Alliance people have shared in the leadership there has been a tendency towards legalism and also a tendency to shy away from [15] struggle and ask only for what it is though the bosses would consent to without struggle. The fact that there has been little attention paid to developing the strike movement is INDICATIVE OF THE RESPONSIBILITY CARRIED BY THE ALLIANCE FOR FAILURE TO DEVELOP THE STRIKE MOVEMENT.

The development of the strike struggle movement is today the single most important task of the revolutionary movement. Nothing will serve more to educate the workers, expose the government's war policies, lay bare the role of social democratic and the reformist agents of the ruling class, than this. The strike movement in B.C. will electrify the labour movement, sharpen the class struggle and hasten new political alignments in the Province.

What is necessary to improve the situation? The following tactics are essential.

1. The Alliance must pick certain fronts in the wage movement where possibilities exist for the development of strike struggles. Every attention should be given to these fronts.

2. It is necessary to intensify all efforts to organize the unorganized in the basic industries (logging, mining, marine) and to bring them up to their natural position as the militant advance guard of the B.C. proletariat.

3. It is necessary to show workers the danger of duration agreements. It is important to win the workers to struggle for increases in their basic rates of pay. In order to consolidate the working class movement and the workers gains and to fight for more it is necessary to break through the bosses' stubborn refusal to recognize trade unions.

4. It is necessary to employ militant job tactics—short strikes, holidays, mass delegations, slow down strikes, etc., even though in some instances these may be in violation of certain existing anti-labour laws. It is necessary at this point to warn against adventurism; i.e. taking strike action under any and all circumstances regardless of how unprepared the workers may be or regardless of how unfavourable circumstances are. This warning should not, on the other hand, be [16] interpreted in such a manner as to stifle the militant leadership of our people. The course of action must, in the final analysis, be taken by the people on the spot after having taken into consideration all circumstances.

5. The Alliance must take energetic steps to overcome its isolation from considerable sections of important workers. The Alliance trade union organization must be established on a more operative

basis. Greater initiative is needed to lead the workers' struggles. Shop or industry papers should be inaugurated wherever possible to carry our line to the workers. Our people must work in such a way as to set an example for other workers to follow; we must strive to win the confidence of the workers and to lead them in their struggles.

6. In those unions where the reformists are seeking to prevent militant action, the sharpest struggle should be conducted against them in such a way as to win the support of the workers for our line. We need to intensify the struggle for inner trade union democracy and, as a guarantee against the labour misleaders, rank and file movements, such as the shop stewards' councils, etc., must be built.[17]

GENERAL

DOUKHOBORS CONTINUE FANATICALLY RESOLUTE

The general situation regarding alternate service work for Doukhobors has developed as follows: After the Conference at Blaine Lake, Sask., on April 24th, 1941, disagreements between the Military Board and Doukhobor representatives tivestiveswere continued. Meetings at the various Saskatchewan and Alberta settlements occurred almost daily and it was finally decided to call a general conference of all Military Boards and Doukhobor representatives from all Western Provinces to reach peaceful solution as to "How Doukhobors could be used for this country without insulting their religious principles."

This General Conference opened its sittings at Calgary, Alta., on May 8, 1941 and, after much talk, all Doukhobor delegates, with exception of John G. Bondareff of Blaine Lake and P. G. Makaroff, K.C., of Saskatoon, unanimously protested and rejected the proposition of the Military Board to accept work on the roads at .50 per day, plus clothing and board. The Conference broke up with no headway being made, the Doukhobors being told to return to their respective communities and work for solution and, failing solution, the young Doukhobors would be conscripted.

On May 18, 1941 some 3000 Doukhobors held a General Meeting at Brilliant, B.C. and unanimously rejected the proposition of the Military Board to do alternate road or any other kind of government work, their general excuse being:-

(a) Although work in itself is acceptable, the Doukhobors do not trust one word of the Government. Doukhobor boys could be taken for work and later transferred elsewhere, or even into the army.

(b) This alternate road work is "regimental work", just the same as service in the army. Doukhobor boys who are not steady in their Doukhobor ideals might be easily tempted to join some branch of military service.

(c) Any collaboration with the Government in war time means the first step towards surrender of Doukhobor exemption rights.[18]

(d) A few prosperous Doukhobors, such as Zibin, Vanjoff, and others who are playing safe from both sides, proposed to ask the Government to give them a certain stretch of road to work on, say 5, 10 or 20 miles close at hand, with only "one English Engineer" to instruct them, that the Doukhobors could do this work of their own free will, without pay, as a present to the country. This proposition was also strongly rejected by the mass of people.

(e) The Meeting was closed without any definite resolution being passed "officially" but "unofficially" the Doukhobors decided to gain time; i.e. find reasons and excuses one after another, to postpone their answer to the Government. They hope that world events will bring big changes in the near future, and the Government might decide to drop the Doukhobor question altogether.

John J. Verigin and his B.C. Doukhobor leaders estimate that a total of some 12,000 Doukhobors in Western Canada will resist any kind of Government Service. It was argued against them that their refusal to meet the Government half way might bring stern action by way of jail or internment camp, but they replied they were ready to accept their fate in upholding their ideals, that the Canadian Government had cheated them and they would stage trouble and to go jail or interment camp rather than make any compromise. Their decision in this regard seems fanatically resolute.

Fred Podovinikoff, [⊁deletion: 1 line] was arrested by the B.C. Provincial Police a few weeks ago and sentenced to a term in Nelson Jail for failing to comply with National Registration.

(Since the above report was received there have been many arrests and convictions of Doukhobors in Langham, Blaine Lake and Yorkton districts of Saskatchewan, for failing to report for road work in lieu of military training).[19]

WHAT IS THE CIVIL LIBERTY UNION?

The Canadian Civil Liberties Union is one of many such unions which sprang up during the last decade in almost every country in the world where there is a Communist Party in operation. It is one of many Communist "Front Organizations" which spring up from one another, as necessity arises and circumstances permit during the onward march of the Communist Party.

The task of the Communists operating within the Civil Liberties Union is to endeavour to make of the Union an organization that will afford protection to the disguised Communist agitator operating within all sorts of bona fide respectable organizations, principally labour unions. In the performance of this task the main weapon is to be that of building up a public and political nuisance value by agitating public opinion. The success of the Civil Liberties Union depends on the ability of its Communist members to attract to its ranks honest, well-meaning and liberal-minded people by hypnotizing them into believing that those who are being prosecuted or interned are being cruelly victimized at the instigation of those who will eventually, if not checked in time, deprive of their Civil Liberties all progressive-minded people.

The Canadian Civil Liberties Union was founded, in Montreal, upon instructions from the Central Committee of the Communist Party of Canada. It was founded in 1935, at a time when the Canadian Labour Defence League which formerly served the same purpose, ceased being effective because of having been too positively exposed as a Communist-controlled organization.

It is not by the number of Communists on the Executive Board of the Union, that the Communist Party controls the Union. The Communist Party controls the Union through the effectiveness of the few of its especially trained and well-guided members on the Executive Board, and a rank and file membership made up of Communists in a proportion of 3 to 1. And this is as the Communist Party purposely intends it to be and to remain. This composition of the executive Board insures a respectable front while the effectiveness of the few Communists on the said Board plus the composition of the rank and file membership make secure the Communist control of the Union.

When the few Communists on the Executive Board find themselves too much at variance with the non-Communist members of the Board on an [20] important question of policy, they demand, as they have a constitutional right to do, that the question be decided by a general membership meeting. This ensures a decision favourable to the Communists. Such a situation arose out of the distribution of a peace pamphlet by the Communists, shortly after the outbreak of the present war. Nine Communists, in Montreal, having been arrested under the defence of Canada Regulations, for the distribution of the said peace pamphlet, the Communists on the Executive Board of the Civil Liberties Union wanted the Union to defend them, while the majority of the Board were opposed. A general membership meeting was called and the Communists had their own way.

Anyone who attended the "National Conference" on Civil Liberties during Wartime held in the Mount Royal Hotel, in the spring of 1940, and arranged by the Civil Liberties Union, at the instigation of the Communist Party of Canada, must surely have come away convinced, without the shadow of a doubt, that the Conference was controlled by the Communists in a proportion of 4 to 1.

For the time being, the Canadian Civil Liberties Union is the most effective weapon of the Communist Party of Canada.

JEW FAMILY GIVES FIVE SOLDIERS

Although the small Jewish settlement of Kamsack, Sask. numbers only

15 families, in response to the call for recruits it gave 13 volunteers for active service overseas, reports "The Israelite Press" of July 4. These include all the five grown-up sons of the family Alfman. Their father came to Canada in 1904 and settled in Kamsack as a pioneer farmer.[21]

SECRET
INTELLIGENCE
BULLETIN

ROYAL CANADIAN MOUNTED POLICE
HEADQUARTERS, OTTAWA

AUGUST 16, 1941

CONTENTS
Communism:
War Series
No. 46

COMMUNISM
"DAILY WORKER" SHOUTS FOR TOTAL WAR

Complete support for the Soviet Union and democracies in their war against Germany and Italy is demanded of the Communist Party of the United States and of Canada. Directives to this effect were published in the "Daily Worker" of New York for June 30.

The manifesto to the Communists of the United States declares:

"There can be no peace for the peoples of the world without the complete destruction of Hitler and Hitlerism. The issue is not Communism. German fascism has set out to enslave all nations and all peoples to conquer the world. That, and only that, is the issue. The people of America are beginning to realize that to defend the Soviet Union means to defend the United States. What is needed is speedy and effective aid to the Soviet and British peoples. It is the duty of the working class to lead the fight to establish American-Soviet-British collaboration for the defeat of Hitlerism and to make this the official and active policy of the government. Defend America by giving full aid to the Soviet Union, Great Britain and all nations who fight against Hitler. For full and unlimited collaboration of the United States, Great Britain and the Soviet Union to bring about the military defeat of fascism."

The Communist Party of Canada makes a similar appeal. To quote in part:

"Hitler's perfidious mad-dog attack upon the U.S.S.R. is a threat

383

not only to the country of socialism and its people, but against the liberty and national freedom of all people throughout the world. The Communist Party of Canada calls upon all anti-fascist people to join hands in a united popular movement for all possible aid to the Soviet people in their just war, to give unstinted support to prosecution of the war against German Nazism and its allies and to defeat any attempt to give aid or comfort to the Nazi regime or its friends and allies in Canada."[1]

The Communist Party of Canada asks for abolition of the ban against it and its press, and the immediate establishment of full diplomatic and trade relations between Canada and the U.S.S.R.

The "Daily Worker" is insisting on the strength of the Soviet Army and has pinned the label of Munichmen on the United States military experts who are pessimistic about the outcome of the Russo-German struggle. There is as yet no indication of what the Communist Party line would be in the event of the capitulation of the Stalin Government.

ANOTHER COMMUNIST IN PUBLIC OFFICE
(Winnipeg, Man.)

As a result of sustained work by the Workers' Election Committee [≈<deletion: 1 line] the radical elements of Ward 3, Winnipeg, succeeded on July 18 in electing M. J. Forkin [≈<deletion: 1 line] to the aldermanic seat left vacant by the internment of Jacob Penner, [≈<deletion: 1 line]. Mr. Forkin's manager was William Kardash, M.L.A., [≈<deletion: 1 line]

Through the indifference of 70 per cent of the 31,000 eligible voters who neglected to use their franchise, Forkin defeated his three opponents, having a majority of 578 in the final count (by transferable ballot).

As pointed out by the Winnipeg Free Press, the newly-elected alderman represents only a small minority of the qualified voters whereas "This extreme radical party made full use of the opportunity offered in a free democracy, while the other citizens notably failed to do so."[2]

MASS SUPPORT FOR SOVIET UNION

(The following comprehensive directive of the Communist Party received from "K" Division, Edmonton, Alta. shows how their former policy of a "People's Peace" has changed to a "People's Victory" for the sake of Soviet Russia and world Communism, while at the same time the domestic fight is to continue unabated "for the complete restoration of all democratic rights" by alliance with all "progressive" parties and trade unions in a mass campaign.)

Dear Friends:

The most immediate necessity at this time is to carry out the policy laid down in the Politbureau motions of June 22, and June 22 statement of the Politbureau to organize a mass campaign to bring pressure upon the King Government to declare itself fully and unreservedly for unlimited aid to the Soviet Union, and publicly to endorse the proposal of the Churchill Government for military and economic help for the Soviet Union......

In his statement of June 22 Mackenzie King only partially endorsed Churchill's line. While much in his statement can be welcomed such as his attack on all war-like peoples, and his statement that Hitler's attack is not a crusade against a 'red menace', it is obvious that there is a serious shortcoming in his remarks. While he give support to the USSR's war against German Fascism and denounces the attack on Soviet Territory, he does not fully endorse the Churchill policy. It is the task of our Alliance to organize at once a great campaign in the labour movement, among the farmers, and the anti-fascist middle class, to demand of the King Government that it requests an alliance with the USSR and at once proposes to the USSR that full diplomatic and commercial relations be established between the two countries.

Such a campaign will have two motivations; first, to increase the support for the Soviet Union, to back up its magnificent fight against Nazism with the offer of all aid from Canada, thus to strengthen the Soviet Union, to back up the Churchill line towards the USSR and to strengthen the favourable position occupied by the Soviet Union among the anti-Fascist forces of the whole world; secondly, it will bring and sharpen the process of differentiation in the capitalist camp in Canada, bringing into the open the Quislings in the ruling class; i.e., those elements who cry for the mutual destruction of the German Fascists and the Soviet Government in the [3] present war, who place the class interests of the big bourgeoise above the truly national interests of the Canadian people, who demand the military defeat of German Fascism.

In this connection, there are some points which we must make clear. (later leaflets, pamphlets, etc., will be sent out dealing with them.) We must take as our point of departure in this campaign that everything that Canada does to continue and step up the war against Nazi Germany is in the interests of the Soviet Union and will render easier the supreme task of the USSR, the military defeat and annihilation of the Nazi war machine. Secondly, the democracy in our own and all countries depends largely on the military defeat of that machine. The victory of the Red Army, which is the main fighting force fighting against the Nazi machine, will restore freedom and national independence enceenceamong the nations subjugated by the Nazis and will be world historic victory for the progressive forces in every country. Thirdly, we must point out that the vile propaganda of the Fifth Columnists to the effect that the Red Army will impose Communism on the peoples of Europe 'against their will' (which is one of the chief weapons in the hands of the Goebells) is a deliberate falsity and a slander aimed at the defeat of the Soviet Union—that the victory of the Red Army will free these peoples from Nazi oppression and enable them democratically to decide their own destiny, their own form of government and their social system. The pre-conditions for the political freedom of the subjugated nations of Europe, for the restoration of their rights, is the defeat of the Nazi war machine, and this defeat rests in the hands of the Red Army. All support which can be given by Canada to the Red Army is consequently support for democracy, for natural freedom, and in the interests of Canadian democracy. On the other hand, should the Canadian Quislings win and press the government to sabotage the fight of the Red Army, placing the hatred of Communism above that of the Hitler Fascist Dictatorship, then the Hitler plan of world domination, based on his undisputed mastery of Europe, faces the Canadian and all other peoples.

Our campaign among the masses must assume a direct, forthright nature and must not be marked by any sectarian thoughts or practices which base themselves on the former political line, and refuse to take into account actual political and class relations at this moment when the decisive thing is to compel the government to render all aid to the Soviet Union, to declare itself ready and willing to conclude an alliance and establish full diplomatic trade relations with the USSR.

Such a campaign must take on mass character. The possibilities for united front activities, for mass agitation and propaganda, for the winning back of democratic rights for the resurgence of the labour movements as great independent political factor able profoundly to influence the [4] actions of the government, for the birth of big popular movements against fascism and for Soviet victory, against Canadian Quislings, must be apparent to every member. In other words, it is our task to take full advantage for the cause of the people's victory for the obvious fact that the Churchill Gov't. and those of the Dominions are forces which by the logic of events and their own desperate position caused by Nazi victories hitherto, have lined up with the Soviet Union in the struggle against Hitler fascism. The outcome of this titanic struggle will determine the future.

The campaign and line of policy herein outlined coincides exactly with the needs of the Canadian people and not by one jot or tittle detracts from their struggle for economic and political rights as against the reactionary attacks of the financial oligarchy. The fight on the economic and political front for the interests of the masses remains in full operation; added to that fight under the new conditions is the tremendous advantage that everything which increases the unity of the Canadian people against the reactionary anti-Soviet sections of the ruling class, increases the strength of the USSR and brings closer the hour of defeat of the Hitler war machine.

The mass campaign here outlined is the supreme task of the whole Alliance. Every Committee, every branch, must react to these directives quickly, forcibly and with all possible ingenuity. Meetings, demonstrations, unity conferences, resolutions and wires to the Government and to local MP's, appeals to the unions, CCF and SC Clubs, left Liberals and

Churchgoers, should be the forms of this campaign. Our slogans, contained in the statement of June 22 regarding a people's victory and the questions of alliance with the USSR, should become the slogans of masses of the people. Such a mass movement can and will cause the government to take full stand which it must take to give body to King's declaration of June 23, and will expose the Quislings and bring into the open all anti-Soviet elements who are working now to weaken the efforts of the Canadian people to help the USSR, and by lies and slanders hope to divide the masses.

The anti-Soviet lies of the Quislings and their campaign of misrepresentation of the aims of the USSR, their assurances that the Red Army will be defeated, their developing campaign to prepare the way for peace with Hitler at the expense of the USSR and the toiling people of all lands, must be met by the mass campaign. One of the main jobs we have to do is to give the fullest, public, description of the achievements of the USSR in all fields, labour, youth, women, army, industry, civil and religious rights, etc., in each district we should make plans for the sale of thousands of copies of the Dean of Canterbury's book on the Soviet Union. Leaflets should be circulated giving the facts; caches of books and pamphlets on this question should be opened up and these sold to the people, steps should be taken to get such pamphlets and books imported from the U.S.[5]

Special efforts must be directed in this campaign to enrol the sympathies and active aid of the hundreds of thousands of Canadians who come from the countries conquered by Hitler and from the regions which were recently liberated by the Red Army but which now have been invaded by the Nazis. The most promising possibilities are open in this field for the building of a great people's movement for the victory of the Red Army over the Nazis, a movement which can and should embrace not only those who sympathize with the Soviet government but all those who are opposed to the Nazi conquerors and want to see the liberation of their native lands. Such a movement will be a powerful auxiliary to the general people's campaign to compel the government to declare its full support of the USSR; it should also come to the aid of the interned anti-fascists and demand their release; the freedom of their banned organizations like the ULFTA and the internment of the fascist among these peoples, such as the Skoropadsky adherents in Canada who are in league with Hitler's Ukrainian henchmen in Berlin and who have up to now been given the protection of the Canadian government.

Trade Unions in the New Situation: It is obvious that the central tasks are now different than they were a month ago and we must face them realistically. It is in this light we must re-examine the June Political Letter which was devoted to our trade union and economic struggles.

The defense of the economic interests of the workers and farmers, the fight against the iniquitous taxation policy, abolition of all oppressive anti-working class legislation and regulations, independent labour political action, establishment of labour-farmer unity, still remain major tasks but they must now be subordinate to, and means by which to achieve, the main objective.

In view of these charges our main tasks in the trade unions, and in the preparations of the forthcoming conventions of the congresses must be:

1. Unqualified Labour Support for the Soviet Union. Every worker should be made to realize that his future and that of all working people in the country is inseparably linked up with the victory of the Red Army. Regardless of his views on Socialism or Communism he must bend every effort to strengthen the fighting people of the USSR and to weaken the pro-Fascist forces in our country. Resolutions pledging such support, declarations emphasizing the special proletarian character of the S.U. appeals to all workers, farmers and progressive people in the country and in other parts of the world to ally themselves with the USSR, should be adopted in every shop, factory, mine and mill meeting, at every local town meeting, trades council and trades Congress conventions. Demands on the Dominion Gov't. to establish direct diplomatic relations with the USSR, to supply the S.U. with all necessary war supplies, should be made everywhere.[6]

Greetings and pledges to the trade unions of the USSR to stand by them until full victory of the Red Army over Fascism is achieved, should also be adopted and telegraphed to the All-Union council of Trades Unions in Moscow, and copies given to the press.

2. Trade Union Unity: The fight should be launched for the closest unity of all progressive forces within each union, between the several unions in one industry and the different trades congresses, around the immediate demands of the workers, the fight for full restoration of democracy in the country, the development of independent labour action for the defeat of fascism abroad and at home. The decisive role of the trade unions in the building of a people's front and in influencing the gov't. should be brought forward in the most convincing manner to all workers.

3. Defend Living Standards But Take the Profits Out of War: Our economic demands: adequate wage scales, national wage scales for each industry, wage equality with the rest of Canada for Quebec, shifting of the war costs to those best able to pay, still remain. The fight for full trade union rights and against the obnoxious orders in council aimed against the S.U. must be continued; in addition we must develop campaigns against the Quisling fifth columnist employers who impede, sabotage and obstruct war production by their fascist opposition to trade unionism and their refusal to grant decent wages and conditions.

4. One Million Trade Unionists by 1942: Our campaign for the extension of trade unionism must now be intensified a thousand fold. The tri-

pling of the trade union membership, the winning of our working youth for the unions and the revitalization of the t.u. movement in the execution of the central labour tasks, is the essential requisite for the successful carrying out of the historical obligations now facing us. One million trade unionists conscious of their role and obligations, will constitute an unbreakable democratic bulwark in the titanic struggle now developing on an international and national scale.

5. <u>To Defeat Fascism We Must Have Full Democratic Rights:</u> The fight against the undemocratic laws and regulations which affect the unions directly cannot be separated from the broader struggle for full democracy in the country. The trade unions must be won for a leading position in the fight for the complete restoration of all democratic rights, to all individuals, groups and parties which are in the fight against fascism. Release of all anti-fascist internees and prisoners, legality of the Party, freedom of the press, etc., are necessary if the war against fascism is to be won.

6. <u>Trade Union Conventions Must Mark Resurgence of Labour's Independence Role:</u> Trade union congresses which will shortly meet in convention must be prepared for by aiming at the election of a majority of progressive united front and pro-Soviet delegates. In addition to all other resolutions, the following major ones must be adopted by scores of local unions, trades councils, etc., and forwarded in time to the several trade union centres.[7]

(a) Greetings to the All-Union Council of Trade Unions, Moscow, USSR, on their heroic struggle against fascism and pledging unqualified support and cooperation of Canadian labour until victory is won.

(b) Demanding of the King Gov't. that it come out with an unequivocal declaration supporting the policy announced by Churchill fo full support to the USSR, and that the Canadian Gov't. immediately establish full diplomatic and trade relations with the USSR and grant unqualified support to the Soviet people and their heroic army.

(c) That the Congress elaborate a "Labour War Program" and approach the other trade union centres in Canada with a request that an all-inclusive Canadian Trade union council be established to carry such a program into effect. The Labour War Program be based on the following main policies:

1. To make the country's war effort truly democratic by the defence of workers' living standards; taking profits out of war; eliminating all anti-labour regulations and orders-in-Council; democratic and just war taxation policy.

2. Oust the Quislings from all high places. To seek the elimination of all anti-labour, anti-democratic Quislings who occupy important positions in the gov't. on various war boards and other gov't. councils.

3. To secure gov't. action against the industrialists who sabotage the war effort by opposing trade unionism and collective bargaining and by deny-

ing fair wages and working conditions to the workers of this country.

4. To guard against the betrayal of the fascist-minded Municheers who will use every opportunity to betray the struggle of the people against fascism and to stab in the back the heroic S.U. because of the deep-rooted hatred for workers' rights, for Socialism, and because of the fundamental attraction which fascism holds for these Quisling financiers.

5. To seek an approach to and the establishment of closest co-operation with, the trade union centres of all countries engaged in the war against Hitler fascism, with the view of creating a unified expression of the trade unionists of these warring countries and making the voice of organized labour heard in the councils of gov't. and thus safeguarding the interests and welfare of the labouring people both during the long days of struggle against the common foe, as well as during the hour of inevitable triumph when peace will be on the agenda.

(d) The organization of a more democratic and more representative national apparatus for the satisfactory settlement of labour problems to protect the rights of collective bargaining, to establish national and regional wage scales, and to gain for labour a greater voice in the development and conduct of war production.

These resolutions and the general approach to the main trade union problems listed above offer the basis for a rapid development of mass work among the workers of the country and for the winning of the trade unions for the People's Victory.[8]

POSITION OF INTERNED REDS UNCHANGED

Until Germany invaded Russia Canadian Communists were the relentless enemies of democracy and of anything that made for its defence. Now, because the Fatherland of Communism is in deadly peril, they deign to join forces with us against the common enemy—until the enemy is destroyed. They have turned their coats but not their hearts and their hatred of democracy burns as fiercely as ever. Should their interned leaders be freed to again stab us in the back? The "Winnipeg Free Press" discusses the subject in a recent editorial. To quote in part:

If the Canadian Communists could only realize it, the intermittent agitation for the release of their interned leaders only provides additional proof of the soundness of the argument in favour of keeping them behind the wire. These people are trouble-makers. The fact that they were Communists and that the Communist Party was likewise a trouble-maker is almost incidental. And today none of the agitators for their release ever show any public token of their conversion from trouble-making. They do not say they are now for the war that they were formerly against. They talk only in the most general terms about how the war—due to Russia's entrance into it— has now become a war against Fascism. How the war which yesterday was a capitalist war and a war of rival imperialisms, etc., etc., has undergone this miraculous conversion, nobody knows—least of all this handful of trouble-makers.

It is significant nevertheless that Great Britain has refused to release its interned Communists, that Australia has likewise refused, and that Canada has also decided to do nothing about it. The shrieks of the friends of the interned men continue to rise to the skies. Injustice is being done, they scream: These men's sole crime was that they opposed Fascism. For this they have been jailed. May the heavens fall upon their jailers! And so on and so fourth.

These Canadian Communists were interned because they were actively interfering with the progress of a national effort, supported by 99 per cent of the population of Canada, to fight Hitlerism. Up to early in September, 1939 (after war had broken out), the Communists were a part of that national effort. They cheered it on. They pledged support. Then, suddenly and without warning, the line changed. The war took [9] on an evil hue. It was a war directed against the workers' interests. It should be opposed. After long delay and with great moderation the most violent Canadian exponents of this creed were interned. Until there is proof, and very complete and extended proof, that these interned men are honestly behind the war, they should stay where they now are. Of that proof there is not the slightest sign or evidence.

For the Communists the war has changed because Russia is now an Ally. But Russian intervention in the war has not affected Canada's position in any respect. Canada declared war on Germany regardless of the Russian position. Canada is pleased to have another ally at this late stage. But the war in July, 1941, is still the war it was in September, 1939. The same issues are involved and the same national resolution is pledged to continue exertions. With these Russia has nothing whatever to do except insofar as co-operation can be made effective to encompass the defeat of Germany. This co-operation is military and not ideological. In that latter sphere there is nothing in common between the ideals of Russia and the ideals of Canada. They are poles apart.[10]

UKRAINIA

FIRST NATIONAL EUCHARISTIC CONGRESS OF EASTERN RITES

The First National Eucharistic Congress of Eastern Rites, held at Chicago, June 25-29, was significant as being not only the first Congress of its kind, but also the largest congregation of Eastern Rites (Greek Catholic or Eastern Catholic Church) ever held on this continent. Its chief purpose was to manifest the unity existing between the Eastern and Latin branches of the Church as well as between the various branches of the

Eastern Church.

However, the "unity" was thoroughly assured in advance by the Basilian Fathers and Bishop Bohachewsky, the organizers of the Congress, who dissociated the Congress from all Ukrainian political parties and kept all public proceedings strictly to religious rites and topics. There was, however, a secret sectional meeting of Ukrainian Catholic bishops and priests at which (to quote a reporter)

"It is presumed that all the important questions affecting the Ukrainian Catholic Church in relation to its attitude toward Ukrainian political movements, here and abroad, as well as to the Ukrainian question in Europe in the present international situation, must have been fully discussed and that certain policies were shaped for the Church to pursue, as a result. What they are, if any, it will soon become evident from the trend the Church will take in the future. Thus, this meeting must be regarded as the most significant event of the Congress insofar as the Ukrainian Catholics are concerned."

That there were numerous divergent and even antagonistic elements in the huge congregation (comprised largely of Ukrainians but also including Carpatho-Russians, Croats, Slovaks, Hungarians, Rumanians, Irish-Americans, Italians, Poles, and so forth, both clergy and laity) was evident at the Congress and afterwards when various leaders were interviewed. It was noted that among those prominent in the big procession were the three supreme directors of the Ukrainian national Association, T. Spikula, R. Smook, S. Kuropas, and the editor of its organ, "Svoboda", Dr. L. Myshuha. (Note: The Ukrainian National Association is a fraternal organization, with headquarters in Jersey City). On the other hand, conspicuous by their [11] absence in the procession were many leaders, local and national, of the Hetman organization and of the Organizations for the Rebirth of Ukraine (the O.D.W.U.), some of them being residents of Chicago.

Also absent were prominent lay leaders of the Ukrainian Catholic Church and expected large delegations from all parishes in the country; also the editors of the two Catholic newspapers, the "Amerika" and "The Way", and professors of the Ukrainian Catholic College in Stanford, Conn; prominent Ukrainian-Canadian priests, namely, the Rev. Dr. W. Kushnir, president of the U.C.C. and Rev. S. Semchuk, of Winnipeg, executive member.

Interviews

Col. Alexander Shapoval, Editor of the "Nash Styah" "Our Banner" official organ of the United Hetman Organization in U.S.A.

Speaking of the Nazi-Soviet war, Col. Shapoval said that it is the act of Providence itself that at last Hitler, described as the greatest genius in all history, decided to smash the iniquitous "Kingdom of Satan", the Soviet Union, and thus give the various peoples inhabiting it an opportunity to free themselves from the unholy prison in which they are enslaved.

Shapoval reflected that the end of the Soviet Union was inevitable. Even a year ago he wrote in his paper articles on the subject in which he had predicted the Nazi-Soviet war. It was inconceivable for two great powers to exist peacefully side by side. This new war will prove a blessing for the Ukrainian people. In the situation prior to the German-Soviet war the fate of the Ukrainians was not too hopeful, in view of the fact that there was nothing in the war aims of the democratic powers which would indicate that the Ukrainians will be liberated. Now that hopeless situation was changed. The Ukrainians will have an opportunity to re-establish their independence on the ruins of the Soviet Union. They will benefit from the "new order" which is being established in Eastern Europe by Hitler. Naturally, it will involve German control; however, this can be compromised somehow. The Ukraine needs German industrial products as much as Germany has need for great natural resources of the Ukraine. Therefore, Ukrainians will work hard in order to satisfy the natural requirements in foodstuffs and so forth of the Germans, in exchange for their industrial products as well as their aid in establishing order and organization in the Ukraine. It is but natural that a German nation of 80 million people must live, and the Ukrainian resources are sufficient to satisfy at least part of their requirements, Shapoval reasoned.[12]

Shapoval went on to say that "it was a foregone conclusion that the Germans will set up a Ukrainian regime in the Ukraine in the same way as they have done in Slovakia and Croatia. Being fed-up with the autocracy of Moscow and the Bolshevist godless slavery, the Ukrainian peasant will gladly accept and support a new order and plow his soil with a revived spirit as he craves for material things that were denied him under the Red regime. He still remembers his God and religion."

In his opinion Hitler would also triumph in the war against England. He stressed the point that "we Ukrainians" should not shed tears on account of the British Empire. It will crumble down because of its mistakes and sins of the past. Britain was never interested in the justice or the fate of subjected nations. She was mainly concerned with her own selfish interests, he declared.

This war, Shapoval stressed, is not being waged as between the British people and the German people. It is a war between the Jewish International and the Nazi Germany, cleverly launched by the machinations of the International Jewry which succeeded in dragging into the conflict the ruling classes of England.

Dr. Luke Myshuha, Editor "Svobada", U.N.A.
and
Roman I. Smook and Stephen Kuropas

Directors of U.N.A.

The chief topic of conversation concerned the Nazi-Soviet war and its significance for the Ukrainian question in Europe. In common with many other Ukrainian-Americans of the patriotic section who thus far had considered the Soviet Union as the only obstacle on the path of liberation of the Ukrainian people, passionately hating both Communism and Russia in the past twenty years, the Nazi-Soviet war was viewed by these men in the spirit of satisfaction, tempered, however, by serious misgivings as to the final solution of the Ukrainian question.

All three desired to see the Soviet Union, described as the "colossus of clay feet", destroyed by the Nazis so the Ukrainian people should be given a chance to emancipate themselves in whatever manner it is possible under the circumstances.[13]

This unexpected turn of the present war was considered the most favourable and opportune for the Ukrainians, in the present unfavourable alignment of powers, to establish independence, regardless of the fact that the people would have to pay dearly for it and that this "independence" would be to a great degree circumscribed by the Nazi lords.

As far as the Ukrainians are concerned, both Stalin and Hitler must be regarded as two evils; however, in making a choice between the two devils, Hitler appeared the lesser evil. The Nazi Germany would never succeed in gaining a complete control of the great Ukrainian nation, the Nazi domination of Europe would not last forever, therefore if the worst happened, whereby the Germans should attempt to subjugate the Ukrainians, they would be dealt with as in 1918, when they were driven out by the popular revolt.

The all-important question now, they concurred, was the liberation of the Ukraine by the destruction of the Soviet Russia. It may not be an ideal way for the Ukrainians to reassert themselves, they reflected, but what other way was there for the Ukrainian people under the present conditions? What assurance is there being offered for the Ukrainians by other powers involved in the war? they asked.

Dr. Myshuha maintained, however, that it is not in the best interests of the Ukrainians in the United States to follow any course of policy which would be contrary to foreign and national policies of the American Government. It was the duty of Ukrainian-Americans to remain loyal to the country of their allegiance and by no means give cause to the Government, or to any anti-Ukrainian elements in America, now calumnizing the Ukrainians in the press, to brand the Ukrainians here as disloyal subversive elements. Enough harm has been done by the two Nationalist groups, the "crazy boys" of the O.D.W.U. (Organization for the Rebirth of the Ukraine) and the bombastic Hetmanites, the United Hetman Organization. Their political antics and puerile declarations in the past have been harmful to general welfare of the Ukrainians, he declared bitterly. Consequently, the Ukrainians here must eliminate some of these extremists in the Ukrainian organized life, and in general maintain a position befitting a responsible people. Regardless of the fact whether the Germans will destroy the Soviets or not, there was no doubt that British and American democracies will finally triumph, and therefore it will be the task of the Ukrainians in U.S. and in Canada to plead the cause of the Ukrainian people in Europe. Thus, if it were for this reason alone, the Ukrainians on this continent must support the democracies. There should be no other policy. This was the policy of the Ukrainian National Association, Myshuha concluded.[14]

(Note: It will be noted that Dr. Myshuha spoke in a derogatory manner with reference to the Hetman and the Nationalist O.D.W.U. organizations and their leaders. He said repeatedly that he has actively opposed the Hetman movement and subsequently the Nationalist O.D.W.U. organization. On this account the leaders of these two organizations despise him, and the feeling is mutual, he said, ignoring the fact that both of his friends, Kuropas and Smook, were Nationalist sympathizers.)

As one of the best informed men on Ukrainian affairs in U.S., Dr. Myshuha expressed an opinion to the effect that co-operation between the O.D.W.U. and the U.H.O. may be possible under certain conditions, particularly in case of a possible alignment of the two Nationalist movements in Europe. At present, these two groups are adversely disposed to each other and continue factional strife along the ideological lines. The two groups have been members of the Ukrainian Congress Committee, but were expelled from that central body a few weeks ago on account of their being identified with two political movements in Europe with headquarters in Germany.

As for the Ukrainian Workingmen's Association, great changes, said Dr. Myshuha, have taken place in this fraternal organization as a result of the recent annual convention, whereby the leadership of the Association was wrested from the hands of intellectuals in the organization and relegated to several radical leaders of the ranks. The reports appearing in some Ukrainian newspapers on a "Communist revolution" in the Association are, in Dr. Myshuha's opinion, somewhat exaggerated. It was true, however, that M. Sichinsky, Dr. M. Lewitsky, Yaroslaw Chyz and several others, have been ousted from their executive positions in the Association and its organ, the "Narodna Vola", the editors of this paper being reduced to a status of "hired men". It was also true, Myshuha said, that the Communist element in the organization has been active in bringing about these changes by inspiring and supporting the radically-minded followers of Korpan, the present president, in this move. Now some members of this organization were in touch with two well-known Ukrainian Socialist intellectuals, Dr. Nicholas Ceglinsky, residing in U.S.A., and Dr. Levinsky of Shanghai, China, in an endeavour to attract them to the editorial positions in the "Narodna Vola", Dr. Myshuha explained.[15]

Speaking of the Church's attitude, Dr. Myshuha said:

"A short time ago I had a conference with Bishop Buchko in New York on the subject of the U.H.O. and the O.D.W.U. and possible consequences for Bishop Bohachewsky and his Church resulting from whatever connections the Catholic Church may or may not have with these two political organizations. I told him frankly and clearly that if Bishop Bohachewsky is anxious to be put in an internment camp or to make a blundering mistake such as made in Canada by Bishop Budka during the last war, let him tolerate, support, or even associate his Church with the two organizations in question."[16]

SECRET

INTELLIGENCE
BULLETIN

ROYAL CANADIAN MOUNTED POLICE
HEADQUARTERS, OTTAWA

SEPTEMBER 30, 1941

CONTENTS

Labour Unrest:
  Stormy Convention of Labour Congress
Communism:
  Three Demands Upon the Government
  National Council for Democratic Rights
  Youth Movement Perverts "V" Campaign
Nazis:
  Western Germans Losing Confidence
Internment:
  Methods of Procedure

War Series
No. 47

LABOUR UNREST

STORMY CONVENTION OF CANADIAN CONGRESS OF
LABOUR

Considerable turmoil and disunity marked the second convention of the Canadian Congress of Labour, held at the Royal Connaught Hotel, Hamilton, September 8 - 12. From the first it was apparent that several of the C.I.O. affiliated unions were determined to embarrass and obstruct the policies of President A. R. Mosher, his executive officers and the majority of the 500 delegates present. Particularly conspicuous in this regard were the Steel Workers' Organizing Committee, the United Automobile Workers of America and the United Electrical Radio and Machine Workers of America, who submitted resolutions calling for all-out aid for U.S.S.R., the repeal of P.C. 7440 and the immediate release of all interned labour leaders. The agitators included E. E. Leary (Dockyard and Shipyard Workers' Union, Vancouver); George Harris (U.E.R. and M.W.); Harold Pritchett (International Woodworkers of America); James Robertson (Labour Council, Vancouver Island).

Two significant incidents occurred early in the convention. First, Mrs. Dorise Nielsen, M.P., addressed the delegates, arousing them to greater efforts in combatting "unjust" war-and-labour regulations and in demanding the liberation of trade unionists; Second, a group of Nova Scotia coal

397

miners paraded with banners around the Hall. Both Mrs. Nielsen and the miners got vociferous applause.

Interned Communists

Considerable excitement arose over the many resolutions calling for the repeal of Sections 21, 39 and 39A of the Defence of Canada Regulations and the release of "all anti-Fascist workers....with special reference to Pat Sullivan, Jack Chapman, Charles Murray, C. S. Jackson and Bruce Magnusson."

George Harris, leading the defence of Jackson, read a long statement written by J. L. Cohen, K.C., which purported to show that Jackson had been interned without just cause or legal trial.

The Government, continued Harris, thus admits for the first time that Jackson was interned for participating in strikes, and he wanted to know if there was any great division between the shooting of trade unionists in [1] Norway and interning trade unionists here. "We must combine all unions in demanding the liberation of Jackson", he said.

Willard Bliss (U.E.R. and M.W.) vigorously supported this move. The internment of Jackson had been a severe blow to the United Electrical Workers, and a serious miscarriage of justice. "We believe that it was no accident that the R.C.M.P. picked him up when he was fighting for justice. These are the same tactics as employed by Herr Hitler. It's the incipient working of Fascism. We appeal to those who have had their leaders taken away and are going to have them taken away, to combine to take action to secure the release of all the trade union leaders of Canada—unqualified unity in this one matter, releasement."

George Warn (same union) endorsed these views and declared that "Jackson was in no way responsible for the General Electric going out on strike illegally."

E. E. Leary was the most dramatic, asserting that he was going to "fight to the last drop of my blood" to have these trade unionists liberated. He said, "you don't have to be a Communist to get in a camp. You only have to fight for labour. You have no democratic rights in Canada today when you can be thrust into a filthy concentration camp. Tomorrow I may be in a camp alongside Brother Jackson and all the other great labour leaders. Tomorrow it may be Mosher (the president) or Dowd (secretary-treasurer)."

M. M. Maclean (Executive Board, C.C.L.) courageously exposed the subversive elements in their true colours. Many of these resolutions and words used in debate carried the brand of the Communist Party, he said. For instance, those formerly called Communists were now labelled "anti-Fascists" and "labour-leaders". "We should recognize what is doing in this convention and I welcome this opportunity to make an issue of it now. The motion under consideration calls for a fair British trial and no more. Now is the time for a showdown between honest labour and subversive elements."

The cheers that followed drowned out the boos, and the resolution (amended by the Resolutions Committee of its objectionable features) was carried by a probably two-thirds majority.

Nova Scotia Miners

Another prolonged and acrimonious debate arose over the treatment of the Cape Breton coal miners engaged on a "slow-down" strike. The extremists, including most of the C.I.O. delegate endeavoured to force the Congress to pass a resolution declaring its complete sympathy and co-operation [2] with the miners, while members of the Executive and others opposed any interference in a C.I.O. "family quarrel".

Speaking to a resolution urging "that this convention condemn the action of the Executive (C.C. of L.) in opposing the struggle of the miners for trade union democracy and a better standard of living, and insist that there be no further such interference in the internal affairs of affiliated international unions", J. A. MacDonald, a United Mine Workers' delegate, explained that, "We didn't stop work altogether because we felt we must produce enough coal to bunker the convoys", that the slow-down was continuing to retard full production by about 40 per cent, and that no early settlement was in sight. He said that he had been a miner for 41 years and that he and his fellow workers felt their democratic rights had been taken away by the U.M.W. executive board in ratifying the Government Conciliation Board offer without consulting them.

Angus McIntyre (U.M.W.A., Nova Scotia), supporting the resolution, said, "Don't let anyone lead you to believe we want to do anything that will cripple Canada's war effort, or any part of it. This slow-down is a long story. It has meant loss of production of 1,700,000 tons of coal and 60,000 man-days in 120 days of curtailed production."

Silby Barrett (Inter. representative U.M.W.A.) explained how the slow-down policy had been forbidden by the parent body and warned the Congress not to interfere with internal affairs of local unions. This, however, did not prevent James Robertson moving a vote of full co-operation with the miners of Nova Scotia; and George Harris shouting, "We must not desert these 10,000 miners to a hostile Government and a hostile company....It seems to be a question of 10,000 miners wanting to get rid of Silby Barrett."

Patrick Conroy, chairman of the Resolutions Committee, warned that if the Congress "did not keep its nose out of the business of United Mine Workers" the international might decide to pull out from the Congress and the Congress might be wrecked. "Let us not play into the hands of reactionaries", he pleaded.

The resolution was finally defeated and replaced by a motion to leave the matter in the hands of the Congress Executive to support the miners in the fairest way possible. As outlined by the Committee:

The president of Congress should use his influence with the government to have the former employees reinstated, it was urged, and upon acceptance of this condition the workers should resume full-time production. The next step proposed was that the president of [3] Congress make known to the international union the willingness of Congress to co-operate, and that a joint committee be named to adopt a basis, after investigating, that will assist in improved wages and working conditions.

The opposers demanded a standing vote. The results were 199 for and 156 against—which pretty well represented the strength of the insurgent element in the Congress.

New Executive

By a vote of 283 to 175, A. R. Mosher, Ottawa, was re-elected president of the Congress of Labour. He defeated Nigel Morgan, Vancouver, international representative of the International Woodworkers of America.

Alex McAuslane of Vancouver, regional director of organization for the Congress, defeated George Burt of Oshawa, regional director of United Automobile Workers of America, for the vice-presidency, on a 264-to-193 vote.

Patrick Conroy, Calgary, was chosen secretary-treasurer over H. J. Pritchett, Vancouver Island Labour Council, on a 281-170 division.

The following were elected to the Executive Committee: M. M. MacLean, Ottawa; C.H. Millard, Toronto; Silby Barrett, Glace Bay, N.S.; and Sol Spivak, Toronto.[4]

COMMUNISM

THREE DEMANDS UPON THE GOVERNMENT
(Edmonton, Alberta)

While Communist underground campaigning against the Government has in no wise diminished since Hitler's attack on Russia it has diverted its efforts into less destructive channels so far as our war efforts are concerned. Instead of employing every method possible to oppose an "imperialist war" it is now trying to force the Government's hands in an all-out alliance with Russia which would include, of course, lifting the ban against the Communist Party of Canada and releasing all interned Communists.

The following Communist party directive enlarges upon these three demands:

Dear Friends:

Here are further and more concrete proposals for mass work in the present period. They are for the purpose of taking quick advantage of the new great possibilities for legal mass work.

There are two lines of mass united front legal work which should be organized at once in each province and locality, and which our leading committees should at once prepare: (1) the formation and organizing of a united movement for assistance to the USSR; (2) a united movement for the release of the interned anti-Fascist and the legality of the CP.

In reference to the first campaign, we propose that in each district committees of a broad nature should be set up at once in all the localities. The aim of this movement is to popularize and build people's unity to compel the King Government to render all-out aid for the USSR, to intensify Canada's active participation in the war against Nazi dictatorship, to use Canada's decisive position in the British Commonwealth to bring all possible backing to Churchill's line of alliance with the USSR, to demand full diplomatic and commercial relations between Canada and the USSR. The concrete forms of agitation on these major issues must be developed with the unfolding of the present situation in Canada and the world, for example it should be possible at this moment to take up the demand that Mr. King goes to London, and to add to that demand the [5] specific proposal that his visit should be for the purpose of negotiating with the representatives of the USSR for a Canadian-Soviet alliance in collaboration with the British Government.

It will shortly be possible to take steps to set up a national committee for this purpose. This does not mean you should wait on that, a local committee of non-partisan nature should at once be set up, to embrace all people and groups who stand for all-out effort to defeat Hitler and who recognize that the Red Army is the main and decisive force fighting the Nazi dictatorship. Such committees should be legal, public bodies, with open offices, and full public status. All manner of activities are possible, public meetings which should serve to form such committees and recruit adherents; the circularizing of resolutions to all groups, the starting of campaigns for raising goodwill solidarity funds for the USSR as a token of Canadian popular support; local petitions on the King Government; the issuance of buttons; special funds raised by groups such as trade unions, etc. In this work the national groups, who have great strength should be incorporated, in addition to the work they do among their own people. Sub-committees of these groups can be set up as auxiliaries of the central committees.

Every effort must be made to get into the press through special press releases to the local paper, interviews (possibly with Mac-Pap vets in some localities), etc.

In Quebec special forms and specialized demands are being worked out to meet the situation there.

In reference to the second campaign, this issue provides the most favourable means of fighting for the legality of the Party and is directly connected with the people's fight against capitalist treachery in the struggle against Fascism. It should be made a special point that for the Government to continue its ban on the CP and its internment of anti-Fascist fighters and militant trade union leaders, is to deny the positive features of King's statements regarding people's unity against Fascist aggression, and is a continuation of the Chamberlain line of preparing for betrayal of the line of red baiting which is the favourite trick of Quislings.

Existing civil liberties groups should be encouraged to take a firmer stand in the present situation and efforts are required to get these middle class groups to issue statements, advantage meetings, etc. and to co-ordinate their actions in Toronto and Montreal. But alongside this we [6] must concentrate on building a big defence movement through the vigorous work of former CLDL cadres, who must in each place get to groups in the labour movement, arrange petitions, etc. for the freeing of anti-Fascist internees and the legality of the CP. Full use must be made of local popularity of the internees. A really broad appeal and agitation can be worked out in every locality around this paramount domestic issue, which mirrors the whole struggle against treachery in Canada. We must use all of our available forces to organize now the movement of the people for civil liberties. Here, too, certain national leads will be given but at once you must start local work.

Yours truly,
J.W.[7]

NATIONAL COUNCIL FOR DEMOCRATIC RIGHTS

A new organization has been launched under the above title for the laudable purpose, it is claimed, of helping "the British and Russian peoples to smash Fascism". Its first public meeting, held in Toronto on August 11, 1941, was advertised by leaflets bearing in heavy type:

DEFEND DEMOCRACY IN CANADA!

RELEASE ALL INTERNED AND IMPRISONED ANTI-
FASCISTS TO HELP DEFEAT HITLER!

and announcing the following speakers:

Lt. Wm. Kardash, M.L.A., Winnipeg, Manitoba
Dewar Ferguson, Canadian Seamen's Union
Alex. Welch, Textile Workers' Union.
David Goldstick, Barrister.

[⊱deletion: 1 paragraph: 4 lines]

Approximately 700 people attended the meeting, the majority being Ukrainians and known members of the disloyal Ukrainian Labour Farmer Temple Association.

A. E. Smith [&<deletion: 1 line] president and national secretary of the Council, explained the aims and objects of the Council are to struggle for democratic rights in Canada, to release anti-Fascist and anti-Nazi leaders from internment, to fight Hitler Quislings and Fifth Columnists on the home front and abolish the Defence of Canada Regulations.

William Kardash urged Ukrainians to rally behind the organization in order to urge all possible aid to Russia and the Red Army. Almost all of his entire speech was devoted to praise of the Red Army and in concluding he appealed to Toronto people to join the National Council for Democratic Rights.

David Goldstick (Toronto Barrister) criticized the Defence of Canada Regulations and in particular regulation 21.[8]

Jessie Storrie (Canadian Youth Council) stated that the Youth Council which she represents is still continuing its activity for the release of anti-Fascists and interned labour leaders, and that the Youth Council of Canada is making extensive preparation for the convention of the International Youth Councils which is to be held likely in the month of November, 1941 at Mexico City, Mexico.

Two days later, at a public meeting sponsored by the Ukrainian section of the Council, Kardash devoted most of his long speech to praising the Russian army and in urging all aid to Soviet Russia. He bitterly criticized the Canadian Government for the internment of anti-Fascist and Anti-Nazi leaders and for confiscation of the U.L.F.T.A. properties. He stated that the aims of the National Council for Democratic Rights are to unfurl energetic action in order to free the interned anti-Fascists and to influence the Canadian authorities to restore the U.L.F.T.A. properties and to restore the legality of the U.L.F.T.A.

A. E. Smith explained that the National Council for Democratic Rights originated from the organization commenced in Winnipeg by the wives of the interned anti-Fascist and anti-Nazi leaders. He stated that it was desired to make this organization nation wide and appealed for the release of all interned anti-Fascists.

The Executive Committee of the Council includes A. E. Smith, General Secretary; Miss Beckie Buhay, Assistant Secretary for Organization and Publicity; Mr. Ted Herman, Treasurer; Mr. Newth, Mrs. Hollwell, and Mrs. Freed.

The Committee announces that immediate plans are under way for the enlargement of the National Committee with representatives from coast to coast, the setting up of councils and branches throughout the country, the issuance of literature for widespread distribution, immediate legal action on cases of anti-Fascist internees and prisoners—for mass meetings, and all forms of activity intended to speed the aims and objects of the National Council.[9]

YOUTH MOVEMENT PERVERTS "V" CAMPAIGN
(Winnipeg)

At a recent Canadian Youth Congress at Oak Glade Park near Winnipeg the idea was advocated of carrying on a "V" for Victory campaign as a means of recruiting for the Youth Movement. It was agreed that members of the Congress should use this deception in their respective districts in approaching organizations and soldiers, ostensibly for developing interest in the "V" campaign, but in reality for winning converts to Communism. During the discussion on "methods of approach" so as to obtain donations from professional and business men in good standing, May Isenor of Vancouver remarked "Bring the sucker list into action".

Since then the Youth Movement's campaign has got into full swing. At the recent Canadian Congress of Labour convention in Hamilton yellow leaflets were freely distributed, hearing such slogans as "Youth of Canada, Unite for Victory!", "Extend Democracy! Fair Wages! Collective Bargaining!" "For A National 'V' Day Nov. 11th", "Open A Second Front in W Europe!", "Organize 'V' Clubs!", "Equality For French Canada", "$1.25 Bushel Wheat", "Abolish P.C. 7440", "Free Transportation For Soldiers".

The inside sheets enlarge upon these slogans, while the back sheet contains a comprehensive appeal to every type and class of youth to join in this "V" campaign.

It is safe to say that the average reader of the text would be deceived into believing that this was solely a call for greater patriotism and war effort on the part of youth, instead of a membership drive for the subversive Youth Movement.[10]

ANTI-FASCIST MOBILIZATION COMMITTEE
(Calgary)

[✄deletion: 1 paragraph: 12 lines]

The Calgary Branch of the Committee got away to a very poor start. There is a lot of dissension in the Party ranks against Lawrence Anderson, and those who are opposed to him refused to take any part in the new movement as long as Anderson has anything to do with it. It was decided that the Committee, if it was to meet with success, would have to be disassociated from Communism, and as a result several prominent persons in Calgary with left-wing tendencies are being contacted to see if they would be willing to accept the public leadership of the Mobilization Committee.[11]

NAZISM
WESTERN GERMANS LOSING CONFIDENCE
(Vancouver, B.C.)

(A student of German-Canadian affairs briefly surveys the present attitude of Nazi sympathizers in Vancouver.)

"On several occasions during the past few days I have had the opportunity of studying closely the different ideas of the local German element in regard to the latest news and political developments. The local Nazi element are greatly surprised at the continued and powerful resistance of the Russian Armies and are greatly disappointed that the 'blitz' method has not worked this time. When rumours first started about a meeting somewhere in the Atlantic between Churchill and Roosevelt the local Germans were sceptical that such a meeting could take place because of the menace of Hitler's submarines. However, now that this meeting is an historical fact, they are kind of flabbergasted and believe that no good can come out of it for the Party of the Fatherland. They are still hoping that the wisdom and luck of their Fuehrer will find a way to final victory. Now that Stalin has united with Great Britain and the U.S.A. in common cause against Germany, it is believed that the war will last much longer than was first expected.

"There are few who believe that a revolt of the German people will take place from within. The mentality of the Germans under the stern and ruthless domination of the Party and Gestapo is such that the German people cannot and will not revolt unless heavy and deciding defeats in the field prove to them that the mighty power of the Nazis is on the downgrade. To a certain extent this same thing also applies to our local situation. Just so long as Hitler rules and wins, our Nazi friends remain boastful, but should the tide turn against their Fuehrer they will loudly proclaim themselves loyal Canadians."[12]

INTERNMENT

METHODS OF PROCEDURE

There has been some misunderstanding as to the procedure followed in regard to internment of enemy aliens and persons known to have engaged in subversive or anti-British activities. Due to this lack of understanding, it was thought in some quarters that internments were the sole responsibility of the police, particularly the Royal Canadian Mounted Police. This is quite incorrect. The duty of the R.C.M.P. with regard to internments begins and ends largely with the investigation of the activities of the persons falling within the categories referred to above. No person other than an enemy alien may be interned except on the Order of the Minister of Justice and, in the case of enemy aliens, on the Order of the Registrar-General of Enemy Aliens.

The procedure followed is simply that when any individual is suspected of having engaged in subversive or other activities prejudicial to the welfare or safety of the State, he is subjected to a thorough police investigation. All evidence of the disloyal actions of the suspected person is obtained and, providing such evidence warrants it, it is submitted to the

Minister of Justice in the form of a Recommendation for Detention. This Recommendation is in turn given consideration by an Inter-Departmental Committee appointed to advise the Minister and if this Committee concurs in the Recommendation of the police, they advise the Minister accordingly, when an Order authorizing detention is issued, pursuant to the provisions of Regulation 21, of the Defence of Canada Regulations.

The person so detained is entitled to object to his detention within thirty days. The detenu is detained in a gaol or other place designated in the Order, pending the hearing of his objection by an Advisory Committee appointed pursuant tot he provisions of Regulation 22 of the said Regulations. These Advisory Committees (of which there are two) consist respectfully of a chairman, nominated by the Minister of Justice, who has held judicial office (judges have been appointed in each instance) and two other members, similarly appointed, with suitable legal qualifications. The Advisory Committee, after hearing the objection, submit their report to the Minister of Justice with a recommendation for release or continued detention. In some cases, before the Minister reaches of final decision, the matter is referred back to the Police to see if additional evidence is available with the request that, if possible, additional evidence be supplied. The Police then further investigate and submit a supplementary report to the Minister of Justice, who gives the necessary consideration to the case.[13]

The above procedure is followed in the cases of all persons who are not enemy aliens. In the latter cases, if the Registrar-General of Enemy Aliens is satisfied that the evidence produced warrants internment, his Order authorizing internment is issued. There is no provision made for enemy aliens to object to internment ordered under these circumstances.

(Note: Canada's internment methods are closely patterned after those in operation in Great Britain.)[14]

INTELLIGENCE
BULLETIN

ROYAL CANADIAN MOUNTED POLICE
HEADQUARTERS, OTTAWA

OCTOBER 25, 1941

CONTENTS

Communism:
"A National Front for Victory"
Is "Victory" alias for Revolution?
Dissension Among Quebec Communists
[✂deletion: 1 line]
General:
Strikers Appreciate Police Methods

War Series
No. 48

COMMUNISM

"A NATIONAL FRONT FOR VICTORY"

Under the above title the Communist Party has issued a pamphlet that replaces all previously issued propaganda relating to the world war and, therefore, is of outstanding importance to Canadian Authorities in directing present and formulating future policies relating to our social security. The pamphlet is signed by Tim Buck and carries the following announcement:

"The Report printed herein was adopted by the Political Bureau of the Communist Party of Canada on August 28, 1941. It is the official statement of the Party's estimation of the war and the tasks it brings forward and the policy to be followed by the Party in the present period. It replaces and supersedes all materials issued previous to its adoption."

The "National Front" advocated would appear to be as broad as the Dominion and to include all people who oppose Nazism. Accepted on its face value it constitutes a document of Communist aims and aspirations that should receive the whole-hearted endorsement of every loyal Canadian and cause him to reverse his whole attitude toward these former revolutionists. To quote from the "Introduction":

Every Canadian who follows events recognizes the transformation that has come over the war and its significance to democracy since Hitler's attack upon the U.S.S.R. The changed character of the war, with the changed alignment of forces and belligerent aims signal-

407

ized most clearly by the British-Soviet Pact and the Roosevelt-Churchill declarations has transformed the tasks and responsibilities of the working class and the general progressive movement.

For the people of Canada this decisive change means that the issue of continued national security of their country, which depends on the victorious outcome of the world struggle to defeat Hitlerism, assumes dramatic proportions. The victory of the democratic peoples and governments over Hitler, with their continued independence, is within grasp—providing that a supreme effort is made to win the war.[1]

The task of the labour-progressive movement today, therefore, is to direct all its energies to the positive task of mobilizing public opinion in support of a united national effort to implement all the plans and pledges, stated and implied, in the British-Soviet pact and the Roosevelt-Churchill declarations. With the King government associated with the governments of Britain and the Soviet Union in the British-Soviet pact, it becomes necessary that the labour-progressive movement direct its main blows against the open and secret friends of Hitler, and not against the King government.

To play its full role in the strengthening of Canada's contribution to the defeat of Hitlerism, it becomes necessary that the labour-progressive movement unite its forces and close its ranks in support of a broad united national effort to win the war.

The Communist Party of Canada which, as a result of the developments indicated above, has changed its estimation of the character of the war and the tasks it brings forward, stands for the broadest national unity of the Canadian people in the fight against the Nazi threat.

The Communist Party urges, and will work consistently to bring about, a united effort of the trade union movement and all the forces of the labour-progressive movement, farm organizations, the Canadian Legion, Liberals, Conservatives, and non-political organizations, English and French-Canadians of all classes and parties, in support of the prosecution of the war to defeat Hitler. Such a movement will constitute, in fact, a National Front. Such a movement will give loyal support to every measure of the King government making for increased support to and co-operation with Britain and the United States and for effective aid to the Soviet Union.

A Just War

Tim Buck takes pains to explain this sudden change of complexion from an "Imperialist War" to a "Just War", asserting:[2]

It is clear from the foregoing that it would be incorrect now to characterize Britain's and Canada's war against Hitler as imperialist. It would be wrong, not only because it would bring grist to the mill of the appeasers, the Municheers and fifth columnists, but because it would contradict the basic fact that a fundamental change has taken place in the character of the war and the international situation.

The Communist Party of Canada, party of the Canadian working class, emphasizing the fundamental, historic change that has taken place in the world situation, frankly re-examines its work, its policies and slogans, and its immediate tasks. In the light of the changed character of the war and the situation characterized by the British-Soviet Pact, the Communist Party of Canada changed its attitude towards the war and called upon all its members and sympathizers to exert all efforts to defeat Hitler. The change thus brought about in our work must now be carried further it must be made complete...

The conflict cuts across class lines. The issue is "For or Against Hitler and Hitlerism". The dominant sections of the British ruling class, under the leadership of Churchill, have realized the implications of the Nazi attack upon the U.S.S.R. and have entered into full collaboration with the Soviet government to bring about Hitler's defeat. There need be no illusions as to their reasons for this. It does not denote any change in the basic attitude of the British ruling class towards the Socialist state. Indeed, Churchill emphasized this fact quite frankly in his historic broadcast of June 22nd. What it denotes is that the Churchill government, supported by the United British people, realizes that the decisive issue confronting it today is the defeat of the Nazi armies. That is the fundamental fact which determines their present policy. The working class must, with ever-increasing efforts and will to self-sacrifice, take up and lead the support of this policy, and ensure: "that complete victory without which our efforts and sacrifices would be wasted. (The Roosevelt-Churchill letter to Premier Stalin.).....[3]

National Front

By the term "National Front" we mean a common front, expressed in identity of aims, of all sections and groups of Canada's people who are for the defeat of Hitler: workers, farmers, business and professional people, including sections of the bourgeoisie, of French, English and other origins, and of Communist, Socialist, Social Credit, Liberal and Tory policial opinions.

Such a front, cutting across the lines of class and party interests, will not be defined by rigid organizational forms or agreements it will not even necessitate formal political agreements or pacts. Support for the measures advocated by the various sections and groupings constituting such a Front will not necessitate membership in any particular political party or other organization and will not necessitate leaving or joining any special or-

ganization. While committees, etc., might be set up under its auspices, the
unity of such a Front — the National Front itself in fact — will be achieved
and maintained as a result of the identity of interest between its various
sections and supporters in bringing about the defeat of Hitler and the
destruction of Hitlerism. Its unity in action will be expressed, in the main,
in the unity of its support, through the activities of its supporters and the
organizations of which they are members, to those central measures which
are essential to victory. The sole essential requisite for such a National
Front, therefore, is the common objective: Defeat Hitler! Win the War!....

War Policies

Not only must the people get behind the King Government's war efforts but they must do all in their power to step up these efforts promising "they will welcome and support every measure taken by the
Government towards ensuring that defeat (Hitler's). The people of
Canada want full and adequate supplies of everything necessary provided
for our forces overseas and a steady increase in Canada's aid to her allies.
The Communist Party of Canada unreservedly supports that position."....

But the Party intends to go further than just give support, and describes
what it considers essentials to a total war:[4]

A.Full collaboration, to the very limit of Canada's resources and
capacity, with her allies associated in the British-Soviet alliance, and
with the governments and people of the U.S.A., China and all other
countries who stand with us in the struggle against Hitler.

B.All necessary measures to expand Canada's war production and to
increase her military and naval effectiveness.

To make these measures even more effective the party declares the following changes in present government domestic policy are highly desirable, and the subject of demands by large sections of the population:

1.Restore democratic rights to the masses of the people.

2.Full rights for the trade unions, on the principles of collective bargaining, to enforce a living wage, and equal participation of the
workers in the organization of the war effort.

3.Parity prices to farmers, and the production of food-stuffs to aid victory over Hitler; participation of the farm organizations in all government farm boards.

4.The Dominion government should take firm action against pro-fascist appeasers of Hitler, who strive to weaken Canada's war effort
by any means, wherever they may be found.

Summary

Governmental policies which embrace the measures indicated above
will unite the great mass of Canada's people in an all-out effort to win the
war. The Communist Party pledges itself to support that effort with all its
strength, and does not place the adoption of its own program for victory

as the condition for its support. Under all conditions, it will maintain its independence of thought and action as a workers' party pledged to the defeat of Hitlerism and the defense of democratic rights and the national interests of Canada. It places the above program for victory before the Canadian people as its considered opinion as to how best and most quickly the war can be won.[5]

It is self-evident that the measures indicated above go considerably further than the policies so far followed by the King Government. This is so because the King Government is not as yet doing "everything necessary to win the war". Its active war policy falls short, by far, of Mr. King's London pledge. The King Government has not acted to encourage the development of democratic initiative in aiding the nation's war effort. It has failed to recognize the changed character of the support which the history-making Churchill policy and the Roosevelt-Churchill Eight Point Program and Pledge have rallied. It failed lamentably to take advantage of the visit of the Soviet Military Mission; it has, as yet, taken no action against the widespread anti-Soviet slanders, which are also contrary to Britain's interests, and which are being used to confuse people concerning the issues and thereby weaken our war effort. The main force of its repressive activities is still directed against the anti-fascists. Mackenzie King has not even attempted to correct the anti-Soviet and anti-British effect of his being quoted as himself expressing the hope that Nazi Germany and the U.S.S.R. would "destroy each other".

These things are obvious proof that much more can be done, and must be done, to make Canada's war effort effective. It will be the task of the democratic people of Canada to press the King Government to make our national effort complete.

In doing so, however, we shall not direct our main efforts against the King Government; on the contrary, we shall welcome and give energetic support to every step it takes in the direction of more effective prosecution of the national war effort. Our main blows will be directed against the appeasers and Quislings who, by doubts, pretenses, clinging to the policies of yesterday, and spreading confusion as to issues and needs, strive to delay or slow down the government's war activity and to weaken or disrupt Canada's effort to make victory sure....

Conclusion

Official authorization of the C.P. of C. to collaborate to the full with the Government throughout the duration of the war, may seem just a little "too good to be true", and it certainly calls for practical evidence of sincerity before it can be accepted. In the meantime, the following questions arise:[6]

1. Will Communists refrain from labour organizing in order to incite strikes?
2. Will they enlist for active service and encourage others to enlist?

3. Will they call off their secret and illegal propaganda campaign?
4. Are they prepared to discipline their own insurgents who continue to make trouble?

If they will do these things then the Party has become an asset instead of a liability and one of our many problems has been solved — at least for the time being.[7]

IS "VICTORY" ALIAS FOR REVOLUTION?

Communist leaders claim to be engaged in an all-out effort to win "the war". In recent months they have launched half-a-dozen movements and scores of committees in the name of Victory and bearing such fine slogans as "Defend Democracy in Canada", "Defeat Fascism", "All Aid to Soviet Russia". Most of these "loyal" organizations have been "explained" in the "Bulletin". They include (among others) the "National Council for Democratic Rights", the "Anti-Fascist Mobilization Committee for Aid to the Soviet Union", the "Youth 'V'-for-Victory Campaign", the Ukrainian People's Anti-Fascist Committee" and the "Peoples Victory Committee"—all of which are Communist "fronts".

The last-named (and the newest) is particularly strong in the West, where for the time being it is to supersede the People's Movement Committee as a medium of appeal to the public at large to rally to the defence of our threatened democracy — threatened (it is asserted) by Quislings in Government and Big Business.

The following report from "K" Division, R.C.M.P., (Edmonton, Alberta), gives a fair glimpse of the subtle methods employed by the People's Victory Committee in promulgating their radical views behind a "front" of well-meaning citizens and in the name of Victory for the Allies:

Mrs. Dorise Nielsen, M.P., addressed a meeting in Calgary on the 21st September, held under the auspices of the People's Victory Committee. Among those who were on the platform was Dewar Ferguson, Acting President of the Canadian Seamen's Union. The chairman of the meeting was Arnold Robertson [⊱deletion: 2 lines]

In opening the meeting Mr. Robertson quoted the following as being the planks of the People's Victory Committee:
1. Effective prosecution of the War.
2. All-out aid to Great Britain and her Allies.
3. All-out aid to the Soviet Union.
4. Maintain the standard of living of the armed forces and the working people.
4a. To build a true anti-Hitler morale among the workers.
4b. To show that working people are not unpatriotic in asking for a decent standard of living.
5. Prepare for a better world after the war, in order that all may retain

their civil liberties and freedom of speech.[8]

Dewar Ferguson was the first speaker. He expressed himself as being whole-heartedly anti-Fascist and that he endorsed the program of the People's Victory Committee. He was critical of the Dominion Government labour policy and contended that the higher profits of the larger manufacturers were responsible for the increase in the cost of living. He appealed to those present to try to effect the release from detention of Pat Sullivan, the former president of the C.S.U.

Mrs. Dorise Nielsen dealt with the war situation and blamed the former Prime Minister of Great Britain, the Right Honourable Neville Chamberlain, and the German Chancellor, Herr Hitler, for the present world chaos. She claimed that we in Canada are doing little more than following a policy of appeasement. Regarding the labour situation in Canada, she claimed that all the strikes were due to the low wages paid and that the employers of labour were really responsible for the strike and that if anyone were unpatriotic, they were. Dealing with industrial production she stated that a General Motors Corporation plant at Oshawa had to close down because there were not enough tools to make army trucks due to the tool makers making tools for a 1942 motor car to be produced in the U.S.A. She said that the assembly lines were being used for the production of the cars for domestic use right up to the eve of the visit of the Duke of Kent, but on the day when the Duke of Kent inspected the factory, army trucks had mysteriously replaced the domestic cars on the assembly line. She demanded that the Vichy representative in Canada be recalled immediately and that a Russian minister be accredited to Ottawa in his place. Mrs. Nielsen stated that the pay and allowances of soldiers and their dependents should be increased.

Mrs. Nielsen concluded her address by stating that she wanted to co-operate with all groups in Canada and co-ordinate them into one great people's movement. Approximately 3,000 persons attended this meeting and Mrs. Dorise Nielsen's speech was enthusiastically received. It is very significant that the Free French and the Danish Consul, who had been asked to attend, were not present.

Two days later the first organization meeting of the People's Victory Committee was held in Calgary with Gordon Wray acting secretary. About 50 persons were present, including representatives of various churches in Calgary, and a number of persons who have been to varying degrees associated with the Communist Party in the past.[9]

During discussion it was announced that the People's Victory

Committee would supersede the People's Movement Committee — the former being closely identified with the Canadian war effort, especially in connection with aid to Soviet Russia, while the latter will confine itself to domestic affairs in Canada.

A membership committee for Calgary was appointed as follows: Mrs. Maude V. Butler, George Taylor, Mrs. H. Kazima, William Wray.[&deletion: 3 lines][10]

ANTI-FASCIST COMMITTEE VERY ACTIVE
(Edmonton, Alberta)

The principal mass organization work being done by the Communist Party is through the medium of the "Anti-Fascist Mobilization Committee for Aid to the Soviet Union". Meetings have been held in all the principal centres of Alberta, at which ex-members of the Communist Party have been the chief speakers. Fairly large sums of money have been raised at these meetings and resolutions have been unanimously passed calling for all-out aid to Russia, the establishment of diplomatic and commercial relations with the U.S.S.R., and for a complete statement by the Canadian Government of their full support of the democratic war effort. The present Government of Canada has been subjected to criticism at these meetings for allegedly allowing industrial concerns to amass large fortunes and for placing the burden of war expenditure upon the working people. They maintain that certain financial interests in Canada are Fascist at heart and that an all-out war effort cannot be expected until these interests are removed.[11]

DISSENSION AMONG QUEBEC COMMUNISTS
(Montreal)

During the past month the Communist Party in the Province of Quebec intensified their campaign along the lines of the new Party policy of "All aid to the Soviet Union". The Party also continued its activities aimed at bringing about the release of the interned Communist Party members who are now being much publicized as "Anti-Fascists". To further their activities they have formed a branch of the National Council for Democratic Rights, composed largely of the wives of interned C.P. members.

The Young Communist League is becoming increasingly active and are organizing meetings under the "All aid to the Soviet Union" front. Various sections of the league are at present in the process of reorganization and activities; are directed by unit leaders who are asked to use their own discretion on matters of policy not covered by the new Party line, until new directives are received.

C.P. propaganda continues to be circulated, but has decreased considerably since the invasion of Russia. Two pamphlets worthy of note were distributed during the month of September. These are entitled "A National Front for Victory" by Tim Buck, and "The Red Army in Action" by Fred Rose.

Rumours reaching the office indicate a considerable degree of dissatisfaction in the C.P. It is felt that the Party has followed an inconsistent and wavering line during the past few years and that instead of keeping the issues clear cut they have befogged the Party line. Apart from the dissatisfaction with the general direction of the Party, there is considerable local dissatisfaction with the Quebec leadership.

A circular of an anti-Communist nature was distributed by mail to many Communist members and fellow passengers during the month. Opinion in the C.P. is divided, one group believing that the anti-Communist circular emanates from the Trotskyites, while another faction believe that the Co-operative Commonwealth movement is responsible. Whatever the origin of the anti-Communist propaganda may be, it has in any event raised a great deal of concern among Party leaders and served to emphasize the present unrest and dissension.[12][Page 13 is missing.]

STRIKERS APPRECIATE POLICE METHODS
(St. Catharines, Ont.)

When 4,000 employees of McKinnon Industries (engaged almost entirely in war production) went on strike on September 11 for higher wages it was decided, under authority of Order-in-Council No. 5830, to place a strong detachment of the R.C.M. Police at the plant to prevent mass picketing and to ensure opportunity and protection for those who desired to work.

On Sept. 14 the Officer Commanding "0" Division, Toronto, four Inspectors and 133 other ranks, arrived at St. Catharines. The effects appear to have been all that could have been desired by all parties concerned, including the strikers. The situation was not only orderly throughout but, due partly to calling strike leaders into conference before plans were put into operation, there existed a feeling of mutual understanding and goodwill as between the members of the Force on the one side and the Company Officials, the workers and the general public on the other. By the time the strike had terminated on Sept. 27, no less than six strikers had made enquiries as to joining the Force, while a number called around to say goodbye when the Detachment were leaving.[14]

SECRET

INTELLIGENCE
BULLETIN

ROYAL CANADIAN MOUNTED POLICE
HEADQUARTERS, OTTAWA

DECEMBER 24, 1941

CONTENTS
Japan:
    Precautions Against Japanese Sabotage
Communism:
        "War Is The Class Struggle"
        Quebec Committee For Allied Victory
        Mass Language Organizations
        C.P. Activity in Trade Unions

War Series
No. 49

JAPAN

PRECAUTIONS AGAINST JAPANESE SABOTAGE

Every reasonable precaution for guarding our West Coat against sabotage from within has been taken by Federal and Provincial Authorities.

The day Japan attacked the United States and Prime Minister King announced Canada was at war with Japan, a selected group of Japanese residents were taken into custody and held for investigation.

All Japanese nationals and those naturalized since Sept. 1, 1922 were called upon to report to the Police in accordance with Defence of Canada Regulations, at which time these people are required to enter into an undertaking to do nothing that would jeopardize Canadian security, and are requested to report from time to time as directed.

Japanese language newspapers were suppressed. Japanese schools were closed. All fishing and other vessels owned or operated by persons of Japanese racial origin were held by order of the Minister of Justice.

A standing committee, appointed by the Government, under the chairmanship of F. J. Hume, Mayor of New Westminster, B.C. and including a representative of Military District No. 12 and of R.C.M. Police, are keeping in close contact with Department of External Affairs, Police and local authorities.

As Japan had long been on the verge of open warfare with the Allies, the Police were given ample time to prepare for the event. Every Japanese-Canadian naturalized since Sept. 1, 1922 and every Japanese national were registered and afterwards re-registered and a very complete record of the history of each, including photograph and thumb-print, was made of each one. Japanese propaganda had been banned from entering the country, while domestic Japanese-language printed matter had been compelled to carry its English translation.

A year ago a Government-sponsored Special Committee on Orientals in B.C. reported upon the problem of Japanese in that province from the point of view of National security. At that time the Committee considered the chief threat to national security emanated from the white majority, and prefaced [1] their recommendations with the following explanation:-

"The police and military authorities in British Columbia have taken precautions which they consider adequate to deal with any subversive activities on the part of individual Japanese and to protect all loyal Japanese against any attack from misguided members of the white community. To reduce the likelihood of any such developments, however, there are certain steps that might be taken which will protect the national interest, reassure public opinion in British Columbia and defend all citizens of whatever racial origin against unjust attack. The recommendations which follow are designed to effect this result."

<u>Recommendations.</u>

1. That there should be continued vigilance on the part of all police authorities in the Province of British Columbia, and that they should as heretofore work on the lines of keeping a close watch for signs of disloyal acts, particularly in the way of sabotage, while doing their best to encourage those Japanese whom they have no reason to suspect of disloyalty to co-operate with the authorities by keeping them informed of conditions in the Japanese community, and in general to impress upon the leading Japanese that in their own interest they must be on the alert to forestall or prevent subversive acts.

2. That the military and police authorities should bear constantly in mind the importance of continuing to provide for the defence of loyal Japanese.

3. That steps should be taken to diminish anti-Japanese propaganda in the Province, by appealing to individuals and to the Press on the grounds of civil security and national defence; and, if necessary, but using the Censorship for this purpose.

4. That wherever possible the co-operation of the leaders of various groups and associations in the Japanese community should be enlisted by the authorities concerned. Such leaders should be invited to accept, in accordance with Japanese tradition, personal responsibility for the loyal behaviour of the members of their respective groups.[2]

5. That, at least for the present, Canadians of Japanese race should not be called up for military training.

6. That training of Canadians of Japanese race in the C.O.T.C. should

continue at the discretion of the University authorities.

7.   That, both for purposes of civil security and in order to deprive persons hostile to the Japanese of a constant and effective ground for complaint, there should be a re-registration of the Japanese population of British Columbia.

8.   That a small standing committee should be set up in British Columbia to supervise the carrying out of such of the foregoing recommendations as are adopted by the Government, and for the purpose of keeping the Government constantly informed as to the Oriental situation in that Province.

9.   That the Government should issue a public statement designed to reassure the white population of British Columbia, and at the same time explaining to the Japanese residents in that Province the advantages which will accrue to them from the carrying out of the measures proposed in this Report.[3]

COMMUNISM
"WAR IS THE CLASS STRUGGLE"

Communists are at present engaged in an all-out class war for the defeat of Capitalism in Canada! Despite their many protestations to the contrary and their assurance of loyalty to a democracy now allied with Soviet Russia, the fact must not be forgotten for an instant that the main if not the sole animating motive for every action is the Communist cause, first, last and all the time.

How do we know? The Communist Party of Canada declare it themselves in their secret directives. It is true, the one published in our last Bulletin (accredited to Tim Buck and endorsed by the Political Bureau) pretended to see why the former "imperialists war" had suddenly become a "just war" and why all political, social and religious parties should now sink their differences in a united front against Fascism, and there was no evidence of duplicity. But subsequent C.P. communications are more revealing of the true part the "Alliance" is expected to play in the class struggle.

To quote (in part) from a directive received by the Calgary C.P. branch since invasion of Russia:

War is the Class Struggle
at its Highest Stage.

It would be the most dangerous to misinterpret the motives which now impel the Imperialist Governments of Britain, the United States, Canada, etc. to ally themselves with the U.S.S.R., or to overlook the contrast between their motives and the ideals which inspire the masses of democratic people.

It must be made perfectly clear to all democratic people that the Imperialist governments are collaborating with the Soviet government because their own Imperialist interests are at stake and co-operation with the U.S.S.R. is the one means by which they may defend and, they hope, preserve their colonial monopoly. In the existing situation and because of the relationship of military forces they can find no way out of their dilemma except by co-operating with the U.S.S.R.[4]

The workers and their democratic allies in the capitalist countries are activated by very different considerations. They want the Soviet people to stop the Nazi onrush; to defeat Hitler; because the Soviet people are fighting to defend the good, glad new life that they have built, the achievement in which workers and democrats everywhere see hope for their own future. The Soviet Peoples are defending not only the fruits of their own struggles and progress but they are also defending the right to, and opportunity for, progress for all mankind. The Soviet People are defending our hope to be able to build the world anew, whilst Hitler Fascism represents all the greed, the thirst for ruthless exploitation, the oppression, the class injustice and the crushing of popular aspiration, all that is worst, most reactionary and vile in the world of Capitalism in decay.

Thus, the Imperialists co-operate with the U.S.S.R. in waging a just people's war—in hope of protecting their own exploiter's Imperialist interests and privileges. The Soviet People, supported by the workers and all true democrats everywhere, seek aid from the Imperialist Governments so as to smash the Nazi onslaught, crush the Fascist beast and keep the road open so that mankind can advance along the path of social progress. The motives of the two main wings of the anti-Hitler front contrast sharply. At the same time interests in the war against Hitler coincide. The interests of all sections of the anti-Hitler front merge, as Stalin so penetratingly explained in his call to action when he said; "Our war for the freedom of our country will merge with the struggle of the people of Europe and America for their independence, for democratic liberties."

To Protect Democracy at Home the Working Class Must Join In and Win the Leadership of the National Effort to Defeat Hitler.

The interests of the dominant circles of the Imperialist Canadian bourgeoisie in defeating Hitler, which impels them to join with the Soviet Government in an anti-Hitler front of governments on the international fields, coincides with the interests of the working class in the struggle against Hitler Fascism, thus creating, at home, the basis for "National Unity to win the war." As a result of this there is already developing a National Front in Canada. As pointed out in the above-mentioned pamphlet,[5] this National Front does not depend upon formal agreements for unity, specific organizational arrangements, or anything of that sort. It comes into being, grows, directly out of life. The motive force which makes it a fact is the widespread and growing determination expressed in the slogan: "Beat Hitler; Win the War."

As pointed out in the pamphlet, the role that will be played by such a National Front will depend entirely upon the role of the working class movement within it. To make the united national effort to defeat Hitler a force for democratic progress, the working class must be the most consistent and the most energetic factor in it....

It is clear, therefore, that the working class movement must be on guard against the danger of becoming a mere appendage to the war plans of the Imperialists. The form which the successful struggle to defeat Hitler Fascism assumes is that of national unity; a National Front. The National Front cuts across the lines of Class and party interests; the basis of its unity is the common determination to defeat Hitler. But national unity to defeat Hitler does not liquidate, or suspend, or even mitigate, class contradictions. The class struggle in Canada continues, indeed it becomes intensified from time to time, within the national Front on a higher plane; the plane of struggle over national policy and for the leadership of the united national war effort. The working class must unite its forces in active support of, and to win the leadership of, the national war effort. If the working class movement fails to do that, reactionary forces will exploit the people's desire to smash Hitler and utilize the Nation's war effort to weaken the democratic forces.

Thus we see that the decisive issue of the class struggle in Canada is becoming the issue of the leadership of the Nation's war effort which, in the situation prevailing today, means leadership of the Nation. Only the working class can give leadership that is in the true interests of the Nation, of the great mass of Canada's people. The labour movement, supported by the farm movement, can win that leadership only by being the most energetic and consistent supporter of the nation's war effort. Labour must unite its forces and become a force in the national front, and win that leadership or there is a danger that reactionary forces will....

To Recapitulate: National unity is developing rapidly in support of the struggle to defeat Hitler. Within the National Front the class struggle continues and will continue to deepen on a higher plane.[6]

Supporting the war to destroy Hitler, striving to increase Canada's production and Military effectiveness, the working class movement must of necessity throw all its energy into the National War effort, win a voice in its direction and, whilst proving itself the most consistent and constructive factor in it, become the leader of that effort. Effective working class action will make the Nation's war effort a vehicle for democratic progress. Failure on the part of the working class to influence its direction would strengthen still more the role of the jingoistic Imperialist bourgeoisie in the nation's affairs.[7]

QUEBEC COMMITTEE FOR ALLIED VICTORY
(Montreal)

Quebec Committee for Allied Victory is the latest child of the Communist Party of Canada. In Montreal, on November 25, a group of about 35 representatives of 16 clubs whose chief aim is the provision of aid to Russia, met at the Y.M.C.A. and drew up a rather ambitious program for increasing their membership and influence.

The Committee explains its aims in its "Declaration of Policy" pamphlet, as:-

(a) To bring home to the people that Hitlerism can be defeated only by the fullest collaboration between the British Empire, Russia and the United States;

(b) To destroy the apathy and doubt which endanger the war effort, exposing all who sow misunderstanding and suspicion;

(c) To stimulate a broad movement of co-operation for Allied Victory among all sections of the population;

(d) To promote unity between all races, classes and creeds in order to ensure the fullest possible measure of support for any programme destined to advance the cause of Allied Victory;

(e) To encourage increased food production and the elimination of waste as weapons against Hitler.

How to attain these ends:-

(a) By the formation of Victory Clubs in every locality and organization, thus affording the civilian a chance to play a role other than that of passive acquiescence;

(b) By radio and other public addresses designed to further the aims outlined above;

(c) By furthering, in every possible way, collaboration between Labour, Industry, and Government for increased war production;

(d) By encouraging greater co-operation between the farmer, the city dweller and the Government for the fullest utilization of our agricultural resources;[8]

(e) By resistance to every effort by groups or individuals to exploit religious, racial, class or political differences between those who are fighting together for Victory;

(f) By condemning and combatting every attempt to exploit war conditions for private, personal and selfish ends;

(g) By supporting our Government in all measures necessary to strengthen co-operation between the Allies and encouraging the further development of this policy.

The Committee, in its desire to sponsor Victory Clubs to participate in war work throughout the city and to obtain names and addresses of possible new members, has issued a circular asking "which of the following activities would you be interested in?":-

Giving your blood for Victory.

Collecting salvage to aid important war production,

Knitting or sewing for our army, navy and air force,

Contributing to and packing V-Bundles for Britain,
Acting as hosts to members of the armed forces,
Serving on committees to help the War Savings Campaign,
Forming groups to further the establishment of day nurseries, to release our women for work in industry.
It has also launched a "Victory Contest" for similar reasons.
[℈<deletion: 1 paragraph: 14 lines][9]
[℈<deletion: 1 line] Roberts [℈<deletion: 2 lines]
It will be noted that the aims and the methods of achieving them are entirely praiseworthy and, if it were not for the Communist element dominating the Committee's component parts, any patriotic society might well lend them support. In view, however, of past history of the C.P. of C. and of present knowledge of the declared intentions of certain elements to use such "Victory" organizations for spreading Communist principles throughout all ranks of society, the Authorities are sceptical of the ultimate good intentions of the Quebec Committee for Allied Victory.

Winnipeg Council for Allied Victory
(Winnipeg)

This Council held a grand rally in the Winnipeg auditorium on Nov. 17. Like the Quebec Committee it is a composite body made from various organizations, the majority being solely pro-Russian in sentiment while a few are definitely pro-Communist. Of the 2000 persons who attended the rally a large proportion were of the first class. The group of three who arranged the rental of the auditorium were Elizabeth Scott and May Melanson ([℈<deletion: 1 line] and Laura Goodman Salverson, a distinguished Canadian novelist.

The collection, totalling over $3,000, emanated for the most part from the societies, councils, boards and parties federated with the Winnipeg Council. The largest donors were Dr. B. A. Victor, on behalf of Jewish Branch, Council for Allied Victory, and Wm. Kardash, M.L.A., on behalf of Ukrainian Association to Aid the Fatherland.

MASS LANGUAGE ORGANIZATIONS
(Toronto)

Following the line of the National Council for Democratic Rights, the various Ukrainian, Russian and other Slav organizations, set up to support the war effort on behalf of Russia, have to all intents and purposes replaced the former mass language organizations affiliated to, and controlled by, the C.P. of C. Perhaps the most striking feature in the activities of these organizations is the large sum of money collected by [10] them at socials, concerts, meetings, etc. for the Red Cross Fund; and the contrast between the apathy of these people prior to the entry of Russia into the War and their present enthusiasm and generous contributions is a definite indication of the trend of their thoughts and the direction in which their loyalty lies. For example: the Russian Committee to Aid the Fatherland has collected over $11,000.00 for the Red Cross since its inception.

Meetings of these mass language organizations are being held all over Ontario and are reported to be well attended and enthusiastically supported.

C.P. ACTIVITY IN TRADE UNIONS.
(Toronto)

The Communist Party continues to endeavour to place itself in a position where it can direct the activity of the Trade Unions and, it must be admitted, among the C.I.O. organizations many of the key positions are occupied by members of the C.P. of C. Particularly is this the case in the United Electrical, Radio and Machine Workers' Union, as is recognized by the Executive of the C.I.O., whose members are becoming concerned about the situation. This concern, incidentally, is prompted more by a fear that C.P. influence will eventually drive them out of office and not necessarily by anxiety inspired by loyalty to Canada. Neither are the A.F. of L. Unions immune from the C.P. infiltration into the Executive.

The Trade Unions have adopted the same attitude as the C.P. of C. towards the wage freezing measure passed by the Government and it is expected that agitation for the repeal of this measure will increase as time goes on.[11]

Index

In compiling the index, we have chosen what we judge to be the correct spelling of persons, places and institutions as index headings. Because no indication of the misspelling or misuse of names has been included in the text of the *Bulletins*, the reader should approach material referenced in the index with as open a mind as possible. The name you find in the text will not always match the name in the index. For instance, the "Walter Albricht" referred to on pages 252-253 is clearly Walter Ulbricht and has been indexed under Walter Ulbricht. In addition to correcting misspellings and errors, the index also uses the currently accepted transliterations of well-known Russian names.

Kanadsky Gudok (Canadian Whistle)
15, 36, 59, 62, 97, 115, 119, 190
Kapustiansky, Gen. N. 317
Kardash, William 104, 372-374, 384,
402-403, 422
Kashtan, Dave 117, 165
Kazima, Mrs. H. 414
Kealey, Gregory 20
Kelly, ___ 146
Kentville, N.S. 242
King, J. G. 111, 132
King, William Lyon Mackenzie 9,
12, 15-17, 42, 55, 57, 79-81, 83, 88,
136, 149, 165, 177, 185-186, 210,
215, 268, 270, 296, 305, 308, 313,
323-324, 338, 350, 372, 384-385,
389, 401-402, 408, 410-411, 416

Kingston Penitentiary 191, 243
Kirkconnell, Watson 302, 318
Kirkland Lake 41, 76, 109, 167, 357
Kitchener 157
Kitchener Communist 344
Knight, William 76
Konovaletz, Col. Evhen 315-316,
317, 319
Korpan, ___ 395
Kossar, W. 316
Krivitsky, Walter G. 193, 320, 322-
323
Kuhn, Fritz 137
Kurmanovich, Gen. Victor 317
Kuropas, Stephen 392-393
Kushnir, Rev. Dr. W. 318-319, 392

L'Eclaireur (The Scout) 139, 160,
185, 188
Labour Forum 49
Labour Progressive Party 17
Labour Review 238
Ladyka, Bishop ___ 318
Laing, Jean 108-109
Langham 380
Lapedes, Sam 126, 146
Lapointe, Ernest 9, 42, 79-81, 215,
277, 296, 335, 372
Larocque, H. 266
Larson, Cedric 245
Laski, Harold J. 50
Laval University 142
Lawrence, Sam 109
Lawson, William T. 108, 120, 126,
135-136
Leary, E. E. 397-398

Lenin, V.I. 54, 62-63, 70, 135-137,
224, 279
Leopold, Sergeant John 11, 17
*Les Libertés Civiles en Temps de
Guerre* 209
Lethbridge 153, 357
Levinsky, Dr. ___ 395
Lewandowski, Tadeusz 117
Lewis, John L. 162, 169, 197, 374
Lewitsky, Dr. M. 395
Liberal Party 43
Liberty 115, 140, 193
Liebknecht, Karl 137
Lignite Coal Company 28, 31
Lind, Mr. ___ 40
Lithuanian Literary Association 144-
145
Lithuanians 140
Litterick, James 144, 234, 241
Lloyd George, David 23
Lockport Company 46, 82, 92
Lockport Fishermens Union 112;
Strike 206
Lockport, N. S. 82, 91, 102, 159,
164, 168, 177-178
Logia, William 294
London, Ontario 25, 42
*L'udovy Kalendar (The People's
Calendar)* 327
Lunenburg 122, 124
Luxemburg, Rosa 137
Lyons, Eugene 193

M.I.5 9
M.I.6 10
MacDonald, Premier Angus 112, 178
MacDonald, J. A. 399
Macedonian Political Organization 92
MacInnis, Angus 167
MacInnis, Clarence 138
MacKenzie, Norman 110, 123-124
MacKenzie, Saskatchewan 196
Mackenzie-Papineau Battalion 117,
227
Maclean, M. M. 293, 295, 398, 400
MacLeod, A. A. 111, 132, 374-375
Macmillan, Lord 65
MacNeil, J. F. 251, 336
Macphail, Agnes 248
MacPherson, James A. 83, 375
MacPherson, K.C., Major ___ 41
Magid, Dr. A. 104
Magnusson, Bruce 398
Maitchak, J. 117